The Goncourt Brothers

Frontispiece
EDMOND AND JULES DE GONCOURT
Photo des Archives photographiques

ANDRE BILLY

The Goncourt Brothers

TRANSLATED BY MARGARET SHAW

ANDRE DEUTSCH

FIRST PUBLISHED 1960 BY
ANDRE DEUTSCH LIMITED
12-14 CARLISLE STREET
SOHO SQUARE LONDON W1
© ANDRE DEUTSCH LIMITED 1960
ALL RIGHTS RESERVED
PRINTED IN HOLLAND BY
DRUKKERIJ HOLLAND N.V., AMSTERDAM

Contents

PART ONE: EDMOND AND JULES

I	Family Connections	11
II	Childhood and Youth	19
III	Beginnings	29
IV	Journalists	42
V	By-ways of History	49
VI	Love Affairs	57
VII	'Body-Snatchers' of History	64
VIII	Etchers	71
IX	Their First Novels	75
X	Pleasures and Friendships	87
XI	Gavarni and Sainte-Beuve	100
XII	Gautier, Flaubert and Others	112
XIII	Princess Mathilde	125
XIV	Two More Novels	131
XV	*Henriette Maréchal*	140
XVI	Their Two Last Novels	154
XVII	The House at Auteuil	167
XVIII	Self Portraits	171
XIX	The Death of Jules	194

PART TWO: EDMOND ALONE

I	The Siege and the Commune	208
II	Life Begins Again	217
III	Four Novels	221
IV	'La Maison d'un Artiste'	235
V	The Cult of Japan	242
VI	'My Friends the Daudets'	247

Contents

VII	The Five Friends	256
VIII	Differences with Zola	262
IX	At the Odéon	268
X	At the Théatre-Libre	279
XI	The Rue de Berri and Saint-Gratien	288
XII	The Academy and the 'Grenier'	296
XIII	The *Journal*	303
XIV	Engagements and Recreations	313
XV	The Last Months	322
	Index	339

Part One

EDMOND AND JULES

I
Family Connections

Paternal

The family of the Huot de Goncourts came from Bassigny, a part of Lorraine where the land has subsided to make on one hand the valley of the Meuse, on the other that of the Mouzon. The upper valley of the Meuse, which possesses all the characteristics of the Lorraine country, presents a perfect uniformity in appearance and customs. Communes are grouped around their crumbling castles: in the plain, each clustered about its parish church, the villages extend in a kind of drab archipelago along the Roman road that runs from Lyons to Trèves, through Langres and Soulosse. The houses are low-built, with porches rounded in the manner of Lorraine or Franche-Comté, and there are dunghills everywhere.

A strange region, as M. Paul Odinot remarks in an unpublished study, *Les Goncourts et le Bassigny Lorrain*, a mysterious region of witches and warlocks, of weird apparitions; a region five times ravaged by invasions, and in winter preyed upon by wolves; a region that does not know where its frontiers lie, nor who is its rightful ruler; where the people are at times as surly as farm dogs and at others as warm and homely as bread; a region where winter is long and springtime chilly, abounding in hunters and poachers, and conspirators.

It lacks neither grandeur nor charm, although the Goncourt brothers would not have allowed as much. 'It seems to me,' says the *Journal*, 'that a region in which people eat so much veal is done for. It has no future, and I am resolved to sell my farms at the very first opportunity.'

Goncourt is situated in the Haute-Marne, in the centre of Bassigny, about fifteen kilometres and a half south of Neufchâteau on the left bank of the Meuse. Its site is pleasant and agreeably cool. A statue of the Virgin, at a little distance from the church, commemorates the fact that the inhabitants of Goncourt had the good fortune to escape the disasters of 1870.

Here, then, is the region where the Goncourts had their roots on their father's side, though neither of them was born here. Their Lorraine ancestry was most apparent in Edmond, who was more serious-minded, more thoughtful, more circumspect and at the same time quicker to take offence than Jules. The latter, who described himself as a Latin in character, considered his brother more of a German.

Bassigny did not awaken any deep feeling of affection in them. Once their childhood was over, they never went back to it except when there was a death in the family or to deal with some business matter, for they had trouble with their tenant farmers which did not come to an end until 1868, when they sold their farm at Breuvannes.

Their great-grandfather, Antoine Huot, was born at Bourmont in 1753, and had become the owner of a little house in Goncourt. Along with this house he had bought the title of lord of the manor of Noncourt and Goncourt. His son, Jean-Antoine, a lawyer by profession, sat as deputy in the National and the Constituent Assemblies until 1791, and after fulfilling other important functions became a judge in the criminal court for Neufchâteau in the Vosges.

Visiting Neufchâteau in 1857 for their uncle's funeral, the two brothers remembered their terrifying grandfather, whose letters their own father, although then a major, would sometimes keep for a week before daring to open them. Edmond remembered having seen him in the dining-room of his house, 'this charming model on bourgeois lines of an eighteenth-century nobleman's residence', 'a little old man with a huge aquiline nose and an imperious chin', mumbling toothless oaths and perpetually puffing at an extinct pipe which he continually re-lit with a coal picked up in a little pair of silver tongs. Beside him was a stick. A harsh man, he did not always keep it there and had used it to intimidate the domestic staff in his house at Somerécourt, where he exasperated the neighbourhood with his angry abuse.

He was godfather to Edmond and is described on the birth certificate as an 'armiger', a 'defender of the throne and of His Majesty Louis XVI in the Constituent Assembly'. His charming house in Neufchâteau, with its façade of white stone decorated with rococo ornaments and posies, its wide main staircase, its dining-room paper representing gardens in Constantinople peopled with fantastic Turks, and its kitchen with a well concealed inside a cupboard, is No. 2 in the place Jeanne d'Arc.

According to the *Journal*, Jean-Antoine's younger son, Marc-Pierre, the father of our Goncourts, born at Bourmont on June 28, 1763, had run away from his father's house to join the army which he entered as a cadet from the Ecole Militaire at Fontainebleau in 1803. In 1808 he became a captain and five years later a major. He was placed on half-pay on July 1, 1818, and in the following year was appointed an officer of the Legion of Honour. He had first married a Mademoiselle de Courtois, the daughter of an officer in the King's service. Napoleon, just returned from Elba, was a witness to the marriage. In 1821, his wife having died, Marc-Pierre married for the second time, his bride being Annette-Cécile Guérin, the daughter of an army contractor who had died in the Russian campaign.

Their marriage contract shows that Marc-Pierre's contribution included, besides personal effects and money, a farm at Brainville in the Bourmont district, and another at Breuvannes in Clermont, both of which, when his parents' share was allowed for, brought in a fair income from the sale of grain. Annette-Cécile's contribution consisted of a trousseau and jewels worth 4,000 francs, goods in kind to the value of 10,000, and a dowry of 30,000 francs.

Did the major mismanage the administration of his wife's fortune? In 1823, 1824 and 1825, with the support of the Comte d'Artois, he asked to be reinstated on the general staff of the fortified towns because of the difficulty he found in bringing up his children. But a black mark had been recorded against him: after Waterloo he had refused to act as aide-de-camp under the new King. The Minister turned a deaf ear to his request, and Marc-Pierre was discharged from the army in 1828. In 1883 he was granted by special order a pension of 2,960 francs, which was in addition to the 1,000 francs he received as an officer of the Legion of Honour.

The major was a staunch Liberal, but without any trace of fanaticism. On March 29, 1831, he wrote to his friend Paul Collardez: 'What shall I say ... in answer to your challenging remarks on politics, except to repeat that in spite of all the opposition that stands in its way, the revolution of July is progressing with great strides and *irresistibly* towards the fulfilment of its destiny. Once again, let us have patience, let us place our trust in the spirit of progress that is permeating the world, in that single trend, though expressed in *diverse* ways, of all nations towards liberty.' There had been a rumour that he was going to be nominated as Prefect of the Haute-Marne. 'Never', he says in the same letter, 'will I wear the *livery* of this present government'.

Reflecting, as he often did, on his own case, for he was not exempt from a certain naïve complacency with regard to himself, Edmond wrote in 1876: 'I believe that no one who is keenly interested in art can spring up like a mushroom . . . the refinement of his taste is produced by an inclination dating back two or three generations . . . My father, a soldier himself, never bought a single *objet d'art*, but in household things he required a certain quality, a perfection, a more than ordinary beauty. And I recall that, in an age when people did not use the finest crystal, he would drink his bordeaux from a glass that a clumsy hand would have broken at a touch. I have inherited this delicacy of taste from my father, and I cannot appreciate either the best wine or the finest liqueur if it is offered to me in a thick glass.'

If old Jean-Antoine Huot made his servants obey by using his stick, the methods Marc-Pierre employed with little Edmond were scarcely less harsh. 'Today', he writes in his *Journal*, 'I am haunted, I cannot tell why, by memories of my old nurse. I can see her, on the day of an important dinner at Breuvannes, when I had just eaten the only ripe apricot off the tree in the courtyard, which my father was looking forward to offering at dessert, I can see her maintaining with fine impertinence that it was she herself who had eaten it, and receiving the thrashing from his horse-whip that my father aimed at me, not believing her, poor dear woman!'

Jean-Antoine's elder son, Pierre-Antoine-Victor, born on June 29, 1783, became a cadet of the Ecole Polytechnique and later an artillery captain, resigned his commission in 1814, re-entered the service during the Hundred Days and rallied the army of the Loire, an act that earned him his dismissal from the army at the request of Louis XVIII. Elected deputy in 1848, he represented the department of Vosges in both the National and the Legislative Assemblies. He died on July 12, 1857. He was, according to his nephews, a perfect gentleman, naturally kind, with a passion for mathematics, and spent his time walking up and down the paths in his little garden.

He had married a cousin, Virginie Henrys, and their daughter Bathilde-Antoinette-Augusta, married Léonidas-Eugène Labille, the son of a lawyer. The Labilles had an estate there where the Goncourts went regularly to stay and where they hunted and fished. It is easy to understand their liking for this pleasant little town bordered on one side by the Seine and on the other by a wooded hill. The river was plentifully stocked with trout and pike and there was plenty of game in the surrounding forests. Besides lands, vineyards and woods, the

Family Connections

Labilles had a garden along the river bank, made more agreeable no doubt by a boat-house, a fish-pond and a kind of rustic summer-house.

Léonidas, so the *Journal* tells us, had something in him of a monk, a pig, a bull, a he-goat and a satyr. Béranger was his god. A fanatical Republican, he had been expelled from the Law School, was unsociable, harsh towards his peasants, liked broad jokes, hated luxury and wore a smock. There were no curtains in the window of his conjugal bedchamber and he slept with his maidservants or drove them out of the house. He boasted that for three centuries his family on his father's side had been commoners, and that on his mother's side he was descended from Robert Bruce, the Scottish king. The son of a man who had been sentenced to five days' imprisonment and a fine of fifty francs for interfering with a religious procession, he used to blaspheme from morning till night.

Maternal

The Goncourts' mother, Annette-Cécile, had a brother, Alphonse, of whom her two sons had very pleasant memories: he used to make much of them both. He had gone into business in England, was ruined by his partner and had retired in the Loiret 'with an edition of Horace's works and a watch-chain'. On April 16, 1863, the *Journal* notes: 'We are left with a feeling of sadness at parting from this old brother of our mother's, who was so kind to us in our childhood, who gave us rides on horseback, invited us to dine with him . . . and took us for walks on Sundays in the country.'

Annette-Cécile also had two half-brothers by her mother's first marriage to Louis le Bas de Courmont: Armand, who was born in 1786 and died in 1832, and Jules. Annette-Cécile preferred Armand to Jules, whose wife she loved like a sister. Armand had been an officer in the Hussars during the Empire, 'a typical example of the handsome and attractive officer of the light horse with his fair hair and moustache looking just as if it had been put into curl-papers'.

Jules, who became chief adviser to the Audit Office, had married Nephtalie, the aunt of Edouard Lefebvre de Béhaine, the Goncourts' great friend until the last, who ended his career as French Ambassador to the Holy See. They used to say of him that he was fundamentally and naturally as kind as other people were ill-natured.

Edmond and Jules

Edmond remembered their grandmother, le Bas de Courmont Pomponne, as an old lady seated in the half-light of a room with a very high ceiling, the furniture draped in dust-covers and with memoirs of the time of her youth lying about everywhere. She never went out except to take a little walk in the passage de l'Opéra on the arm of an abbé. Her tall figure, extremely sensitive to cold, was always enveloped in cashmere shawls, and her pale, still beautiful, but severe and taciturn face greatly intimidated her grandson.

Cousin Cornélie Le Bas de Courmont (the 'Mlle de Varendeuil' of *Germinie Lacerteux*), who died at the age of eighty-three, was her grand-daughter. 'We climbed up', says the *Journal*, 'to see our old cousin Cornélie in her poor little room on the fifth floor. She was obliged to send us away, so many ladies, and schoolboys, and people of all ages who are related to her by blood or marriage come to see her. She has not enough chairs to let them all sit down, nor sufficient room to keep them long. It is one of the good features of the nobility that it does not shun people because they are poor.'

The Goncourt brothers had two sisters. The first had died as a child of tender years; the second, Emily, born about 1823, died some nine years later. On April 12, 1889, the *Journal* notes: 'This evening I have been burning some of my mother's grey hair, and my little sister Lili's fair hair, golden as an angel's. I recall her as she was in that year 1832, when she came with her nurse to Goubaux' boarding-school to fetch me, to escape the cholera epidemic... Poor child! The very next night, in the coach that was bearing us away towards the Haute-Marne, she was attacked by cholera. Imagine this journey with this dying child on our knees and my father and mother not daring to stop at any of the villages or the little towns we were passing through for fear of not finding a doctor able to give her proper attention. We did not arrive at Chaumont until she was, practically speaking, dead.'

The great-grandparents of the Goncourts' mother belonged to the family of Laurent de Villedeuil, and the combined influence of the social environment of the Villedeuils and the Courmonts on both brothers was profound. It was to this side of the family that their preferences inclined; it was the family of their Parisian mother to which they, and more especially Jules, attached themselves most willingly. They had inherited from Annette-Cécile her delicate perceptions and her sensibility. Her aristocratic connections had awakened in them pretensions to nobility which, as they themselves were aware, had only a feeble justification. 'As men of letters,' they confessed, 'we cannot clear ourselves of two things that make the public doubtful about us: the suspicion that we are rich and of noble birth. And yet we are not rich and very far from being noble.' They clung passionately, however, to their 'nobiliary' name, as they termed it, and to their prefix. In 1858, when Vapereau's biographical dictionary referred to them as: 'Goncourt (Edmond and Jules Huot, styled *de*), French writers, born at Goncourt (Vosges) *circa* 1825', they insisted through a solicitor on a correction in four of the leading newspapers. 'Allow me' (Vapereau wrote to them) 'to beg you not to bring a suit against a man who has fallen upon rather unhappy days after completing a task that makes him stand in the eyes of Europe as a personification of biographical learning'. When Louis Ulbach in *Charivari* repeated the reference in Vapereau's book, they again obtained satisfaction.

In 1860 the *Bulletin des Lois* announced that M. Ambroise Jacobé and his son Louis, born at Goncourt in the commune of Matignicourt, were authorized by decree of the Emperor to add to their patronymic that of Goncourt. The two brothers, supported by their cousin Lefebvre de Béhaine, brought an action against the Jacobés before the department of disputed claims of the Council of State. The Minister objected on the grounds that the Goncourts' situation was identical with that of the Jacobés, whose great-grandfather had bought the estate of Goncourt in the Châlons-sur-Marne district, in 1790, just as theirs had bought that of Goncourt in the district of Marne. To this they replied, not without reason, that the forbear of the Jacobés had bought property annexed by the State, whereas theirs had bought a lordship for which he had sworn allegiance to Louis XVI. In the end, they abandoned their suit for 'lack of confidence in the sort of restitution which the government that has robbed us would give'. Their sole consolation was that of drawing an episode in *Renée Mauperin* out of this affair.

On December 30, 1860, Labille, the husband of their cousin, wrote from Bar-sur-Seine to Paul Collardez, son of the family's solicitor, who occupied himself with looking after their affairs: 'I have received several letters from these gentlemen who *get on my nerves*. To tell the truth, I have not answered them. More recently, they have written to ask me if I had any title-deeds relating to the farm at Goncourt to support their lawsuit against M. Jacobey, who takes the liberty of claiming the right to call himself de Goncourt. I sent them my title-deeds by Mme Labille to avoid having to write to them. All the same, I cannot see why two low-born, simple commoners like Huot and Jacobey, whom I do not know and whom I believe to be very worthy people from a bourgeois standpoint, but out-and-out commoners none the less, should not both bear the name of Goncourt.'

After the days of June, 1848, Edmond made to Collardez a profession of faith in the future of socialism, to which he added: 'Shall we see the shipwreck, or shall we bequeath it to our grandchildren? That is the whole question. For myself, and as a descendant of Louis the Well-beloved, I tell you frankly that I hope all my wishes for a postponement will have the help of the powers that be, of which, however, I despair.' This allusion to a mysterious royal descent remains an enigma.

If the Goncourts were passionately attached to their name, they do not appear to have been so to their family. 'Every man of letters', they remarked, 'ought to adopt a pseudonym to keep his family from inheriting his name ... My father's family do not seem in any way related to me. They are worthy people I might have met when travelling by coach, but I have made a mistake in getting myself linked with them.' This was not very gracious towards their cousin Labille who entertained them so often at Bar-sur-Seine.

On June 28 Labille's son Marin and his sister, Mme Le Chanteur, 'a stylish little cousin, neat and dainty as a doll just out of a box', came to Auteuil in a landau to ask Edmond's permission to adopt his name. The young woman whom Marin was about to wed thought the name Labille vulgar and wanted a prefix. Edmond, who was fond of Marin, granted the wished-for authorization; but it was bitter to him to see the name he and his brother had done so much to make famous become 'the trade-mark of silly little provincial nobodies'.

II
Childhood and Youth

Edmond de Goncourt was born at Nancy on May 26, 1822, at 33 rue des Carmes. When he was eighteen months old his parents went to live in Paris, where they installed themselves at 22 rue Pinon (today rue Rossini) with a cook and a children's nurse. It was here that Jules was born on December 19, 1830.

The house stood on the corner of the rue Laffitte. 'Windows, why do you look at us so?' wrote the Goncourts in 1852. 'So sadly too, and with such tender, lingering glances? From these windows, when we were tiny children, we used to see fine gentlemen and beautiful ladies passing in the street. O windows! you stand for our happy childhood and our chief memory of death . . . "Your father's not very well today, children," our mother would say to us, "don't make a noise." And he, seeing us sad at having to stop playing, would take us both on his knee, and laughing with us, would tell us things that seemed like fairy tales, about the Russian campaign, and how he had taken part in it with his shoulder broken, and sometimes tied to a cannon . . . He would make us pass our little hands over his battle-scarred head, and our little fingers would run lightly over his seven sabre-cuts. Then we would play with his officer's cross, that cross he pinned on his major's uniform at the age of twenty-five, at a time when such decorations were dearly bought!'

The major died, broken in health, on January 7, 1834. His widow, left with a pension of 500 francs, viewed with some misgivings the difficulties ahead of her. To cut down expenses, she went at first to live with her brother Alphonse at 13 rue de Provence; then in July, 1838, she moved to a flat at 12 rue des Capucines belonging to a friend, Françoise Mangin, who in 1842 left her a legacy of 2,000 francs. Edmond always remembered the dances his mother gave there on Shrove Tuesdays for his little friends and their sisters. 'Poor Mother, what a life of sorrow and misfortunes! The loss of two little girls, life with a husband in constant suffering from the effects of his wounds and the breakdown in his health, which had been ruined by the Russian campaign... Then left a widow, with a slender fortune in lands, in farming rents that were difficult to recover. Ill-fated, too, in every undertaking that might have seemed wise and reasonable in the mother of a family, losing through unlucky speculations the investments she made with a view to her children's future: investments made possibly only by saving and herself going short.'

The Pension Goubaux (also called the Pension Saint-Victor) where he went as a boarder, had been started by Prosper-Parfait Goubaux, one of the authors of *Trente Ans ou la Vie d'un Joueur* and a collaborator with the elder Dumas, Legouvé, Eugène Sue and many others. It was said he had taught himself to read by studying shop signs in the streets. The Pension Goubaux, which was bought much later by the city of Paris to become the Collège Chaptal, is recalled in *L'Affaire Clémenceau* by the younger Dumas, a pupil in the class immediately below Edmond's. 'The establishment was big enough to take about two hundred and fifty boarders... In the Upper School a few pupils of merit were grouped around M. Frémin (*i.e.* Goubaux) and formed a nucleus of work, of emulation and success that maintained the high reputation the school had formerly won for itself. M. Frémin devoted himself entirely to these young people, leaving to the junior masters those who were not worth troubling about, and who, in the hands of his partner Delauneau, who was simply a man of business, represented the money-making side of the enterprise. What went on among these latter pupils is unbelievable. A taste for pernicious literature, ... immorality and impiety provoked by the over-strict conditions of the age, slackness and idleness, precocious libertinism, such were the current vices of this true republic.' Edmond was doubtless not among those pupils in whom M. Goubaux took an interest; the boy was almost always in detention on Sundays.

Of his year at the Lycée Henri IV, which he entered next as a fourth form pupil, his memories were principally of fights with his school-fellows, and of being sent to Coventry because of his need to assert his independence. His master, Caboche, an intelligent and eccentric Benedictine with a slightly bitter and ironical turn of mind, was one of the first to awaken in him a love for exquisite style.

Edmond also spent a year in the sixth form as a day-boy at the Collège Bourbon. 'I am very pleased with him,' said his mother, 'he works hard, and having him with me brings more joy into my home'. Mme de Goncourt did not know that this big son of hers was going to

Childhood and Youth

balls at the Opera, thanks to the complicity of her servant, Rosalie Malingre, known as Rose, who used to open the door for him at daybreak.

On January 30, 1843, he was served with his call-up papers and in one of his letters he alludes to the medical board before which he had passed prior to joining the National Guard.

Edmond has preserved for us in *La Maison d'un Artiste* some delightful recollections of the property at Belleville owned by Jules de Courmont in about 1836. It was not far from the Pension Goubaux. 'In those days, going back to the year 1836, one of my uncles owned some property at Ménilmontant, a large dwelling in the shape of a temple, with the ruins of a theatre, in the middle of a little wood ... In the summer, my mother, my aunt and another of her sisters-in-law ... used to spend the whole of the summer on this estate; the three families lived in a kind of friendly community all day long. I was at the Pension Goubaux, and every Sunday when I had leave this was more or less my time-table for the day: towards two o'clock, after a light meal at which, as I remember, raspberries were always served, the three women dressed in gowns of light-coloured muslin and shod in little prunella slippers with ribbons crossed round the ankles, such as one sees in Gavarni's drawings in *La Mode*, would saunter down the slopes in the direction of Paris. Together these three women made a charming trio: my aunt with her brunette's face, full of intelligent and spiritual beauty; her sister, a blonde from the colonies, with her bright blue eyes, her white skin faintly tinged with pink, and the lazy ease of her figure; my mother with her sweet, gentle face and her tiny feet.

'My aunt was at this time one of the four or five people in Paris who had a passion for old things, for what was deemed beautiful in bygone ages, for Venetian glass, carved ivory, marquetry furniture, *point d'Alençon* lace and Dresden china. We would arrive at antique shops just when their owners were getting ready to dine ... when the shutters were already closed and only the door, still half-open, let a ray of light trickle through the dusky shadows of an accumulation of precious things. In this dim and dusty chaos, there would be three radiant women rummaging, making a pitter-patter like mice in a pile of rubble, and stretching out neatly-gloved hands into shadowy corners, a little afraid of getting them dirty, and daintily drawing back tips of feet shod in prunella, then bit by bit thrusting forth into the full light of day pieces of wood-carving or gilded bronze piled up on the ground against the wall... And always, at the end of the foray, there would be some lucky find... It is those far-off Sundays that have made of me the collector of bibelots I have been, and still am, and will remain all my life.'

Of Nephthalie de Courmont, who was to have so great an influence in shaping Edmond's sensibility and tastes, her nephew wrote: '... she let me stay beside her almost all day, giving me all her little commissions, letting me go with her to the garden to carry the basket in which she put the flowers she chose for the vases in the drawing-rooms, finding amusement in my *whys*, and doing me the honour of answering them seriously... I used to keep a little way behind her, as if I were possessed with a feeling of religious adoration for this woman who seemed to me to be of another substance from that of the women of my family... the welcome she gave you... her bearing... her speech, and the caressing expression on her face when she smiled, had an influence that I experienced with her alone.'

In Paris Nephthalie lived at 15 rue de la Paix and later in the rue Tronchet. '... my eyes have kept a *far-off memory*... of her hair billowing out around her like a halo, of her pearl-white rounded forehead, her eyes deep-set and dimly seen in their dark circles, the delicate bone-formation of her face, in which life-long consumption kept the slender lines of youth unchanged, the imperceptible bosom tightly swathed in floating folds of material, the austere contours of her body; the memory, in short, of her spiritual beauty which, in my novel, I have moulded and mingled with the psychic beauty of Madame Berthelot.'

On October 7, 1871, Edmond gives another memory of his childhood: 'This evening I receive news of my dear cousin's death.' (This was Augusta, the daughter of his uncle Pierre-Antoine-Victor, who was married to Léonidas Labille and who had been a pupil in a boarding-school in Paris.) 'This news', he adds, 'has kept me absorbed in our family's past all this evening and taken me back to our youth which we spent together. I remember when her old nurse used to come to fetch us on Sundays, my cousin from Cousinot's, me from M. Goubaux's school. I remember the walks she had to take on the heights of Montmartre because of my being kept in, and how the nurse, to prevent my being scolded by my father, would always lay the blame on the poor girl. I see her again, when we sometimes went to spend the evening with the prim and proper Villedeuil ladies, on whom my father commented severely ... I see us again in the first year of her marriage, fighting with each other like the children we became the moment her husband turned his back.'

Other pleasant memories of Edmond's childhood included the family's house at Breuvannes where, sunk in an old easy chair in the bakehouse, he had read a copy of *Robinson Crusoe* which his father had bought off a pedlar; his grandfather's house in Neufchâteau, and long walks through the countryside, gathering mushrooms, eating meals in a woodland hut, picking up small birds caught in a snare.

Among other delightful spots were the Collardez's house at Breuvannes, and cousin Léonidas Labille's estate at Bar-sur-Seine: 'I was just twelve years old when my cousin, getting out of the coach at Troyes, bought me a white smock to put over my little Parisian's suit. What an eventful month that was! To begin with, I fell into the Seine, where I thought I should drown, and a few days later a powder-flask burst in my hand—fortunately in its box—and a thousand other rash moments.' The next year Edmond, now grown sober and serious, passed his nights in reading and his days in dreams.

Jules went as a day-boy to the Collège Bourbon. 'My brother', Edmond once wrote, 'was adored by his mother. He was her last-born ... the prettiest child in the world, and extremely delicate. When he began his lessons, my mother, in order to spare him the hardships of life at school, withdrew from the world entirely and secluding herself at home, became the kind and indulgent supervisor of his studies. Jules's pretty face had the gift of arousing the hatred of his school-fellows; they would willingly have fallen on him tooth and nail ...' several times they attempted to disfigure him, and this 'without his ... even having contact with them, but out of that rabid hatred of democracies for aristocracies, no matter what their nature.'

Jules was mischievous, but his health gave cause for anxiety. He was in the lowest form of the middle school when he made his first communion, offered for the health of his aunt Nephthalie, at that time ill in Rome. During that year he had a master, who, says Edmond, 'made his whole childhood miserable, driving him pitilessly on to try for prizes offered in a general competition between the schools'. In the competitive examination of 1844, at the end of a year in the lowest form but one, Jules won two second prizes for translations from Latin and from Greek. Later on, in the fifth form, he had a master whom he offended by making as many puns as he did, and equally bad ones.

Edmond and Jules

In the upper sixth, where he had Prévost-Paradol as a fellow-pupil, he illustrated *Notre Dame de Paris* with pen-and-ink sketches, and on the terrace of the monastery of the Feuillants, oblivious of time, except for the music of the guards on their way to relieve those at the Palais Bourbon, he composed a drama, *Etienne Marcel*, of which Colonel Corbin, a former schoolfellow, later said in writing to Edmond that it seemed to him superior to the *Bohémiens de Paris*. 'I remember particularly', he wrote, 'an arresting scene in which a halberdier on guard on the ramparts—or maybe at the town hall—however I am inclined to think it was the ramparts—had just delivered a long tirade celebrating, I think, the beauty of the night or of his beloved mistress, when a treacherous creature, approaching the unlucky and unsuspecting sentinel, drove his dagger in a masterly fashion clean between the man's shoulders. To the dagger was attached, as is right and proper, a thrilling letter of denunciation.'

Jules spent many happy days at Gisors, where the parents of his schoolfellow, Louis Passy, owned an old Franciscan convent in the rue des Fontaines. The *Journal* has some delightful pages on Gisors— the front steps smothered in roses, the clumps of lilac, the river, the old ferry-boat, the island with tall poplars, the summer-house in the watch-tower, the iron-wire footbridge, the conservatory and the theatre with its make-up, the fine hussars' uniforms worn by the little actors in *Le Chalet*, Louis Passy's handsome wig, and Jules's false beard which prevented Edmond from recognizing him. All sorts of games, endless dinners, evening dances, amateur theatricals, in fact all the pleasures of both town and country life were to be found in this children's paradise.

The ties of affection binding Jules to the Passy family were to last for more than twenty years. On September 15, 1858, he writes: 'There is something beautiful, and nobody can deny it, in the Passys' bourgeois pattern of life, with its family feeling, its sense of unity in a group wherein each unit feels itself linked with the others in a delightful fellowship of old and young.' Later he wrote: 'This is a place where I feel I can expand.' The appraisals of the two brothers were rarely as favourable as this.

★ ★ ★

In 1841, Edmond entered the office of a solicitor, a Maître Fanier (or more probably Fagniez), in order to study law. His mother cherished the ambition of seeing him as a lawyer attached to the Supreme Court of Appeal.

Childhood and Youth

In an undated letter to Paul Collardez he writes: 'This year, with the joy of schoolboy in the lowest form, I have left both the solicitor's office and such people as Duranton, Delvincourt & Co ... I really ought to write to you every day ... in one hour's time I shall become a lawyer's junior clerk ... it is no longer possible to draw back ... I submit myself to it. Posts are so over-loaded with applicants, jobbery pushed to such extremes, patronage so well-established in high places, that when you have not the good luck to be born the son, or grandson, or nephew of a deputy you have simply got to win a place for yourself in one of those careers adorned with the appelation of independent. But the trouble is that those to which a solicitor's job does not serve as an introduction are few and far between. Here I am, then, freshly installed amidst all this moral filth for, in whatever form it may present itself, what is a lawyer's office but a slough of evil passions? People say this makes a man. Why then, so much the better! Though I rather fear that all this may fill him with the deepest disgust ...' As a Bachelor of Law, Edmond might have acquired in legal practice where his probationary period was longer than Balzac's, the experience that made the latter an inspired and ingenious chronicler of middle-class disputes. His passage through a solicitor's office is only revealed in the second chapter of *Charles Demailly*, where the biographical sketch of the solicitor Nachette is so Balzacian in feeling that one might think it was a pastiche.

It was round about this time, when his allowance did not exceed 1,200 francs, that he made a bid at the auction rooms in the rue des Jeûneurs for a terracotta by the sculptor Clodion, which started at 200 francs, and rising to 520, escaped his grasp. This terracotta, the loss of which he regretted all his life, was the maquette for a monument which, in 1787, Louis XVI had decided to erect to the glory of Montgolfier. The impecunious young lawyer made up for this by buying one of Boucher's water-colours, discovered in a portfolio on a bookstall in the place du Carrousel, and also the Boutourlin edition of *Télémaque*, for which he paid 400 francs.

Many old drawings were on sale beneath the arches of the Institute and along the embankments by the Seine. Here, for two francs, Edmond bought nine rough sketches by Saint-Aubin for an illustration to *Zadig* that had not been engraved. Near the chapel of Saint-Nicolas, at the top of the faubourg Saint-Honoré, he picked up a Cochin for three francs, and one of his Watteaus came to him from a man who sold

Edmond and Jules

curious weapons and Red Indians' heads dried in smoke.

His increasing need of money forced Edmond to abandon law for the Ministry of Finance. Mme de Goncourt wrote to Paul Collardez in November, 1847: 'You have heard that my big boy Edmond has got a post at the Treasury worth 1,200 francs; this is not brilliant, but it is at any rate a beginning.' (Did she suspect that, sick of his life as a junior civil servant, Edmond was contemplating suicide?) 'As for Jules,' she continued, 'he is far from engrossed in learning, first of all because he has a gay disposition, which is prejudicial to any kind of serious study, and because he has had a master in the fifth form who did not prepare him properly for work in the classical sixth. However, he works a little, so I hope the result, if not brilliant, will be good.' A salary of 1,200 francs; Mme de Goncourt was well justified in saying this was not brilliant. In 1848, she was reduced to selling her silver, the agent handling her affairs in the Haute-Marne showing a neglect of her interests that came near to being unscrupulous.

On June 22 Jules wrote to his friend Louis Passy: 'In spite of my horror of this stifling atmosphere of classicism or the *dolce farniente* of my bed, I am working fairly well for M. Nisard. I swot away composing French discourses for him. As for the Latin translations you recommend to me on pain of your curses, know that my last Latin exercise was on Lucretius, that I translated it, and into French verse too, and that all the translations from Latin he gives me I turn into French verse. The academically-minded Nisard has not recoiled in too much horror before this *monstrum horrendum*.' Nisard was his pet aversion. After the outbreak of trouble in June of that year, the young student in rhetoric wrote again to Louis Passy: 'M. Nisard, as you may well imagine, is almost off his head with terror. He utters mountain-rending sighs, this poor classical Jeremiah!'

Edmond was beginning to think of following his cousin Léonidas Labille's example by standing as a candidate at the elections in the Haute-Marne. This unfortunate notion had, however, no consequences. By the time he learnt that Paul Collardez was also a candidate, he had already given up the idea.

During there volutionary outbreak of June, 1848, Edmond's company of the National Guard had some ten of its members killed, and Edmond himself was able to see the insurrection at fairly close quarters. His reflections are marked by a political sense which increasing age was in some measure to obliterate. 'Yes,' he wrote to Collardez, 'it was necessary

Childhood and Youth

to be severe with the ringleaders; yes, it was necessary to be pitiless towards the perpetrators of atrocities that brought dishonour on their party. But after their revolt had been suppressed, instead of falling back on reactionary measures, care should have been taken to show clemency and to indicate by progressive action that if the Republic set its face against violence it was not calling a halt on the road to democracy. And was there not something better to do with 6,000 prisoners than shooting them or deporting them to Cayenne? It should not have been forgotten that fifty to sixty thousand men were fighting under the red flag and that half Paris supported the triumph of the new doctrines with its good wishes, and is it not a known fact that ideas are more formidable when they are watered with the blood of their martyrs? . . . Are not socialist ideas, however absurd they may appear, the bases on which a new society, replacing the old, will establish itself, and will not property in a quarter of a century go to rejoin nobility, its elder sister, sent to execution in 1792? And will not Louis Blanc, by his doctrine of equality of wages, have prepared the way, in a much more distant future, for a revolution against talent? For nobility, property and talent, these are the three ways by which a man enters society as a privileged person, and the new doctrines seem ready to improve upon the distributive equality God has ordained among men.'

Twenty years later Edmond set down a few stray sketches on the February revolution which had preceded these outbreaks: a tinsmith in the rue des Capucines knocking down with his hammer the words 'to the King' which followed 'tinsmith' on his sign-board; in the Tuileries a roebuck's head cut from its body, the statue of Spartacus capped with a Republican bonnet, and a revolutionary rigged-out in Louis-Philippe's dressing-gown. 'Today,' he writes, 'while passing again through the rue des Capucines, I looked by chance at the sign-board, and there, in the place of "tinsmith to the King", I read "tinsmith to the Emperor".' In *Charles Demailly* there is another reference: 'I went once to the town hall of the city. That time I saw there, in the Saint-Jean Chamber, the men who were killed in the February riots lying very neatly embalmed in muslin shrouds.'

In 1848, a great misfortune befell them: their mother died at the house of her cousin, the Marquis de Villedeuil, at Magny-Saint-Loup, in Seine-et-Marne. Jules wrote to Louis Passy: 'My poor mother died, as I wrote to tell you, on September 5. On Tuesday she was thought so ill that the Sacrament was administered to her at two o'clock. When

Edmond and Jules

this heart-rending ceremony came to an end my mother said to us: "It's all over then?" She did not see the approach of death, she did not know she was going to die! A mother holds so closely on to life! Then she imparted her last wishes to Edmond and joined our hands together. She was in the last throes of death at a quarter past four. An hour later we were orphans.'

The two brothers spent a great part of the following year at Bar-sur-Seine with their cousin Léonidas. In December, 1848, Jules, who for the past year had been running wild, had passed his *baccalauréat* brilliantly at the same time as Louis Passy.

In 1871 Edmond cast a backward glance on the period of their youth that is full of bitterness: 'I think of those school-days which were harder for me than for others, on account of a sense of independence which, all those years, made me fight with boys who were stronger than myself, and forced me to live in that kind of quarantine which the despotism of incipient tyrants imposes on the cowardly spirit of men-children. I think of my vocation as an artist, of my vocation as a student paleographer at the Ecole des Chartes, both of them thwarted by my mother. I see myself again . . . as a student, as a penniless lawyer's clerk, condemned to sordid love affairs, ill at ease among companions and friends of low, vulgar, bourgeois mentality, who understood nothing of the aspirations towards art and literature that tormented me, and chaffing me about them with the ripe sagacity of affectionate uncles. Finally, there was I, who have never known precisely what two and two add up to and have always had a horror of sums, condemned to totting up figures at the Treasury from morning till night. Two years in which the temptation to suicide came very near to me.'

III

Beginnings

Their mother's death had left them with a fortune which, though modest, was sufficient for the independence to which they aspired. Their money difficulties were none the less pressing, at least for the moment, which was the fault of Parison, their mother's agent. A letter from Jules to Paul Collardez on September 19, 1848, is instructive on this point. 'You ask us', it says, 'if the taxes on the sum you receive from Flammarion (one of their farmers) must be paid. We must confess to you that at this moment we find ourselves completely insolvent . . . we were counting on Flammarion's payment to meet the expenses inseparable from a death and to give us something to live on until December.'

No serious vocation had as yet commended itself to either of them. 'I have made a very firm resolution', wrote Jules to Louis Passy, 'and nothing will make me change it, neither sermons, nor good advice, even from yourself whose friendship I have fully experienced. *I shall do nothing*, to employ an expression which is incorrect but in general use . . .' During a visit to the home of their uncle Alphonse near Orleans, in May, 1849, Jules had however written two hundred lines of a little humorous and satirical novel in verse. Attracted by the Ecole des Chartes and by archaeology, Edmond, in order to get himself elected a member of the Société d'Histoire de France, had undertaken to write a history of medieval castles. He had no desire for fame. 'It is a positive fact', he wrote on November 29, 1895, 'that in rummaging among my memories I cannot discover in myself, throughout the whole of my youth, any desire to become a famous personality. I had no ambition but that of leading a life of independence in which I would occupy myself with art and literature, but as a dilettante, and not, as it has turned out, a galley-slave of fame.' This expression, applied by Balzac to himself, was, we must admit, somewhat less applicable to Edmond.

Edmond had been to the art school run by Dupois, and Pouthier, a Bohemian and one of his old school-friends, introduced them to the art students' world. They often went to see Peyrelongue the picture dealer, and the painter Servin, a devotee of the bottle, and as Jules had illustrated *Notre Dame de Paris*, and copied caricatures from *Punch* and some of Gavarni's lithographs, they decided to become painters.

A journey to Italy was at this time considered an indispensable preliminary to every artist's life, but the political and social conditions of the peninsula seemed as unstable as those in France. Mazzini and Garibaldi in Rome, Gioberti in Piedmont, Montabelli in Tuscany were maintaining a state of unrest. In Venice, Manin had just proclaimed a Republic. On the steps of the Chancellery in Rome, Pellegrino Rossi, Minister to the Vatican, had been assassinated. The Pope had taken refuge in Gaeta. Was this the moment to pass beyond the Alps and roam the highways? They decided to replace Italy by the South of France. Having bought the equipment then considered proper for out-of-door artists, a white smock, cap and gaiters, knapsack, parasol, etc., they set out from Bar-sur-Seine, en route for Burgundy, Lyonnais, Dauphiné, Provence and Algiers.

It was Jules's first entry into life. What had Edmond's experience of it been, now that he had arrived at man's estate? What passions had he known? At the age when one is naturally romantic, he had been living through the romantic age of his century, but this dual romanticism had affected him little. As a child he had had a revelation of the physical side of love through suddenly coming into the bedroom of his newly married cousin Fanny Curt, when her husband was preparing to make love to her. At a later date he gives a description of his own sensations: 'When I was beginning to be a young man, I remember that going through the countryside in spring, I had a sort of languid and melancholy impression of this earth with its wretchedly sparce show of greenery, its spindly trees, and all the painful puberty of nature; and I found myself taken unawares, with tears in my eyes and full of swelling desires, the glands in my breast throbbing painfully, and my whole soul, as it were, bursting into bud. At this period of my life, I felt a desire for a woman, not hotly sensual, but rather as an aspiration towards her. A feeble, sickly, puny sort of yearning, an aspiration giving something of the impression one gets looking at a statuette of a Gothic virgin . . .'

Round about the same period we can place his love for a sister-in-law of his mother's, Marie Lefebvre, the mother of his dear cousin Edouard de Béhaine, a fair-haired, white-skinned creole with blue eyes. At this period too comes the episode of the pleasant little woman at Bar-le-Duc, three months married to a solicitor, who always lagged behind for Edmond to accompany her when they were out hunting, and once complaining of a bad heart, made him lay his hand on her chest as they were going uphill; he made up his mind to have her on the next occasion, but her sister-in-law suspected this and did not leave them alone for the whole of that day. It was with his thoughts taken up by this 'charming little woman' that one Sunday, a fortnight later, when he had leave from school, he received his sexual initiation from Mme Charles, 'a creature to give one a permanent disgust for the physical side of love, an undersized woman, with a trunk in the form of a rhomboid, attached to two little arms, and two little legs, which in bed made her look like a crab turned over on its back'.

When he had only just left school, he had felt a slight inclination to marry a young gentlewoman called Lerche, who many years later, in June, 1886, came to see him in Auteuil. A healthy middle-class matron, still very youthful-looking, with fine, dark eyes like a Spanish woman's, she was now a widow, and had a daughter aged thirty who would have liked Edmond to arrange for the publication of a novel of hers in a newspaper. 'And we talked,' writes Edmond, 'of the house in the rue Franklin, and of the one with the large garden in the Allée des Veuves, and chatted about the men and women, now dead, who had been in our circle.'

Edmond's experience of love at the age of twenty-seven was, in fact, fairly restricted, at least if we refuse to admit that owing to his modesty he had always objected to exposing the secrets of his heart; but the rest of his life clearly shows that for himself, as for his brother, the kind of love in which feeling has its place hardly counted. These diligent observers of human nature were never in any degree romantic; realists in art, they were also, and primarily, realists with regard to love.

If we know what Edmond's initiation had been, we are ignorant of Jules's. At fifteen, while spending the holidays with his uncle Alphonse near Orléans, he had drunk more than he should during dinner at a friend's house, and in trying to touch the knee of his hostess, he had stretched his leg too far and fallen off his chair. The husband had not taken offence at this, but Uncle Alphonse, who was as much the worse for drink as his nephew, felt himself obliged to fight a duel in the youngster's place. This anecdote *à la* Paul de Kock seemed to portend a career as a seducer of women; we hesitate however to believe that

Edmond and Jules

Jules, so gay, so obliging, so witty, so innocent-looking with his golden hair, was ever one of set purpose. A certain Maria Lepelletier, with whom he had relations in the rue d'Isly during his last year at school, and who is perhaps that little Maria, whose first lover had been Edmond and who died of consumption—the story is told at length in the *Journal*—was doubtless not his first conquest; he would have said so otherwise.

'I remember her in the rue d'Isly, in the little flat facing south in which the sun darted about and perched like a bird. I would open the door in the morning to the water-carrier. She would go out, in a little bonnet, to buy two cutlets, standing in her petticoat to cook them, and we would have our lunch on one end of the table, with a single set of electro-plated cutlery, and drink out of the same glass. She was a girl such as were still to be found in those days: something of a grisette's heart still beat beneath her cashmere shawl.'

Realists they were, and equally so in politics. In this respect, as we have seen, their experience had already been fully developed by 1848. They had acquired the conviction that the future lay with socialism, that the aristocratic and middle-class civilization to which by origin, upbringing, and tastes they both belonged was drawing to its close, and they had decided on their course of action. They would henceforth take refuge in art, an attitude to be adopted by almost the whole of their generation of writers, who had completely lost all the grand illusions of 1830. They had discovered their own purpose in life, and this lay neither in the love of women, nor in that of humanity, but in the beauty of art and in the truth of human nature as conceived by intelligent, refined and disillusioned minds of the time.

In spite of this community of ideals, they were, and remained, very different. Edmond, taciturn, misanthropic, slightly stiff, with the soldierly stiffness of the Goncourts, a little formal, a little morose; Jules, the spirit of mischief, gay and lively, exceedingly whimsical, and full of the charm that distinguished the Villedeuils. Their age, their characters, were contrasted, yet complementary. This was the secret of the profound understanding between them. The elder brother protected the younger as would a father or a mother.

On the roads of Burgundy and along the valley of the Rhône as they set off on their journey to the South of France, their two figures presented so marked a contrast that Jules, clean-shaven, fair-skinned,

Beginnings

slim and graceful, was taken for a young woman in disguise whom Edmond might have abducted. The latter was amused by this, and possibly flattered.

At Mussy, where they arrived on the first evening of their journey, worn-out, with bruised and aching feet after walking twenty kilometres in new shoes, they sketched in the thirteenth-century church an old Descent from the Cross which is thought to be the tomb of Guillaume de Mussy and his wife. Other churches, other old houses, other statues detained them on their journey. 'For beginners', says François Fosca, 'their water-colours are extremely attractive. They reflect the manner of Hervier and are treated with a great freedom of execution. The picturesque old tumble-down places are rendered without baldness and with a very good sense of the possibilities of painting in water-colour.'

The notes they made on their journey, containing at the outset hardly anything except the menus of their meals and the number of kilometres covered in the day, became by degrees notes of a more literary character. Edmond declares that this little diary of their travels made writers of them, and this is true, but what was it made them collaborators? On this point we have only a brief indication from Edmond: 'He *(i.e.* Jules[was often heard to say: "... I was born to write, in the whole course of my life, a little duodecimo volume of the kind La Bruyère wrote, and nothing but this little duodecimo!" It is therefore solely out of tenderness for me that he co-operated with me right up to the very end...'

They reached Marseilles towards the end of October, 1849, and on November 7, they disembarked from the *Philippe-Auguste* at Algiers. From the moment of their arrival, with either pencil or paint brush in hand, they roved night and day round the town and its suburbs. They spent six hours in a state of enthusiasm watching the negresses, the beggars and the dogs in the place du Burnous. They climbed up to the Casbah, visited the cemetery of Sidi-Abder-Rhaman, installed themselves at tables in arab cafés and dance halls, lounged about the bazaars, attended swimming displays at the Moorish baths, took the bus to the Mustapha quarter surrounded with pleasure gardens, walked in the Jardin d'Essais, made their way into the Grand Mosque, climbed up to the Emperor's Fort to admire the panorama of the city, explored villages inhabited by French colonists.

Algiers was therefore far from a disappointment to them, although

Edmond brought back with him a tendency to dysentery which caused him agonizing pain for two years and permanently affected his health. 'On each page, my dear Louis,' Jules wrote to his friend, 'there are arresting pictures, pictures in the manner of Decamps, as I would say to you if you understood painting ... Decidedly, my dear chap, there are just two cities in the world: Paris and Algiers. Paris, everyone's city, Algiers the artist's ...' In Paris, Jules would never again pass a shop that sold things from Algeria without feeling himself back once more in those lovely days in Algiers. 'Nothing in the Western world has given me this; it is only over there that I have drunk this air of Paradise, this magic philtre of oblivion, this Lethe flowing so quietly from everything around me and drowning memories of my native Paris.'

Writing on December 26, 1849, to Paul Collardez, he remarked: 'Life as a traveller on foot is so full of interesting variations! This road along which he journeys in a leisurely way, without anything to hurry him on, stopping in the shade, drinking at an inn and sometimes spending the night there, and chatting with the natives, is so prolific in contrasts; this continual succession of hotels and taverns, of genial hosts and sullen lodging-house keepers, this uninterrupted switching from a snack to a dinner of several courses, this vagabond life in which one sees so much on one's own, this panorama that has unrolled itself for five whole months before us, from the hillsides of the Vougeot so fertile in misty September to the cacti of the Mitidja desert peopled with jackals, from Bar-sur-Seine to Algiers, has been full of delightful impressions for us.'

Later on they were to change their opinions. 'It is strange,' runs a note of January, 1869, 'how at this moment we have come to feel a kind of distaste and contempt for the vulgarity of this colourful land that we once loved so much ... Our interests are no longer there, but with a country of odd and eccentric human beings and complex social groups such as England or Russia, in which the main source of the picturesque is found in men.' They could, of course, speak with confidence on England and Russia, never having visited either of these countries.

Their short stay in Algiers none the less remained for the moment the happiest time of their youth. They had been so taken with North Africa that they thought of pushing on as far as Timbuctoo as members of an expedition planned for the following spring.

Beginnings

On their return to Paris on December 17, 1849, they settled down in the rue Saint-Georges in a dark ground-floor flat where Jules spent the whole winter making a fair copy of their notes and putting finishing touches to his water-colours, most of which he subsequently burnt. From the ground-floor they moved up to a flat on the third floor, at the far end of the courtyard. There they were to remain for twenty years.

In their *Manette Salomon* Coriolis paints an excessively terrifying picture of the Bréda, or Saint-Georges, quarter, but the example of the Goncourts themselves and of many others proves that one could work there very well. As with all the houses in the quarter, theirs was none too respectably inhabited. The *Journal* mentions 'a harlot of the name of Garcia' who lived in a flat let for twelve hundred francs on the second floor and borrowed money from Rose, their servant, when the rain prevented her going out to pick up a man. On the same landing as themselves, where one night a woman was almost murdered, lived Anna Deslions with whom they got on friendly terms, and doubtless Jules became her lover. She used to send her maid with her nightgown to the man with whom she was going to sleep and had a different set of things for each of her lovers in the colours he preferred. The little window of their water-closet looked out on a flat belonging to an actress called Lagier, whom they could hear shouting at her lover in fits of jealous rage.

In the spring of 1850, they visited Switzerland and Belgium. In September they stayed at Sainte-Adresse, at the Château Vert. They had given up the idea of going to Trouville, 'that branch-establishment of the boulevard des Italiens', to Dieppe on account of its pebbly beach, to Etretat which they knew of only through Alphonse Karr, the novelist, who later became editor of *Le Figaro*. 'Sainte-Adresse, my dear Louis,' writes Jules, 'is the Asnières of Le Havre. It is a seed-bed of little villas, grouped in lines on a hill that dies away into the sea ... We did not catch ourselves feeling bored for a single minute. The sea is really a huge source of entertainment. It is as good as the finest landscape in the world.' Besides this they had Shakespeare, Rabelais, and their work. 'To provide myself with some distraction in between two tides I amused myself with composing, as an exercise in style, some nineteen chapters which I dare not call original, nineteen completely disjointed chapters with nothing to weld them together. I put into them every kind of stylistic ornament, I piled up daring phrases, words that clashed with each other, and by putting a great deal of colour into this serious pantaloonery, I believe I have enriched my palette.'

Shortly before this visit to Le Havre and Sainte-Adresse Jules contracted the syphilis that he was to die of twenty years later. About the same time, he passed before the military court of appeal in Paris, by which, in spite of his short sight and the blue spectacles he had donned for the occasion, he was declared fit enough to become a hussar. 'By the way,' wrote Edmond in their first novel *En 18..*, 'Jules has been caught!—The humbug, he is as short-sighted as a couple of governments!'

Not counting a monograph on *La Cuisinière* that Edmond sent to the publisher Curmer for *Les Français Peints par Eux-Mêmes*, their first literary effort was not, as has been believed, a sketch written for the actor Sainville. The archives of the Comédie-Française contain this unfortunately undated letter from Jules: 'Saturday evening. Sir, I have just finished a sketch in three acts in verse. But before you consign this first work of mine to the files of the Comédie-Française I should be exceedingly happy if you would be so kind as to put yourself to the trouble of reading it. I am very young, and, more than that, unknown; these two things, I trust, will count in your opinion as claims to your respect. There is a third I will not insist upon; it is that of the play: *Hégésippe Moreau*. If you have the time and the goodness to listen to my work, would you be kind enough to write to tell me on what day *at the beginning* of next week and at what hour I may have the pleasure of presenting myself at your house?'

Neither Jules nor Edmond ever mentioned this *Hégésippe Moreau* in three acts in verse, one scene of which, sent by Jules to his friend Louis Passy, has been published in the paper called *L'Intermédiaire des Chercheurs et Curieux*.

Working opposite each other at a large table specially made for them by a carpenter in Goncourt, they next had the idea of composing, with the help of a paint-brush dipped in Indian ink, a piece for Sainville, an actor at the Palais-Royal. Sainville, who in his day enjoyed great popularity, usually played the part of a dull-witted bourgeois. They rang his bell 'as one rings at a dentist's door'. A pretty housemaid showed them into the drawing-room where they began to read their play, which they had called *Sans Titre*, to the actor, beside whom was standing a tall individual who was his customary adviser. 'At home, this easy-going, jovial actor on the stage assumed for the audition of a play an expression of sullen and impenetrable reserve which gradually took on something of the venomous look on the faces of those grand mandarins one sees on vases of the Celestial Empire issuing orders for execution.'

After an icy silence, Sainville told them that *Sans Titre* had not enough couplets, spoke of an eventual collaborator and asked them to leave the manuscript with him for a fortnight; at the end of which he sent it back to them. He had handed it 'to the person responsible for reading plays submitted' who had found in it 'a good deal of wit, but not enough dramatic quality'. The following year a play that was not theirs, *Le Bourreau des Crânes*, met with some success at the Variétés; its opening, a box on the ear administered in the auditorium, was the same as that of *Sans Titre*, which they promptly burnt, as they did *Abou-Hassan*, its younger brother, also rejected by the Palais-Royal.

In 1851 they were at Louèche, in the heart of the Valais mountains, where later on Maupassant came to take a cure. There they took hot baths, went on expeditions, had very poor meals, played dominoes, read, and in a leisurely fashion started to write their first novel, *En 18 . . .* Towards the end of August they were in Neufchâteau at the marriage of their cousin Fédora Henrys to Léon Rattier. What a wedding! The celebrations lasted from August 23 to September 6 for six hours a day!

Lingering behind in the lovely house in the Place Jeanne d'Arc, where they had absolute freedom and a garden in which to walk, they took possession of the library in order to work there. At the end of October they were back in Paris. At about this time a review of work by young writers, *La Revue de Paris*, was on the point of appearing under the patronage of Théophile Gautier. 'If it doesn't give us an article', they remarked, 'it will belie its claims'. By now their novel was ready for printing. 'Printing! By jove, the very word excites me!'

Set in type, printed and bound at their expense, *En 18 . .* was left with the publisher Dumineray. The dominant influence revealed in it is that of Heine. He and Poe were the masters of their youth, two masters of morbid genius towards whom one would suppose that Jules, with his inclination to fantasy, would have been more attracted than Edmond, had not the latter written in 1875: 'If my sluggish soul experiences the need of a slight poetic stimulus, it is in Heinrich Heine I find it; if my mind, weary of the commonplace character of life, needs to find relaxation in the supernatural or the fantastic, I discover it in Poe. Nevertheless it vexes me to be stimulated or supernaturalized by foreigners alone.'

En 18 . . is a typical beginner's work, self-conscious, vague, pretentious, incoherent, and rather colourless, but a work that casts light upon the state of mind of the younger generation in 1851. The Goncourts' favourite subjects of inspiration already appear in it: the *femme fatale*, the eighteenth century, the French Revolution, Japan, and contempt for Molière. Edmond, who brought out a new edition of *En 18 . .* in 1885, was on the whole rather proud of it, even though he wrote in his *Journal*: 'On re-reading the proofs of *En 18 . . .* I sometimes fly into a temper over the artificiality of the book which makes me fling the printed pages on the floor and kick them away . . . Then I go and collect them again.' In the preface to this new edition he wrote: 'This book is badly composed, or not composed at all, if you like! On the other hand, what proud impulse of revolt, what reckless bursts of indignation, violent blasphemies against every kind of religion, bold assertion of literary and artistic independence, and haughty revolutionary principles are preached in these pages, and then what scrupulous regard for learning, what inquisitive interest in knowledge—and in what example of light literature written by a novice will you find this same crossing of swords in lofty arguments, this nimble juggling with paradoxes, this vitality which later, having gained full mastery over itself, will give relief to the bravura passages in *Charles Demailly* and *Manette Salomon;* and also this stirring up of problems such as are ventilated in the most serious writings, and, from beginning to end of the volume, the striving and the aspiration of its authors to reach the highest peaks of thought.'

★ ★ ★

On the morning of December 1, 1851, the Goncourts, overcome with emotion, and highly excited because the publication of their book had been fixed for the following day, were just getting up when their cousin Villedeuil's 'confidential companion' M. de Balmont, a former officer in the Life Guards, now an asthmatical, cross-grained conservative with hair going grey, burst in upon them like a gust of wind. 'Good God!' he cried, 'it's happened.' 'What on earth has happened?' 'Why, the Revolution!' 'Oh, confound it! And our novel was to be published today!' They rushed into the streets to find troops were in possession of the offices of *Le National*, and looked everywhere for the poster which was to make France and the world acquainted with their names. Not a poster anywhere! In order to reach their uncle Courmont's house in the rue de Verneuil they had to cross the Seine. Near the headquarters of the Legion of Honour and the Audit Office the soldiers all were tippling beside their stacked-up rifles under a radiant sun. When they reached their uncle's they found he had been arrested.

Gerdes, their printer, and also that of the *Revue des Deux Mondes*, whose printing works had been invaded by the troops, had thrown the posters into the fire; the title and certain sentences in the book might have been taken for political allusions. *En 18*.. did not therefore appear until December 5, and then without any posters to advertise it and minus certain passages from a chapter dealing with politics. 'Six months before this happened,' said the Goncourts, 'we had made the most dangerous allusions to what are only now accomplished facts.'

A pleasant surprise, however, awaited them: an article by Jules Janin in the *Débats*, in which their novel was reviewed with *La Dinde Truffée* by Varin and Léris and *Les Crapauds Immortels* by Clairville and Demanoir. 'A fantastic farrago of our book and some current sketches', wrote the Goncourts, 'in which he talked of everything in reference to us and of us in reference to everything.' The famous critic scolded them in a fatherly way for the daring liberties they took with style, without apparently suspecting that these were derived from himself. His article consoled them for their disappointment over the publication of their book: 'It is a joy,' they said, 'that takes one's breath away, one of those joys one cannot expect to meet with again any more than the joys of first love. The whole of that day we did not walk, we ran.' Janin welcomed them with bluff good-humour: 'Well I'll be damned, this is just how I imagined you!' They were waiting for other encouraging articles when one arrived from the *Revue des Deux Mondes* (it was by Pontmartin, the Catholic critic) 'savage, ferocious, almost impolite... which repudiated us from top to bottom, stuck a dunce's cap on our heads, and dismissed us with the epithet of tap-room pedants'.

Sixty copies of *En 18*.. were sold. Shortly afterwards Dumineray begged them to take the ones that were unsold off his hands. These were about 1,000 copies, which they deposited in an attic in the rue Saint-Georges. 'Some two or three years later, having gone up to this attic, I no longer know why, we each sat down on the floor in a corner and began to read a copy picked up from the heap; and that day we found our first novel so feeble, so imperfect, so childish that we decided to burn the whole pile.'

Edmond and Jules

'If you want to succeed,' Janin had told them, 'there's nothing but the theatre'. They got the idea of a New Year's Eve revue, which would consist of a conversation between a lady and gentleman during the last hour of December 31, and would be performed on that evening. It would be called *La Nuit de la Saint-Sylvestre*. It seemed to Lemoine-Montigny, the manager of the Gymnase-Dramatique, insufficiently scenic. On Janin's recommendation they took it to Mme Allan, of the Comédie-Française, who received them as she was putting the last touches to her costume in front of a triple mirror. The tone of her voice was harsh, without any relation to the one she used on the stage. An appointment was made for the following day, when they received a charming welcome, with many murmured flatteries. Having accepted the part, the actress promised to learn it by December 31. It was now the 21st. They rushed off to Janin, who could not see them, being busy on his article, but referred them to Arsène Houssaye, manager of the Comédie-Française. Off they went to see Houssaye, who received them standing: 'Gentlemen,' he said, 'we are not putting on any new plays this year. That has already been decided, I can do nothing about it.' But he added, 'If Lireux will read your play and make a report on it, I will put it on if I can secure a special reading.' Off to see the journalist Lireux. 'We made our way into the den of a typically Balzacian man of letters, reeking of bad ink and the warm smell of an unmade bed.' Lireux promised to make a report the next day. Off to see Brindeau, who should play opposite Mme Allan. He was out, but would soon be back. At half past four they wrote to Lireux. At five o'clock they went back to Brindeau's house. At six o'clock still no Brindeau. At half past seven they caught him in his dressing-room just after his performance. Running with sweat and naked under his dressing-gown, he agreed to listen to their play and was pleased with his part. So they took their manuscript to Lireux, and then returned to Mme Allan's house, where they found her surrounded by her family, and gave her an account of their day. Two days later, sitting on a bench on the stairway of the Comédie-Française, they suddenly heard the ugly off-stage voice of Mme Allan, from behind a door closing on her. 'That's not decent of you, it really isn't!' Lireux had decided to refuse their play.

Edmond has passed this judgement on their little sketch: 'It's a witty little drawing-room piece, but its wit has rather too many airs and graces.'

Beginnings

In April, 1852 they made a fruitless attempt to approach Lemoine-Montigny, manager of the Gymnase-Dramatique, with a play based on *En 18*... Still undiscouraged, they composed for the Théâtre-Lyrique, in which their cousin Villedeuil had an interest, a farce in the style of the old Italian harlequinades, entitled *Mam'selle Zirzabelle*, in which prose was intermingled with verse. But this attempt met with no more success than the previous ones.

IV

Journalists

One morning in November, 1851, a solemn young man with a beard rang their door-bell. He was Pierre-Charles, Comte de Villedeuil, and their cousin, being related to them through their mother's family. 'When quite a child, he tried to pass for a man . . . Sitting beside him at dinner when I was only fifteen, he would talk to me of orgies that made me open my eyes very wide. Already he was dabbling in literature, and . . . at twenty he held republican opinions and had a great beard, wore a light brown sugar-loaf hat, referred to "my Party", wrote for *La Liberté de Penser*, drafted terrific articles against the Inquisition and was lending money to the philosopher Jacques. His father was reported to have had a touch of sun in India. Pierre-Charles, Comte de Villedeuil, seemed to be the offspring of this sunstroke.'

Villedeuil was looking for collaborators in a biographical work. Family ties, and the common bond of age and ambitions drew him and his cousins together. In a café in the vicinity of the Gymnase, they amused themselves by trying to think of a title for a newspaper. *L'Eclair*, that was it! 'What about starting such a paper?' With an income of 50,000 francs, the capital of which he had already eaten into considerably, Villedeuil made a tour of the money-lenders, and imagined a front-page picture of lightning striking the Institute. Although the Board of Censors banned the picture, *L'Eclair* was given official sanction on December 2. It appeared on January 12, as a weekly review of literature, drama and the arts. Its programme was romantic. There was an article by the Goncourts on the actor Fechter (who was to create the role of Armand Duval in *La Dame aux Camélias*) and articles by Villedeuil on *En 18* . . . The editor and his two cousins did all the work. Subscribers did not hurry to enrol. 'When a red-haired mistress of Villedeuil's, Sabine by name, who is the only person who comes to this office, asked us one day: "Why does that gentleman over there look so sad?" we answered in chorus: "He's our accountant!"'. This was Pouthier, the Bohemian they had known at school, whose name often appears in the *Journal*.

Journalists

To prolong the life of the paper Villedeuil sold a collection of *Ordonnances des Rois de France*, a money-lender advanced him five or six thousand francs and collections of standard works were offered as a free gift to principals of educational establishments and headmasters of lycées. A ball was organized for subscribers (there were finally about 250 of them), for contributors, and for all the friends of *L'Eclair*, among whom some female 'acquaintances' introduced themselves, when Nadar (the 'Couturat' of *Charles Demailly*), an expert in practical jokes and in advertising, who was beginning a series of caricatures in the papers, flung open the windows, and invited the passers-by to come in.

The Goncourts had a passionate admiration for Gavarni—they put him on the same level as Balzac, and even went so far as to copy his lithographs—and the idea occurred to them of getting Villedeuil to ask him for some drawings. During a dinner at the Maison d'Or, which marked the beginning of his friendship with them, a friendship that was to result in their becoming portrayers of manners, Gavarni proposed the series entitled *Le Manteau d'Arlequin*. His first two designs were engraved on wood (the others were lithographed) and they alternated from week to week with drawings by Nadar.

Gavarni lived at the Point-du-Jour, next to a tavern that bore the sign: *A la Renaissance du Perroquet Savant*. His mind was incessantly in search of new ideas that would completely revolutionize the life of his day. He would often go on working while the Goncourts were there and they used to spend whole evenings with him, quite forgetting the time of the last boat from Versailles as they listened to him talking of Lamennais, Proudhon, Delaroche, Delacroix, Balzac, and all the other famous men he had known.

They went on visiting Janin, always cheerful, always beaming in spite of his gout, but the man they went to see most often was Peyrelongue, the picture-dealer, a fat man who looked almost as if he were wrapped in a gold-beater's skin. He liked to have five or six people at his table, and every month his mistress would slip away with one of the guests, Pouthier for preference. Among the company were Hafner, the Alsatian, Valentin, who made drawings for *L'Illustration*, the foppish Deshayes, a rather drab personality, the fair-haired colourist Voillemot, the young painter Servin, and others. The whole lot conducted themselves riotously.

L'Eclair was just managing to struggle along as a weekly when, on

Edmond and Jules

his cousins' advice, Villedeuil decided to bring out a daily paper modelled on *Le Charivari*, which would be called *Paris* and would be concerned only with literature. Gavarni would contribute a lithograph every day. The first number of *Paris* bears the date, October 20, 1852, and contains a leading article by Edmond and Jules. The paper came out at half past four, giving information on closing prices and a list of current theatrical performances.

The offices of *Paris* were at first in the buildings of the Maison d'Or, and later in the rue Bergère, above the offices of the Assemblée Nationale. Here Villedeuil gave orders, made harangues, introduced innovations, and every day invented new ways of attracting subscribers. His accountant, Lebarbier, the grandson of an eighteenth-century engraver of vignettes, came, like Pouthier, from the lowest circles of Bohemia. The paper was put together by a deserter from *Le Corsaire* (a rival paper), one Venet (the Malgras of *Charles Demailly*), a 'tartuffe' and possibly a police agent, 'one of the few writers', says the *Journal*, 'who had escaped from the dragnet in which the government had collected the journalists on December 2'.

At the *Paris* office the Goncourts became associated with Aurélien Scholl, who had been a reporter on *Le Corsaire* and *La Naïade*. 'A nervous little fellow, delicate and bashful, given to blushing—a violet on a bench in the ante-room of a newspaper. There is something of the woman and of the girl in him . . . he comes from Bordeaux, writes charming verses, and a rather wild sort of prose. We try to put him at his ease by shaking his hand very cordially, we introduce him to Villedeuil, we help him and we like him.' Scholl was to be Jules's best friend for a very long time.

On the editorial board of the paper were the lachrymose Murger, Banville with his smooth, hairless face and his falsetto voice, his 'subtle paradoxes and humorous character sketches', Alphonse Karr, Eggis, a lean individual with long, greasy hair, who had a private grudge against the Academy, Henri Delaage who had a passion for occultism, had already written several curious works, and was later to become editor of *La Chiromancie*. Of Forgues, the translator and intimate friend of Gavarni, the *Journal* tells us that this 'congealed Southerner' had 'something about him of an ice fried according to the Chinese recipe'. He was the author of a laudatory article nine columns long in the *Athénéum* of April, 1894, on the Goncourts' *Histoire de la Société Française Pendant la Révolution*. Louis Enault, critic and translator of *Uncle Tom's Cabin*, is hardly better treated; the *Journal* describes him as 'garnished with cuffs, and with a sinuous figure like that of a singer of drawing-room ballads'. The *Paris* team reached its full complement with Félix Gaïffe (the Florissac of *Charles Demailly*), a handsome, indolent fellow, for whom literature was 'a state of violence in which one can only hold one's own by extravagant measures', and Roger de Beauvoir, 'often bubbling over in the office like the foam on champagne', sparkling, overflowing with good spirits, talking of murdering his wife's lawyers, and throwing out vague invitations to dinners that never came off.

After cruelly ridiculing each contributor, the *Journal* praises the group as a whole. 'At the present moment, the paper is getting under way, it isn't making money, but it makes a stir. It is young, since it has as its heritage the literary convictions of 1830. In these columns are displayed the ardour and the fine enthusiasm of a host of marksmen on the march, without order or discipline, but full of disdain for subscriptions and subscribers.' The Wednesday number was edited throughout by the Goncourts. In the issue of April 15 there appeared their double portrait by Gavarni.

★ ★ ★

One day towards the end of 1852, on his return from seeing Latour-Dumoulin, controller-general of printed publications, Villedeuil announced in a theatrical voice that an action was being brought against *Paris* because of a review by Alphonse Karr and another one in which there were some verses. 'Who was it put some verses into an article this month?' 'We did,' said the Goncourts.

The article, which was called 'A Journey from 43 rue Saint-Georges to No. 1 rue Laffitte', reviewed in a satirical fashion, after the manner of Sterne, the business concerns, the odd chemist's shops, the dealers in pictures and bric-à-brac which the brothers passed every day. Referring to a picture by Diaz exhibited in a shop that was run by a former artist's model, the Goncourts had quoted a few lines of verse by Tahureau taken from Sainte-Beuve's *Tableau de la Poésie au XVIe Siècle*. This Diaz had been sent by Mlle Nathalie, of the Comédie-Française to Mlle Rachel, who had sent it back to her. 'Why should I', she asked, 'deprive you of a picture that I myself would have to keep hidden?'—and she cited Molière's Arsinoé as a woman fascinated by nudities, a remark that showed a singular ignorance of the repertoire, as Mlle Nathalie did not fail to point out to her illustrious colleague. It was this correspondence that the Goncourts had published in *Paris*, and it had come to them from Janin.

An action against them for verses quoted more than twenty years before by a member of the Academy! It was really due to resentment against the independent spirit of *Paris*, against Villedeuil's aristocratic insolence, his dealings on the Stock Exchange, his disdain of invitations from the Tuileries and from Nieuwerkerke, lover of the Princess Mathilde, the supposed Orléanism of the two brothers, who were friends of the Passys, their refusal—this was an idle rumour—to write a cantata at the government's command. It was also, so Edmond wrote to Collardez, because they had attacked 'Mlle Rachel in person'!

Their uncle Courmont, chief adviser to the Audit Office, went to see Latour-Dumoulin. The latter at first believed the affair to be a question of blackmail. Better informed, he had used his influence with M. de Royer, the Attorney-General, but Armand Lefebvre de Béhaine, counsellor of State and cousin of the accused, pleaded in vain with M. de Royer, the staunchness of whose opinions in favour of the government had earned him the appointment of chief advocate to the Supreme Court of Appeal; the eminent magistrate replied that he himself, after due investigation, had given orders for the prosecution. As a preliminary measure he advised the delinquents to address a petition for pardon to the Emperor. A few days later the examining magistrate summoned them before him and was surprised to learn that the lines from Tahureau had already been reproduced by Sainte-Beuve.

There was a stay of action in the suit, but the report in a Belgian newspaper of their interrogation, in which the examining magistrate was called an executioner in a frock coat, and also a statement by the police originating from people intimately acquainted with *Paris*, resulted in the reopening of the case. Summoned to appear before the 6th court of summary jurisdiction, whose indulgent attitude with regard to suits concerning the Press was known, they went with their uncle to visit their judges, as was the custom. 'We went first,' says the *Journal*, 'to our presiding judge, Legonidec. He lived at the top of the rue de Courcelles, possibly in order to be nearer to the place Monceau, where, according to public report, he used to go in search of lovers.' ... He was as dry as his name, cold as an old wall, sallow, cadaverous, bloodless, with the air of an inquisitor. 'Next we saw the

Journalists

two other judges, Duraty ... who ... did not appear to find us particularly guilty, and Lacaussade, a bewildered sort of creature, who looked like Leménil taking a foot bath in *Le Chapeau de Paille d'Italie*.' The deputy public prosecutor, charged with summoning the brothers to appear, showed himself disconcertingly affable. He considered them innocent, but Latour-Dumoulin had given him his orders. 'And this man who was comfortably off, who had an income of several thousand pounds, was about to ask the maximum penalty for an offence of which we were not guilty. He announced this naïvely, cynically, to our faces.' Their uncle, in spite of his egotism and although he was 'a tough old bourgeois', was highly indignant about this.

In the waiting-room at Latour-Dumoulin's, whom they were intent on seeing personally in order to raise the question of suspected blackmail, they were kept hanging about so long that on seeing their angry faces the high functionary believed at first they were going to challenge him to a duel. He was quite prepared to recognize that it could not be a question of extorting money, but *Paris* was a paper connected with the theatre. 'Blackmail, for instance, such as asking to sleep with the actresses.' 'I declare, sir ... we do not know any actresses ... ' Latour-Dumoulin set himself to soothe his interlocutors with fair words. 'When he had thoroughly sickened us with this sudden sugary change of front and the trite little catchwords of a man who does not want to make enemies, we took our leave of him with all the contempt one feels for a hypocritical persecution and for an Empire that sends you with its compliments before the courts.'

The hearing took place the next day, February 12. Villedeuil had ordered for the occasion a cinnamon-coloured coachman's coat with five collars. He took the Goncourts to the Palais de Justice in his yellow barouche, 'a barouche that had something of the look of a Louis XIV state-coach and also of an operating table. "I am much guiltier than they are," he cried to the usher who wanted to bar him from the court. "I am the owner of the newspaper." Since the beginning of the action he had been torn between two feelings—a desire to play the leading part and anxiety for the interests of his paper.'

The presiding magistrate made them sit in the dock, the place reserved for felons, whereas it was then the custom to allow journalists to remain beside their counsel. 'They had a rehearsal yesterday,' said Alphonse Karr as he took his seat beside them between the gendarmes. Their voices trembled with anger as they stated their identity. After touching on what was urged against Karr—an old epigram of Lebrun's recast by him, that Nieuwerkerke had taken as directed at himself—the deputy public prosecutor did not find much to say concerning the lines from Tahureau, or about a passage in the article referring to a woman coming back from a dinner with her stays wrapped up in a newspaper, but he inveighed against Villedeuil, who could no longer contain his joy and pride at having cast doubts upon feminine virtue. Coming back to the two brothers, he represented them as corrupters of morals, men who had regard for neither law nor gospel, low-born scoundrels, apostles of physical love. Their counsel, as had been foreseen, groaned, burst into tears, and depicted them as virtuous young men, but a trifle feather-headed. His major argument was that they had an old servant who had devoted herself to them for the past twenty years. Finally the case was adjourned for a week. In the interval, M. Rouland, later to become Minister of Education, Vice-President of the Senate, President of the Council of State, and Governor of the Bank of France, most fortunately succeeded Royer, the Attorney-General whose hatred was to pursue them for a long time.

On February 19 Alphonse Karr, the Goncourts and Lebarbier, the managing director of *Paris*, were acquitted Although the indictable passages in the article were judged licentious, the court allowed that the authors had not intended to outrage public morals or good manners.

As may be imagined, after such a trial the two brothers were hardly satisfied, and indeed with the political and social regime established by force some two years before they were not satisfied at all. 'It means a flood of... corruption and dishonour, the abdication of the human conscience', wrote Jules to Collardez. 'Here is decadence in its vilest form, and it would appear that the new society is getting ripe for a new invasion of the barbarians.' By degrees, however, all that had been disagreeable and even a little frightening in their adventure was forgotten, and a feeling of pride and satisfaction became dominant in their minds. 'It is really strange that the four men most completely without any trace of narrow or mercenary motives, the four pens most entirely consecrated to art, should be the ones summoned to sit in the dock in a police court: Baudelaire, Flaubert and ourselves.'

V
By-Ways of History

Dedicated to Gavarni, *La Lorette* was published in the summer of 1853. In it these reputed romantics boasted of being the first to protest against apologias of the courtesan in love. *La Lorette* was their fifth work, the others being, besides *En 18...* and *La Nuit de la Saint-Sylvestre*, *Le Salon de 1852*, a series of articles reprinted from *L'Eclair*, and *Les Mystères des Théatres* (1852). On the cover of this little work, written like the others on themes propounded in *L'Eclair*, there figured side by side with their own names that of Cornélius Holf, a pseudonym for Villedeuil. On the back cover was an announcement of *Le Camp des Tartares*, by Edmond and Jules de Goncourt, a monograph on the Palais-Royal that was later to be developed into *L'Histoire de la Société Française Pendant la Révolution*.

At Dentu's bookshop in the Palais-Royal *La Lorette*, 6,000 copies of which were printed, was sold out in a week and a little later it was reprinted with a vignette by Gavarni.

In their reviews on the theatre the Goncourts showed themselves pioneers, not by reason of their coruscating style, but in their way of talking about themselves, their friends, and their own personal affairs and of admitting on occasion that they had not seen the play they were writing about. Of criticism in its truest sense there was little or nothing.

The editorial staff of *Paris* enjoyed itself as people did in those happy times. On Sundays they would go in a body to a little country retreat belonging to Villedeuil, in the garden of which the only shade was provided by a stone table. After dinner, Landelle, a novelist who wrote stories of life at sea, would bellow shanties at the top of his voice, Venet hum pastoral airs of Colin and Colinette, and Mlle R... sing a fragment from some opera, while the master of the house would discourse with certain eccentric gentlemen on the monopoly in leeches in Morocco. On their return, they would take a ride on the roundabouts in the Champs-Elysées.

The two brothers had collaborated less with *Paris* since their misadventure with the law; Royer had told them semi-officially that they were being watched and would be wise to occupy themselves a little less with journalism. So much had their morale been affected that they thought of going into exile in Belgium, as Sainte-Beuve had done five years before, there to start a paper free from government control. This idea of a paper of their own continued to haunt them for a very long time; in it they would have published reviews on art exhibitions, articles on prostitutes, the money market, etc. In January, 1858, their cousin Alphonse Lefebvre de Béhaine was still advising them to be prudent, and they returned to the idea of exiling themselves in order to show the government that they had 'certain qualities as pamphleteers'.

An article of April 27, 1853, on the writer Edouard Ourliac was the last they contributed to their cousin's paper. 'With this, dear reader, we bid you farewell! For six months, every Wednesday, we have taken you by the arm and chatted with you. A book of historical biographies now claims our whole attention, and at the point we both of us have reached I see no reason for keeping its title from you: it will be called, when finished, *Les Maîtresses de Louis XV*.' A supper that went on until six o'clock in the morning put the finishing touch to their career as boulevard reporters. They had not relinquished it with a light heart. 'Each morning rousing Paris from sleep with one's ideas! Each day sounding the charge, and hurling back sarcasm in a counter-attack, driving France back and keeping her hanging on the point of one's pen! This battle, this daily battle! Resting, but never sleeping! Making war with one's head, in short! Ah! what a glorious, though tiring, task!'

During 1852 they had published some twenty articles in *Paris*, and ten in the following year. Some of these were assembled by them in *Une Voiture de Masques*, and some later on by Edmond alone, in *Pages Retrouvées*.

Both *Paris* and *L'Eclair* ceased publication in 1853. In vain had Villedeuil appealed for help to the younger Dumas, to Montépin, and to Baudelaire, whose translation of Poe he published, in vain had he multiplied advertisements, programmes of entertainments, reports on racing events, financial news, railway time-tables, etc.

The Goncourts' transitory experience of journalism had not been without its use in their formation as writers; it had given more polish to their style and had taught them many things they were to turn

to advantage in *Charles Demailly*. 'I think', we read in this work, 'that men of wit and intelligence pass through journalism and do not remain there; it is for literature like garrison life for the army.'
On leaving journalism, Jules said goodbye to his youth.

At first they had not thought of anything more than a monograph on the Palais-Royal during the Revolution: *Le Camp des Tartares ou l'Histoire du Plaisir sous la Terreur*. With an abundance of documentary material at their disposal, their ideas grew wider. 'For this attempt at the reconstruction of a society at once so near to us and so far away', says the preface of *L'Histoire de la Société Française Pendant la Révolution*, 'we have consulted about fifteen thousand documents of the period: newspapers, books, pamphlets, etc. Behind the smallest fact put forward in these pages, and behind the most trifling remark, there is a document we hold ready to offer to our critics.'
Neither the *Journal* nor the *Letters* gives any indication of the researches they had to make. There is only a note at the end of February, 1854, which reads: 'All this winter, furious labours for our *Histoire de la Société Française Pendant la Révolution*. Every morning we carry off in one fell swoop some four or five hundred pamphlets from M. Perrot, who lodges close by in the rue des Martyrs.' This M. Perrot had made a collection of rare pamphlets, which he had bought for a penny each on the embankment, sometimes having to pawn his watch to buy them.
They did not visit the Bibliothèque Nationale, which was far from offering the same facilities it offers today: its books and documents were only handed over after endless difficulties. All day long they worked at home on papers and pamphlets either lent to them or bought with their own money. At night they wrote their book. No women, no pleasures. They had given their dress-suits away so as to make it impossible for them to go to evening parties; all they did was to take a walk after dinner along the outer boulevards.
The manager of the Porte Saint-Martin had put up in the foyer of his theatre some of the portraits by Gavarni reproduced in *Paris*. A young and pretty woman called Céleste Laveneur, at that time Aurélien Scholl's mistress, had fallen madly in love with Jules on seeing the portrait of him. Scholl was not in love with her any longer, but from the moment she was false to him, he became jealous. He was a strange sort of man, with an envious nature. Obsessed with

a fear of seeming ridiculous even in love, which with him was somewhat platonic, he would take pleasure in humiliating a woman in front of other people, and then make a show of repentance. 'Go to bed with Edmond,' he said to Céleste one day, 'then you can tell me what he's capable of.' She had tried to drown herself in the Gironde, but a dog had pulled her out of the water. Jilted by a lover, she had taken herself off to a brothel. When Jules wanted to break with her, she went and badgered him. He did not conceal from her that he thought her too foolishly romantic. In 1870, after his brother's death, Edmond received this little note: 'I have this moment read in the *Courrier du Gard* of June 23: "M. Jules de Goncourt is dead!" I have spent some time musing over *this single line*, recalling the memory of Jules, so fresh-coloured and so fair, but a few short years ago. There are tears in my eyes as I write these lines, still hoping you will tell me it is not true. After so long a time, perhaps, the name that follows will not recall anything to your mind. For my part I have the memory my heart supplies, and I remember having loved Jules very dearly.' The letter was signed 'Céleste, operatic artist'.

At the beginning of 1854 the brothers published a short work of thirty-six pages, *La Révolution dans les Mœurs*: under several headings —The Family; Society; Old Women; Young Men; Marriage; Rich People; Literature and the Arts; Social Decorum; Catholicism—it was a savage satire on contemporary family life as opposed to that of France in the good old days.

A few weeks later, appeared the 480 pages of *La Société Française Pendant la Révolution*, published at their expense by Dentu in an edition of 1,000 copies. They had not lost much time.

Their collected correspondence contains some forty letters and notes from Dentu. The earliest of these, dated March 29, 1854, informs the authors that the government supervisor of printed publications had refused permission to advertise the work.

Custom required that authors should take their own steps to get their work reviewed. 'When I tell you that we are having a rest', wrote Jules to Scholl, 'I only refer to a rest from writing, for in using our legs, making overtures, paying visits, putting on white gloves, leaving cards, and volumes, climbing stairs, and taking critics by assault, we are as active as two Napoleons or one Gaudissart.' Sainte-Beuve, Rémusat and Victor Hugo paid them compliments by letter. In October a friendly article from Pontmartin added to their satisfaction. Some objections, however, had been urged against them: an excessive use of anecdotes and over-elaboration of detail, on prostitution in particular, lack of references to provincial life and indifference in the matter of politics.

In the preface of *La Société Française Pendant la Directoire*, their next production, they invoked in their own defence Plutarch, Saint-Simon, Juvenal and their grandfather Antoine Huot. It might have been enough for them to reply that what they were blamed for was precisely what they had wished to do, and what they had wished to do was sufficiently justified by its novelty.

A few months later Jules did not hide his discouragement from Scholl. The picture he gave his friend of the state of contemporary literature was heart-breaking, but then pictures of this kind usually are. In May, 1854, they had gone to see him in Bordeaux, his native town, where he was editor of a newspaper, and where he was shortly to be condemned to two months' imprisonment for fighting a duel. There they discovered the local mushrooms, Médoc wine, Madras muslin, etc., and in the whimsical roundabout manner that was habitual with Jules, communicated their discoveries to the readers of *L'Artiste*. With Scholl and Monselet, in whom it is possible to see one of their precursors, they extended their journey as far as the sandy wastes of Provence.

This same year they paid a visit, the first the *Journal* mentions, to their uncle Jules de Courmont's country house at Croissy-Beaubourg. They spent August at Sainte-Adresse, at the Château-Vert, taking nearly all their meals at the house of one of Cherubini's grandsons, a M. Turcas, to whom they had been introduced by Asseline, editor of *Le Mousquetaire*, and who conceived an almost passionate affection for them. His mistress, Brassine by name, an actress at the Palais-Royal, had a woman friend called Dubuisson, and Jules has given an account of how he once climbed up to her balcony and, climbing more quickly than Asseline, had spent the night with her.

'I really think,' writes Jules, 'that I shall never experience love... except in such sudden gusts. This kind of thing rises up, chokes you, and carries you away to a paradise that vanishes before your eyes... She told me the story of her life, a host of sorrowful, even sinister, things, breaking off short with a *What do I care?* that seemed to swallow her tears. There appeared to me, in this common hussy's skin, an indescribably sad little figure, pensive, dreamy, sketched on the wrong side of a playbill. After each amorous embrace her heart went tick-tock like a cuckoo-clock in a village inn; a funereal sound, like pleasure singing a death-knell.' Jules was not a light-hearted lover. Relating this incident of the balcony again in 1881, when he was publishing *La Faustin*, the first scene of which it inspires, Edmond gave it the finishing touch. Asseline, who had remained in the street with him, had drawn him down to the sea, and there had proclaimed aloud his love for the faithless woman. 'A magnificent outpouring of passion', writes Edmond, 'which I have attempted to transpose in my book'.

Bordeaux, Croissy-Beaubourg, and Sainte-Adresse hardly halted them in their work, since their *Histoire de la Société Française Pendant la Directoire* appeared only eleven months later than *La Société Française Pendant la Révolution*. The former had less success than the latter; it must, however, be looked on as superior, since it shows a closer correspondence between technique and subject-matter. The *Journal* makes mention only of a laudatory article by the aged Barrière in the *Débats*. Co-editor with Berville of *Mémoires sur la Révolution Française*, Barrière was a good judge. His article had not been accepted without some difficulty. Jules had had to go and see the advertising manager. 'Really, sir,' said the latter, 'last year you advertised in many papers, but not in *Journal des Débats*. This exception seems very ungracious. And yet it is the best paper for advertisements.' Jules pleaded the meagreness of their resources and the little advantage the advertisements had been to them in the previous year; they had decided to put no more than five lines in the leading newspapers. After some haggling an advertisement costing a hundred francs was agreed on, 'on condition that the paragraph ... is inserted two or three days from now'. 'I will send the money for the advertisement today,' added Edmond. 'You give me your word of honour that you will put in an advertisement for a hundred francs this very day?' 'Yes, within the hour, for a hundred francs.' This passage from the *Journal* ends with a cry of horror: 'Blackmail, even with the *Débats!*'

They had sent a copy of *Société Française Pendant la Révolution* with their compliments to Montalembert,[1] who had at least approved of the spirit of their work. As candidates for a *prix Monthyon*, they sent him their *Directoire* and went to see him in his vast and peaceful

---

[1] Catholic politician and political writer.

residence in the rue du Bac. He told them the reason for their lack of success with the selection committee, of which he himself was not a member. 'It was your lively tricks of style that ruled you out. The Academy is a lady who does not like that sort of thing.' The Comte added: 'I should like *Le Correspondant* to take notice of your book... Have you any friend who could write it? It must be someone who can do it in a way to suit presbyteries as well as the landed gentry.' He liked their talents and more particularly their character, which, so he wrote to them in reference to *La Femme au XVIIIe Siècle*, 'allows you to interest the public without pandering to any of its base and servile tendencies'.

Their researches on the Directorate gave them the idea of a sketch entitled *Incroyables et Merveilleuses ou le Retour à Ithaque*. They took it to the Théâtre-Français, and then to Edouard Lemoine, manager of the Théâtre du Gymnase. 'Your study of French manners at the time of the Directorate is certainly original,' Lemoine replied. 'But would it have enough scenic effect? We rather doubt it.' Banville, who was well acquainted with the theatrical world and gave them a somewhat malicious description of it, was doubtless of the same opinion. 'You would have to have great actors, and you won't get them.'

Barrière remained their friend; they listened to his conversation and welcomed his advice. On the subject of their *Portraits Intimes du XVIIIe Siècle* the kindly old man chided them for wasting their talents on insignificant topics. 'A new and original kind of history, if it departs from the general form of ordinary historians, will not give the twentieth part of what is given by a voluminous compilation in which we have to wade through pages of details on what we know and have heard *ad nauseam*.' A savage attack on their *Directoire* in the *Débats* by the weighty and prolific economist Henri Baudillart was not calculated to reconcile them to 'the party of university professors, of academicians, eulogizers of the dead, critics, men incapable of producing ideas, men devoid of imagination, all of them made much of, fêted, entertained, given pensions, houses, bedecked with braid, with stars and crosses, stuffed and gorged with good things in the reign of Louis Philippe, and who always made their way in the world by merciless criticism of the intelligent minds of their day.' Up till this time their nonconformity might have passed for a sign of youth; from now on it would seem to be a settled habit.

Edmond and Jules

The attack, which took their historical methods as its objective, very probably discouraged them from writing a history of society under the Empire which they had already planned, as also a study of Paris in the eighteenth century, for which Jules had undertaken to engrave some plates. After *La Société Française Pendant la Directoire* they published a little work of some fifty pages, *La Peinture à l'Exposition de 1855*. That year they became friendly with the illustrator Célestin Nanteuil, with whom they went to stay at Bougival, a visit from which resulted some very successful pages in the *Journal*.

VI

Love Affairs

In the autumn of 1855 they decided to make the pleasant journey that political disturbances had prevented in 1849; relinquishing their plans for a weekly periodical, they set off for Italy. Now that the business of correcting the proofs of *Une Voiture de Masques* was off their hands they felt a kind of homesickness in reverse, a sense of satiety with their native country, a need for other skies.

Louis Passy accompanied them to look after their expenses. At Domodossola they bought a notebook bound in white parchment with a little leather strap, which is now in the Louvre. It might perhaps have been more convenient if each of them had had his own; this little detail says much for their close communion in thought and work. To these notes, which are mostly descriptive, Jules added sketches in pencil and water-colour. There are some excellent pages in *L'Italie d'hier*, which Edmond left unpublished until 1894: the carnival in Florence, where Jules had an adventure 'as silly and insipid as a novel', is a sparkling piece of work. And what amusing details of manners and costume, and of that Italy which before its unification was still a romantic country! While Jules strolled lazily round the streets and into museums, Edmond was busy copying letters in the libraries. In Venice, where they met the writer Armand Baschet, who had been sent on a special mission by the Minister of Education, Jules had a first idyllic affair to which allusion is made in one of Baschet's letters: 'This delicate wisp of red silk, which might be taken as the proud forerunner of that which I shall one day see on your lapel, has been snipped from the throat, from the bosom, whose whiteness and contours it will one day be given you to admire. I had announced your presence in '57, she had at first understood '56 and had smiled with so exquisite a smile that I will not venture to define it. Her eyes shone, *her lips grew moist*, the ripples of a most Venetian smile stole over this most Venetian face! And she exclaimed *Ah, Jules!* almost in the way of the *Ah, Armand!* in *La Dame aux Camélias*, with more modesty, however, of tone and expression.' To this letter Jules replied:

'Tell her that this thin strip of red is maid-in-waiting to my heart—I must have read that expression in a sentimental song... Say also to this dear creature that two minds that embrace each other without knowing it, that are in love without saying so to each other, make the tenderest of all communions, and that the memory of a single second plays, though I know not where within you, little symphonies without words that make mock of maidenly and innocent ideas...'

Still in Pisa on February 9, they did not reach Rome until a few days later. There they spent the month of March. From Naples, where they arrived on April 4, Jules brought away this charming impression which he noted the following year in the *Journal*: 'Whenever I drink a cup of chocolate, I am back again in Naples. It is midday. The sun is always shining, etc.'

Why are notes of this kind not more numerous, instead of descriptions of pictures, which, in spite of a certain virtuosity of style, make the book somewhat heavy? Nowhere does Jules's talent shine more brilliantly than in such passages. The assassination scene, with which the chapter on Rome comes to an end, is a page worthy of Mérimée.

In Rome, where they had taken up their quarters at 24 Via San Andrea della Frate, at the foot of the hill on which stands the church of the Holy Trinity, and where they led a rather gay life, now at the Villa Medici, now at the Embassy, the news had come to them of Heine's death. 'A great man has died,' wrote Jules to Baschet. 'Better to have had the whole funeral procession in the grave... than the man whose hearse they followed. I see none but dwarfs now left to bend Ulysses' bow.' To Scholl, on February 28, he had written: 'If you only knew what a volume we are bringing back from Italy! When we have put it into shape, let them put their heads together to try and understand it, and let them declare us raving mad. I give them permission to with all my heart. On the whole we are delighted that the battle against the fantastic school is not dying down. Opinions not exposed to clash after clash will never spring to life.' The following month, in a letter to Baschet, Jules once more recalls with satisfaction the controversies excited by the fantastic school. 'It appears there is a veritable crusade against Fantasy. They do us the honour of aiming the greatest and most violent blows at us, as at its standard-bearers, and they consign us, with all the pomp and ceremony of criticism, to the best padded room in the asylum of Bicêtre. Do you know what

Love Affairs

I think of that? It delights me. What are attacks but success in intaglio; it only needs time to bring it into high relief.'

They were back again in France in May. On the whole, Italy had disappointed them. Besides having found the light too crude, they were not much interested by antiquities. Rome was to please them better on their second journey.

They found some difficulty in getting re-acclimatized to life in Paris. 'Not a single young man, not a single young writer, not one bitter feeling. No public left, but a certain number of people who like, while reading, to assimilate a plain, transparent sort of prose such as you find in a newspaper.' For these fanatical lovers of the eighteenth century had a horror of a smooth and simple prose. What they liked in the eighteenth century was its furniture, its rococo ornaments, its works of art, its women, its manners—everything, in short, except its style.

Gavarni, who no longer had a mind for anything except mathematics, was not one to reconcile them with the world of letters.

It was during this period that they discovered Edgar Allan Poe, and caught a glimpse of a new kind of literature: 'Imagination by means of analysis, Zadig as an examining magistrate, Cyrano de Bergerac Arago's pupil.' Goodbye to love, in short!

Une Voiture de Masques, later to become *Quelques Créatures de ce Temps*, was published by Dentu in a very small edition and at their expense. These are portraits of real or imaginary people, either fanciful or based on records, sometimes written in the form of dialogues, and discussing almost everything published in the newspapers. About this time they got the idea of a book devoted to 'the good folk of Lorraine', based on a chronicle of Breuvannes and its neighbourhood. 'It is one of my regrets', Edmond confessed, 'that I did not write this book'.

We might be tempted to think that the idea of *La Fille Elisa* dated from this time if the Goncourts had not still been far removed from naturalism. One evening during this period they had gone to a house licensed by the Ecole Militaire, which Edmond was later to use as a background for his novel. A note of February, 1862, on the effacement of personality among prostitutes gives some authority for believing that they visited such places regularly. The *Journal* speaks of another 'abode of love', in which 'ten women dressed in variegated colours, blue, pink, white and yellow, were sprawling, flopping, wallowing

59

on divans in coquettish, animal poses, and with silly little quivers of their red heelless slippers . . . I go up into a room; it is like some wretched bedroom in an inn at a village where the stage-coaches no longer pass'.

On July 15, 1856, the two brothers had a conversation with Aubryet on the question of the kind of love affairs a writer should have. 'We ended by concluding that, for us especially, the ideal woman for a man of letters could never be met with in a brothel, and that since a man of letters is nothing but vanity personified, the mistress for him is a mistress ready to admire him—a Mme d'Albany or a Mme Arsène Houssaye.' Love that springs from the heart was foreign to their natures. 'I see love everywhere,' we read in the *Journal*, 'in books, in the theatre, and in other men's lives. People talk about it, harp upon it everlastingly. It is a thing that seems to exist and to take up much attention. However, here are we, both of us well formed and apt for the service of the heart, having the wherewithal to get clean shirts and pay for a bouquet, and devil take it if I can recall having been in love more than once for more than a week together.' Their chief grievance against passionate love was that the time and strength expended on it was so much time and strength lost for literary creation.

As we have already remarked, in love they were by no means romantics. 'After a few transports, and a few bursts of passion, a tremendous moral nausea takes hold of us and makes us, so to speak, spew up the orgies of the night before. Gorged and drunk with material things, we leave these beds adorned with lace as though we were leaving a museum of anatomical specimens, carrying with us I know not what sort of distressing surgical memories of these pleasant and agreeable bodies.' The notion that the identity of their natures implied in this plural could have found expression in acts was not at all repugnant to them. In a note of October 28, 1858, we read: 'M. de Vailly [1] has made a prediction about us that may perhaps be realized. He declares that if we fall in love we shall do so together, and that laws and morals should make an exception in favour of our phenomenal duality.' This exception was realized in the case of Maria Lepelletier, whose lover Jules had first become in 1851 during his last year at school. In May, 1857, Jules wrote: 'Men like ourselves need a woman of little breeding or education, who has nothing besides her

---

[1] His identity is uncertain, but he appears to have been some sort of fortune-teller.

Love Affairs

gaiety and her natural wit, since such a one will delight and charm us in the same way as a little animal to which we can become attached. But once a mistress has mixed a little in society, has a slight acquaintance with art or with literature, wishes to commune on an equal footing with our ideas and our feeling for beauty, and has the ambition to associate herself with us in the book we are bringing to birth or to share our tastes, she becomes as insupportable to us as a piano out of tune—and very soon an object of antipathy.'

On May 23 the *Journal* notes: 'My mistress [Maria Lepelletier] told me today that she had congestion of the lungs and hadn't enough money to buy the leeches ordered so that she could get well. She told me this, poor girl, in a way to arouse one's pity. But what is that compared with the terrible sufferings of those who can buy as many leeches as they like! The whole thing is to know whether a man who is dying of love or of diseased ambition suffers more than one who is dying of hunger? And for my part I sincerely believe he does.' For talking of the pangs of love and judging them more cruel than hunger, Jules, it will be agreed, was not very well qualified.

At the beginning of 1865 Maria Lepelletier, now a professional midwife, was attracting the interest of both of them. 'For some time', they wrote, 'we have been engaged in studying a midwife as interesting as the gateway into human life'. A few days after they made this note Maria told them the history of her life, part of which they were to use for the story of Romaine in *Sœur Philomène*. (It was with Maria, incidentally, that Jules at this time went to visit a fortune-teller in the rue Fontaine-Saint-Georges. 'You have nothing to fear,' she told him, 'from a sword thrust or a pistol shot, you have everything to fear from a stroke of the pen'.)

Maria was the daughter of a poor boat-builder, born in a little village on the banks of the Marne, where she was assistant in a pork butcher's shop. At the age of thirteen and a half she had been seduced by a young nobleman, the Comte de Saint-Maurice, who, after taking her to the Théâtre-Français and then to the Plat d'Etain, installed her in his house, where he had left her alone at the mercy of household gossip and with nothing to do but read wearisome books. For six months he had no relations with her but sometimes had girls brought from Paris with whom he amused himself by chasing them round his park, naked under their muslin gowns. On these occasions he shut Maria up indoors. After a year, in the course of which she had

61

attracted the attention of the Duc d'Orléans and his valet, the Comte, seized with remorse for his actions, blew his brains out. Pregnant, and with her sole possessions consisting of a watch ornamented with pearls and some diamond earrings, Maria went for her confinement to a midwife, who, after robbing her of her jewels, sold her to a masterbuilder, or it may have been to a pawnbroker. Her child died, but later she had another, a girl, who up to the age of eleven was looked after by an old nurse in La Villette, and then, for four years, by the nuns of Saint-Ouen. After some other adventures Maria had apprenticed herself as a midwife to the woman who had delivered her first child. At the maternity hospital, a nun surprised her wearing a lock of 'some loved one's hair' that was intended for another woman, and which she promptly swallowed. In *Germinie Lacerteux* can be found a picture of the epidemic of puerperal fever that she witnessed. Dismissed from the hospital, she entered a private nursing home in which was performed the Caesarean operation on a dwarf which the brothers cut out of *Sœur Philomène* but which Edmond has inserted in the *Journal*.

What attracted them in Maria, of whom Jules made an engraving, was her skin 'as fine as the tissue paper through which one can clearly see the circulation of the blood under a microscope', her gaiety, her laugh, her altogether delightful appearance, her open-armed embraces, the fairness of her wavy hair, the strange sweetness of her eyes, her fully rounded figure such as Rubens might have painted, her legs as slender as Diana's, her statuesque feet, her knees ... 'At certain times', they confessed, 'a man feels the need of indulging in some coarseness of language, and above all a man of letters, in whom matter held in bondage by the mind will sometimes take its revenge.' Other avowals are even plainer. On December 23, 1858, we are told that Maria accepted their 'collaboration'. As men of letters at all times, however, even in the arms of their mistress, they were still concerned with taking notes. The confidences of a midwife were of thrilling interest; in *Germinie* as in *La Fille Elisa* they made copious use of them. In their definition of love as they conceived it they gave priority to Marcus Aurelius over Chamfort. 'Love is a minor convulsion.'

In July, 1862, their attitude to love finds further definition: 'There is deep down in me, ready waiting but not yet having found an outlet, one single ambition: the ambition to possess a woman worth the trouble, to remain impenetrable to her, and while appearing to abandon

Love Affairs

myself to her, to break her on the wheel, as they said in the eighteenth century. Not that I like injuring people or inflicting pain, but it seems to me a pleasant form of superiority to keep one's mask on while making love and to appear as nothing but a child to a woman, while being in fact her master ... What I find the greatest and most beautiful thing in love is for a woman never to possess you. To enter upon a role in the same way as you enter a house, would that not be exactly the opposite of what one ought to say? ... I will go further. I will practise some experiment or other on my mistress; I will astonish her in some kind of way; I will bind her indissolubly to myself by some sort of low and carnal tie; hide, in fact, a species of Valmont under a Chérubin. I have an idea that the opportunity of diverting myself with this and finding interest in it will one day come my way.'

Against the risk of forming a serious attachment their mutual affection protected them; it gave them all and more than they could desire. 'Women, whoever they may be,' we read in *Les Frères Zemganno*, 'do not like men to be on closely intimate terms with each other, it gives them doubts about the amount of affection one man will allow another to show them; their love in a word, and for good reason, takes fright in face of great masculine friendships.'

VII
'Body-Snatchers' of History

In 1856, Dentu's published a booklet of sixty-four pages, called *Les Actrices*, again at the Goncourts' own expense. 'Dentu', they wrote, 'is in despair about an unseemly chapter of *Actrices*. Declares the play on words incomprehensible. Desires—what folly—to understand the things he publishes. Maintains that this vulgarity will do us harm. His ideal is something refined and touching. You would get a good price from him for a novel in which all the men wear gloves and all the consumptives were attended by Andral.[1] Sentimental as a hurdy-gurdy.'

All the same, at the close of the year Dentu decided to publish their work himself. We find the note: 'Sold to Dentu for the sum of 300 francs' (he had at first offered them 150) 'our *Portraits Intimes du XVIIIe Siècle*, for the making of which we have bought two or three thousand francs worth of autograph letters'. This figure raises a question. Their mother had left them only a modest fortune and there were two of them to keep. Their books had cost them money. In spite of this they could buy 2,000 or 3,000 francs' worth of autographs. And they travelled too. And they had spent seven months in Italy. In November, 1859, moreover, they engaged a groom, the nephew of their old servant, Rose Malingre, a groom in a large green top-coat and nut-brown breeches, with a white tie and a hat with a black cockade. And they went on accumulating *objets d'art*, engravings, hand-woven rugs and embroidered hangings, and pieces of Venetian glass. Marvels of sagacity and careful calculation?

At the headquarters of *L'Artiste*, to which they brought their impressions of Venice, Théophile Gautier did not at first sight impress them very favourably. A jaded, heavy face, a sleepy expression, his hearing sometimes poor and occasionally capricious. He kept lingering lovingly over the words: 'Ideas spring from form', which Flaubert had said to him that morning. But it was not long before they felt

---

[1] A celebrated physician of the day.

attracted towards him: 'This man, who at first seems a little irresponsive, or rather as if he were buried deep down in himself, has really great charm and in time becomes in the highest degree sympathetic.'

Their *Venise, la Nuit* appeared in two numbers of the paper, in spite of opposition from Aubryet who, with Arsène Houssaye, had put up the money for this new *Artiste*. It was an utterly crazy piece of work, he seems to have argued; the city and provinces would have withdrawn their subscriptions in a body. This *Venise, la Nuit* is a curious essay in literature dealing with the interpretation of dreams which should have earned the two brothers a place in Albert Béguin's *Le Romantisme et le Rêve*. They have recounted many of their dreams in the *Journal*.

Edmond has given an explanation of their intentions with regard to literature at this time; they had not as yet any leanings towards realism. 'Very much to the contrary,' they wrote, 'we found ourselves in the same lyrical and symbolic frame of mind as other young minds of the present time, with, deep in ourselves, a certain scorn for the transcription of what was true, what was *non-imagined*, and still deeper submerged in our contempt for it by Champfleury's lack of talent and of style. And the studies from life we were then making of Italy were for us only the *stratum* of a book of poetical, fantastical and lunatic prose—a book of dreams offered as the product of a series of nights full of hallucinations.' Echoes of the quarrel between the fantastic and the realist schools can be heard in *Charles Demailly*, just as those between the 'Ingristes' and the colourists in *Manette Salomon*. In 1859, their evolution towards realism had not yet started.

At the offices of *L'Artiste*, the Goncourts also met Flaubert and Feydeau. Of the latter they wrote: 'Feydeau, the epitome of self-infatuation, self-contentment, and swollen pride, but so genuine and so naïvely childish that it disarms you.' On Flaubert there is nothing; at first sight they were not attracted to each other.

In the autumn of 1856, they had stayed with the Passys at Gisors, where the idea of *Renée Mauperin* first began to germinate. This happy period was followed by a series of worries and disappointments: 'Little treasures of a new kind of history, refused by *L'Assemblée Nationale* because of certain crudities, by *La Gazette de Paris* because of the length. So many efforts and even minor successes, leading nowhere. The publishers still not confident after our two volumes of history—this history of French society during the Directorate into

Edmond and Jules

which we have put all possible counter-irritants, sold for 500 francs.'

Sophie Arnould was published in 1857 by Poulet-Malassis and de Broise, and republished by Dentu in 1877 after Edmond had greatly improved it. In 1855 they had bought a bundle of papers from Charavay, a dealer in autographs, without any idea of what it contained, but in which they found a medley of documents, notes, extracts, fragments, the rough draft of a study on Sophie Arnould, some memoirs this singer had left unfinished, and some copies of her letters. Other documents relating to Sophie were transmitted to them, and they wrote their *Biographie de Sophie Arnould d'après sa Correspondance et ses Mémoires Inédits.* The first edition, of 500 copies, brought them 125 francs. Thus began, a long time before it was continued by Edmond alone, the series of studies devoted to actresses of the eighteenth century. It was based on the idea, today entirely refuted by facts, that the evolution of history would henceforth proceed without violence, and that historical works should consequently have a psychological character and be concerned with individuals. It was no longer only the public lives of great men that were of interest to us, it was their private lives, which were the proper concern of 'intimate history', of this 'true novel' that posterity will one day speak of as human history. Now the sources of this history were not to be found in treaties and official correspondence, but in private letters. We will not insist on what is over-weeningly ambitious and defective in this theory. Certainly the Goncourts—after Sainte-Beuve, who introduced private life into history and criticism, as well as Alexis Monteil, the talented author of *L'Histoire des Français des Divers Etats*—opened the way to a complete scheme of research which we have seen multiplied and which can be called secondary history, more picturesque and anecdotal than the history of diplomatic negotiations and military achievements. But what the Goncourts did not foresee is that side by side with the history of great and conspicuous events there would spring up the history of great events behind the scenes, that is to say: economic and social history, which is considered by some as supplying the only valid explanation of the former. It is difficult not to smile when the Goncourts advertise their claim to having entirely reconstituted the eighteenth century with the aid of private letters. 'An age', they said, 'of which one has not a sample of a gown or a menu, is not seen as a living age in history'—a paradox which

'Body-Snatchers' of History

contained some truth, but which accentuates the narrow and superficial character of their work.

Their *Portraits Intimes* are of unequal value. There are some which are admirably finished, such as those of Piron and the Comte de Caylus; others boil down to the reproduction of one or two documents given just as they stand. We must remember that the Goncourts were serving their apprenticeship. Nothing had prepared them for the profession of historians unless it were their taste, their curiosity, their love of quaint and pretty trifles, which had been developed in Edmond since childhood.

Les Portraits Intimes and *Sophie Arnould* earned them the nickname, given by Barbey d'Aurevilly—the 'Sergeant Bertrands' of history. Sergeant Bertrand was a monster, a body-snatcher! It made Jules livid with rage.

The Empress having made Marie-Antoinette fashionable, they decided to write her life. A great subject, this time! For their *Histoire de Marie-Antoinette* they found at last, thanks to old Barrière, a reliable publisher: Ambroise Firmin-Didot, printer to the Institute. He asked them to make some corrections in their style, which, of course, did not please them. 'We who have an ideal ... who really try to write, who love our own way of writing, and wish to be ourselves, should we allow a thing of naught, a numskull, an idiot to touch and fiddle with what we have brought to birth, and cover up our children and reclothe our ideas with the aid of Prudhomme's scissors? Definitely no ...' In the rue Jacob there was a scene that lasted for three hours. 'But it is pure ideology!' exclaimed the old publisher tartly. 'No, sir, it is a religion.'

With *Marie-Antoinette*, published in June, 1858, they made a big step forward in the type of biography for which they evidently had an aptitude. It was their most moving, their most thrilling work; in it they make use of eloquence, even grandiloquence. The writer, Rosny the elder, took them to task for showing a bias in the queen's favour, but added that 'if they are traditionalists, they are also passionately resolved to tell the truth, and for them, from the point of view of literature and of history, every truth is fit to be told ... *Marie-Antoinette* is first and foremost an honest book.' So, without being traditionalists like the Goncourts, who were not narrowly or blindly or systematically so, but were so by nature and inclination, we too can approve of their conclusion: 'The 16th of October, 1793, will teach us what tricks a revolution can play on a people who the day before were the most lovable in the world. It will show how, in a moment, a city, an empire, can become like that friend of Saint Augustine's who was persuaded to attend a combat in the arena, suddenly finding a taste for violence and delighting in their own barbarity. The 16th of October will have its message for systems of humane philosophy. It will rise up against those too youthful hearts, against those too generous minds, against the whole army of Condorcets who die without wishing to renounce their pride in their illusions.'

They had been expecting a success, but on September 23, 1858, we find the entry: 'Claudin [1] informs us that the editors of the *Moniteur* feel some embarrassment as to what to say about *L'Histoire de Marie-Antoinette*. The matter has been referred to the Minister,[2] who has told them to wait. This makes it clear to me why Sainte-Beuve, who up to the present has acknowledged all our volumes, is lying low about this one, waiting for the word of command and fearing to be compromised.'

In *Le Réveil* they had a carefully written article from Barbey d'Aurevilly whom they thanked courteously. 'My friend M. Barbey d'Aurevilly,' wrote Escudier, the editor of the paper, 'has told me that you have written him a very kind letter with regard to his article on your fine work, *Marie-Antoinette*, with which he is most agreeably pleased. I am happy to have opened the columns of *Le Réveil* to this appreciation which in some parts is perhaps a little severe but is certainly dictated by a high sense of equity.' There followed a request for a contribution from them which elicited the following bitter remark: 'It is strange how in this present age the people who insult you harbour a grudge against you for so short a time.'

In spite of the refusal of certain booksellers to display their work, in spite of the delay in publishing certain advertisements of it, people talked of *Marie-Antoinette*. The Russian Embassy ordered three copies. This gave it official sanction. The Comte de Chambord, to whom they

---

[1] His novels of Parisian life and articles under the pseudonym of 'The Gentleman in Black' are a precious source of information on life in the boulevards.

[2] It is not known to whom this refers.

had sent a copy with their compliments, thanked them for it in a short note in which they thought to find a trace of haughtiness. The Comte Henri de Laborde congratulated them on having 'made some progress on the lines of true historical criticism'. In 1859, they brought out a second edition, revised and enlarged. They also submitted *Marie-Antoinette* for a prize awarded by the Academy—'I naïvely confess that it was not for the honour but for the money.'

When in 1862, François-Adolphe de Lescure announced that he in his turn was about to publish *La Vraie Marie-Antoinette, Etude Historique, Politique et Morale*, followed by a collection assembled for the first time of all the queen's letters known up to the present, they claimed the right to forbid use of the letters published by themselves. Lescure jibbed at this: the letters did not belong to them, they had merely been communicated to them by kind collectors. In 1869, when he announced that like themselves he was giving up history for the novel and the drama, they only made the comment: 'This man's feet are always in our shoes! fortunately in this case plagiarism will be more difficult.' However, there was never a complete breach between them.

No one could give attention to *Marie-Antoinette* or *Madame de Pompadour* without the Goncourts being upset as if it were a theft, a violation of their special privilege. On January 21, 1868, they remarked: 'Nothing any longer but gleaners and second-hand dealers in our history... Campardon having already battened on our *Marie-Antoinette* now thriving on our *Madame de Pompadour* and lowering himself so far as to offer his history as a guide for carnival costumes.' Would they not have done better to remark that they were exerting an influence and to have been delighted about it? They were right, nevertheless, in complaining that in their report on the progress of history since 1848, Geffroy, Zeller and Thimot had omitted to mention them with Michelet as well as Thimot himself, as recent historians of the eighteenth century. This lighter type of history was not yet officially recognized.

A visit to the Courmonts at Croissy-Beaubourg in 1857 caused them to feel still more deeply their separation from 'the bourgeois world' and the 'base realities of life'. An artist's attitude that was to be that of so many others, from the romantics to the symbolists, and in which no one flaunted himself with more assurance or more artlessness than they.

Edmond and Jules

In July, 1857, their uncle the captain had died at his fine house in Neufchâteau. With the drawing-room transformed into a mortuary chapel, his cross of the Legion of Honour and his deputy's sash on the coffin, and assembled round it old comrades-in-arms with their faded red ribbons, black-hatted farmers dusty from travelling a long way on foot, old servants and their sons grown wealthy in business, and members of the National Guard drawn up in line on either side—all this pomp of death was simple and dignified.

At Breuvannes they saw once again the summer home of their childhood, now turned into a factory for making files and corkscrews, and since they did not like the inn, they accepted the hospitality of Paul Collardez, 'the hospitality of a farmer or a patriarch'. M. Paul Odinot has given us information on this 'old accomplice' of their father's in electoral contests, this old *harbourer* of the family from father to sons, the infinitely kind friend who looked after the business side of their farms and who, when necessary, advanced them the money to pay their taxes. The Goncourts describe him as a stoutish man, with a head at once both socratic and porcine, little round sparkling eyes, fat lips and a double chin, but also as having a noble spirit, the equal of Gavarni's and Berthelot's, developed by solitary meditations, familiar with the works of many great writers, rather loquacious in his conversation, but capable of handling the most important questions and knowing how to confine his ideas within neat, incisive formulas, as clear-cut as newly minted medals, tender of heart, inflexible in politics, a character after Danton's pattern, to whom nothing had been wanting except favourable circumstances, 'ready for anything, and worthy of anything'. Such forceful eulogies as this are rare in the *Journal*.

Their holdings in Breuvannes caused them too much worry. 'Last year, for the cleaning out of a river about which I care nothing and which I cannot see at all from my farm, the government took 1,800 francs from me out of a total revenue of 2,700; this year it takes 1,442 francs. It is astonishing how everything nowadays seems inimical to inherited property.' In 1857 they sold their share of land-dues, and then their farm at Fresnoy, and after Collardez's death, sold the remainder to buy the house in Auteuil.

VIII
Etchers

After the intensive labour of writing *Marie-Antoinette* these two very highly-strung individuals experienced several months of relaxation, idleness and mental torpor. Then followed *L'Art du Dix-Huitième Siècle*, published at their expense by Dentu in twelve instalments: *Les Saint-Aubin* (1859), *Watteau* (1860), *Prud'hon* (1861), *Boucher* (1862), *Greuze* (1863), *Chardin* (1864), *Fragonard* (1865), *Debucourt* (1866), *La Tour* (1867), *Les Vignettistes Gravelot, Cochin-Eisen, Moreau*, in two instalments (1868-70). The whole collection was finally published in 1875 as *L'Art du Dix-Huitième Siècle* with short notes, additions, and errata, and a preface by Edmond. 'All the etchings,' says a note, 'are engraved by Jules de Goncourt, with the exception of Saint-Aubin's *Saint Augustine seated on a stool* and the series of *Divine Justice and Vengeance pursuing Crime*, which are engraved by Edmond de Goncourt.'

In the preface to the original edition we read: 'This book was begun by two brothers, in the years when they were young and in good health, in the confident belief of carrying it through to the end. Laying aside each year, for one whole month, their dark and melancholy studies of contemporary life, this was the task by which, during happy sunny holidays, their love of past ages was stimulated anew. And there was a kind of rivalry between them both in giving form and meaning to a sentence and making a word express that almost inexpressible something to be found in a work of art. This was their favourite book, the book that gave them most pains.'

Jules was to die before the completion of the series. In 1870 Pater, Lancret and Portail still remained to be dealt with. They were to have had as their setting a study of Watteau's influence and a general survey of eighteenth-century sculpture, in particular that of Clodion. 'This old man', wrote Edmond in 1875, at the age of fifty-three, 'does not feel he has the courage and—why should he not say it?—the talent to write, alone as he is, the two studies which are lacking in the book. Besides, if he did feel capable of doing this, a feeling of piety that a

Edmond and Jules

few will understand, would impel him, indeed impels him today, to wish that it should be with this book as with the room in which someone we love has died, where things remain just as they were when death found them.'

Pol Neveux points out that Gillot, Nattier, Oudry, Peronneau, Hubert Robert and Louis Moreau do not figure in this work: the Goncourts had not enough information about them. 'They never allow themselves', he adds, 'to speak of an artist of whom they have only superficial knowledge, whom they have not examined at length, not only in public and private galleries, but also at home.' We rather believe that if Jules had lived the gallery would have been complete. For the rest Pol Neveux is right in placing the Goncourts above Théophile Gautier and Fromentin as art critics, but with the reservation that they only took an interest in the eighteenth century, and that as regards the nineteenth they were lacking in perspicuity in placing Gavarni, among others, too high. 'The Goncourts,' says Pol Neveux, 'speak as great writers, judge and give grounds for their decisions as men who have made literature their profession. They have an admirable knowledge of the forms and harmonies of language, a sureness of touch and a sense of values. A general command of rhythm, ingenuity in the arrangement of particular details, the most swift and subtle changes of mood, the most fleeting variations of light and shade, all the secret charm that lies hidden from inexpert observers, these they discover for us in quick succession.' The only things they needed were less narrowness of taste and the power of observing from a superior level the evolution of the plastic arts.

In addition to the six etchings by Edmond already mentioned the following should be noted: *Jules by the fireside in 1859*, *Autumn*, after one of Watteau's figures, *Mademoiselle Dangerville's Masque*, after La Tour, *The Beggars* and a *Head of a Man*, after Gavarni. Besides those etched by Jules for *L'Art du Dix-Huitième Siècle* we have some etchings of his which their old and close friend Philippe Burty published in 1876, together with wood-cuts of some of his water-colours. Seven of their etchings not included among either of these collections are taken from various artists, one of them from Gavarni. An etching of Henri Monnier's *Madame Lafarge* earned for Jules this word of thanks from the artist: 'Never have I been better interpreted, and if I had been interpreted in this manner, my work today would have been considerable. It would have given me courage.'

Etchers

Not one of Edmond's original drawings has been preserved; a certain number of them however remain as illustrations to a work of Paul Lacroix, entitled *Le Moyen Age et la Renaissance*. When destroying his own work Edmond only spared two portraits of his brother: a pastel sketch of him in the uniform of the French Guard, now the property of the Académie Goncourt, and a fine water-colour of him smoking his pipe, seated with his heels above his head. An etching from this water-colour, painted on April 29, 1857, was later made by Jules, of whose own water-colours and drawings a large number exist which were made during their travels in France and Algeria in 1849, in Belgium and France in 1850 and later, and also in Italy.

As a black-and-white artist, a water-colour painter and an etcher, Jules is superior to most of those writers of his time, except Hugo and Fromentin, who like himself handled a pencil, a brush, or an etcher's needle. Neither Mérimée nor Gautier nor yet Baudelaire can hold a candle to him. From 1861 to 1865, he exhibited his work at the Salon as a pupil of Gavarni's. Possibly he had taken lessons also from Decamps. 'Jules de Goncourt,' wrote Philippe Burty, 'possessed the same firmness of touch as Decamps in the rendering of accessory details; he knew all the tricks of the trade, the process of mopping up, of smearing, scratching, sponging lavishly with water, and making little marks with a lithographer's pencil. He has rendered surprisingly well the sturdy decrepitude of the by-streets of old Paris, giving relief with a reed dipped in sepia, against the general tone of dim grey light and shade, to the salient lines of the picture which in some way disguise the skeletal fragility of the composition.' Roger Marx has rightly said that his eighty-six etchings would have been sufficient to keep his name from being forgotten.

On February 17, 1859, Jules describes the experimental printing of his first etching, the portrait of Augustine by Saint-Aubin, etched for *L'Art du Dix-Huitième Siècle*. '... nothing in our life has taken such a hold on us as these two things: drawing formerly, and now etching ... which makes you completely forget not only time but also the vexations of life, and everything else in the world. For whole long days together you live entirely absorbed by it ... Never, perhaps, in any circumstance of our lives, so much desire, impatience, or frenzy to arrive at the next day, and the success or the utter failure of the printing. And to see the plate washed, see it blacken, see it grow clean, see the paper getting wet, and to set up the press and spread the coverings on it, and give the necessary two turns, this makes our hearts flutter in our breasts, and our hands tremble as we seize this dripping sheet of paper on which shimmers the misty semblance of a picture that has hardly taken shape.'

It is clear that painting and etching were not for Jules a mere dilettante's pastime. He was a painter and an etcher every bit as much as he was a writer, by virtue of that same vocation, that same aptitude for grasping and expressing everything he saw. We should understand nothing of his talents as a writer if we treated it apart from his talent as an engraver.

IX
Their First Novels

While they were writing *Marie-Antoinette* the Goncourts had also written a play, aimed at the prevailing dominance of Bohemia, their pet aversion. It was of this that they were thinking when they wrote: 'Why, good heavens, every man is for sale. It is simply a question of his price and the way it's offered. If he does not want money, you can buy him with odds and ends of fame or decorations. You must not, on the other hand, ask him to do anything outrageous, such as sawing a man's head off with the rung of a chair. Some would refuse to do it.'

At the Café du Helder, to which their group had moved in a body from the Café Riche, their play was presented to Goudchaux, manager of the Vaudeville, by Mario Uchard [1] and Saint-Victor, and was immediately accepted. They did not learn until a fortnight later that Beaufort, who in the meantime had taken over the management of the Vaudeville, did not dare to produce it at the moment. This news which a few days before would have caused them real sorrow, did not arouse more than a slight sense of disappointment in them. Their eagerness to have their play performed had slightly worn off in the interval.

The manager of the Gymnase-Dramatique, Lemoine-Montigny, who had already rejected their *Nuit de la Saint-Sylvestre*, again refused to take a chance. 'The theme of your work,' his brother Edouard wrote to them, 'is not well chosen, in the sense that it is a true picture —this one must recognize—of the manners and morals of certain men of letters. But would this picture interest the public? ... the details are little related to the action, if indeed there is any action in the accepted meaning of the term. All this ... consists of conversation that is nearly always witty but has little scenic quality. Your fifth act comprises a long and painful death-bed scene, recalling that of *La Dame aux Camélias*, but ... brings nothing to a conclusion.'

[1] Novelist and playwright. The central figure of the little group of journalists and artists depicted in *Charles Demailly*.

Edmond and Jules

Two years later, *La Guerre des Lettres* was again rejected, this time by Charles de La Rounat, manager of the Odéon. Disgusted with the stage, they fell back upon the circus and its clowns—'when all's said and done, the only actors whose talent is incontestable, absolute as mathematics, or better still, as a somersault'. Their hearts being set on *La Guerre des Lettres*, they made a novel out of it which they called *Les Hommes de Lettres*.

They summed up their evolution from history to the novel thus: 'Our path in literature is somewhat peculiar. We have passed through history to arrive at the novel. That is hardly the usual process, and yet we have acted logically. On what is history written? On documents. And the documents of the novel, what are they but life itself?'

They offered *Les Hommes de Lettres* to *La Presse*. As yet only partly written, it was returned to them unread. They had felt the blow coming, provoked by Gaïffe, the author and journalist, on behalf of the good name of Letters and the respect due to journalism. Nevertheless their disappointment was keen. After the book had been turned down again, by Michel Lévy and the firm of Amyot, they sold some of their capital and took the manuscript to Dentu, by whom, at their own expense, *Les Hommes de Lettres* was published in January, 1860.

It was a day of feverish activity. After visiting Flaubert, who offered them his congratulations, they wandered about the whole evening, inspecting the bookshops on the boulevards, calculating the chances of a duel and those of a success. There was no duel, but there were protests. Jules Janin accused them of having written a satire against their own 'corporation' and of holding literature up to scorn. 'Yes, indeed,' they wrote, 'it is thus the critics speak of this book, the best and the most courageous action of our lives. This book that only makes the depths of literature so low in order to make its heights all the higher and the more worthy of respect.' They addressed an explanatory letter to the *Journal des Débats*: 'Our book, as our conscience bears us witness, is not at all the bitter work you imagine, devoid of pity and of good cheer. If it touches on things that bring dishonour on the profession of letters, on men who compromise its reputation, it also speaks of those high passions and generous spirits that ennoble it.' The *Débats* agreed to insert their letter, but never spoke of them again.

To set themselves right with Janin they went to see him at his chalet in Passy. In fact, in this novel warm praise is given the guild of Letters as a whole, 'a great and noble race of men, a free race, and fierce, which is restive under any kind of domination, does not recognize the divine right of money, and has not yet been domesticated by the gift of a five-franc piece'.

Their natural pessimism, and possibly the ambitious design of replying to Balzac's *Les Illusions Perdues*, possibly too the irritation provoked by the evil practices of the Bohemians, led them into gross exaggeration of their picture. How they hated this Bohemia! How they despised 'those dregs of coffee in which embryonic reputations and great men who have not made their name are christened, in which are brewed those successes of Bohemia, to which every man contributes self-sacrificing devotion, as if he crowned himself in crowning some individual of the gang!' They did not speak favourably of criticism either. 'With us newspaper criticism is strictly controlled, related more or less to the colour of the paper's opinions, to its tendencies, and if not to its prejudices, at least to its principles. It is accordingly exposed every day to giving precedence to the opinions of a book over its real, intrinsic value. Criticism, in short, is hardly allowed to applaud a work from another camp, nor to hoot at one from its own.'

An article by Barbey d'Aurevilly in *Le Pays*, severe, but courteous, rather took them aback. 'A thorough dressing-down, but on the surface polite, drops upon us from the heights of *Le Pays* and from M. Barbey d'Aurevilly's pen. A strange man, this critic. A Catholic and a Monarchist, he serves this government and Mirès, the owner of *Le Pays*. A critic of morals, he has published *Une Vieille Maîtresse*, etc. A critic of literature, he takes other men to task for their metaphors and their lively turns of style, and with what a spate of metaphors himself! This critic, as you see, is comprehensive.'

A kind letter from George Sand consoled them a little. 'It is so well painted, so well presented, so arresting that it must be true . . . What strong and vigorous satire! You write forcibly and your indignation is eloquent without being over-rhetorical.'

Les Hommes de Lettres was their first real novel, romantic in its gloom and in the appalling character of the tragedy with which it ends. The little touches of direct observations scattered freely through it, although taken from life, have not as yet their source in realism. Demailly's nervous disorder, in which all the symptoms described in Esquirol's *Mental Diseases* are, as it were, scattered *ad lib*, strangely foreshadows the illness by which Jules was to be carried off ten years later. On May 4, 1876, his brother wrote: 'My eyes were filled with tears today as I was correcting the proofs of *Charles Demailly*. Never, I believe, has it happened to an author to write in advance, in a manner that is also dreadfully true, about the despair of a man of letters suddenly feeling a sense of powerlessness and emptiness in his brain.' In his bitterness and discontentment Charles Demailly resembles his authors even more than in his unfortunate and nervous disposition. 'Why,' he exclaims, 'did I not write day by day, at the beginning of my career, about that harsh and horrible struggle against lack of recognition, about all the stages of my progress through indifference and insults, that public that one seeks but which evades one, that future towards which I made my way, resigned, but often despairing, that battle of an eager, impatient will against the age and against seniority, one of the great privileges in the world of letters? No friends, no influential connections, every door closed to you!... Ah! that dumb death agony within yourself, without any other witnesses than a pride that bleeds and a heart beginning to fail you! That monotonous, uneventful death agony, set down on the spur of the moment, hot from experience of suffering, this would be a very fine study, but one that no one will write, because a trifling success, the finding of a publisher, the gain of a few hundred francs, a few articles at twopence-halfpenny or threepence a line, your name made known to some hundred persons unknown to you, two or three friends and a little puff or two, will cure you of past ills and fill the cup of forgetfulness for you!' What an avowal of the desire for notoriety that consumed them! And in what follows, what a confession of their sensitivity to criticism! 'Certain articles, read before dinner, would close the passage to his stomach and take away his appetite as completely as the news of some great misfortune. With his mouth dry and bitter, he would drop into the sort of stupor produced unconsciously by organic disturbances which invariably precede the passing of bile into the blood.'

Charles Demailly, full of disorder and confusion, remains as interesting evidence of the Goncourts' inner life and their particular state of mind. Borrowings from the *Journal* are numerous, indeed too numerous, but their hatred of women and their theory that the state of celibacy is indispensable for the artist are already in this book and give it psychological interest.

Their First Novels

In the same year as that of the publication of *Les Hommes de Lettres* there appeared *Les Maîtresses de Louis XV*, which Edmond recast in 1878 and '79 in three volumes, *La Du Barry, Madame de Pompadour,* and *La Duchesse de Châteauroux et ses Sœurs*. The work was dedicated to their cousin Edouard Lefebvre de Béhaine, at that time minister plenipotentiary in Bavaria. Edmond himself has pointed out the defects of a work in which lack of experience was still largely apparent: too much literary affectation, too many flowery passages in arbitrary juxtaposition. 'We were at that time too passionately fond of unpublished material and were possessed, a little mistakenly, with an ambition to write an absolutely new kind of history, full of extravagant disdain for ideas and works that had been popularized.' According to Alidor Delzant, the brothers' first biographer, Edmond recognized another fault in this book: excessive indulgence with regard to Louis XV. This was not Flaubert's opinion: he considered the portrait of the king a masterly one and said he was thrilled by Mme de Mailly. He was pleased with everything in these books: their style and this original way of writing history. 'Here one continually sees the soul behind the body, the psychological aspect is not smothered by the abundance of details. Morality runs beneath the facts without overemphasis or digressions. The book is alive, a rare merit.' On July 12, 1860, they were able to write: 'Our *Maîtresses*, so it appears, are going very well, the book is a success. This leaves us as cold as if all this were happening to someone else.'

On Sunday, February 5, 1860, they were lunching at Flaubert's house with Louis Bouilhet [1] who told the story of a sister in the hospital at Rouen who had been in love with a friend of his who had hanged himself. Bouilhet was watching beside his body: the nun came in and without paying any attention to him stayed for a long time praying in front of the corpse. When she got up Bouilhet handed her a lock of hair intended for the dead man's mother. She took it and withdrew without a word. Since then, though she had never spoken of the incident to Bouilhet, she had always shown herself extremely obliging towards him.

Soon the idea of a novel drawn from the incident took shape in their minds. Taking inspiration from a niece of Rose Malingre,

[1] Friend of Flaubert and author of historical plays.

Rosalie Domergue, for the story of their heroine's childhood, they there and then began to write *Sœur Philomène*. Flaubert recommended them to two doctors among his friends, Dr Cloquet and Dr Follin, who gave them an introduction to a house physician at the La Charité Hospital, who was later to become their own doctor. After getting up at half past six, they paid their first visit to the hospital on a cold, damp morning that was hardly calculated to put them in good heart.

A week later, on December 26, unable to stand it any longer, they gave up going. Apart from a dinner at Saint-Antoine's Hospital at which they were present two months later (and from which they brought back the idea that the most intelligent class in society was that of the resident medical staff) they had only spent about ten hours in a hospital.

Their first impression of this type of institution is rather odd: 'Strangely enough, the underlying horror is so well concealed beneath the white sheets, the cleanliness, the order and the discipline that there remains—it is difficult to strike the right note—an almost sensually pleasant and mysteriously stimulating impression. We retain from our view of these women, vaguely caught sight of on their blue-white pillows and with faces transfigured by suffering and motionless repose, a picture that titillates the imagination in a sensual sort of way and attracts you by reason of this awe-inspiring veil. . . . It is strange, that we who have a horror of suffering, and of any painful excitation, feel ourselves more than ordinarily in the mood for love.'

Truth to tell, the few pages in the *Journal* devoted to the La Charité Hospital are worth all the 240 pages of *Sœur Philomène*. In spite of its ingenious construction and instances of subtle analysis, in which the part played by sensations preponderates over the genuine spirituality of the work, this novel suffers from the same defects as *Les Hommes de Lettres*: conversations developed at too great a length following laboured descriptions, action insufficiently fused with its accessory elements, details of observation and recording of aural and visual impressions set down without any attempt at transposition. However, *Sœur Philomène* still has something in it to appeal to fastidious minds. It is a remarkable book, and one of the most original of those written by the Goncourts. Had it been treated as a novelette, *Sœur Philomène* might have been a masterpiece.

What urged them to write it? Had the subject or the setting really anything in it to inspire these sceptics, coldly disposed if not hostile towards religious matters and religious people, who did not choose to see anything more in this theme than an outlet granted to women's amorous demands? What change of mental atmosphere did they look for in it? They themselves wondered. 'You do not write the kind of books you want to. There is a sort of fatality in the first chance event that dictates the idea of it to you. Then there is an unknown force, a superior will, a kind of compulsion to write that controls your work and guides your pen; so much so that sometimes the book that takes shape in your hands does not seem to have come from yourself; it takes you by surprise, like something that was in you but of which you were not conscious.'

This novel, which Michel Lévy, finding its subject too gloomy, had not felt inclined to accept, was published in 1861 by the *Librairie Nouvelle*, which had bought it from them at the rate of twenty centimes a volume for an edition of 2,000 copies. On July 11 they themselves took charge of its distribution to the bookshops.

It was their first step, and a decisive one, on the road to the realist novel. 'One of the particular features of our novels,' they had remarked in January, 1861, 'will be that of being the most *historical* ones of this present age, the novels that will furnish the history of morals and manners in this century with the greatest number of facts and indisputable truths.' On another occasion they wrote: 'History is a novel that has been written; the novel is history as it might have happened.' Or in other words: 'Historians are narrators of the past, novelists narrators of the present.'

They had therefore, almost without knowing it, been led to realism by the study of documents, and to documents of contemporary life by way of those of the eighteenth century. Their evolution in some slight way recalls that of Balzac, led by way of the historical novel to the modern novel. But the novel was never for them an exclusive preoccupation. They did not fling themselves into it heart and soul as did their great predecessors or contemporaries, Balzac, George Sand, Flaubert, Daudet and Zola. Is this an indication that the novel did not move them to the depths of their soul, that in fact they were not born novelists?

George Sand was only half-pleased with *Sœur Philomène*. 'It is sad, like everything well done and carefully thought out, it is indeed a good piece of work, and you will come to be great artists once a gleam of idealism or passion, something even a trifle mad, mingles with this high understanding of the real. This strain of madness is perhaps the defect needed to bring the faculties into full play. Young people of today do not have it, those of my generation had it perhaps too much. But for you moderns, and for you two especially, I believe in a maturity full of power.' Flaubert, in a long letter, declared himself fascinated; he would not have been astonished if the book had met with great success.

Before all this they and Saint-Victor had taken the train to visit Holland and the banks of the Rhine. There they took no interest in anything except painting.

On their return bad news awaited them: the *Librairie Nouvelle* had gone bankrupt. Instead of 400 francs they received only 100. *Sœur Philomène*, however, seems to have had its moment of success. At Bar-sur-Seine they noted in their *Journal*: 'A letter this morning from Saint-Victor tells us that our book is taking wing. On the water, in the boat, dazed and stupefied, we remain bewildered, our thoughts away in Paris, with impossible figures of sales beating hard against the walls of our brain.' 'The Jesuit boarding school in Fribourg, where I was educated,' wrote Saint-Victor, 'was the male counterpart of your convent. As I was reading you I felt my old enthusiasms revive: *veteris agnosco vestigia flammae*. In truth, I became as maudlin as an old serpent who is shown his young skin.'

The preface of *La Femme au Dix-huitième Siècle* (1862) an important work dedicated to Saint-Victor and to which Sainte-Beuve devoted two of his Monday articles, takes up the theme of history as they conceived it, but applying it to the eighteenth century, 'up till now disdained by history'. 'The historians', they maintained, 'have held aloof from it as from a study that would compromise the respectability and dignity of their historical work. It would seem they are afraid they would be set down as frivolous if they approached this century whose levity is only its surface and its mask.' An opinion which puts too low a value on the work of Sainte-Beuve, Michelet, Monselet, and others but which, taken on the whole, is fairly true. We must not deny the Goncourts the merit of having, especially in the picturesque, worldly and anecdotal side of history, opened the way to innumerable successors.

La Femme au Dix-huitième Siècle was to have been one of a series of four works: *L'Homme, La Femme, L'Etat, Paris*. Even more than lack of time, the increasing attraction which the novel held for

Their First Novels

them prevented them from realizing the whole of their project.
This part of their life comes to an end in the summer of 1862 with the death of Rose and their first visit to the Princess Mathilde. Jules saw here 'one of those breaks in one's existence where, as Byron puts it, destiny changes horses'. The beginning of the Magny dinners and their own definitive evolution in the direction of realism soon marked a new phase in their career. Between *La Femme au Dix-huitième Siècle* and *Renée Mauperin*, that is to say between 1862 and 1864, they published nothing except different parts of *L'Art au Dix-huitième Siècle*.

For twenty-five years Rosalie Malingre, known as Rose, had been in their service. There was nothing she did not know about them; she read their letters, had the keys of their bureaux, and received their confidences. She had bought apple-turnovers for Jules out of her own money, and used to open the door to Edmond when he came back secretly from a dance. Every evening she tucked them up in bed, and every evening there were the same jokes about her ugliness. 'There is a great spirit of irony in this world,' they wrote, 'and, as it were, a cunning vengeance exacted by things. We who have arranged our lives so as to be free, and who appear the freest people on this earth, we for whom woman plays nothing but an animal role—we who are neither married, nor in love, are almost subjected to the yoke of marriage by our maid and are the slaves of her nervous outbursts.'

Suddenly, in July, 1862, at Bar-sur-Seine, where they had brought her, already ill, for a change of air, Rose began to cough. Her coughing used to wake Jules, who was already afflicted with that obsession about noise that was to give warning of his end. It was tuberculosis. They took her back to Paris. Her features, her expression, her gestures, all were changed; she seemed to shed her personality. 'It's the end,' said Dr Simon, the former house-physician at La Charité, on July 31, 'there's no hope, it's just a question of time. The disease has made very quick progress. One lung is done for, and the other is almost as bad.' Distracted, they left the house, walking haphazardly round Paris and at length, completely exhausted, sat down in a café where a rebus in *L'Illustration* struck them as a prophecy: 'Against death there is no appeal!'

On August 2 the *Journal* describes them applying cupping-glasses to their old servant. 'What torture for the nerves! Our hearts

shuddered, our hands trembled at throwing the flaming paper on to this pitiful body, this skin so shrunken and so near to the bones...'
In her attic, which the sun coming through the skylight made as hot as a greenhouse, poor Rose lay in torment. It was decided to take her to hospital. Out of bed she looked as though she were already dead; her legs were as thin as broomsticks. The charwoman having packed her things in a parcel, a little clean linen, a set of pewter cutlery, a glass and a cup, she got into a cab. Jules held her up against the pillow placed behind her back. She managed to walk as far as the main hall of the hospital where Jules sat her down in a wicker armchair close to a little barred window. After a clerk had filled in a few forms, a hospital orderly and the charwoman each took one of her arms. 'And then,' said Jules, 'I made my escape. I ran to the cab. A nervous contraction of the mouth kept me swallowing my tears for an hour on end. I burst into sobs that came thick and fast and choked each other. My anguish rent me.'

On August 14 the brothers found Rose confident that she would soon be cured. The next day Jules wrote: 'I am very glad to be going to the fireworks this evening, to merge myself in the crowd and drown my sorrow there. It seems to me that sadness is lost among so many people. I look forward with pleasure to being jostled by common folk as one is tossed about by the waves.' Next day, at seven o'clock on the very morning of the day on which they were invited for the first time to dine with the Princesse Mathilde, Rose died from a haemorrhage, without knowing that she was dying.

They did not have the courage to identify the body. 'We will send someone', they said, and they rushed away to report the death at the mayor's office. They had to collect the dead woman's papers and clothes and tidy up the medicine bottles and the linen she had left. 'It was terrible to go back again into that attic where, in the hollow of the half-open bed, there were still the crumbs of her last meal. I threw the bed-clothes back over the bolster like a sheet over the ghost of someone dead.' Mass was said on August 18 in the chapel of the hospital over three or four coffins.

Rose was buried in a common grave in the cemetery at Montmartre, to which Jules was to return in February, 1863, to paint a water-colour that remained in front of their eyes while they were writing the last chapters of *Germinie Lacerteux*. In 1888, when the play that Edmond had made from *Germinie* was being put on, he entrusted the water-colour to his friend Porel, the theatrical manager, with these words: 'Here is my brother's water-colour, a view of the cemetery drawn from life... as it was at the time of Germinie's death—not the cemetery of the boulevard des Italiens that your scene-painter has cooked up for you. It is the cemetery with its skeleton-like winter trees, its surroundings at that time devoid of houses, with the last gas-lamp of Paris and the last windmills of Montmartre. Below the cutting to the left and the little hillock which should rise a trifle more above it was the entrance to the communal grave, a door made simply of planks gaping open at the bottom and topped with a sheet of zinc on which was hanging a workman's overall left there by one of them who was digging a trench close by.'

Two days after the funeral, Jules went back to ask the nun in charge of the Saint-Joseph ward how Rose had died. There followed a stupefying, a frightful, revelation: Maria, up till then bound to observe professional secrecy, informed them of the other side of Rose's life: an existence unknown to them, hateful, repugnant, utterly lamentable. She had run up debts with all the tradesmen, had signed promissory notes, had had relations with men, had furnished a room for the dairywoman's son, and had taken her masters' wine, chickens and all sorts of provisions along to another man. By the dairywoman's son, Alexandre Colmant, who was a boxer, 'a sort of slender Hercules with a pretty head like a woman's', she had had two children, one of whom had lived six months. In order to pay for her debaucheries, she who used to preach a religion of honour to her nephew the groom, she who in the eyes of her masters was the very soul of devotion and honesty, had been robbing them, had been taking from them 'twenty-franc pieces from a packet of a hundred francs so that her paid lovers would not leave her'. She had fits of crying, for which she said she did not know the reason, and felt such remorse for her misdeeds, such a terror of hell, that she had taken to drink. Once, when completely drunk, she had had a miscarriage on the parquet floor. The pleurisy from which she died, she had contracted one winter's night keeping a watch on Alexandre to find out what woman had taken her place!

'Poor creature!' they wrote. 'We forgive her and even feel a great sense of compassion when we take account of all she has suffered... But for the rest of our lives a mistrust of the entire female sex will possess us... We are filled with horror at the fundamental duplicity of her nature, of the intense capacity, the skill, the consummate genius for lying inherent in her . . .'

They had not waited to be told about this unhappy woman before becoming misogynists, but the discovery of her intemperate follies led them to hold more firmly to this opinion, and this revelation gave the death-blow to whatever remained of fantasy in them, making them realists, men without illusions, and adding the final touch to their experience of life.

X

Pleasures and Friendships

Their participation in the life of the boulevards extends from about the time of their first publication of *L'Eclair*, in November, 1851, to the autumn of 1862, the date of their first appearance at Princess Mathilde's house and at Magny's restaurant. There was nothing Bohemian in their way of living except their frequenting of certain places and hob-nobbing with certain friends and colleagues. Bohemians, spongers, topers, men who did nothing and who had failed in everything, were to be met with in plenty on the boulevards. They had invaded the Café Riche which the Goncourts went to regularly and where they rubbed shoulders with Baudelaire. The galley-slave's air that he affected was not the only thing that alienated them from him. They had been told he had taken up his quarters in a little hotel near the railway and had chosen a room on a main corridor where, with his door wide open, he offered the spectacle of himself at work, 'diligently applying his genius, with his hands busy rootling for thoughts in his long white hair'. Between himself and them there was complete incompatibility, in spite of the affinities which should have drawn them together. 'It is a very dangerous game,' wrote the brothers, 'for oafish and provincial minds to get drunk on paradoxes. One day they become overwhelmed by them, which is the case with Aubryet.[1] I am rather inclined to believe that madness does not attack men of strong will or of great talent, but only gets hold of a Baudelaire here and there, that is to say an exasperated type of Prudhomme, a bourgeois who has spent all his life trying to acquire the elegant distinction of appearing somewhat mad. He set himself so earnestly to manage this that he died insane.' When he wrote these lines on December 15, 1868, poor Jules had no idea of the disease which he was to die of a year and a half later.

In October, 1857, the Goncourts and their little group took refuge at the Café du Helder; at the Café Riche, where their presence had

---

[1] Journalist and author of *Les Idées Justes et les Idées Fausses*.

attracted many undesirables, they no longer felt sure their identity would be sufficiently concealed.

The Moulin Rouge had also been one of the favourite haunts of their coterie. This was a fashionable restaurant in the Champs-Elysées. 'At the bottom of the garden, at all the windows on every floor, in the lighted depths of private rooms, just as in boxes at the theatre, women's heads could be seen nodding left and right to former companions of their nights, or possibly to some of their yesterday's guineas.'

They were to be seen also at the Librairie Nouvelle. Established in 1849 by Jacottet and Bourdilliat, it occupied the ground floor in the Jockey Club building, 15 boulevard des Italiens. It started the series of one-franc novels among which appeared those by Balzac and George Sand, and it also published *Sœur Philomène*. The journalist Gustave Claudin (represented in *Charles Demailly* under the name of Bourniche) was also a member of the group at the Café Riche and the Moulin Rouge. 'The journalists and men of letters who came to the Librairie Nouvelle', he says, 'formed themselves into several groups. The one to which I belonged included Théophile Gautier, Edmond and Jules de Goncourt, Paul de Saint-Victor, Aubryet, Charles Edmond [1], Gustave Flaubert, Gustave Doré, Mario Uchard and Arsène Houssaye... I cannot possibly explain the strange and original nature of the collaboration between Edmond and Jules de Goncourt. These two brothers were in fact only *one*. The one would take up a sentence begun by the other, and speak, not in the plural, but in the singular.'

Life on the boulevards was studded with affairs of honour. Duels of romantic origin between journalists were still frequent under the Second Empire. The fencing school was, as it were, an indispensable adjunct to an editor's office. The Goncourts, as might be imagined, took lessons in fencing.

They frequently went for long walks through a Paris that had not yet lost its old picturesque character, exploring the Central Markets, the less reputable districts and the brothels, taking part in rat-hunts with Morère, a friend of Gavarni's, going down into the Catacombs, and discovering Haussmann's new Paris, still under construction. With Scholl and Murger they visited seamstresses of easy virtue and

---

[1] Dramatist and sometime librarian to the Senate.

clinked glasses with their disreputable male companions. They went to boxing matches in which their maid's lover, Alexandre Colmant, took part. All this is noted down by Jules with remarkable keenness of observation. He was a master of a type of rapid sketch of which he left all too few examples. What an amusing picture he might have given us of Paris under the Second Empire!

They were diligent first-nighters, though their taste inclined more to the circus and the dance-hall, to which Jules in quest of amusement dragged his brother, indulgent as a father to him. 'Yesterday,' Jules writes, 'we were in Princess Mathilde's drawing-room. Today we are at a dance attended by lower-class people at the Elysée des Arts . . . I like these contrasts. It is tackling society as if one were mounting the stairs to different floors of a house.'

Hunting for bibelots was Edmond's favourite diversion. Jules, who had a reliable memory and incomparable taste, was content merely to advise his brother. He would have limited himself, so Philippe Burty says, to choosing a few things of superior quality. Together they visited the 'junk-merchants' or 'dealers in old iron' on the boulevard Beaumarchais, the boulevard des Filles-du-Calvaire and the boulevard du Temple, also Vidalenc's den, its tiled floor covered with dust, crammed full of treasures, woodwork, quaint old bedsteads, and armchairs of every shape and kind, amidst which they were guided by Mme Vidalenc in the costume of an Auvergnat peasant with a bonnet of old lace. They also went to a dealer in a side-street who sold drawings and engravings and from whom, for lack of money, Edmond had failed to buy a series of sanguine sketches by Fragonard at eight francs apiece. The *Journal* describes their visiting Chambe, the hunchbacked dealer in old iron in the rue de l'Ecole Polytechnique; here were remains of carriages, mouldy harness, cast-iron stoves, broken crockery, bits of uniforms, and in the midst of it all a marvellous hoard of engravings and drawings—twenty Bouchers and a superb Watteau. Another time they were to be seen at the central auction rooms at an exhibition of eighteenth-century costumes in every delicate shade imaginable, crushed-strawberry, dove-grey, sulphur-yellow, misty pink and opaline colours. 'I do not believe,' we read in the *Journal*, 'that an admirer of lovely things can be a patriot. My portfolios and my drawing-room are my native country. A work of art gives you a distaste for the market-place, it creates in you a kind of spiritual and idealistic egotism.' Another day they wrote: 'Few people know the great happiness of looking at old drawings while smoking cigars with opium in them; one mingles the cloudy contours of the line with a dream that rises with the smoke.'

Though they clung firmly to their reputation as initiators in matters concerning the eighteenth century, it was only half-deserved. As proof of Théophile Gautier's priority in this domain Adolphe Boschot, the music critic, has recalled the fact that Gautier, while still a youth, borrowed a hundred francs from his publisher, in order to buy one of Boucher's sketches. Gautier seems to have been the first to awaken in collectors and artists a taste for the major and minor masters of the preceding century. The author Pol Neveux has politely given the lie to the legend according to which the Goncourts were discoverers and pioneers in this field. The way had been shown to them by others: Mario Uchard, for instance, Paul de Saint-Victor, Gavarni, and Philippe Burty. Jules Claretie, a member of the Académie Française, attributes to Arsène Houssaye the merit of having discovered rococo while Gothic was still in the fashion. The members of this little artistic confraternity, says Neveux, continually dined together in order to communicate their discoveries to each other. It is thus that the Goncourts were able to admire in the place de la Sorbonne the ceiling Boucher painted for his engraver Demarteau, that at Chambe's, the rag-and-bone man, they were introduced to the aged collector of autographs, Fossé d'Arcosse, that Burty got them the entrée to the studio of Carrier the miniaturist, to whom they were indebted for their taste for gouaches. Already there were numerous private picture galleries devoted to the eighteenth century to which the Goncourts had access, in particular the one owned by Marcille, the well-known collector, who died in 1856. His two sons, Camille and Eudoxe, were real friends to the Goncourts.

Camille Marcille had visited all the museums in Europe. After marrying the daughter of Baron Walkenaer and buying an estate at Oisème, near Chartres, he lived there in close retirement, hardly leaving it except to carry out his duties as keeper of the Chartres museum. His brother Eudoxe, keeper of the museum in Orléans, had received as his share of his father's possessions a series of marvellous Chardins, while to Camille had fallen thirteen interiors, still-life studies, and scenes of family life by the same master, together with nine Prud'hons, and a few Latours, Fragonards, Greuzes, etc.

The Marcille family, provincial but worthy people, with very

Pleasures and Friendships

different personalities and highly entertaining, greatly attracted the Goncourts. In this happy atmosphere, they could relax. There is a witty letter from Jules to one of the little girls, probably the one who showed herself so affectionate towards him that the mother jokingly called him 'my son-in-law'. Mme Marcille they had thought at first rather cross-grained, stiff and reserved, in short, the new type of female pedant. She showed Edmond so much affection however that her husband took offence. Her letters, which have been preserved, indicate clearly that even after 1870, out of modesty and virtuous discretion, she had almost always taken care to disguise her feelings for the elder brother by memories of the younger. 'What a letter Mme X... will write after Jules's death,' said Edmond. 'How ill her love conceals itself beneath her friendship, and how, in spite of her impeccable virtue, in spite of her passionate devotion to her children, each line confesses: "*I love you.*" Today, in this second letter, which arrived this morning, I note the curious disposition of her heart and the unutterable affection she offers me in the semblance of love of God... Very touching, these self-imposed deceptions of a noble and sensitive woman's heart, whom tender devotion leaves defenceless against the illusive idea of pure affection, of guiltless love.'

It is certainly to Mme Marcille that Edmond refers when writing on July 29, 1872, of a meeting at a wedding, his consequent agitation, a feverish shaking of hands, a half-inarticulate promise to go and see her. He did so; it was a sad, an almost funereal, occasion. She asked him to tell her the site of his brother's grave so that she might go there in secret. After her husband's death in 1876 she had to sell her collections, which Edmond and Eudoxe helped her to do. That same year Edmond chose as the frontispiece for an edition of his brother's engravings one representing *La Passion des Mesdemoiselles Marcille*. In 1884 she returned to him some letters from Jules she had recently discovered and invited him to Oisème, but his health prevented his going. In June, 1885, on the anniversary of Jules' death, he found on his grave two bouquets of roses and carnations she had placed upon it. How can one doubt that Edmond made an allusion to her in 1886? 'The few women whom I have loved with exalted passion, loved with a little of my brain intermingled with my heart, these I did not possess—and yet it is my belief that if I had wholeheartedly wished to have them, they would have been mine. But I have found a pleasure in the indescribably exquisite sensation experienced in seeing a woman led to the brink of committing a wrongful act and allowing her to live exposed to temptation and in continual fear of yielding to it.'

While frequenting collectors and antique dealers they also inspected archives and went to public auctions, to which, in order to kill time, they took a copy of La Bruyère. Visits to dealers in autographs were particularly Edmond's affair; he was the amateur of bibelots, the collector by vocation.

Round about 1860 a large reproduction of a Rubens in water-colour and gouache, a copy of the *Saint Bonaventure* in the Grenoble museum, decorated their little hall. The walls of their dining-room were adorned with panels surrounded by rare drawings. Their drawing-room, a fairly large one, was furnished with chairs covered in Beauvais tapestry and adorned with drawings by Latour and Boucher. Above the fireplace was Edmond's portrait of Jules in water-colour, with Clodion's statuette of a seated nymph, some unusual bronze candlesticks, and fine Sèvres vases. For their study they made use of Edmond's bedroom.

The Magny dinners, the Princess, and their growing love for bibelots drew them more and more away from their old connections, until in February, 1867, they wrote: 'Odd sort of Parisians in Paris are we who are as solitary as wolves. For three months we have been only just kept in contact with our fellow-creatures by the Magny dinners and those at the Princess's. Three months with hardly a visit or hardly a letter, hardly a single meeting with one of our acquaintances during our walks at eleven o'clock at night. Half by choice and half by determination we gather solitude around us, at one and the same time happy not to be wounded by contact with other people and sad to be by ourselves.'

Meanwhile, they were at home to friends every week, at first on Wednesdays and later on Thursdays. Their dining-room was the scene of cheerful dinners and suppers to which Janin, Gautier, Murger, Beauvoir,[1] Garvarni and others were invited, all men of lively intelligence, incited to laughter by a certain Léoville and that singular character Saint-Péray. Presiding over the kitchen was a cook skilled at making English puddings, pasta, curry and other exotic dishes. With the idea of introducing Paris to the real Lorraine style of cooking,

---

[1] Pseudonym of Eugène Roger de Bully, novelist and author of melodramas.

Pleasures and Friendships

Edmond engaged a woman from the Vosges who was unrivalled for her crayfish soup and stewed woodcock. Frantz Jourdain the art critic, who was a friend of Edmond's, speaks of him as a gourmet. Doubtless, as often happens, he had become more of one as he grew older.

Through their connection with *Paris*, the daily paper their cousin Villedeuil had started after *L'Eclair*, they had become friends with Scholl, then making his first appearance as a journalist. 'Don't you realize that you have got into my blood and that I am one of your ribs?' he wrote to Jules from Bordeaux, to which he had returned as chief editor of a paper, and where he was bored to death and short of money to the extent of borrowing fifteen louis from them. They were amazed at his impertinence, his waspish character, his witty remarks, his fits of temper, his whims, his amorous adventures, his duels, his spotty face, his spells of imprisonment, his flights into Belgium, whence he would return penniless and homeless to seek refuge in their hospitality. But a very different Scholl from the lively and aggressive man of the boulevards was one day unexpectedly revealed to them. His mistress had written to tell him that, weary of his tyranny, she had taken another lover, and he, in tears, recited to the brothers some verses that this betrayal had inspired.

After making them passionately interested and even a little dazzled, he embarrassed them by his vanity, his futility, and his taste for scandal. Having become the lover of the golden-haired Doche, the actress who created the role of the heroine in *La Dame aux Camélias* and other dramas, he made himself impossible, not to say ridiculous, by his affections and his ostentatious vanity. 'On seeing Scholl now, changed from the youngster he was when I first saw him, twiddling his gloves on a seat in the *Paris* waiting-room, on seeing him today so cock-a-hoop and so insupportable, I think how badly a little soul, a plebeian soul, can stand good fortune and to what extent success makes such men ridiculous.'

The *Journal* of December, 1857, shows us Scholl 'consumed with cares... maddened by evil ambition... contemplating a series of articles in which he will wreak vengeance on the heads of the public for not yet being a famous man.'

At a New Year's Eve party in 1859, Jules had a conversation with Doche which doubtless it only rested with him to carry further. In December, 1860, Scholl is spoken of as living with a certain Rosita.

Edmond and Jules

In May, 1861, we are told of him as grown sick of Doche—she was then forty-three—and wishing to go back to a hotel to live. In January, 1862, he was living in a flat in the rue Laffitte, and was the lover of the charming actress Léonide Leblanc, but jealous of her as of all his other women. An unhealthy life, but full of excitement; a novel into which he flung the tattered fragments of his life and love affairs, shortage of money, restaurants, cafés, brothels, mean but wild and feverish ambitions and, last but not least, spiritualism, for Scholl was a medium. '... A type representative of all that is lowest in literature, of the fretful activities of men with little talent and the desires and appetites of diseased minds...'

In December, 1866, the Goncourts dined in his flat, cluttered with pictures of nudes, photographs of actresses, papers and books. He was living there with a young woman with a Polish accent who had a huge mop of red hair and strange green eyes that glittered like the eyes of the black cat in the house. That evening the brothers found Scholl still bristling with resentment, sarcastic, boastful, with his mouth full of his novels and plays.

In September, 1867, when Edmond received his decoration, he was attacked by Scholl. 'A venomous attack such as one must expect from a man who has received nothing but friendliness from you, and from the police an order to leave off wearing a decoration imitating the rosette of an Officer of the Legion of Honour.' In 1892 Daudet brought about a reconciliation between Edmond and Scholl.

Entirely forgotten, even more so than Scholl, is Mario Uchard. Originally a stockbroker's clerk, he became a writer of novels and plays. He had had his play *Le Retour du Mari* rejected by the Comédie-Française, and then his *Fiammina*, which was given a second chance, however, under influential patronage, but proved a failure.

In Uchard's *La Seconde Jeunesse* there is a scene entirely composed by Jules. 'The only scene that introduces a slightly jarring note into the play by showing some trace of ideas, some semblance of wit, some shadow of French style... And as I heard people laugh and applaud, I thought a little of the pride of a man face to face with his conscience, yet borrowing thus from others, and I could not understand his elation at this success which includes so many peacock's feathers.' Elsewhere the *Journal* harks back to Uchard's vanity and lack of perception. 'The most curious literary infatuation I have ever seen is that of Mario puffed up and full of shameful pride over plays he has not written himself. To believe one possesses the talent one steals is perhaps the last limit in literary conceit; a man cannot go any further.'

Charles Edmond, with whom the Goncourts had been friends ever since they had been contributors to *Paris*, and who later became secretary to the Prince Napoleon, was known as Chojecki; he was born in Poland in 1822. The Goncourts used to dine with him at his house in Bellevue where he lived with a mistress called Julie. The house had a tiny garden with a terrace running alongside a lane that led out into the country. It was pleasant there in the evening in Saint-Victor's company to recall memories of the classics. 'Nothing here that stinks of the squalor of those transient Bohemian *ménages* in furnished suburban lodgings, which in Murger's novels are set down at table opposite a bottle of bad wine and put to bed in dirty sheets—a thing that utterly destroys a woman, since women can only exist in conditions of certain elegance...'

In January, 1852, the *Journal* presents to us a Charles Edmond 'of flaxen fairness, with a gentle voice, but deep and loud as thunder when he becomes animated; a man full of tales of Roman adventurers and of Poland, of legends and Russian atrocities, talking well and slowly, in a vague and sympathetic way, of wild and preposterous ideas, with the gentle, caressing smile one sees in the eyes of Slavs, and the slightly asiatic and cat-like charm of this people... They felt a particular respect for him, appreciating his capacity for hard work. I take Charles Edmond to a rehearsal at the *Bouffes Parisiens*. He is weary and utterly exhausted, with a face as wan as the face of the dead. I tell him he ought to rest. He replies that he is expecting seven people to dinner and that he has to earn forty thousand francs in order to leave Julie an income of two thousand. "If I happened to die, everyone would abandon her, that I know." And we confess to ourselves that he is a better man than we are.'

Charles Edmond's marriage and his appointment as librarian to the Senate did not please them. In this palace that seemed to them like 'a corsair's villa washed by the Nile', and where they were served with bad wine, they thought the married couple boring, stingy and deceptively friendly.

Edmond About, who was also a member of the coterie at the Café Riche, never had any great charm for them. The Goncourts met him at Charles Edmond's and went for a stroll with him through the

Bellevue woods. His conversation was largely about himself. 'He represents success in the first person, but not too grossly so, nor too insupportably, since it is compensated for by witty little monkey tricks, by little literary pats on the shoulder given to men of letters who are present and for whom he serves up quotations from their books. But in his conversation there is nothing that is not worldly, narrowly Parisian, or like the stuff one gets in some inferior newspaper.' Their antipathy for him increasing, About seemed to them a man of no imagination without a gleam of wit—a kind of ill-bred child, a bourgeois who boasted of his connections and flaunted his successes with women in paradoxes that might have come from a commercial traveller.

At the Café Riche, Murger sat down beside them. 'Murger, completely penniless, lived as he could, on money borrowed from newspapers, by wangling payments in advance. The man himself had no more sense of delicacy than the writer. An entertaining and comical sort of fellow, he did not shrink from becoming a parasite, accepting dinners, suppers and drinks he never paid for and which he could not return. Neither a bad nor a good companion. I always found him indulgent—especially towards people without talent. He would speak more freely of these than of the others; an accomplished egotist.' Had he been one of their intimate friends, would Murger have been given a better funeral oration?

The reviewer and critic Xavier Aubryet must have inspired them with some respect when in October, 1857, they invited him with Paul de Saint-Victor and Mario Uchard to a reading of *Les Hommes de Lettres*, but in an entry in the preceding June we find some rather unflattering remarks about him: 'A Prudhomme masked in paradoxes, a good fellow on the whole, but boring in his speech and gestures, who takes himself seriously because he has squandered money on *L'Artiste*, talks at the top of his voice, is as cynical as a schoolboy, poses as a Lovelace ... and takes women of the town for rides in his carriage, a man of many illusions, who ... exhausts himself speaking of other people in order to get himself talked about ...'

Aubryet gave a dinner at which were present, besides the Goncourts, Charles Edmond, Saint-Victor, Flaubert, Ludovic Halévy, Claudin and Gautier. 'A fifth-floor flat in the rue Taitbout through which a prostitute's upholsterer has passed. A drawing-room padded with dove-coloured silk with a ceiling by Faustin Besson. A dining-room furnished with those pretty odds-and-ends of porcelain and glass that Arsène Houssaye had made the fashion.' According to Claudin who, as a contributor to the *Moniteur*, was in a position to reveal the underside of the official press, Aubryet was one of the most original figures of boulevard life round about 1860. 'Whimsically gay and excitable by nature, he wrote about nothing but serious subjects, and spent his time fighting on behalf of principles in contradiction with what he said and did.' Most of the witty remarks people quoted to each other came originally from him. Eventually, the Goncourts lost sight of him. It is without a line of commentary that, on March 7, 1886, Edmond reports the dismal account the painter Ziem gives him of his last meeting with Aubryet, smitten with the same disease as Alphonse Daudet.

The little space given in the published version of the *Journal* to Adolphe Dennery, the one-time linen-draper's assistant who had become a capitalist and an author of successful plays, bears no relation to the place occupied in the manuscript by himself and Gisette (Clémence Desgranges), the mistress whom he married. The author of *La Reine des Blanchisseuses* is not spared in this part of the *Journal*. 'As for Dennery,' we read, 'he has a very simple recipe for wit by which he has earned himself an easy reputation as a witty person. It's always "you old swine" and a perpetual string of disagreeable remarks, as, for example: "I was bored in Venice, it seemed to me I was at one of your plays".' As with all their friends' homes, Dennery's, a typical interior of the Second Empire, shocked these amateurs of the eighteenth century. 'It has a drawing-room,' they wrote, 'such as a millionaire in the rue Sentier would approve of. Rosewood furniture, portières, curtains of crimson silk damask; and everywhere those horrible pieces of Buhl manufactured in the vulgar Faubourg Saint-Antoine.' Dennery's guests were in keeping, a thing which did not, however, prevent the Goncourts from going, on Dennery's invitation, to visit him at Cabourg, where he was mayor. Whence came the pleasure they found in Gisette's company? 'Up till now,' says the *Journal*, 'I have only met three intelligent women among the different classes of society: the Princess, Lagier,[1] and Gisette. The first had the gift of eloquence and a savagely caustic tongue, the second that of

---

[1] A well-known actress, on whom Edmond based the likeness of Mme Bourlemont, keeper of a gambling den described in *La Fille Elisa*.

telling ribald and marvellously racy stories, the third that of quick repartee and a genius for making witty remarks. In each of them was the reflected image of some great man, in the first that of Mirabeau, in the second of Rabelais, in the third of Beaumarchais.'

The fortune Dennery had made in the theatre allowed him to build a superb town house for Gisette with a marble staircase. Here the Goncourts rubbed shoulders with a mixed society of mothers, children, and young girls in whose presence any liberty was permitted. People kissed and cuddled and when Dennery had left, they danced the can-can, skirts flew up and legs were displayed. 'You leave this house,' says the *Journal*, 'these women, these velvet gowns with a sad contraction of the heart, with the bitterness in your mouth of someone who has taken a bite out of a lovely fruit that is rotten, sour, and hollow.'

It was also at the time of their connection with *Paris* that they had become friendly with Théodore de Banville, an affectionate and striking portrait of whom, under the name of Boisroger, is contained in *Charles Demailly*. On December 13, 1856, they wrote: 'We visit Banville's house... on the boulevard Clichy, a tiny dwelling with little rooms like those one takes in the summer in the neighbourhood of Paris—a few costume designs from the Bullier theatre, a photograph of Louis Melvil, a painted panel of Gothic virgins, *The Green Monster* [Banville's mistress] in Banville's dressing-gown... a lack of furniture disguised by a few chairs idly placed round an armchair, an indescribable feeling of a life of hard work... a home at the mercy of chance. I know not what story of sadness, what struggles, and what anguish these silent walls record. Nothing is so cheerful as a solid bourgeois home! Happy people! How well they are revenged on those who think and write and dream! What simple healthy delights compared with this solitude shared with a woman of low repute.'

Three months later they wrote: 'We have been to see Banville; we find him in bed (an iron bedstead) suffering, according to the homoeopathic doctor who attends him, from attacks of pain that have their seat in the stomach. A little painter's cap on his head, his thin face underneath it. Sitting up in bed and looking, in a way impossible to define, like a pierrot or a mountebank at a fair, laughing in a sweetly sharp falsetto voice and making us laugh with him at his own troubles and the troubles of humanity.'

The correspondence contains several letters from Banville, one of which, undated, encloses some verses sent at the request of the Goncourts, apparently for one of their plays. At that period at least, if we are to go by an opinion expressed in November, 1868, they did not think very highly of Banville. 'It is possibly a prejudice but I believe that a man must be well-bred and a bourgeois of good standing to be a man of talent. I judge by Flaubert and ourselves in comparison with the great men of Bohemia, its novelist Murger, its historian Monselet, its poet Banville.'

When the poet died, in March, 1891, Edmond and he were coldly disposed towards each other, but on account of the article Banville had written about Jules after his death, his old friend remained grateful to him.

Feydeau did not find favour with the Goncourts, and the truth is that the author of *Fanny* seems to have aroused little sympathy for himself in the circles he frequented. What people found fault with most of all was his gross and childish self-conceit. He lived in a magnificent flat in the Parc Monceau, which the Goncourts, ever sensitive to styles of decoration, describe as 'appropriate to a great courtesan or an important jobber, with something dubiously rich about it, that smells of other people's money'.

Feydeau was looking round for capital with which to start a newspaper. In August, 1870, Edmond received an urgent letter from him asking him for the loan of five hundred francs. In October, 1872, he appeared and demanded that Edmond should immediately let him have five hundred francs for a portrait of his mother by Gavarni, and make *Le Bien Public* accept his sketch of Gautier. 'As he leaves me', writes Edmond, 'he says, "There were only five francs left in the house; I spent them buying a pancake for Gautier. My wife scolded me. She said that a man in my circumstances doesn't buy pancakes for his friends." Thereupon this "palsy-stricken wangler" gets into a fine, comfortable carriage and goes off to rejoin a wife tricked out in velvet and lace in a handsome flat in the rue de Copenhague.'

Except for their relations with Banville, Saint-Victor and Dennery, all these acquaintanceships were hardly more than casual. The two brothers had some that were more serious.

XI
Gavarni and Sainte-Beuve

'We loved, we admired Gavarni. We spent much time in his company. For many long years we were almost the only close friends the misanthropist had. For the younger of us he felt a kind of fatherly affection; and the solitude of the Point du Jour would resound to us with this kindly greeting: "My boys, you fill my house with joy!"'

Twenty years senior to Edmond, Gavarni was as much a master to them as a friend. Master of drawing, master in philosophy, master in the art of observing and noting things that happened from day to day. Henry Céard, author of the introduction to Jules's *Letters*, has rightly remarked his important influence over them; he opened their eyes to the life and manners of their times. 'Little by little, under his pervading influence, MM. de Goncourt were awakened to an interest in reality, to curiosity about things close at hand. They began to understand the place that still remained for them to take in the novel of contemporary life that had been so neglected since Balzac's death.'

The whole of the first part of the *Journal* is full of Gavarni. They devoted a book to him, on which Jules was working when he fell ill. He treated them as his children and allowed them to be present while he was at his labours, which, 'having taken a hand in them', they have described in minute detail.

The Gavarni they knew in 1851 still had a fine appearance, with something of a military air about him, hair and beard of golden-red, a ruddy complexion, an expression of bland and witty good humour. He grew old before his time and from then on began to suffer from melancholia. This was the Gavarni after his stay in London, a repudiator of all the graces and all the elegance he had painted with such affection, the Gavarni, in short, of *Thomas Vireloque*. But sometimes in the evening after his day's work was over, he became cheerful, and dressed in a long frockcoat and with trousers strapped under his instep, a silk handkerchief round his neck and his elbows on the table, would enjoy himself amid glasses of hot punch. This would sometimes last for an hour or two. As the night advanced the artist's thoughts would become more

Gavarni and Sainte-Beuve

exalted, their compass wider, revealing a Gavarni who was a philosopher, a materialist, an atheist, with a passion for mathematical and geometrical research, who would hold his young friends in a state of expectation well after the hour when the last boat from Versailles should have taken them back to Paris; and there would be variations played on the sciences, rambling off into digressions on what he called the music of numbers. All this took place in a garret warmed by a cast-iron stove up under the roof of his house, the lower rooms of which were unoccupied. On the walls were plans for altering and embellishing the Palais-Royal, which he would have liked to see transformed into a sort of huge flower-market—one of his pet fancies; there were also T-squares, rulers, a thermometer in a gilt frame, and mahogany bookshelves. The table was covered with books, portfolios, bundles of lithographs, mathematical notebooks, and also the skull of his dog Trilby. In a corner was a green velvet divan and a desk on which were displayed the plans of his house and garden.

One thing shocked them in Gavarni's house, as it did in most other houses: the lack of distinction. 'This Gavarni, whom posterity will picture as the master and the very epitome of elegance, he who has mingled in his sketches so much silk, so much luxury and the pick of the Paris basket, Gavarni has a home and tastes that are almost those of the working-class. A common wine-seller's glass is good enough for him to drink his wine in at home. At a dinner he has a horror of everything that smacks of studied refinement, extra attention to details, dressed-up dishes, and he calls a dinner exceedingly distinguished where there is no distinction at all.'

After the death of his son, Jean, his ideas became hazy, capricious and tiresome. He remodelled his garden, dug it up, replanted it, built bridges and put up railings, hollowed out ravines and made little lakes, erected a monumental table and constructed bedrooms for his dogs. He also bought a huge meadow that separated the garden from the Seine. He ruined himself for his garden, but it was his heart's delight.

He would turn up unexpectedly in the rue Saint-Georges, sometimes for dinner, sometimes only for a chat, and would start talking about geometry, painting, mortgages, horticulture, photography and women. The Goncourts used to go shopping with him and would sit down with him at the Café de la Gondole, where he went by the name of M. Guillaume. One day he felt a desire to go back and see one of those balls at the Opera that his pencil had immortalized and which were in some degree his work. After spending the evening at the Cirque, and stopping at a little café where he talked to them about the mathematician, Biot, then still living, they went to the Opera. And there, held up by them, and lost in the crowd, 'like a king forgotten in his ancient kingdom', he went up the stairs and spent an hour contemplating the spectacle of the masquerade from a box. They took him back with them to spend the night in the rue Saint-Georges. 'On the way he seemed to be dragging his feet. He did not utter a word. He took a long time getting up our stairs, stopping to rest and getting his breath with some difficulty on almost every landing. Finally, by the fireside he told us all about it. He had felt cold at the Cirque, the heat of the ball had stifled him, and on coming out into the street he was seized with a sort of fit of nervous choking, for a moment he had wondered if he could put one foot before the other.' He made jokes as he went to bed, but he was still troubled by the sort of slight stroke he had had. Two days later they went to Auteuil to ask how he was. 'I don't like things I can't understand,' he told them.

They went on going with him to those queer eating-houses, ancestors of our bistros, which he called 'bistingos', particularly to a certain Café du Mail where the cooking was abominable, but the owner of which he suspected of having been a comedian at the Palais-Royal. At his house there were frequent improvised dinners at which were assembled by chance such guests as, for instance, his son Pierre, the Goncourts, a lieutenant-colonel in the Zouaves, an actress from the Comédie-Française, and Henry Monnier. It was at Gavarni's also that the two brothers became acquainted with Constantin Guys.

From 1861 onwards his health began seriously to decline. The indifference of the public grieved him, he left off drawing and became absorbed in mathematics and in putting his affairs in order. A crazy whim seized him: to transform the big meadow he had bought at the bottom of his garden into a nursery with a greenhouse, covered walks, a landing stage and a boat service for the transport of his trees. He did not, however, forget his great project for rejuvenating the Palais-Royal, which included making a stream across it, which if he had realized it would have brought him millions. His friends encouraged him in this, but he complained of the difficulty he found in getting about, and the trouble of taking steps to accomplish the project. If he had had the use of his legs he would have moved the world!

On July 14, 1862, having been invited to dine with Princess Mathilde, he borrowed a black suit from them. It was in the autumn of that year that, in order to provide him with some distraction, his friend Dr Veyne, who was also a friend of Sainte-Beuve, took the initiative in starting the dinners, soon to be known as the Atheists' dinners, the Magny dinners, or those of the Gavarni circle.

The Goncourts would appear to have judged Gavarni very well in writing that there were two men in him: the one keenly interested in the most important questions, and for whom, as for Goethe, the revolution of 1830 would have seemed an insignificant incident compared with a letter from Cuvier to the Academy; the other, somewhat narrow-minded, sharing the trivial tastes of the Restoration, and who is to his counterpart as his first drawings are to those of Vireloque. Isolation, so they elsewhere noted, made a greater man of Gavarni, women's society diminished him and made him dull and stupid. At each visit his declining health depressed them more and more. In 1863 the expropriation of his little property dealt him a mortal blow. 'This expropriation, his disappointments, his worries, his stroke, the failure of his dreams of buying Tambourini's house at Meudon when the purchase was nearly completed, all this I fear may finish him, and in killing him the worthy citizens of the expropriation committee, the master builders, slaters, etc., will be well revenged on this immortal joker at the expense of the Bourgeoisie.'

In October, 1868, while going with him over the property he had contemplated buying, they were struck to see him more and more bent, weakened, feverish, congested and apoplectic, and inclined to be something of a petty bourgeois in his ways.

He fell 'into the most frightful state of poverty'. 'He would have been driven out of the house he had bought for 26,000 francs if M. Trelet[1] had not died. On top of all this there are still debts outstanding that were thought to have been settled.' On March 30, 1866, they wrote: 'Seen Gavarni lately. He no longer has any notion of time, of hours, days, or months. He is nothing more now than a pure abstraction, an idle dream. He does not draw any more, is not interested in doing anything, nor about anything at all.'

Finally on November 25 of that same year, when visiting Bar-sur-Seine, they read in *La France* the news of his death at the very moment he was being buried. 'We shall not find ourselves walking behind the

---

[1] The explanation of this incident is not known.

coffin of the man we loved most, and most admired. We shall never see him again.'

On their return to Paris they got his son to give them an account of his death. In the avenue de l'Impératrice they caught sight of the artist's old house and thought it had a funereal, deserted air. 'In spite of everything we are still glad to see this house still standing! It brings back memories of him.' Pierre Gavarni entrusted to them the manuscript of his father's memoirs. It disappointed them: there was nothing in it about themselves, nor about other friends. The whole of it was devoted to women and mathematics, there was an amazing inequality in the level of ideas, the highest speculations mixed up with the maddest nonsense.

Pierre Gavarni, whose friend Edmond remained, confided other papers to them. In the excitement of preparing their book about him they thought to discover in Gavarni something dark and Machiavellian that made them compare him with Laclos, the author of *Les Liaisons Dangereuses*, and they made the additional comment: 'This man... who is always speaking to himself of truth, lets one see all sorts of sides of himself without freely, plainly, or frankly disclosing them. In his soul, in his mind, he has the habit of twisting his thoughts and his sentences, of resorting to that kind of philosophical quibbling that is never the first impulse of an idea that springs from the heart. And in all his actions, in all his writings: women, always women, scribbled between the lines ... there are many men in this man, and men very different from the one man we knew. What a strange thing history is when one writes it about people one has known and loved! We cannot in our book tell the whole and absolute truth. That his father, for instance, seems to have been a rascally old revolutionary, that he himself was legitimatized by marriage, and that his mother was a seamstress.'

Their admiration for the artist, however, remained whole-hearted to the very end. 'The last time his already trembling hand ran the etching-needle over the copper,' so Philippe Burty writes of Jules, 'and his disordered will made it bite into the metal, it was to reproduce an example of his favourite masters' art, a small-part actor, a raw-boned peasant, repeating anxiously to himself the few, brief words he will say to this lord when he comes on the scene.'

On November 22, 1862, the first of the dinners that took place at

Gavarni and Sainte-Beuve

Magny's restaurant in the rue Contre-Escarpe-Dauphine was thus recorded in the *Journal*: 'Gavarni has organized a dinner with Sainte-Beuve which is to take place twice a month. Today is the inauguration... dinner at Magny's where Sainte-Beuve is a regular customer. Today there are only Gavarni, Sainte-Beuve, Veyne, Chennevières [1] and ourselves. But the dinner will be bigger later on and include other guests.'

This gathering is foreshadowed in *Charles Demailly* in the dinners at the Moulin Rouge: 'Intimacy, an intimacy complete and without reservations, had established itself between those who dined there every Thursday, and as it so happened the diversity of political creeds, the variety of opinions on literature, and even the clash of temperaments had at least contributed as much by their harmonious opposition as did the community of tastes and the similarity of humours to the mutual sympathy of each individual member for the others. The basis of this society, its essential groundwork and its charm, consisted in a sense of security, a fearless trust in one another, freedom of speech, of thought, of conscience, a certainty that one's personal likes and dislikes would never be betrayed. A rare pleasure in this little world of letters, that of being able to let one's mind and heart expand freely, of being able to open out completely without furnishing weapons to gossip, to indiscreet tittle-tattle, to jealous or wounded companions, or indeed any copy for a newspaper or notes for a biographer to use!' Between the dinners at the Moulin Rouge, which actually took place, though the novelists of *Charles Demailly* idealized them, and the dinners at Magny's, there are many differences. The diners at the Moulin Rouge, if not young men, were at least still youthful and full of illusions; those at Magny's were full-grown men who had learnt from experience the precarious stability of the most firmly grounded friendships.

The first dinners were very pleasant, but by June, 1865, the spell was already broken. 'We have come to feel contempt and distaste for the Magny dinners. To think that this is a communion of the most liberal minds in France! For the most part, from Gautier to Sainte-Beuve, they are certainly men of talent, but what a miserable scarcity of ideas among them, of opinions which their own nerves and their own sensations supply! What an absence of personality, of temperament! With all of them what a bourgeois fear of excess, of ideas in advance

[1] Art critic, curator of the Luxembourg Museum.

of the times! This evening we almost got stoned for saying that Hébert, whom no one at the table had read, had some talent. Sainte-Beuve declared that the proof he had none was that his contemporaries had not recognized it in him. They are all of them servants to current opinion, to prejudices that have the strength of laws, to refined and scholarly Prudhommes...'

Refined? One would doubt this if one had to rely on the scene on February 22, 1863, which enables one to dismiss the idea that here was a platonic banquet. 'Most of us are there and our discussion touches upon every sort of subject. "Boileau is very much more of a poet than Racine," cries Saint-Victor. "Bossuet's style is poor," so Flaubert affirms. Renan and Taine put La Bruyère above La Rochefoucauld. We give vent to peacock screeches. "La Bruyère is deficient in philosophy," they exclaim. What does that mean? Renan wanders on about Pascal, whom he proclaims the finest writer in the French language. "Pascal! A mere clod!" cries Gautier. Saint-Victor spouts some Hugo. Taine says: "Generalizing the particular, that's all Schiller amounts to. Particularizing the general, there's the whole of Goethe." People fight about aesthetics, they discover genius in the rhetoricians, homeric contests take place on the value of words, on the music of sentences. Caught between Gautier and Taine, Saint-Beuve gazes dolefully at them with an anxious eye; everyone is talking, and out of each man's mouth come professions of faith in atheism, fragments of Utopian philosophy, shreds and tatters of stereotyped discourses, systems for nationalizing religion. And I am present to see the fine spectacle of Taine, who has just been sick out of the window, coming back again, still looking quite green... and professing, for an hour on end... his faith in the superiority of his Protestant God.'

★ ★ ★

They had been in touch with Sainte-Beuve ever since he had warned them in 1854 not to hope for a review of their *Histoire de la Révolution Française* 'in the rather rigid and antiquated setting of his articles in *Le Moniteur*'. In 1857, they had sent him their *Portraits Intimes*, their *Sophie Arnould*, on which he had complimented them, and some time later their *Marie-Antoinette*. Now, in 1857, they already detested him. In fact, they did so as early as 1851, since in the first chapter of *En 18..* we read: 'Volupté! Priapism in the sacristy!—Stuff and nonsense! centipede sentences, pure caterpillar twaddle!' They refused to see in the *Causeries du Lundi* anything more than a biographical *Dictionnaire de la Conversation*. An unfrocked romantic, that was Sainte-Beuve! A frigid style, a doubtful, hypocritical character, cowardly, narrow-minded, more attached to correctness of grammar than to style in its real sense, envious, fond of platitudes, 'slithering with his little arms over statues of great men and clinging on to their feet of clay'.

On September 1, 1861, he wrote to them: 'Messieurs de Goncourt have always been for me the most likeable people in the world. I have received their fine volume. *Sœur Philomène* is a novel which gives the perfect truth, directly studied from life. I hope I shall not always remain on such a footing with Messieurs de Goncourt as to thank them from a distance. Besides their being very charming people, I know they have a treasure-house of curious things in art and literature which they delight in showing to their friends, and they treat me (and rightly so) as if I were one. I will ask them to be so kind as to let me look at the eighteenth century, their own century, with them . . .' They met each other and found themselves more or less in sympathy around Gavarni's table, on which, after the latter's death, they were to help Sainte-Beuve write his article.

The Magny dinners quickly bore fruit. On December 18, 1862, Sainte-Beuve supplied *Le Constitutionnel* with an article on *La Femme au Dix-huitième Siècle*. At his rooms in the rue de Montparnasse the Goncourts were shocked by the mediocrity of his surroundings, as they had been by his manner, like that of a 'half-refined little provincial draper'. On that occasion, he had worked himself into a rage over Flaubert's *Salammbô*. 'Progress, by Jove,' said Sainte-Beuve that evening, 'I will tell you how I see it; like a series of terraces. There comes a moment when humanity is about to drown. A rescuer arrives, and carries it up to a terrace; there it is laid down, it begins to recover, and then the water rises, it overruns the terrace. And so on and so on, a system of rescues from terrace to terrace.' At the end of dinner, in a confidential aside, Sainte-Beuve let slip the cause of his deep and hidden melancholy, the secret of a buried but still living grief. 'He would have liked to be handsome, to have a good physique, seductive charm, that immediate conquest of women, who are his temptation, his paramount concern . . . the focus of his being, his desire, his curiosity . . . and which form an old man's dream and his abiding shame. There is a disappointed, melancholic satyr deep down in this little old man who feels himself to be ugly, unpleasing and, to put it briefly, old.'

Edmond and Jules

The Goncourts' preoccupation with art interested and even intrigued him, but what a divergence of ideas and opinions! About Heine, for example, whom Jules had so highly praised some ten years before, and whom Sainte-Beuve spoke of as a rascal.

At Magny's Sainte-Beuve was the most important guest and showed himself friendly to the Goncourts. On June 6, 1863, lumbago prevented him from accompanying them to Saint-Gratien where Princess Mathilde had a house. However, he gave them directions for getting there, a superfluous attention since they had already been there in November. He told them his secrets, he whispered in their ears an abridgement of his philosophy, which was the same as Sénac de Meilhan's. Had he any idea of the severity with which they judged him, as did Flaubert and Gautier? Did he suspect that Jules was carefully collecting everything that was said about him at the Princess's in his absence?

In 1864, they made a careful record of Chesneau's [1] jealous recriminations accusing Sainte-Beuve of compromising his position, his future, and his contract with the *Constitutionnel*. They had got Levallois, who had been Sainte-Beuve's secretary four times, to talk about his former patron. 'He is short and thin,' they wrote of Levallois, 'with one of those faces on which poverty has left its mark and which bear the imprint of Bohemia. His beard, his hair and his complexion are pitiable, he wears a shabby frock-coat and wretched carpet-slippers. The man is as lean as his house.' In talking of Sainte-Beuve, the poor fellow revealed to them the lack of decision, the timidity of his own first judgements. 'There are always bunches of women in his life . . . He is inexhaustible and very interesting on the subject of Sainte-Beuve, about whom he tells us stories, whom he mimics and ridicules with that admirable aptitude for revenge to be found in men who have ministered to someone else's fame or talents . . . He depicts for our benefit the man with that mistress, Mme de Vacquez, whom he firmly believed to be Spanish and whom he would religiously consult on whatever Spanish literature came his way, such as Calderon and others . . . Then he returns to his own moments of hesitation, his endless quest for public notoriety, for other people's ideas and the opinions of women of no importance, to the curious fear he has of huge, husky fellows . . . He tells us of the way in which he lost his illusions about the famous

---

[1] A critic of art and literature.

critic, who set out to write an article on George Sand's *Villemer* without knowing the first thing about it, and who remarked after a day's reading: "Well now, I'm going to take a plunge, I'll swim later. Instead of making it into two articles I'll make it three in order to have time to read it."'

On the subject of *Germinie Lacerteux* Sainte-Beuve wrote to say: 'I have been attracted by this simple story, true with the kind of truth so little courted, but so much in accordance with reality, and in which not a single detail is left to chance or adapted to suit convention ... But already one thing strikes me, that to judge this work properly and to talk about it, one would need an altogether different conception of poetry from the old one, adapted to the productions of a new type of art, a new kind of elegance. And it is already very praiseworthy for a book to have raised a question of this importance, to have broken away to such an extent from old conceptions...'

The intrigue that wrecked *Henriette Maréchal* found him on their side. When, too, they had a violent dispute on the subject of Homer with Saint-Victor at Magny's, the critic intervened in a friendly way on their behalf. On the occasion of Gavarni's death he wrote to them expressing his regrets. In the same letter he told them he was glad they had been absent from Paris at the time of the last Magny dinner: 'Otherwise I should have been afraid that what happened on that other ill-omened Monday had something to do with your absence. I could not have borne this and I would rather stop coming to the dinner if you did not come any more. But I greatly hope we have not reached this point.'

In August, 1867, a visit to the rue Montparnasse gave them cause to write some very severe lines about Sainte-Beuve. 'One peculiarity of his ... that indicates ... very clearly the essentially democratic character of this man ... is the costume he adopts in the privacy of his home: his dressing-gown, his trousers, socks and bedroom slippers, those plebeian woollens that make him appear like a hall-porter suffering from gout ... And involuntarily, as he was talking, we were thinking how a single article from a caustic and truthful pen, a single pin-prick from a sincerely honest man, would deflate this wind-bag posing as a martyr on a salary of thirty thousand francs—an article which would recall that, alone among men of letters, this Sainte-Beuve was the writer who, in 1852, during the white terror in the realm of literature, when we were summoned before the courts at the time of Flaubert's trial, in that period of silence and universal slavery, was... the official supporter of the government. And it would be amusing to recall that it was a pay-sheet that served to enlighten him and make him a convert to the cause of liberty and that courage only came to him with his salary as a permanent official and with those senator's palms he gained by serving with the perfidy of a priest all the vile rancours of December 2.'

There can be no question of the independent spirit, of the disinterestedness of the Goncourts, but there is nothing to be seen in their lives that might have authorized them to speak in such a tone of a critic to whom but a little time before they had addressed such lavish protestations of admiration and friendship. Why did they not write this article 'from a caustic and truthful pen' themselves? Sainte-Beuve's attitude towards them had always been irreproachable, and more than that, friendly. Very much their senior, he could have assumed a high tone with them; he never did so, any more than with anyone else, unless his feelings had been wounded. Three days after Jules had written what has just been quoted, Sainte-Beuve, very probably because they had asked him to do so, was writing to the Princess: 'I found the Goncourts on their return from Saint-Gratien better in health with their minds refreshed and in high spirits. Will that little ribbon, which apparently pleases when one is young, come to them within reasonable time and not in shreds? Your own kind self has it in mind, but elsewhere there is so little kindness.'

He proved his genuine sympathy for them to the point of threatening not to go to Magny's any more if they stopped going there, but it was only superficially returned. Could these artists, these aristocrats, in actual fact, be on really good terms with a man who dressed like a doorkeeper, the interior of whose home was like that of a provincial doctor, and who in one of Gavarni's lithographs mistook the shadow cast by one figure for another person?

They congratulated him, however, in connection with the controversy raised in the Senate by his intervention against the placing of certain books on the index, and on the duel that almost resulted from it between himself and Lacaze, the right-wing senator. 'We have followed with an interest you will not suspect,' they told him, 'all this already historical controversy. At first we were a little afraid of the shock to your health and then we saw your pen in such good state that the writer has reassured us regarding the physical condition of the man. We hope very much to be rather better confirmed in this opinion when we see you.'

In April, 1868, while studying in preparation for *Madame Gervaisis* the works Sainte-Beuve had consulted for his *Port-Royal*, they made the comment: 'I knew very well that he had always borrowed from others. He is nothing but a chameleon who has made a tour of all the ideas of his time.'

XII

Gautier, Flaubert and Others

From certain entries in the *Journal* it is doubtful whether, up to the time of the Magny dinners, there was any sort of real understanding between the two brothers and Gautier, but from the year 1862 they seem to have become friendly with him. On March 3 of that year they paid their first visit to his house at Neuilly, where the 'sultan of the epithet' had been living ever since he left the rue Grange-Batelière. It was a jerry-built plaster-cast house, its courtyards overrun with fowls. They found in the interior 'a mean, shoddy sumptuosity like the home of an old retired actress'. The oriental indolence and freedom of speech of the poet's daughters made a very great impression on them.

In the presence of the Goncourts and Prince Radziwill, Flaubert performed the dance of the Fool of the Drawing-Rooms. 'He borrows a coat from Gautier, he turns up his shirt-collar; I don't know what he does with his hair, his features, his expression, but all of a sudden there he is transformed into a frightful caricature of crass stupidity. Seized with a desire to emulate him, Gautier takes off his frock-coat and dripping with sweat, his great posterior overshadowing his shins, dances in his turn the Creditor's Jig, and the evening ends with Bohemian ditties, wild melodies into which Prince Radziwill introduces an admirably strident note.' A merry party in which joy is not entirely unrelated to the Pouilly.

In discussing aesthetics and philosophy all three of them were generally of the same opinion. The two brothers did not however approve of Gautier's system of grammar. 'A great artist,' they called him, 'but a fool at syntax'.

Gautier has left behind him the memory of a poor man. This was not the opinion of his two friends, however, in 1868. 'Our good Gautier is one of the richest of those modern starvelings of literature, with his librarian's post, say 6,000 francs, his pension from the Emperor's privy purse, say 3,000, and almost 20,000 a year from the *Moniteur* and the royalties on his books. Who among writers is as rich as that today?'

They would, if need be, have forgiven him for his wealth, but not for his ambition to become a member of the Academy, nor his son's position as chief of the official censors of the Paris press. They were particularly hard on him for his vulgar obsequiousness towards the Princess at whose house they met sometimes. 'It is amazing how this man becomes brutally inhuman and assumes an air of boorish malevolence in the face of official favours and concessions. Obsequiousness aggravates the baseness of his nature, and he presents to his friends at this moment a distressing and painful spectacle of the lowest degradation, of the vilest servility . . . and, so to speak, maddest "swank" of the most ill-bred poet that ever lived.'

On March 10, 1864, they happened to be at his house with the younger Dumas, who was there as an old friend and neighbour, 'now grown thin, with a receding forehead, hair *en brosse*, a retreating chin and with something angular and faded about him that hardly made it possible to recognize that large face bloated with health and self-complacency of former days'. They were present at the first night of Dumas' *Les Idées de Madame Aubrais*. 'Dumas has one great gift. He knows the secret of speaking to his audience, to this public that comes to first-night performances; he is their poet and he serves up to men and women of society, in a language they can understand, the idealized form of the commonplaces their hearts delight in.'

George Sand had sent them a cheering letter on *Les Hommes de Lettres* which had seemed to them like the handshake of a friend. On March 30, 1862, they rang her bell at 2, rue Racine, and the engraver Manceau opened the door to them. In spite of her seemingly curt and formal manner, her placidity, her gravity, she showed herself very pleasant and full of praise for their work. They thought she had a kind and gentle face with more delicate features than appeared in her portraits. All the same, it is doubtful whether they rated her as highly as Renan and Sainte-Beuve had done at the Magny dinners. Her transparently clear and smooth style of writing could not have been to their taste. On February 12, 1866, she made her appearance at Magny's. Jules was struck by her shyness, her silence, and the delicacy of her hands. They met her again the following May, in a peach-coloured gown, 'a costume which was, I believe, entirely in Flaubert's honour'. The twenty volumes of *L'Histoire de Ma Vie* made them less unjust towards her.

There is nothing to show whether the Goncourts had met Flaubert before April 11, 1857, when they found themselves in his company with Gautier and Feydeau at the offices of *L'Artiste*. Although in the interval they saw him on several occasions and even invited him to dinner one Sunday in November, 1858, with Gavarni, Saint-Victor and Mario Uchard, they let two years elapse before drawing this portrait of him: 'Flaubert is extraordinarily like the portrait of Frédérick Lemaître in his youth. He is very tall, broad-shouldered, with fine large eyes protruding from slightly swollen eyelids, plump cheeks, a heavy drooping moustache, a weather-beaten complexion mottled with red. He is spending three months in Paris, going nowhere, only meeting a few friends, and leading the same unsociable life that we all of us lead.' In November of the same year, one of them, who had gone to Rouen to copy some of Mme de Chateauroux's letters met him as he was taking his mother and his niece to the station. That either Jules or Edmond should have visited Rouen without letting Flaubert know is a sign that at this period their friendship had not yet taken definite shape. In January, 1860, they invited him again, this time with Saint-Victor, Scholl, Charles Edmond and his mistress, Julie, and Scholl's mistress, Mme Doche. He talked to them of the life of retirement he led in Paris, of his methods of work, his literary crotchets, his favourite authors, the boredom that consumed him and his disgust with life.

When *Les Hommes de Lettres* was published, feeling the need of his approval, they paid him two visits almost on top of each other—'in his study, brightly illuminated by the daylight from the boulevard du Temple, in which a Buddha in gilded wood serves as a clock. His large, round table, with his manuscript upon it, and over by the window, a big metal dish ornamented with arabesques, and above the wide leather-covered divan at the farther end a plaster cast of the Naples Psyche.'

He replied to their visits with an invitation to dinner with Bouilhet; a meeting from which resulted *Sœur Philomène*. He told them of his adventures, his first attempts at literature, his youthful jokes and escapades, his invention of the imaginary character of *Le Garçon*, his love affair with Louise Colet. He invited them to his flat with the actress Lagier, a cynical woman given to ribaldry and with a weakness for officers.

They were at the dinner for which the reading of *Salammbô* supplied the setting: 'First, I shall begin to howl at four o'clock,' wrote Flaubert.

Therefore come about three. Secondly, at seven o'clock, an oriental dinner ... Thirdly, after coffee, the punic slanging-match will continue until the listeners burst. Do you like the idea?' In December, 1861, the hermit of Croisset begged them to find out something for him about the process of dying of starvation for his episode of the death of the mercenaries. In return, they asked him to copy some of La Popelinière's letters in the Rouen library for them, and they got into the habit of going to see him regularly on Sundays when he was in Paris. 'Those Sundays spent in Flaubert's flat on the boulevard du Temple save us from Sabbath boredom. Here we have friendly talks that spring from peak to peak, go back to the origins of worlds, dig deep into religions, review men and their ideas, going from legends of the East to Hugo's lyricism, from Buddha to Goethe.' On another occasion we read: 'I come away from a Sunday conference at Flaubert's with feelings of amazement and disgust at the servility of the ideas I meet with everywhere. They make a pretence of investigating paradoxes, and their paradoxes are almost always a species of catechism.'

It would be a mistake to attribute to the Goncourts the same admiration and—the term is not too strong—the same kind of affection that Flaubert's followers accorded their great master, and which, so it seemed to them, all his friends should have felt. 'You are decidedly a part of ourselves and we, although two, feel ourselves somewhat incomplete when you are not there,' so Jules wrote from Bar-sur-Seine, on July 10, 1861, to the friend whom he defined as 'a man of great sensibility'. The two brothers, however, considered Flaubert very inferior to his work. How is it that this eminently lovable individual, so open-hearted, so frank, so affectionate, had not completely won them over? It was because they had hardly any capacity for feeling sympathy with anyone, and because their conception of art and of life, both narrow and finical, was directly opposed to his. Flaubert would let himself go and throw away all restraint in their presence without noticing that they were observing him in cold blood and, incapable of attaching themselves to anyone, were holding him responsible for whatever reservations they felt with regard to himself. 'In reality,' they remarked, 'in this frank, straightforward, open, wildly expansive nature there are wanting infinitesimal links that lead on from acquaintance to friendship. We find ourselves at the same point now as on the day we first met him, and when we speak to him of coming to dine with us he expresses his deep regret, but he is only able to do his work at night.'

Flaubert's art itself remained alien to them. What these industrious observers of the outside world, these collectors of minute details, of facial expressions and scenic backgrounds found fault with in *Madame Bovary* was that it represented 'a very material side of art and thought' and that it was a work 'which paints things for the eyes much more than it speaks to the soul'. What follows, coming from men whose ambition it was to apply the methods of painting to the art of writing, is even more surprising: 'The noblest and strongest part of this work belongs much more to painting than to literature.' They grant that truth is the foundation of all art, its essence, its inner guide, but why, if they allow *Madame Bovary* to be 'the very last word on truth in the novel', do they ask 'why is the spiritual side of the mind not completely satisfied with it?' And thereupon they draw a comparison between *Madame Bovary* and *Paul et Virginie*, 'which will always remain an immortal masterpiece, whereas *Madame Bovary*, a more vigorous work by reason of the strength that maturity supplies compared with youth, observation with imagination, a study from the life and of human nature with a poetical composition, *Madame Bovary*, I feel, will remain an example of stupendous industry and will never be a work like the other, a Bible of human imagination.' There is some truth in this comment, but was it for them to formulate it? Did it not express an emphatic denial of their ideals and their ambitions as artists?

If Flaubert had guessed their mental reservations he would certainly not have written to the Goncourts as he did on September 13, 1862: 'What! three weeks without seeing you? I miss you strangely. Paris seems empty to me without my two dear boys.'

In October of that year the *Journal* contains this note in Edmond's hand: 'Something of a questionable nature has come to light since he involved himself with Michel Lévy, the publisher, in connection with a prize of 30,000 francs for *Salammbô*; the underside of his nature, so frank on the surface, of which I already had a presentiment, is now apparent to me, and I have conceived a mistrust for this friend, who said that a genuine man of letters should spend his whole life working on books for which he should not even seek publicity, now that I see him juggling so cleverly in order to sell his own.' This was an allusion to an agreement between Flaubert and Lévy to allow, and even cause, it to be reported, that the manuscript of *Salammbô*, for which the author was actually paid 10,000 francs, had been bought for three times that price. A very innocent publicity measure which the Goncourts might certainly have agreed to had it been proposed to them.

On November 21, 1862, the *Journal* notes: 'Flaubert, whom I meet with Saint-Victor, seems ill at ease with me. There is, I feel, a certain coldness suddenly come between him and me, no doubt on account of the article Sainte-Beuve told me about on Sunday when asking for the proofs of *La Femme au Dix-huitième Siècle*. There is something Norman and extremely sly and pig-headed, so I begin to believe, deep down in this fellow, who is apparently so sincere, so expansive on the surface, who shakes your hand so heartily and openly turns up his nose at success, at reviews, at advertisement, and whom I find, since that shocking business of his sham contract with Lévy, secretly accepting notoriety and influential connections, working up success for himself like anyone else, and pushing on with an air of modesty towards open rivalry with Hugo.' One of their greatest grievances against Flaubert at this period was that in effect he did compare himself with Hugo. Equally they found fault with him for the variation in his attitude towards Sainte-Beuve, his lack of artistic sense and want of taste, and more generally, for being at bottom nothing more than 'a provincial genius'. The Magny dinners did not make them more indulgent towards him.

At the close of 1863 they went to Croisset. The *Journal* contains the most detailed description we have of Flaubert's house. 'For a man's interior is the man himself, his tastes and his talents. An interior fully displaying the coarser side of Eastern culture and through which peeps forth the underlying barbarity in this artist's soul.' Their friend's hospitality, moreover, seemed to them on the parsimonious side. He read *Le Château des Cœurs* to them; they saw nothing in it but the most commonplace of fairy tales.

Flaubert did not escape the reproach of servility which they lavished so freely. 'There is a curious difference,' they wrote, 'between Flaubert and Saint-Victor in their servility towards the powers that be. The latter, with the natural thoughtfulness he owes to his Latin temperament, has halted on this road, restrained by a kind of paralysis of purely physical origin, a stiffness of the head, the muscles and the spine. The former, in spite of wild theories, yells of independence, a vigorous affectation of anarchy, is an out-and-out servitor, a sycophant of the Austrian Court.' Even his health was a kind of offence to them. In talking of someone's illness, he shocked them by 'the easy, off-hand manner' in which he tried to cheer them up and the way in which he exclaimed as he left: 'It's amazing, but at this moment it seems to me I inherit the vigour of all my friends.' A remark that, addressed to a couple of neurasthenics, was not perhaps excessively tactful, but may it not be that Flaubert, afflicted as we know him to have been, was trying to disguise this from himself?

In April, 1868, they had dedicated their *Idées et Sensations* to him. He had certainly deserved this dedication, having written in a letter to the Princess in February: 'I consider them the greatest gentlemen alive. I know nothing so seemly in literature. They are real good fellows. Put your trust in them.' On March 11 the brothers wrote: 'Truly Sainte-Beuve is missed in the Princess's drawing-room. There ideas sink and voices rise, and Flaubert, who sprawls about, turns it into a provincial salon. With every story that is told you may be sure in advance that he will say, whether or not the story is finished: "Oh! I know a better one", and of every person mentioned, "I know him better than you do". A vulgar, a decidedly vulgar mentality.'

Paul de Saint-Victor possessed at that time a reputation that surprises us today, but if his sparkling rhetoric seems to us a little hollow, his skill as a writer of articles was past dispute. The Goncourts and he had made friends in 1857 in a room at the back of the Café Riche. Two years before this he had left off writing leading articles for *Le Pays* to take on those of *La Presse*. This son of a Breton Royalist who had thrown Charlotte Corday a rose as she was being led to execution and who, after being imprisoned during the Empire for conspiring in favour of Louis XVIII, had not received his share of public money because he had not been an *émigré*, this son of an historian of Paris, whom Lamartine had had recourse to for the publication of *Les Méditations*, was a man who appealed to their aristocratic tastes. To have been Lamartine's secretary and the friend of Barbey d'Aurevilly were not negligible qualities either, in their eyes. They only thought him a trifle haughty. 'We met Saint-Victor,' they wrote, 'still carrying his head as if it were a brand-new epithet, a half-handsome fellow hovering between the type of a Velasquez portrait and that of a barber's assistant, with a primly waxed moustache, a cold, abrupt manner, a little walking-stick in his hand, at times condescending, at others boring because of the trouble he takes to get hold of a word that escapes him.' It was friendship that had to be started afresh at each meeting. A pity! They had so many ideas, so many preferences, so many prejudices in common.

'In the present state of literature,' they remarked, 'this man Saint-Victor, this writer whose thoughts are continually dwelling on giving a fillip to art and thrashing out great ideas and important problems, is a truly noble literary type.' The fascinating Remouville of *Charles Demailly* is an exact reflection of the idea that, up to the time of the bickerings and broils at the Magny dinners, the two brothers had formed of this reviewer.

On their return from the trip they made with him to Holland they were already outlining a character-sketch that was hardly flattering. According to them, his conversation was too flowery, there was too little of a personal point of view in his ways of thinking and judging, which were more acquired than instinctive, he was only interested in what was labelled and classified, his eyes were shut tight against life in the world around him, he was only attracted by pictures and statues, had absolutely no imagination, was meekly subservient to the precepts of hygiene, superstitious, violent in his speech but weak in character, giving way to childish fits of despair and childish whims, self-centred, and casual, but charming in his simplicity and his gaiety. 'For us who have been so spoilt by our life at home together, he is the only travelling companion who is almost entirely congenial to us and whom we could bear to have with us for a whole month. And this is no meagre praise.' In January, 1862, they wrote: 'Saint-Victor has no faculty of observation, no perception or intuition of people and things. All his experience is limited to experience derived from books. Thus with regard to men and things he judges them from pictures. These are for him the mirror in which he sees everything reflected.'

Rachel, the famous actress, had four sisters: Sarah Félix, older than herself, Rébecca, Lia and Dinah. All of them were on the stage. Lia had successfully created the role of Claudie in George Sand's play. Although she was not beautiful, she could strike attitudes. 'Lia Félix, a Jewish comédienne, knowing very well what she wants [to get Saint-Victor to marry her] tells him in a whisper that she is plain, that she has nothing to keep his attention, that she is neither witty nor intelligent . . . And there he is, at her feet or taking her on his knee . . . Hercules at Omphale's feet . . . become this woman's obsequious admirer.' The theme of *Manette Salomon*, at least in part, may possibly have sprung from this. They had a daughter, Claire, to whom Edmond was godfather, and whose beauty sent her father into fits of wild enthusiasm.

The Goncourts were invited to Lia's house at Montmorency. 'Saint-Victor,' they wrote, 'is no longer a man, but a father. Oh! what a strange sight to see the critic of *La Presse* pushing his child's little pram along the High Street in the midst of these bourgeois villas.' On January 18, 1863, they remarked: 'I have more respect for Saint-Victor's talent than anyone. As for his character, he is a Greek of the Empire in its decline.'

Their criticisms of their friend grow more and more severe. He was no longer anything but a weathercock, and one that needed oiling. 'Never a personal or impartial judgement, and then too, in all this violent tension, there must be a quarrel with Lia in the background, and the nervous irritability of a man who gambles on the Stock Exchange, to make him so intolerable and full of contradictions.' The opposition of their characters was aggravated by an opposition of ideas. Saint-Victor was a passionate admirer of Voltaire and spoke ill of *Le Neveu de Rameau*. In discussions, his anger would turn to frenzy.

A bitter dispute over Homer, whom Jules said he preferred to Hugo, came to an end at Magny's in October, 1866, with a rather chilly shaking of hands. 'As he is leaving, Saint-Victor holds out his hand to us. On the whole, I would have preferred him not to hold it out. This is a friendship we find burdensome, and in which sad inner conflicts are provoked by our literary sympathies, the pain we suffer by reason of the narrow pedantry, the intolerance and intermittent lack of friendliness in this individual, and the underlying feeling of contempt aroused in us in spite of ourselves by all that we know of him and all that we guess.' It is not surprising to find Saint-Victor accused a year later of having stolen some of his ideas from the Goncourts and some from Gautier.

On Jules's death a reconciliation took place between Edmond and Saint-Victor, but their friendship did not recover its former warmth. 'I who need such affection,' said Edmond, 'and who for so many years have been so spoilt in this respect, cannot be content with the cold and trivial friendship of other people. And when I have spent an evening with this marble statue known as Saint-Victor I come home filled with a longing to weep.' On June 24, 1879, he noted in his *Journal*: 'Today at this republican dinner at Brébant's, in an atmosphere of seemly piety, one man alone had something odious to say concerning

Gautier, Flaubert and Others

the death of the young Prince [Imperial], one man alone vociferated against this honourable and unhappy corpse. This was, as can already be guessed, M. de Saint-Victor, whose unceasing fear of losing the position given him by the Napoleons perpetually puts him to the trouble of imagining utterly futile acts of meanness.'

Edmond was staying at Jean d'Heurs with his cousin Rattier when, in July, 1880, he learnt of Saint-Victor's death: 'I was on bad terms with him,' he wrote ... 'But, after all, he was my comrade in letters for many years and he had the seductive charm of a highly intelligent mind. And my thoughts today go back to our past and also to his daughter whom I see once again, a new-born babe, in her embryonic nakedness, in front of her mother's bedroom fire.'

They did not like Taine, and, indeed, there was nothing in him to attract them. His mentality, that of a philosopher and a professor, was poles apart from theirs. 'Our worthy philosopher Taine,' they wrote, 'is at this moment importuning the Princess to arrange a wealthy marriage for him.' In July, 1868, they added the note: 'Taine, whom we have not seen since his marriage, makes his reappearance this evening. He is rigged out in his Sunday best, puffed up, ill at ease and stouter. He remarks in a fatuous way to the Princess that if he has not brought his wife with him it is because she is not very well, and asks me how "M. Flaubert" is keeping! I thought it rather cheek of this professor, this former student of the Ecole Normale now become a respectable citizen, to be already assuming an air of importance as a high official of the University and speaking as if from the seat of a minister-to-be ...'

Under Sainte-Beuve's ill-natured attack on *Madame Gervaisis* they thought they could perceive the influence of Taine, 'this friend who does not like us'. Princess Mathilde did not feel any sympathy for Taine either, to judge from this passage in a letter she sent the two brothers: 'Taine has written to Saint-Victor to tell him that he has invited married friends to his wedding. He is with his wife at Viroflay, in his father-in-law's house, and seems very pleased with his new estate. He is working hard, according to what he writes to me, in order to prove that a married man is not a goose fattened for slaughter. There you have a man who, in order not to act like everyone else, will not even allow himself time to be happy.'

Renan was at first as antipathetic to them as Taine. 'We have written to Gautier to acquaint him with our contempt for this book [*La Vie de Jésus*], our antipathy to its author's physical appearance, our horror of his bad taste and the vagueness of the thesis he sustains, his lack of candour, the childishness of this God who is not God and yet is more than God himself.' The fact of sitting near him at the same table little by little dispelled their prejudice against him, and in the end close contact was established. As they came to know him better they liked him more and more. He seemed to them in spite of his physical ungainliness a type, as it were, of moral beauty. 'There is in this apostle of doubt the lofty and intelligent kindliness of a priest of knowledge.' He gave them his biography of his sister which, on account of their own 'brotherhood', brought tears to their eyes. This did not last. During the siege of Paris Renan's lack of patriotic zeal made Edmond feel indignant and when, in 1891, the *Journal* made its appearance everything between them was utterly ruined.

In Berthelot, the renowned expert in organic chemistry, they admired a great and brilliant constructor of hypotheses. Together with Charles Edmond, his neighbour, they went to see him at Bellevue. 'A little house in the woods, a drawing-room full of women. Mme Berthelot, of a rare and unforgettable beauty; a beauty that has intelligence, depth and magnetism, a beauty of the mind and soul resembling the creations of Poe's supernatural world.' The whole day was spent in walking through the woods of Sèvres and Viroflay.

Although he was not one of those at the Magny dinners, we will put Michelet beside Renan, Taine and Berthelot. Already, in 1858, the *Journal* proclaims their admiration for the stylist and the historian. Great was their pride when they found themselves mentioned in his preface to *La Régence*. Together with Hugo's approval, that of Michelet consoled them for many attacks and many deliberate omissions of their name. They could not do less than go to thank him at his house near the Luxembourg. His interior was that of a bourgeois who regularly attended auctions. He talked to them about furniture, one of their favourite subjects, and of many other things, and they took away with them the impression of a petulant man with a small private income, and with long white hair falling over his cheeks. They were invited by him to a fancy-dress ball, at which Mme Michelet's friends would be attired as nations. 'You would have believed yourself,' says the *Journal*, 'at an evening party given by the principal of some provincial art-school'. And what a contrast between himself and his wife, 'the wife of a junior clerk'. There are some amusing lines by Jules Levallois on the evening's entertainment: 'I see them still at the latter's at an evening fancy-dress party... There was dancing, and Mme Renan, dressed all in white, had that kindly giant Flaubert, far from agile and graceful in his movements, as her opposite number. What struck me most was Michelet's behaviour; always in bed at nine o'clock, he wandered disconsolately from room to room, wondering what so many illustrious mummers were doing in his house, and why he was condemned to go to bed so late.'

A few days after this, Mme Michelet told the Goncourts that she found it a treat to read them. Recalling in 1884 their visits to their distinguished friend, she wrote to Edmond: 'I still see both of you sitting beside each other in my study where he used to receive his friends so that I should be there. He would be seated on the sofa. I have not allowed anyone to touch it since then, liking to see his place where the springs had sunk down from long usage. It is just as if he were going to come back and sit there again.' 'Michelet!' Jules would exclaim. 'The genius who at this present moment has an influence on everything and on everyone. There is something of his *La Mer* in Hugo's *Les Travailleurs de la Mer*. Today I open Renan's book, it is Michelet adapted to Fénélon's manner. Michelet has taken possession of contemporary thought.'

On coming away from Sainte-Beuve's house, they spent a day at Michelet's, whom they found sitting on his little sofa, his hands on his thighs in the attitude of an idol and with a beatific smile on his face. He spoke to them of Rousseau, of Mirabeau, both of them driven to the last extremity by unhappiness and despair and bending destiny to their will. On another occasion there was talk of his book, *Le Prêtre et la Femme*, which a father confessor had authorized some nuns to read. '... when I was told that,' said Michelet, 'it was a great blow to me!'

In May, 1869, they saw him once more, still youthful, still full of lively talk, of original ideas, and genial paradoxes. Without belittling the sympathy and admiration they felt for him, it can be supposed that the admiration he himself showed for them in his letters, his consulting them on details, and even going so far as to say he was their debtor in matters relating to the eighteenth century, had something to do with this. He parted company with them, however, over Marie-Antoinette. And why? 'She would have liked to greet Voltaire. She invited Gluck and Piccini to supper. And France remembers that.' He did not share their anti-semitism either. 'I like the Jews,' he said, 'although they are the fathers of Christianity, and I should indeed have a little to say on their behalf, but you have depicted [in *Manette Salomon*] what is inexorably true. Such they are and such we have made them.'

Philippe Burty had paid his first visit to the Goncourts in 1859. He had mentioned their study of Augustin de Saint-Aubin in the *Gazette des Beaux-Arts*. Like them, he had learnt to draw and paint, like them, had a horror of academic methods. On March 16, 1865, they remarked: 'We have spent the day at Burty's house, in the rue du Petit-Banquier, in a remote and countrified quarter of the town, which smells of cattle-breeders and horse-markets. An atmosphere of cordiality, of innocent, lively children, of a happy family life that takes one's thoughts back to the households of artists and bourgeois in the eighteenth century. It is a rather gay and sunny house, such as one imagines the house of a man like Fragonard would be.' Pol Neveux has spoken in praise of Burty's charm, his clear-sightedness, his good taste, his independence, his courage and the wide range of his intelligence; we shall have an opportunity later on of questioning whether Edmond would have endorsed such praise.

XIII
Princess Mathilde

Princess Mathilde, having read their *Marie-Antoinette*, confided to Saint-Victor her wish to make their acquaintance. Let him bring them to dinner one Saturday! She herself invited Gavarni. She did not foresee that Vieil-Castel, the official writer of memoirs to her salon, who had quarrelled with her lover Nieuwerkerke, and since then had left off coming to her house, would have successors in them.

The impressions they carried away from their first dinner at Saint-Gratien, on August 16, 1862, were not very favourable. They had taken the train with Gavarni and Chennevières, and then the Princess's little omnibus. The house, described in detail in the *Journal* of November, 1874, was a comfortable one, full of flowers, the walls hung with chintz in old-fashioned designs, but entirely without any *objets d'art*. The drawing-room had a veranda where one could look out over a fine stretch of lawn and a large park. The Princess came down; they were introduced to her. Forty-two years old, she was a large, stout woman, the remains of a beauty but with a slightly blotchy complexion, receding features and rather small eyes whose expression could not be seen; her bearing was that of a middle-aged courtesan whose familiar manners did not altogether conceal an underlying harshness. At the dinner Nieuwerkerke, whom they addressed as Nieuwkerque, was naturally present, an old bachelor, strongly built, with gentle eyes and a gentle voice, as much at his ease as if he were master of the house, free as an artist in his manner, courteous as a man of noble birth. Also present were Giraud, historian, man of letters and legal authority, a petulant old fellow with grey whiskers, a joker and a grumbler, his brother Eugène, the painter of domestic scenes; and an aged lady companion, Mme de Fly, or Defly, or Dieudé-Defly, who had had an illegitimate daughter by Mathilde's uncle, Prince Paul of Wurtemberg, and who was the personification of etiquette. The cooking was indifferent, the conversation 'as in the house of a humble courtesan on her best behaviour'. They talked about table-turning, sleep-walking, of the marital jealousy of Girardin, a publisher of popular mass-produced journals, of the actors Bocage and Lemaître, and of Musset's drunken habits. People smoked openly in the drawing-room. There was a visit from the schoolmistress and the recently decorated curé, whom the company assailed with loose ambiguous remarks from Viollet-le-Duc, Admiral de la Roncière, some Russians and Princess Cantacuzène. Seated in the inner drawing-room, close to the pug-dogs that never left her side, Mathilde indulged in violent abuse of Haussmann, who had taken away 1,200 metres of her large garden in the rue de Courcelles.

Such was the Goncourts' first evening at the house of one whose company was about to transform their lives. From that time onwards, their close ties of friendship with backstage or café companions began to slacken. This was also the effect of a certain process of growing older, of rising in the hierarchy of literature and society. 'Here we are with the best literary connections in the world. If we had no talent, if we had neither distinction, nor originality, nor a name, and if we acted like everyone else, everything would be open to us, newspapers, magazines and all. It is only our talent that holds us back. Eunuchs' fortunes are the soonest made.'

The great house of Saint-Gratien, built by the Comte de Luçay during the Second Empire, and of which there remained only a lodge that the Princess later lent to the Goncourts during Jules's last illness, contained eight guest rooms on the second floor. Like many others, they came there to stay, but at first for fairly short visits. Mathilde, who had a great number of friends, was anxious not to awaken any feelings of jealousy.

At their second dinner, at the beginning of December, in the rue de Courcelles, where Gavarni, Chennevières, Nieuwerkerke and Mme de Fly were again present, they found the Princess very likeable. They saw in her a type of modern woman with artistic leanings, speaking the language of the studio, regretting that she had not come upon any intelligent women, showing masculine interests, expressing lofty and original ideas. They visited her studio, 'cluttered up with those things that are of artistic value to women only: a pastel wrongly attributed to Boucher, and similar pastels in imitation of Chardin. Nieuwerkerke points these out to us in all seriousness. He believes in them, that is some excuse for him.' On December 31 there was a third dinner, without their sponsors Gavarni and Chennevières, but with Sainte-Beuve, de Musset and others. The Princess had given them her approval.

Princess Mathilde

For their part, they still reserved their judgement. They found this society very dull, very bourgeois. 'It never happens that a princess like that does anything more extraordinary than giving you dinner; she will not ask you to wait in a room where *Le Diable au Corps* lies on the table. No, nothing unexpected; they have not got any feeling for that sort of thing. Even when they are harlots, they have mended their ways. You stupidly believe it will be like a novel, it is merely a drawing-room. There are no princesses left.'

From that time invitations followed uninterruptedly. In January, 1863, they sketched this portrait of Mathilde: 'The princess has a very enigmatic cast of face. All kinds of expressions flitting across it, eyes that escape definition, with glances shot suddenly at you that pierce you through and through. Her wit is a little like that glance, all of a sudden comes a sally, a casual, sly remark, a picturesque epigram, originating from a free and easy and individual volubility, as for instance, when she says of one gentleman, "His eyes have a hazy look like the film on a picture".' Very positive in her opinions, she detested Prud'hon and *Paul et Virginie*, which they on the contrary greatly admired.

Had she any heart? They wondered. 'The Napoleons have for a long time had the habit of doing without one, but she is charming and shows the most gracious frankness in her dealings with other people, and she has above all what one rarely finds, even in men, an original wit, abounding in sudden flicks of the whip, lightning flashes and sometimes peals of thunder through which runs a reminder, or as it were an echo, of her uncle.' Yes, indeed, she was certainly a Bonaparte! 'Nothing delicate, nothing subtle, nothing tender; strength, intelligence, eloquence, everything that appeals to people in the mass and nothing that attracts individuals.' On one occasion they defined her as Marguérite of Navarre in a Napoleon's skin.

The evenings spent in her house were lacking in zest and animation; there were some dull occasions when the guests seemed to them to be dead. 'The conversation drags and languishes. The game of lotto Nieuwerkerke and the Bonaparte princesses are playing is sinking to sleep in a corner. The Princess sits listless and drowsy over her needlework; a great shadow seems to be cast by Mme de Fly's large lampshade, and amid the silences that grow longer and longer in the sleeping drawing-room, you might believe that there will be a knock on the door and in will come, holding out his hand to the Princess, the figure of Exile under the ridiculous guise of her hunchbacked gentleman-in-waiting, General Chauchard.'

One evening Saint-Victor brought back the report of a violent outburst by the Princess against Gavarni, as an artist and more particularly as a man. 'It's extraordinary what little discretion this woman has. How is it she doesn't understand that the people who are there turn over in their minds this device on tombs: *Hodie mihi, cras tibi*. Saint-Victor is aghast at the torrent of gall that poured from her mouth. Whatever can Gavarni have done to her?'

Choleric, coarse, capricious and swayed by her instincts, she was neither treacherous nor malicious, and this pleased them as a contrast to the hypocrisy all around them. They appreciated in her a sort of kindness at the same time unrefined and delicate, and occasional unexpected liberties. She delighted them when, the first time she came to see them in Auteuil, she snatched up a hunk of bread and plunged a spoon into a pot of jam. But at Saint-Gratien it took a day or two before her friendship warmed up and passed from 'sir' to 'my dear'.

She enjoyed making word-pictures of the people who came to see her on Tuesdays (she did not even offer them refreshments) and was not past finding fault with the Goncourts themselves, for their materialism and atheism, and, with the blood rushing to her face, would complain that everyone around her was an unbeliever, hardly even a deist. Their contempt for Molière used also to infuriate her. She did not spare her own father, who, in his wife's presence, would get his mistress to apply leeches to him, and had rendezvous with maidservants in the lavatory. She depicted the Murat family sleeping in a promiscuous huddle, Anna, ten years old, and always in her shift, in love with a footman, Joachim, smoking a cabman's cutty-pipe, Caroline refusing to wash her feet, and, in a fit of hysteria, howling at the moon. 'And a long conversation starts between us and her about hysteria, the *globus hystericus*, the physical characteristics of the hysterical woman, and all those questions to do with love-sickness about which she has an almost greedy curiosity.'

Beneath her imperious, haughty airs she was preoccupied with love. 'Let a man be polite, attentive and pleasant to a woman and she will be by no means grateful to you for it. She demands that you should allow her to imagine you love her carnally, that you desire her.' Nothing forbids us to suppose that she had shown herself provocative with Jules.

Her sudden changes of humour puzzled them and held them back on the brink of an unreserved friendship. A note of February, 1869, appears as the last words uttered by Jules, for whom death already lay in wait, on this woman to whom their hearts had never been fully given. 'As regards the Princess, we waver between various and ever-changing feelings. At moments we are seized with sudden vague instinctive fears of being exploited in a friendship, an attachment truly affectionate and sincere. Then that is chased away by brief moments of tenderness and real feeling on her part towards us, in which, almost without a word, there passes between us something like a nervous current in our consciousness of affection shared. Then again, all at once, in this extremely complex woman, in whom chance has mingled so many different strains, we seem suddenly to see the Italian woman with her double nature, or the lady of Wurtemberg with Germanic arrogance and coldness, take the place of the Frenchwoman who was near to you and entirely yours.'

At first, the drawing-room at the rue de Courcelles had seemed to be frequented by disinterested, independent and courageous people, whose freedom of judgement the mistress of the house respected and whose objections and criticisms she would accept. Things changed, however. On August 15, 1869, they wrote: 'Here there are none now except beggars, lackeys, base minds, base hearts and a servile chorus of flatterers. Little by little, in the midst of this circle, she has become used to not being contradicted and to stifling the least little objections under the weight of her silly, blind and childish fits of temper.' And as for the less important *dramatis personae* of Saint-Gratien, this 'little German Court', there was 'Mme de Fly with her haphazard way of dressing, her blind gaiety, her broad Voltairean jokes, her blunders, her hallucinations... Mme de Galbois with her sharp, pointed nose, comical in her utter stupidity... that fellow Soulié, the doltish courtier full of idiotic paradoxes... and Claudius Popelin, the painter of enamels, an intruder everywhere, an artist become rich while remaining bitter, with a tormented nervous expression, a cutting, aggressive, contradictory manner of speaking... Popelin, the maker of pseudo-antique enamels, has just been decorated. This honour he obtained by means of innumerable little underhand acts; those I know of give me an idea of those I suspect.' The friendly relations we shall see later on established between the painter and Edmond did not last until the end.

M. Joachim Kuhn, author of a biography of the Princess, has pointed out that the gatherings in the rue de Courcelles had no harmful effect on the Magny dinners; on the contrary, they were of use in curbing those rash indiscretions of the Princess's new friends that might at first have embarrassed the members of her intimate circle. Saint-Victor was introduced to the rue de Courcelles by Flaubert and the Goncourts. Taine was never much looked upon with favour. Renan only became acclimatized there with difficulty.

At a party in the rue de Courcelles one evening the Goncourts came in contact with Napoleon III, the man they had considered their personal enemy ever since his magistrates had brought them before the courts. They have drawn a lurid portrait of him which receives support from a remark of Gautier's: 'He looks like a ring-master who has been sacked for getting drunk.' They were no more indulgent towards his cousin the Prince Napoleon, whom they saw 'sunk in an easy chair, in a clumsy posture, his legs apart . . . The Emperor's head seems to have fallen on to his shoulders from a great height. He is ungainly and squat—in short, a lubberly Caesar.'

They were on very good terms with Nieuwerkerke, who like themselves was a member of the Magny dinners and who used to invite them to the flat he occupied in the Louvre as Superintendent of the Beaux-Arts. A sculptor not entirely without talent, although he was accused of not being the author of works to which he had given his name, a man of the world, a handsome man, and the appointed lover of the Princess, he had at once fascinated them by an affability which he showed ungrudgingly to everyone. When he was accused of having lent masterpieces from museums too freely to his friends, they took his side and refused to contribute articles to the *Gazette des Beaux-Arts* which was attacking him.

XIV

Two More Novels

'And then,' Jules wrote to Flaubert in March, 1863, 'we tackled a young woman of the bourgeoisie fair and square, full-face . . . painting the bourgeoisie is like making a tour of a five-franc piece, you tread the same ground over and over. Perhaps because it is dull, our novel is growing longer.'

Renée Mauperin is a project that goes back to 1853, the year in which they had renewed their friendship with Louis and Blanche Passy and the circle at Gisors, and which had taken real shape in July, 1862, at Bar-sur-Seine. Their idea in writing it had been at first to paint not only the young woman and the young man as the Liberal and parliamentary régime had made them, the one, Renée, free of all the obstacles put in the way of her development by traditional methods of education, the other, her brother Henri, a species of Rastignac, practical, cold, calculating, commonplace and devoid of ideals, and around them three generations of the bourgeoisie, in short, a whole society, but this too vast design reduced itself to the study of a particular group.

An episode in the book recalls a pencil-sketch preserved by Edmond that Jules had made in a little studio built for Blanche Passy at the bottom of the garden: the young girl is shown in profile in front of an easel, with a few roses twined in her hair, a rounded forehead, dark eyes, a loosely knotted man's tie falling over a turn-down collar; above the drawing are the name and the date, September 19, 1859. Renée is thus Blanche Passy, Louis's sister, of whom Jules said that she had a man's cordiality and sincerity allied with a young woman's charms, mature in reason, young in heart, and with a mind full of high ambitions. Ill at ease among the lies and subterfuges of society, she was entirely spontaneous, with a surface gaiety above an underlying melancholy. She was passionately fond of horses, had a superstitious dread of Fridays and the number thirteen, and the sight of blood made her feel ill. She combined certain weaknesses with original forms of coquetry, for instance with regard to her feet, which were the smallest in the world. Misjudged and adversely criticized by women and by anyone who had a horror of sincerity, she was destined to inspire a passionate friendship in those who, like herself, had a hatred of the meanness and hypocrisy of the world.

But however sympathetic, however pleasing, poetical, and charming the character of Renée, the Passy family considered the resemblance offensive. The heart disease from which the heroine of the novel dies reminded them of the cardiac trouble of the girl who had served as a model for the Goncourts; there was a breach between Gisors and the rue Saint-Georges, the family album kept by Blanche which contains the names of those who visited the Passys—Rosa Bonheur, Burnouf the famous Orientalist, the critic Nisard, etc.—makes no mention of the Goncourts.

Blanche Passy took after her father; it would have been preferable if she had resembled her mother, whose portrait, painted by Prud'hon, is well known. Besides her bedroom, kept intact since her death and in many of its details exactly like Renée Mauperin's, the country house at Gisors, now the property of the Comte and Comtesse de Bueil-Passy, holds many souvenirs of her, among others her portrait by Octave Roland, her drawing master. In this she appears in a white dress with a broad blue sash, leading a goat, and looking a very fascinating little girl with sad, dark eyes. She had the gift of making people love her and was well in advance of the young women of her generation, being endowed with a quick intelligence and an air of distinction which later assured her a place in Orléanist drawing-rooms.

Full of high spirits, keen on riding, an amateur actress of extraordinary self-possession, she was perfectly at ease among her cousins and her brother's friends. It is not surprising therefore that Jules was somewhat stirred by her, as is indicated by the enthusiasm with which he speaks of her in the *Journal* and in his letters, noting down the slightest details of her character and ways.

One wonders whether politics may not have been the underlying cause of the rupture that occurred after the publication of *Renée Mauperin*. The Passys were fervent Orléanists. Blanche, until her death, was in close contact with the princes and princesses of the House of Orléans and so violent was her aversion to the Empire that she looked on the defeat at Sedan almost as a victory. Who knows if the publication of *Renée Mauperin* was not merely a pretext for her ceasing to meet the friends of Princess Mathilde?

She never married. After her father's death, she spent the greater part of her time with her half-sister, Mme Dailly. The disfiguring attacks of rheumatism that made her a martyr at the end of her life did not rob her of her usual elegance. Stretched out in a silk gown, her little feet set off by those slippers with rosettes that Jules speaks of, she always received her friends with the same charming grace.

In March, 1896, Edmond Lefebvre de Béhaine got himself introduced to her at the Duc d'Aumale's house. When she discovered his kinship with Edmond and Jules she exclaimed: 'My dear friend Jules de Goncourt!' and she and the diplomat chatted for a quarter of an hour about Jules, about Mme de Goncourt and the little fancy-dress tea-parties on Shrove Tuesdays in the rue des Capucines. Edmond was touched by this. 'I was afraid she might have retained a disagreeable memory of the Goncourts from her reading of *Renée Mauperin*, in which however I had painted her with her pride, her nobility and her independence of character. No, it will be her brother who kept her from seeing us again. After all, she can only reproach us for having made her die prematurely of heart disease, and her present sixty years provide a triumphant denial of our ending.' She died in Paris, in the rue Pigalle, on May 13, 1901.

The Goncourts went on seeing Louis Passy, but the *Journal* of February 5, 1866, contains this note: 'Our play [*Henriette Maréchal*] had certainly put to flight two of our school friends: Pouthier and Passy. Pouthier out of cowardice, Passy purely from envy of the publicity created by our failure.' And on May 15 of that year comes the comment: 'I am going to my ex-friend Louis Passy's wedding. What complexity in human feelings! This fellow, envious of me ever since we were at school, intoxicated by future prospects of marriage, riches and the Institute, embraces me madly and breathes into my ear: "I love you with all my heart"; and for the moment he believes it. Try then, after that, to make men all of a piece in a novel!' When in July, 1874, Edmond learned that his 'former friend' Louis Passy had been appointed Under-Secretary of State to the Treasury, he gave way to an outburst of disgust about the parliamentary system.

During December, 1863, and until about the middle of February, 1864, *Renée Mauperin*, or rather *Mademoiselle Mauperin*, appeared as a serial in *L'Opinion Nationale*. The literary critic of the paper, Jules Levallois, to whom Jules had read some passages 'in the manner of a skilful virtuoso', had made the editor Geroult accept it. 'For three days now our novel *Renée Mauperin* has been appearing in *L'Opinion*

Nationale. Three days during which our friends have rigorously abstained from speaking to us about it ... We were getting a little hopeless about this thing ... fading away in silence when this morning a very kind letter arrived from Féval which shows us our child is stirring.'

The type of *L'Opinion Nationale* was used to print a small double-column octavo book of eighty-nine pages, in a cover without a title, of which only a few copies were printed. The novel, with a dedication to Théophile Gautier, was published shortly afterwards by Charpentier. The Goncourts had first called it *La Jeune Bourgeoise*, a title that, in 1873, Edmond thought of changing to *La Jeune Bourgeoisie*.

Flaubert declared himself enchanted with *Renée Mauperin*. 'There are some stunning bits,' he wrote, 'some portraits in the best style. The dialogue between the married couple is delightful and the scenes of mourning superb.' Flaubert's approval did not reassure them. 'All these past days, in connection with our book, sadness, vexation, uneasiness, dull anguish, a tendency to see the dark side of things, a weighing-up of chances of failure, a squirrel-like activity of the mind within the same circle of ideas, of doubt, of failing courage, of despair. The life of a man of letters is indeed a horrible one, in which after suffering from doubts about the work itself, one suffers from doubts of its success. We say nothing to each other, but are perfectly aware of the ideas that rack us and which each of us is trying to hide from the other.' Three weeks later they wrote: 'The pain we feel springs mainly from insatiable, festering literary ambition, all those bitter rancorous feelings, in fact, originating in the vanity of authors, when the paper that makes no mention of you offends your pride and the one that mentions others drives you to despair.'

Renée Mauperin did not have a bad press. Monselet, of the *Figaro*, found Renée's character inexplicable, but added: 'It is hardly possible to show more lively intelligence; and above all a more modern spirit.' In *La Presse*, Saint-Victor congratulated the authors on having created a clearly drawn and living character, possessing the reader's imagination and never to be dislodged from it. Cuvillier-Fleury, of the *Débats*, complimented them on having combined truth of observation with honesty of purpose. Vapereau, in *L'Année Littéraire*, found Renée too true to be lifelike. In the *Revue des Deux Mondes*, de Lagenevais admired the truth of certain characters, but thought the bathing episode unconvincing and indecorous.

Two More Novels

The Goncourts would not have been the writers they were, endowed with little imagination, yet keenly attentive to life around them, if, once they had recovered from the first surprise, the disappointment and shock to their pride, the revelation of the kind of woman their dear old Rose had been had not inspired them with the idea for a book. From the beginning of 1863, we find them on the look-out for odd corners to describe: the ballroom at the Elysée-des-Arts, for instance, or the outer boulevards. They read studies on hysteria. In search of background scenes for *Germinie Lacerteux* they went to the Porte de Clignancourt near the fortifications surrounded by rag-pickers' huts. Since the year before they had been exploring the dance-halls near the gates of the city and it might have been thought it was for *Germinie*, but actually it was for *La Fille Elisa*. On October 12, 1864, they handed some chapters of their novel to Gervais Charpentier, who had already published *Renée Mauperin*. At the page where it said that Germinie, on her arrival in Paris from Breuvannes, was covered with lice, Charpentier interrupted them: for the sake of the public 'lice' must be replaced by 'vermin'. 'The devil take this public from whom the raw truth of everything must be hidden! What dainty lady is this public then, and what right has it to demand that a novel should always lie to it, and always hide all the ugliness of life from it?' They themselves recognized a few days later that there are limits in literature to effects of disgust and horror; they cut out of the manuscript a Caesarean operation on a dwarf.

Germinie Lacerteux appeared on January 16, 1865. Renewed anxiety. 'We are ashamed of feeling a certain nervous emotion. To have the superabundant mental energy we possess and to be betrayed by nerves, by morbid weakness, with a base fear in the pit of one's stomach, and one's body in *rags and tatters*. Ah! it's too bad not to have physical energy equal to one's mental vigour!'

The preface explained their purpose: given that one lived in an age of universal suffrage and democracy the lower classes had as much right as others to be made a subject of study for novelists. If they had been confronted with *Les Misérables* and *Les Mystères de Paris* they would have replied that those novels were untrue to life, whereas their *Germinie* was a novel that told the truth about it. 'Nothing alive,' we read in the *Journal* of April, 1862, referring to *Les Misérables*. 'The people in it are made of bronze, of alabaster, of everything except flesh and blood. The lack of observation strikes and offends you everywhere. In situations and characters Hugo has built up his novel on a semblance of truth, not on truth itself, which adds the finishing touch to men and things in a novel by introducing a note of unexpectedness that makes them whole and complete. The title is unjustified. It colours poverty. No hospitals. Prostitution barely touched upon.' This last remark refers to *La Fille Elisa*, which they then had in mind, and for which, while staying at La Cômerie in the following September, they went to visit the women's hospital in Clermont. Their evolution was complete; they had gradually progressed from romanticism to realism at the same time as Jules had passed from youth to maturity.

They had screwed up their courage beforehand against the attacks of which they would be the object. 'Now, let this book be slandered, it matters little to it! Today, now that the novel grows broader and bigger, now that it begins to be the great, the serious, passionate, living form of literary study and inquiry into social questions, and becomes, by means of analysis and psychological research, a history of contemporary morals and manners, now that the novel has imposed on itself the studies and the duties of science, it can claim the same liberties and privileges.' It was perhaps a trifle too out of keeping for such subtle artists thus to evoke, as Zola might have done, science and humanity in connection with an anecdote of secondary importance, more startling than typical, which they would doubtless never have stopped to consider if the heroine of it had not been their own servant.

Attacked by Charles Monselet—'meticulously fabricated filth'—by Merlet—'literature gone rotten'—by Villetard and Lagenevais in the *Revue des Deux Mondes*, praised coldly and not without reservations by Levallois in *L'Avenir National*, *Germinie Lacerteux*, concerning which Flaubert wrote to his niece that it was arousing universal disgust, found a champion in the person of young Emile Zola, writing in a Lyons paper, *Le Salut Public*. His first letter to the Goncourts, dated February 3, 1865, with the heading of the Librairie Hachette, whose publicity he handled, asked for a copy of the book. He praised their work as showing 'indomitable energy, a sovereign contempt for the judgement of fools and cowards, a generous and magnificent boldness, extreme vigour in its general tone and ideas, a carefulness and an artistic conscience rare in these days of hurried and poorly produced publications'. After putting the Goncourts on an equal footing with Balzac and Flaubert from the point of view of inspiration, Zola concluded: 'For me the work is great in the sense that it is, I repeat, the manifestation of a strong personality and that it draws its life freely from the life of our age. I am not interested in any other kind of merit in literature.' In his opinion, *Germinie* had besides this the virtue of bringing the common people for the first time into literature. They went to Hachette's to thank him, but they did not find him there, so they wrote to congratulate him on having so well defended 'the right to speak the truth about contemporary life, to reveal the poignancy of things that move us and make our nerves quiver and our hearts bleed' and also to tell him of the emotion aroused in them by *Thérèse Raquin*.

Later on Edmond declared: 'I have given the complete formula of Naturalism in *Germinie Lacerteux*, and the books that have followed it have been made exactly according to the method taught by this book.' A claim that is hardly an exaggeration; the importance of *Germinie Lacerteux* is not to be denied.

About the same time as Zola took their side, Jules Claretie did so in *La Nouvelle Revue de Paris*. 'You believe as we do,' Jules wrote to him, 'in a great movement in the novel, on the march towards the precision of the exact sciences and the truth as it is given in history.' This was not, we can well understand, Pontmartin's opinion. 'MM. de Goncourt were worthy not to have written *Germinie Lacerteux*. I can only prove my sympathy with them and keep faith with them by showing my anger. If I spared them, they would have the right to tell me I was insulting them.'

'You have surpassed Champfleury,' wrote Flaubert, a reference to the novelist who was considered the leader of the realists. 'The work from beginning to end is horrible and sublime. The great question of realism has never been so clearly stated. One could have a fine dispute upon the aims of art after reading your book.' An appreciation in which some trace of mental reservations is clearly perceptible.

Victor Hugo was pompous as usual: 'Your book, my dear sirs, is as pitiless as poverty itself. It has this great beauty: truth. You get to the very bottom of things, that is your duty, it is also your right.'

Princess Mathilde told someone that *Germinie* had made her literally sick, and at their next visit she drew them aside. 'She is infinitely puzzled', wrote the Goncourts on August 17, 1865. 'why people like us write books like that... this servant girl arouses no interest in her and... what revolts her in it is that she herself should be condemned to make love in the same way as these miserable women.' A letter from the Princess herself is more explicit. 'I read the book without once putting it down all the way from Dieppe to Paris, saying to myself the whole time: "How can decent, well-bred minds discover such monstrosities ... and follow them like this to the very end without insuperable disgust?" I need to believe there are not many Germinies and to hear you say so ... Has my frankness carried me too far? I am not afraid, since I am writing to people who know me and understand me. *Germinie Lacerteux* made the same impression on my mind as the *Wreck of the Medusa* on my eyes. I think you have attained your end. Try to find another one.'

This was by no means one of their intentions. They were firmly resolved to persevere in the same vein. 'Because,' as Edmond wrote in 1871, 'it is in the lowest depths, in the eclipse of a civilization, that the character of things, of persons, of a language, of everything, is preserved, and because a painter has a thousand times more chance of making a work that has style out of a mud-bespattered street-walker in the rue Saint-Honoré than out of a courtesan of the rue Bréda. And why? Because I am a well-born man of letters and the common people, the riff-raff, if you like, have for me the particular attraction of races unknown and undiscovered, something of that *exotic* quality which travellers go in search of at the cost of many hardships in far-off lands.'

Not only was *Germinie* in their eyes neither a coarse nor a vulgar book, but they maintained that it could only have been written by aristocrats.

Germinie fixed them in their vocation as realist novelists. In May, 1865, they wrote: 'At this moment, there is only one great interest in our lives: the thrill of studying from the life. Without that, boredom and emptiness. We have, to be sure, galvanized history as much as is possible, and galvanized it by means of a truth that is truer than that of other men, and by turning reality inside out. In short, the truth that is dead no longer means anything to us.' This was, of course, proclaiming that they had abandoned history. When he feels creative imagination dried up in him Edmond will return to it once more.

Germinie Lacerteux is generally considered the Goncourts' most perfect and most important work. The progress made in it is considerable in relation to their preceding novels; in balance, continuous development of plot, and harmonious distribution of descriptions and dialogues. The interest is maintained or carried forward, the dramatic tension increases, the sense of fatality deepens from episode to episode, as in Balzac or in *Madame Bovary*.

Criticism from university quarters having generally been severe towards the Goncourts, it is all the more agreeable to quote Jules Lemaître's opinion of *Germinie*: 'We must overlook many things in anyone who could write *Germinie Lacerteux*. The whole story of Mme de Varandeuil is a pure masterpiece. That of Germinie herself is deeply moving in its truth and its humanity. Our ears are assailed with talk of Russian novels and their compassionate realism... That is all very well, but as for poor Germinie, at once heroic and vile and who, in all the shameful, mad bodily excesses, preserves so large a heart, and in her "darkness"—to speak like Tolstoy—the pure flame of a true and absolute self-devotion, is not this an instance of puzzling contradictions of character somewhat like those we admire in the Russian novelists? Am I mistaken if this or that passage in *Germinie Lacerteux* moves me in the depths of my soul to such strong and lasting compassion that, above and beyond the particular sufferings there described, it extends to the wider sphere of human misery and thus takes on a religious character, every bit as much as if the text were translated from the Russian?...'

XV

Henriette Maréchal

Since 1838 the Vaudeville theatre had stood opposite the Stock Exchange in what had formerly been the playhouse of the *Nouveautés*. The two brothers took *Henriette Maréchal*, which they had finished writing in December, 1863, to show to its manager, Beaufort. The following summer he rejected it. Feeling discouraged, they flung the manuscript into a drawer and, absorbed in *Germinie*, completely forgot it was there, so when in the spring of 1865 one of their friends asked to read it, they could not find it at first. Their friend predicted that the play would be performed, which they did not believe, knowing only too well, since the episode of *Les Hommes de Lettres*, the repugnance managers felt for the works of those who were really writers. However, their interest in *Henriette Maréchal* had been renewed, and shortly afterwards they offered it to Harmand, who had succeeded Beaufort as manager of the Vaudeville.

They were waiting for his answer when Banville, who, according to Alidor Delzant, had been struck by 'the sparkling flashes of wit in the dialogue, and the free flow of the play as a whole', spoke of it with his customary enthusiasm to the distinguished scholar Edouard Thierry, who was manager of the Comédie-Française. Thierry, said Banville, admired them and had written kindly of their work, and having at the moment to put on a play set in the time of the Directorate, he was steadily reading their *Histoire de la Société Française*.

This overture left them sceptical. *Henriette* with its masked ball at the beginning and its pistol shot at the end, seemed to them impossible at the Comédie-Française. One evening on their way to an evening party, they called at the theatre. Thierry could not see them, but was anxious to read *Henriette*, so they sent it to him (Jules's letter is dated April 22) and as Harmand had promised them a reading of the play after Feydeau's *Monsieur de Saint-Bernard*, they asked for it to be returned on April 27. Thierry sent it back the same day with some very kind remarks that raised their hopes. 'We go out madly excited, getting drunk with merely moving about, with walking ... our

'Henriette Maréchal'

hands trembling feverishly, like people who have just broken the bank, wildly agitated, walking, gesticulating, putting our happiness into words.' They took their play back to the Comédie-Française and a fortnight later, on 8 May, obtained a reading. 'We are in front of a table covered with a green cloth, on which there is a reading-stand and something to drink, and facing us is a picture of the death of Talma. There are ten of them there, grave, impassive, silent. Thierry begins to read. He reads the first act, the Opera Ball, in the midst of laughter and sympathetic glances directed at our fraternal partnership. Then he starts at once on the second act and passes on to the third. In our brains, during this reading, very few ideas; deep down in us, anxiety which we try to suppress and drive away by setting ourselves to listen to our play. Gravity has gained possession of our audience, an inscrutable gravity under lock and key, which we seek to examine and surprise. It's finished. Thierry ... takes us into his study ... The minutes seem endless. Through one of the two doors, the only one closed, we hear voices, among which predominates that of Got, whom we fear; then there is a soft, successive, metallic little sound of balls falling into the zinc container. My eyes are on the clock ... it is 3.35. I cannot see Thierry come in, but someone shakes my hand and I hear a soothing voice that says: "You are accepted and very easily, too." Thereupon he begins to talk to us about the play, but after two minutes we ask him if we can make our escape, and fling ourselves into an open carriage, cleaving the air with our hatless heads.' There had been nine white balls and two red.

On May 10 they wrote to Thierry: 'Dear Sir, We felt so much emotion on Monday that we expressed our gratitude to you very badly. Kindly allow us to write these few words to express it—not any better—but in words that remain. To you we owe our entry to the theatre ... our début at the Comédie-Française ... What can we say to you? That we are extremely touched; and that we will try to thank you on the first page of a play of which you are the true and original godfather.'

Mme Arnould-Plessy accepted the part of the mother. 'It's the first time I've played the role of Mamma,' she said, 'but after all she is such a guilty woman!' Delaunay took the part of Paul de Bréville, Got that of Pierre, Lafontaine that of M. Maréchal. Victoria Lafontaine was to be Henriette, and Dinah Félix, Thérèse.

Coquelin, through Banville's agency, had asked to be given a part.

Thereupon Delaunay, on the pretext that he was not young enough, but in fact because he was not paid enough, gave up the role of Pierre. Camille Doucet intervened without success. In vain a line was added making Paul de Bréville a little older. The authors, who had already had to plead with Mme Arnould-Plessy and invite Got to lunch, saw their play being ruined. On September 19 they wrote to Thierry. 'Dear Sir, we have thought of something. If M. Delaunay should definitely refuse to act in our play, would it not be possible to fall back on a young, versatile and original actor, rising in popularity, and whom the Comédie-Française might perhaps be persuaded some day to engage—I mean Febvre.' A letter of September 25 to Thierry says: 'Dear Sir and friend, forgive me for not having answered you sooner, but we were setting out for the country when your letter arrived. I thank you a thousand times and ask you to wait two or three days longer. I have some grounds for supposing that M. Delaunay has reflected a little about his refusal, and I am trying a last and entirely personal approach to him. I will tell you what it is when I let you know what comes of it.' On September 28 Thierry informed them that it was impossible to put on their play at that moment.

They went off to Cernay, and then to Barbizon, in order to forget their troubles and to work on *Manette Salomon*. At last Delaunay, harried by journalists, by Sarcey, critic of *Le Temps* in particular, and worried by fears that a young comedian called Delessart would be put in his place, gave way. *Henriette* was announced for December 1.

On November 5 they wrote to Thierry from Bar-sur-Seine: 'Write and tell us plainly and frankly if our presence is necessary before next Saturday. If it should be, we would come back immediately. Could they not begin by rehearsing the second act? We should like to come to an understanding with you about the casting of the minor roles.'

On November 10 the play was rehearsed for the first time on the stage. 'What strikes us is the lengthy drawl the actors assume when speaking. They begin to rehearse by reciting rather like children. You feel their need of having their parts drummed into them, of their being wound up and warmed up. They fumble over intonations, they make a bad shot at gestures. All the way through they misinterpret the text in such a way as to give the opposite meaning to what you have written. And how long they seem in getting into the skin of

'Henriette Maréchal'

your role! Exception however must be made of Mme Plessy.' After rehearsals, the ceiling of their flat seemed to weigh down upon them, sleep was a bore, the nights seemed empty. They no longer lived for anything except the first performance.

The committee in charge of readings had counted on the Board of Censors to bear the odium of having cut passages out. Princess Mathilde obtained a promise from Marshal Vaillant, a senator and grand marshal of the palace, that he would restrain these officials in their zeal. On December 2 one of them, Plante, issued a license for the production. Thierry was only moderately delighted. He had too much experience of the theatre not to foresee that certain daring expressions in the play would lead to protests.

On December 2 the dress rehearsal took place in an atmosphere of general cheerfulness and confidence. Everyone believed it would be a triumph. It was twenty years since a play so well produced and so well acted had been seen at the Comédie-Française. On the 5th, after a good night's sleep, the authors left cards on the critics: Roqueplan,[1] whom they had already gone to see to ask him to announce the performance, and Janin who, no longer stirring out-of-doors, practised dramatic criticism at home.

In the Latin Quarter a wind of revolt was brewing. Besides the serious grievances they had against the Empire, the students had not yet recovered from the dissatisfaction caused by the suppression of the nursery garden in the Luxembourg and the disfigurement of the Medici fountain. These so-called embellishments had occurred at the same time as the measures of expulsion passed by the Council of the University against those who had paraded their materialist doctrines at the Congress of Liège.

From two o'clock in the afternoon, in spite of the cold, a long queue had lined up under the arches of the Théâtre Français. Students, real or make-believe, were in the majority. They made animal noises, sang songs and played innumerable jokes. They were hoping to occupy the pit, but during the morning Thierry had received a visit from two young editors of *L'Art*, Catulle Mendès and Louis-Xavier de Ricard, who had come to ask for seats for themselves and their friends. Thierry had given them all the remaining tickets for the pit. Those who had queued, furious at being relegated to seats in the

---

[1] Writer on Parisian life, sometime managing director of the Opéra.

Edmond and Jules

balcony and the upper gallery, protested and continued to sing popular songs in the theatre itself.

Horace and Lydia, a dramatic trifle by François Ponsard which served as a curtain-raiser, received the first volley of boos. Gautier's prologue in verse was listened to with attention however, and it was almost the same with the opening of the first act. The tempest was only loosed when reference was made to subscribers to the *Revue des Deux Mondes*—a little revenge by the authors on the magazine which had been so hard on *Germinie Lacerteux*. At a given signal everything was booed, even the scene in which Mme Plessy stood silent in a black domino with a large bouquet of violets in her hand. Pale, and with nerves on edge, the authors, standing in the wings, did not flinch, by their example impelling the actors to stand firm. Eleven years later Alphonse Daudet, who was pointed out to Edmond but whom he did not see again until they met at Flaubert's house in 1873, wrote: 'In the lighted empty foyer, feeling the solemnity of the occasion and conscious of disaster, the two authors, trembling, and pale with indignation, strode up and down . . . convulsed with sudden nervous spasms as they faced the question one asks oneself under every injustice of fate: "Why is it? What have I done?" Fortified by their inward knowledge of themselves as writers, of their lives so laboriously spent in the service of art, they tried to bear up, to conceal beneath a smile of bitter resignation the intensely painful emotion they felt; but for those who could look behind this mask of conventional good-breeding, it was easy to see their despair and to guess what weariness and what disgust would be released in solitude after all this hubbub.'

The pistol shot provoked a sort of riot which was prolonged in order to prevent Got from announcing the name of the authors. 'M. Edouard Thierry,' writes Delzant, 'relates that Maître Marie, one of the gravest and most well-behaved people you could meet, and who, as President of the legal advisory council of the Comédie, was connected with it by the closest of ties, did his utmost to drown Got's voice and prevent the names of the guilty parties from being heard. He made this unusual obstruction out of respect for an ancient tradition. Formerly, in that epic age when the pit had succeeded in making its jurisdiction supreme, to refuse to hear the name of an author meant damning his work for good and all. It would never appear again. Got managed to get over the difficulty very cleverly,

'Henriette Maréchal'

finally flinging out the names of the Goncourts into the midst of the tempest. Let him who could do so hear them, but the names had been pronounced.'

Having made their way out of the theatre past tumultuous groups, they had supper at the Maison d'Or with Bouilhet, Flaubert, and their friend the Comte d'Osmoy. Flaubert thought his two 'dear boys' magnificent, in spite of an attack of nerves that made them want to vomit each mouthful. They went home at five o'clock in the morning utterly exhausted.

The next morning an article by Jules Vallès in the *Chronique de Paris* unexpectedly defended the play while making some reservations: 'If it had pleased heaven to give the last two acts the insolent boldness of the first, *Henriette Maréchal* would have been the *Hernani* of realism. Why, we were all of us there, we who are not bald or toothless or prematurely aged, to protest or applaud whenever truth in modern dress, with laughter on her lips and a drop of champagne in her eyes, tore with her carnival spurs at the gowns of... Clio, Thalia and Melpomene. People applauded enthusiastically, booed relentlessly. There was a stubborn body of hostile opinion up in the gods... It was a defeat, but it was a very good evening.'

Goncourt was always grateful to Vallès for defending *Henriette*. In 1879 he promised to contribute articles to *La Rue*, the paper Vallès was then directing from London. In a letter written about that time to Edmond the author of *Les Insurgés* said: 'When on May 28th, 1871, I found myself in the middle of a lake of blood at the corner of a deserted street, and threatened on all sides by death, I hunted through my tired brain for the names of those who had been insurgents like myself on the battlefield of letters. I thought of you and of going to ask you for shelter.'

On the 7th, the performance of the play was almost possible. The kiss which ends the second act and the dramatic effect in the third, where Mme Maréchal flings herself into Pierre's arms, had both been cut. Mme Lafontaine was not booed. On the 9th, they heard that on the first night some ten or twelve disturbers of the peace had not been thrown out; the police superintendent, called upon by some of the spectators to allow them to hear a play for which they had bought seats, had replied that he had been given no orders. On the 11th disturbance was at its height, the first act gave the effect of a play in dumb-show. Bressant's courage was superb, and Mme Arnould-

145

Plessy's no less. 'Some friends of mine', she wrote to the Goncourts, 'heard this said yesterday: "They have taken good precautions tonight, they want to crush us, but they won't always be so well armed and we'll have our revenge." Have courage. I myself am like a lioness. Be comforted... Your friend, Arnould-Plessy.'

A circular had been distributed throughout the Latin Quarter, inviting law students to prevent the curtain from rising after the first act. Signed 'Pipe-en-Bois', it appeared in *L'Opinion Nationale*, which was edited by the former Saint-Simonien, Adolphe Guéroult, and was said to have been inspired by the Prince Napoleon. The pseudonym of 'Pipe-en-Bois' has been thought by some people to conceal the identity of a certain Georges Cavalier, who was among other things a reporter attached to some minor republican newspaper. It was said that he had already been the instigator of an intrigue at the Odéon against *Gaétana*, a drama by Edmond About, who like the Goncourts was guilty of having relations with officialdom. Unlike *Gaétana*, *Henriette Maréchal* did not lead to any arrests. The atmosphere of the Comédie-Française was not the same as at the Odéon.

M. de la Guéronnière, a writer and politician, who was said to be acquainted with Napoleon III's secret thoughts, attacked both the play and the Princess's salon which was reputed to be Liberal. Etienne Arago, another writer who was also a politician, cried out against their profaning of the Revolution. At the Sorbonne a certain Professor Frack trampled on *Henriette Maréchal* 'to the great joy of all the "Pipes-en-Bois" at the lecture'. In Notre Dame, Père Félix called down the wrath of heaven upon the two authors. But it was the attacks of Anatole de la Forge in *Le Siècle*, demanding the suppression of the play, that the authors felt most deeply. Jules wished to send his seconds to the reviewer and would have done so if Edmond, who eventually took no action, had not claimed the right to do so in his place, fearing that because of his lack of agility his brother would run too great a risk, whereas he, the elder, who was a very bad shot had a tricky way with weapons which was disconcerting to those who shot well.

On the day of the sixth and last performance there appeared, at the same time as the text of *Henriette Maréchal* with a preface by its two authors, (published by Villemessant, who had paid them 3,000 francs) a pamphlet entitled: *What I think of Henriette Maréchal, of its preface and the theatre in my day* by 'Pipe-en-Bois'. At a dinner on

'Henriette Maréchal'

December 12, given by Nadar to Préault the sculptor, Asselineau, Baudelaire's friend, and a very young civil servant, Iveling Rambaud, who was in a hurry to get himself talked about, *Henriette Maréchal* had been much discussed. Nadar had had the idea of producing a pamphlet and Rambaud had adopted it. The matter was arranged on condition that the pamphlet appeared in two days' time. In spite of its being a silly trifle, seven thousand copies of it were sold.

Some of the weekly articles on the theatre, appearing six days after the first performance, protested against those who had booed the play. 'This,' Saint-Victor declared in *La Presse*, 'is the bulletin of an ambush, not of a defeat'. In *L'Evénement*, Roqueplan inveighed against the premeditated action of those who had come armed with whistles. In *Le Moniteur Universel* Gautier praised the authors for their skilful adaptation of their style to dramatic dialogue. There were, however, many papers that dealt more severely with the play. The *Revue des Deux Mondes*, in particular, against which a remark by a masquerader in the first act had been directed, completely lost its temper with the authors.

In the *Figaro-Programme* of December 19 five students expressed their opinion on the question of a cabal against *Henriette Maréchal*. Undoubtedly there had been a concerted attack by students holding republican opinions against two authors whose play, so they imagined, had only been performed out of favouritism; it is surprising all the same that on the first night the hubbub created by these students should have been tolerated by the police and that at the third performance their superintendent should have alleged, as a pretext for refusing to intervene, that he had no orders. It was only at the fourth performance that some fifteen persons were expelled from the theatre, an action against which *La France* protested on December 17, the very day on which Marshal Vaillant, more or less directly inspired by the Tuileries, banned the play. This blow would therefore have certainly come from the Empress, who was the Princess's enemy, as Jules himself said in a letter to Flaubert.

In their story of *Henriette Maréchal*, which was written for the second edition of the play, and in which the preface to the first is partly repeated, the Goncourts thanked their friends and supporters. Their independence, their aloofness, their disdainful bearing easily laid them open to attack. Supported by the Princess's circle alone, they were looked on with suspicion by all parties. This was the real underlying cause of the almost general hostility that had been unleashed against them. One wonders whether they really understood this. Did they believe, or did they make a pretence of believing, that the younger generation of students bore a grudge against them because of the prefix to their name and their supposed wealth? On this occasion, after insisting on their ancestry on their father's side, they wrote as follows: 'We have laboured for fifteen years, withdrawn from the world... intent on our work. We have experienced all the setbacks, all the sorrows, all the fits of despair, all the insults that belong to a life devoted to literature. For many long hours, unknown to the world, our pride has bled within us. For years our books have hardly paid for the wood and the oil we burn at night. Step by step, book by book, we have made our way, forced to contend for everything and win everything ourselves. It has taken us, in short, fifteen years to reach the Comédie-Française. As for our wealth, we have not quite a thousand pounds income between the two of us. We live on the fourth floor and have a maid-of-all-work to attend to us. And as for our happiness, that must not be too much exaggerated: we have, the one neurasthenia, the other a disease of the liver... two ailments that perhaps will one day end by killing us, unless we should happen to die of something else, both of us together, as has been forecast by a threat that someone has been good enough to make.' The Comte d'Osmoy besought them in vain to cut out this last sentence which, so he said, was calculated to make them appear ridiculous.

The preface was dated December 12. The Goncourts have described the circumstances in which it was written: 'Correcting proofs of the play, making additions to it, writing twenty letters a day, reading all the newspapers, receiving people who come to see us, driving round part of the day in a carriage, getting an audience together, assigning roles, attending all rehearsals right up to the end in order to keep the actors up to the mark, taking friends out to supper in the evening—and, on top of it all, finding time and sufficient composure to write our preface, in bits, in sentences hastily jotted down in pencil, whilst driving about, whilst eating, in cafés, in the wings of the theatre; it is as if one were spending ten years of one's life, of one's nervous system, of one's brain within the space of ten days.'

On the morning of December 15, Thierry, 'this craven hero, this semi-courageous man, caught betwixt the cabal and the government, the most fickle of all authorities,' came to see them, bringing the first copy of their preface. They understood at once it had killed their play by the protest it raised against the tyranny of beer-shops and pubs. 'For that's what it is above all, this cabal, and perhaps those people who find it funny because it only strikes at us will not be laughing about it later on.' Showing them an appeal in *La Gazette de France* to taxpayers whose money provided the public grant to the Comédie-Française, its manager requested them to withdraw their play. This they refused to do, they would wait until it was banned by the government. That evening the performance was a triumph. At the least sound of a boo the whole house rose in protest. Nevertheless Thierry could not promise them a further performance. On the 17th Marshal Vaillant pronounced sentence on the unlucky Thierry, caught between the cabal and the government, with these stern words: 'Sir, I look at you, and condemn you.' The Princess had received some anonymous letters, promising her that the first torch would be used on her house.

In all, there had been six performances. The fourth had been the stormiest, the fifth the most peaceful. The suppression of the play had done so little to calm people's minds that on the 17th Sainte-Beuve, fearing lest the dinner at Magny's the next day would be disturbed by demonstrators, appealed to the police to keep watch on the restaurant, but their intervention was not needed.

Worn out and ill, the Goncourts took the train for Le Havre. They spent their time walking about on the beach in the fog and wind under a leaden sky, beside an angry sea that stung their faces. A severe and bracing diversion. On December 31 their last thoughts for the year were of a performance of their play which was being given at Marseilles.

On January 6, they dined at Croisset. 'Tell me now,' Flaubert had written to them, 'is it true? Your play has been withdrawn *by order?* Why so? I imagine your preface is not unconnected with this. Someone has been offended by something or other? You have said all there was to say. I only found you too sincere and *too modest.* When people are as brave as you are, they can be *bold.* When they have your talent, they ought to be proud. I have read *Henriette* twice over. *It's good . . .* I suspect some clerical influence in your cabal . . . And then, over and above everything, you have *style,* a thing that people never forgive . . .'

For a long time this banning of their play weighed heavily on their minds. On January 1 they wrote: 'This government is truly despicable. In the report on the State theatres during 1866, we find secret congratulations offered and transparent encouragement given to 'Pipe-en-Bois', to whose judgement they hand over, in the person of the public, the task of controlling taste.'

Henriette Maréchal was performed not only in Marseilles but also in Montparnasse before an audience of workmen and retired hall-porters. The authors went to it. The audience seemed to them to take everything very well. As they came out they overheard this comment from a workman: 'I don't care, but it must be jolly fine among the nobs!' During the whole evening they had suffered 'like a man who sees his mistress familiarly accosted in a wine-shop by men from the slums'.

The bitter feelings aroused by their reverse were still perceptible when, after the success of Bouilhet's *La Conjuration d'Amboise*, they had supper with the author and Flaubert: 'Our thoughts were on the vulgar conduct of success, the way in which one works it up and in which an author without subtlety but with a gift for declamation that appeals to the public can carry it off, and also on this mass of idiots from which an audience is created, all those judges whom we whole-heartedly despise and whose judgements and applause we are yet weak enough to seek.'

It is possibly in a letter from Sainte-Beuve to their cousin Lefebvre de Béhaine, at that time First Secretary at the French Embassy in Berlin, that we find the most just and sympathetic note concerning them in all this: 'You cannot imagine the absurdity and the senselessness of all this rumpus stirred up by our friends' play. The only sensible and plausible objection that men who follow tradition and set conventions could make is that the play would have been better anywhere else than at the Comédie-Française; but they did not confine themselves to that. The notion of its being under the Princess's special protection dominated the minds of ill-intentioned people and gained a hold over the decent public which does not believe there is such a thing as an out-and-out lie and imagines that a calumny must be more or less well-founded.'

According to Edmond, *Henriette Maréchal* should be interpreted as evidence of the attitude of mind of its authors 'when the younger of them fell in love'. More carefully formulated and expressed in a more literary style, it reproduced the ironically affectionate bickerings which

'*Henriette Maréchal*'

see them at loggerheads with each other, the one of them armed with the impetuous fire of youth, the other with the experience and scepticism of riper age. It is possible that in 1865 no one noticed that Paul de Bréville in the play is Jules, and Pierre, Edmond. Today this is obvious.

In spite of the fanciful humour of its first act *Henriette Maréchal* is not a good play: it offends by the unexpected brutality of its ending, it departs from probability in the coincidence that allows Paul de Bréville, wounded in a duel arising out of an incident at the masked ball and which Mme Maréchal had provoked, to be given shelter in this lady's house. The Goncourts vainly adduced the experience of a cousin of theirs, the victim of an accident near the house of a young woman who had not been allowed to marry him, being received in this house and finally marrying the object of his passion. On the whole *Henriette Maréchal* is neither better nor worse than most plays of the period, and that is the most that can be said in its favour, while at the same time there is a touch of daring in its blunders, and in this respect it deserves both attention and indulgence.

Théophile Gautier found in it a quality peculiar to its authors; a literary form of speech. 'And for me,' said Edmond emphatically, 'a new language is the only renewal of which the theatre is capable. A language in which there will no longer be bits and pieces out of books, no longer any phraseology in which the witticisms of the professional writer can be traced, yet one which nevertheless makes an audience feel that a man of letters has invented the words that come from the actors' mouths. There is the revolution to be attempted! And this revolution, we have tried to effect, but only tried. Ah! if we could have written a second play with a love interest, I guarantee it would have been swept clear of any kind of romantic or *bookish* jargon!'

The failure and the banning of *Henriette* had not discouraged the Goncourts so much that they abandoned their idea of seeking compensation for their losses in the very same theatre. 'All things considered, a drama must either be an epic or a work of pure imagination. A comedy of manners, coming bump up against the contemporary novel of manners, what a caricature! What a trifle! What idle nonsense!' They would write an epic drama.

At Princess Mathilde's house they had heard General Ducrot

predict an imminent war with Russia, a forecast which their cousin Béhaine confirmed in his letters to them. Their patriotism, their knowledge of the eighteenth century, as also, so Henri Céard [1] claims, their annoyance at seeing their researches made use of by the dramatist François Ponsard in *Le Lion Amoureux*, combined to inspire them with the idea of writing *La Patrie en Danger*, a drama in five acts on the siege of Verdun, the first title of which was *Mademoiselle de la Rochedragon*.

Supplied with documents by the historian Camille Rousset, who had sent them a bibliography and the index numbers of works in the Archives of the Ministry of War, they wrote from Bar-sur-Seine to the manager of the Comédie Française: 'We have a historical play in five acts completely finished; this play we intend to read at the Comédie Française as soon as the Comédie is good enough to listen to it...' On December 6 they noted: 'Been to see Thierry to ask him for a reading of our five-act play on the Revolution, *Blanche de la Rochedragon*. His polite reception of us makes us tremble.' On the 31st they wrote: 'The fair copy of the manuscript of *la Rochedragon* has been handed to us, we were almost afraid of it as of something out of which will spring the hellish torment of theatrical passions.'

By February 23 they were becoming anxious. 'Dear Sir, We have no news of the five-act play we handed to you six weeks ago. We should be greatly obliged if you would fix a moment convenient to the Comédie-Française for having it read.'

The reading was fixed for March 7. They went to see Régnier a well-to-do pretentious bourgeois', Coquelin, who received them undressed in a bathing establishment, Leroux, another actor, in a 'palace', the 'peasant' Got in his little house in the hamlet of Boulainvilliers. They had asked Gautier to announce in his weekly article in *Le Moniteur* that they were preparing to read a drama on the Revolution. He had promised he would, but did not do so. 'What a thing this Revolution is! How frightened people are of it. Oh! The Terror! It's well-named!' The very day of the reading, on learning of the existence of an old lady of the name of Rochedragon, they adopted a better title—*La Patrie en Danger*.

The work was accepted on condition that they made some alterations; the Board of Censors would never countenance such a display of

[1] Civil Servant and member of the Médan group of writers.

'Henriette Maréchal'

revolutionary sentiments. They did not press the matter: 'The committee has let us see all Thierry's machinations; he has doubtless shown the manuscript to Doucet [the Academician] and taken orders from the Censors, then worked upon his committee and got it going, as he knows how to, by means of his skill in intrigues and priestly manipulations.'

In August of that same year they were at Trouville when a letter came from Hostein, the manager of the Châtelet Theatre, which since 1862 had taken the place of the Cirque, asking them for *La Patrie en Danger*. Puzzled and sceptical, they returned to Paris, where Hostein received them on August 31. His verdict was discreetly weighed: 'There is no trace of drama in your five acts. There's no interest. It's the Revolution in a drawing-room. It lacks movement... It has style, oh certainly style! Portraits, and characters!... But it would have to be perfectly acted... nothing but scenic effects... Witty remarks! But the Censors would have to leave them in...' The Censors had neither to leave them in nor to take them out. Hostein became bankrupt. His idea of putting on *La Patrie en Danger* had only been the quick reflex action of a manager with his back to the wall.

La Patrie en Danger did not leave Edmond's portfolio again until 1873, to be printed then with *Henriette* and a preface in a melancholy vein: 'Today, now that out of the two collaborators I alone remain... with somewhat failing energy, I do not feel I have the courage to take the necessary steps, to endure the pin-pricks, the vexations, the petty mental tortures an author most ordinarily meets with from a theatrical management, when, at the end of a success so dearly bought, one may be confronted by a heart-breaking veto.'

In 1868, however, undiscouraged by the banning of *Henriette Maréchal* and the rejection of *La Patrie en Danger*, Jules was thinking of writing comedies in which they would have satirized their times. One of them was to have been called *La Blague*—Humbug. It would have been a good title.

XVI
Their Two Last Novels

The brothers had been toying with the idea of *Manette Salomon* ever since 1850, but the first mention of it in the *Journal* is with reference to an evening in 1865 when they had called on Tournemine, the orientalist and painter of Turkish landscapes, to have a look at some letters he had written to his wife from Turkey. They had drunk coffee made in the Turkish way and eaten jam brought back from Constantinople.

Ever since their youth they had mixed with painters. In 1852, along with a group of some dozen art students and writers, they had spent a few days at Saccaux's inn at Marlotte, where Murger was 'convalescing on absinthe'. In July 1853, they had taken lodgings at Gretz-sur-Loing, where Saint-Victor had come to join them 'in a rustic inn frequented by artists, with full board for 3.50 francs a day, living in white-washed rooms, sleeping on feather beds, drinking the local wine and eating a great number of omelettes'.

In June the following year they were again at Gretz. 'Yesterday,' wrote Jules, 'I ate my food off silver-plated dishes; today off earthenware; I like these contrasts.' They went for walks in the moonlight with Saint-Victor, visited the Fairies' Pool, the Gorge of the Wolves, the castle of Fontainebleau, Bas-Bréau and Barbizon, to which they returned in June and October and where they were filled with wonder at themselves for having put up with so much discomfort for the sake of literature.

The studio described in *Manette* was the one in the rue de Fleurus occupied by Anatole de Beaulieu, a friend of Mme Daudet's father. Freely based on wide reading on the aesthetics of painting, on the Jews, on the whole tribe of harlots, and so forth, this novel, the most voluminous of all the ones they wrote, took a year and a half's work. On August 6, Jules wrote to their cousin Béhaine: 'For the past six weeks we have been working madly, and with dogged regularity... Heaven be praised! we are now at the end of this huge contraption.'

Manette Salomon, at first called *L'Atelier Langibout*, and which, in its study of artistic circles, formed a kind of pendant to *Charles Demailly*, was completed at Trouville on August 21, 1866. Submitted to Adrien Hébrard, editor of *Le Temps*, by Charles Edmond, the novel appeared in that paper at the beginning of 1867. In the autumn of that year it was published in book form with a dedication to 'the guests at Magny's table'. On November 25 the Goncourts made this brief entry in their *Journal*: 'Bar-sur-Seine. In the country and staying with relations to give ourselves a change. We leave behind us *Manette Salomon*, now enjoying a great success.' A success, perhaps, but not with the Press, in spite of a good review by Vallès, a writer of revolutionary inclinations. 'In 1867,' writes Alidor Delzant, 'when the Press, tightly muzzled whenever it wished to poke its nose into politics, gave literary events an attention which it doles out to them very sparingly today, the appearance of *Manette Salomon* was hardly noticed except by one or two writers of weekly articles.' Albert Wolff, of *Le Figaro*, found fault with the authors for not knowing how to speak to the soul, a reproach which they themselves made of Flaubert's work; on the other hand, he admired the execution of certain passages. Albert Duchesne replied to him in the same paper: 'It is impossible for me not to recognize in MM. de Goncourt two writers of great talent and high ideals and in *Manette Salomon* a work of remarkable literary value which one could not refuse to esteem most highly without offending both against justice and good taste.' Jules Lermina, in *Le Corsaire*, expressed a different opinion: 'What is the use of all this? What idea inspired the authors of this novel, or to speak frankly, this piece of drivel?... They are the high priests of futility.' Flaubert wrote to his friend Jules Duplan, remarking: 'The dear boys' *Manette Salomon* seems to me to have put on so long a jacket that it could pass for a shroud: the book is worth reading all the same.' From their dear Flaubert's pen, ordinarily more enthusiastic, such an appreciation was lacking in warmth. In writing to them he had said: '*Manette Salomon* has held my attention all day long. I am astounded, dazzled, completely struck with it... As for talent, it's cram full of it. What richness, by Jove! Never in your lives have you been more *you*, and that is the most important thing.'

Viollet-le-Duc, who had supplied them with copious notes on 'how to achieve success' at the Académie des Beaux-Arts, told them that their book was going to let loose the wrath of the whole world of painters against them. The picture they had given of it was only

Their Two Last Novels

too true. Le Figaro found fault with it for its generally grey tone, but the fact is that the Bohemia of the artists, unlike the Bohemia of men of letters, did not indulge in flashes of wit. 'You have created for us,' wrote Viollet-le-Duc, 'that disjointed, futile existence, full of ancient stereotyped conventions, with a truthfulness that breaks the heart of anyone who knows this particular world.'

While asking them to contribute to the *Revue des Lettres et des Arts* which he had just started to publish, Villiers de l'Isle-Adam also promised to write an article about them: '*Manette Salomon* absolutely inspires me. I will do my best to give a good account of this meticulously careful, masterly and lively style, which has the sharpness and depth of a painting and comes near to producing a physical sensation. The pages full of that dreadful comic side of modern times, drawn from life, are truly confirmatory evidence for the use of future historians.'

Taine, in a letter, took the book to pieces with scrupulous care. In it he praised a passion for flesh-tints and colour which was not to be found to such a degree in either Gautier or Saint-Victor; but their style was that of writers who did not think enough about the public. 'You write for specialists, men of the same profession as yourselves... People get out of breath in trying to follow you... On the whole, this produces an almost painful bewilderment, an almost continual jolt...' Then followed suggested amendments which must have made the two novelists shrug their shoulders. What a pedant, this fellow Taine!

Taking up the theme of *En 18*... and of *Charles Demailly*, *Manette Salomon* is in certain parts an indictment of womankind in general and in particular of the Jewish woman and the pernicious influence she is capable of exerting over an artist. By debasing his art and his character and humouring his lowest aspirations, she leads him on to working only to gain honours and money. Charles Demailly, the victim of a former mistress, dies insane. Coriolis, Manette's victim, sinks to the condition of a brute.

From what source did the Goncourts derive this misogyny and this anti-semitism? Was it the product of an ancient grudge? The interest of the book however lies elsewhere, in a style that transposes painting into literature, in the picture of an artist's life under Louis-Philippe and the conflict between the 'Ingrists' and the Colourists. The glory of French painting in the eyes of the Goncourts lay 'in the

Their Two Last Novels

great movement towards the return of the art and the men of the nineteenth century to *natural* nature, in the sympathetic study of things to which old civilizations resort to renew themselves, in the passionate pursuit of the simple, humble, innocent beauties of this earth, which will remain as the charm and the glory of our present school of thought'. The painter they most admired was Théodore Rousseau.

The champions of anti-academic art, but despisers of Courbet, whom they accused of having discovered something uglier than ordinary ugliness—mindless ugliness, in fact enthusiastic admirers, too, of Decamps the painter, with whom, by the way, they compared themselves, the Goncourts do not seem to have had any idea that the very year in which they began to study documents for *Manette* the protests of artists rejected by the Salon had been so violent that Napoleon III had gone himself to the Palais de l'Industrie to have their pictures shown to him there. From this visit sprang the Salon des Refusés, which included such artists as Manet, Whistler, Fantin-Latour, Pissarro, Bracquemond and others. 'In the farthest room,' writes the artist Cazin, 'Manet made a hole in the wall with his *Déjeuner sur l'herbe*.' The public laughed at them.

If they went to the Salon des Refusés, we do not believe the Goncourts laughed, but although M. François Fosca, whose pages on the Goncourts and painting are intensely interesting, believes that we can hail them as precursors and heralds of impressionism, they were certainly not aware of the future in store for painting in bright, clear colours. Apart from two passages in which he is cited as the painter of Zola's portrait, Manet, whom Edmond met now and then in the house of the painter and sculptor, Nittis, is never mentioned in the *Journal* except in terms of scorn. On May 18, 1889, for instance, Edmond makes this comment: 'With Manet, whose methods are borrowed from Goya, and with the painters in his train, came the death of painting in oils, with that lovely warm and crystalline transparency of which Rubens' "Woman in a Straw Hat" is an example. Now we have opaque and lustreless paint, plastered on with all the characteristics of painting done with a gluepot.' The year before Edmond had written: 'The impressionists? Odd sort of artists who have never been able to make anything whatever seem real.'

Notwithstanding the general fault found with the Goncourts for not having succeeded in identifying themselves sufficiently with their

Edmond and Jules

characters, *Manette Salomon*, which is less well-balanced than *Germinie*, affords more lively interest to the reader. It is what today we would call an excellent documentary on the life that artists led in the nineteenth century, and also an authentic, anecdotal and artfully varied picture of manners, beside which Murger's *Scènes de la Vie de Bohème* seems even weaker and more conventional than ever.

They had depicted middle-class life in *Renée Mauperin*, the lower classes in *Germinie Lacerteux*, artistic and literary circles in *Charles Demailly* and *Manette Salomon*. Now they were seized with the idea of returning to the middle class with a novel at first called *Mademoiselle Tony-Freneuse*, but later changed to *Madame Gervaisis*, about a woman of the upper middle class.

On April 2, 1867, they briefly noted: 'We are setting off for Rome', a simple mention of a fact that no previous note had foretold, although letters from their cousin Lefebvre de Béhaine tell us that they had made preparations beforehand for their arrival in that city.

Going on board the *Pausilippe* at Marseilles, they disembarked at Civita Vecchia on April 6. At six o'clock that evening they were in Rome, possibly staying, as did their Mme Gervaisis, at the Hotel Minerva. They had come to Italy to get material for their novel, only setting out from a sense of duty and 'devotion to literature' but, as it happened, they now experienced an unexpected feeling of deliverance and lightness of heart.

They have indicated that their monograph on Mme Gervaisis is really one on their aunt Nephthalie de Courmont, who had died in Rome. 'The story of Mme Gervaisis's life, of my aunt's life, in Rome, in our occult novel, is pure and authentic history. There are literally only two instances of juggling with the truth in the whole book. The affectionate but dull-witted child, whom I have portrayed under the name of Pierre-Charles, had died of meningitis before his mother left for Italy, and I have burdened this poor, attractive little boy with the heart-breaking sorrow and mental anguish suffered by his younger brother during the time his mother was afflicted with religious mania. Also, as a matter of fact, my aunt did not die in the Papal audience chamber, but while dressing to go to this audience.'

Alphonse de Courmont had told them about his mother's last years and the pangs of conscience that had led her to seek religion. They had undoubtedly been impelled to write *Madame Gervaisis*,

Their Two Last Novels

a character-sketch of a woman up till then imbued with the philosophy of the eighteenth century, out of curiosity about a realm of psychology which had always been closed to them, but the tendency of the work, at least in the second part, is distinctly anti-clerical and anti-religious. 'We whose personal and racial sympathies incline us towards the Pope, who feel no hatred for the priesthood, are here writing, impelled by some irresistible force that is in the air, a book that speaks unfavourably of the Church. And why? But does one know the why and wherefore of what one writes?'

The question of relations with Rome was in the foreground of current affairs, and Princess Mathilde's set as well as the Prince Napoleon's were resisting the Pope's claim to temporal power. Unconsciously or not, the Goncourts had been influenced by the atmosphere they breathed in the rue de Courcelles with Taine, Renan, Sainte-Beuve and Flaubert. Their personal and racial sympathies for the Pope were certainly very superficial, being nothing more than a natural liking for history, tradition and art; a genuine feeling for Christianity did not enter into it. The ceremony of washing the feet of men in the pilgrim's hostel only moved them because in Christian charity they saw one of the sources of modern sensibility.

The *Journal* gives us very few details of their stay. In evening dress, pumps and white ties they were received in public audience by the Pope and given his blessing in Saint Peter's Square; they dined at the French Embassy, to which Lefebvre de Béhaine had given them letters of introduction, were entertained by the painter Hébert at the Villa Medicis, went with a letter from Charles Blanc, the critic and engraver, to see another painter, Chenavard, across the Tiber, paid several visits to the Vatican Museum, where the Belvedere Apollo appeared to them as the supreme and absolute masterpiece, and where Raphael's 'Transfiguration' gave them the impression of badly painted paper. A note from José-Maria de Hérédia allows us to think that they visited the Catacombs of Saint Calixtus in his company. This entry in the *Journal* is worth noting: 'Rushing off as soon as we're up to make a quick study of some church or some ruin, breakfasting at a rickety table in the Café Greco, or in the shade of our own room, smoking cigars as we write our notes, with a bunch of white roses with sulphur-yellow centres in front of us; then towards four or five o'clock a carriage drive round the outskirts of Rome: that is the life we lead from day to day.'

They certainly spent a great part of their time in the streets and the scenes of popular life count among the best pages in *Madame Gervaisis*. But Philippe Burty tells us that Jules, already ill and wrapped up in himself, did not make any drawings or paint any water-colours while he was in Rome. They began their return journey on the *Hermus* on May 14. 'Italy makes us homesick for grey skies. The rain, on our return, seems like one's native country.'

In the summer of 1867 they made a long stay at the Hotel Madrid in Vichy. 'As for the hotels in Vichy,' Flaubert had told them in a letter, 'they are all wretched. There's no district where the food is worse.'

On their return to Paris they went several times to stay at Saint-Gratien. Trouville seemed horrible to them that year: the Hotel du Bras d'Or full of bourgeois, two rooms the size of a cigar box over a stable, a child cutting its teeth, and to crown everything, Thiers striding up and down the floor in white trousers, like 'a Punchinello dedicated to the Virgin's service'. It was enough to make one commit suicide. Even Edmond's nomination to the Legion of Honour did not bring back their zest for life.

'As with all joys, this one arrives incomplete, and the man to be decorated is dissatisfied ... Some pride however in this decoration, which will have the rare distinction of not having been asked for or even solicited by a word or an allusion, but snatched by a friend who thought of it on her own and by the sympathy of unknown persons.' The Princess had thought of it first, but Sainte-Beuve, as we have seen, had reminded her of it at an opportune moment.

They hung up a plan of Rome on the wall in front of their eyes and at the beginning of 1868 settled down to write *Madame Gervaisis*. The novel was completed on December 22, 1868, in the midst of all kinds of domestic and other worries. An instinctive horror of noise was beginning to torment Jules. On July 21 they had read one or two chapters of their novel to Gautier, who had spoken in praise of it to the Princess. Her curiosity aroused, she asked to hear from them about it. The Goncourts knew that every kind of reading bored her, even if it were of a masterpiece, but they read her some of their book. 'She listens in dismay, with the peevish air of someone offended by heaven knows what in our style of literature. But good God, why then do princes want to take an interest in things that do not interest them?' Gautier had vainly interjected a few such comments as, 'That's very good, that bit!'

Their Two Last Novels

On January 1, 1869, they took their manuscript to the publisher Lacroix and armed with a recommendation from Taine, suggested that an extract from it should be published in the *Journal des Débats*, but the editor, Edouard Bertin, was not at his office. Then followed days of serious mental strain aggravated by stomach troubles. On January 20, they sent three chapters to Zola, who brought them out in *Le Gaulois* with an introductory note by himself. The previous month they had had him to dinner for the first time. He had impressed them as a lean, young student, robust yet puny, looking somewhat like Sarcey, and with a bloodless, waxen complexion. 'A very young man, with delicate moulding like the finest porcelain in his features, his upper eyelids and his hands; somewhat fashioned, in general appearance, like those individuals he makes up of two opposite types, those faces in which he mingles male and female characteristics; and even in his mind, which discloses some stray resemblance to these beings he creates with a curious ambiguity in their souls.' All in all, a troubled, anxious type of man, deeply thoughtful, complex, evasive, difficult to read. He told them of his money troubles, his desire to write a story of a family in eight volumes, his dislike of journalism. After a moment's silence he added: 'I have so many enemies . . . And it's so difficult to get oneself talked about!'

On February 2, they wrote: 'We must confess we are filled with some pride on reading the first printed pages of *Madame Gervaisis*.' On the 5th, at midnight, they finished correcting the final proofs, and on this occasion they took care to make things clear in their *Journal*: 'People may think that this woman's death as she steps across the threshold of the Papal Chamber is pure imagination, and yet it is almost the exact truth. That woman, that relation, whose character we have developed in this novel, died just as we have made her die, while dressing to go to an audience—all we have done is to postpone her death for a couple of hours.' They also admitted that their references to consumption had been based on remarks they had heard Dr Robin (to whom they had shown the final proofs) make at the Magny dinners and which they had adapted in their book. 'For that to which we have given definite shape and character would never have come from this learned person, who was struck by the style and daring of our writing—for he himself, when faced with putting this on paper, would have shown the same drivelling bashfulness and produced the same rather timorous amendments as those he sent us in the margin of our proofs.' On the 17th, after a consultation with a doctor whom Edmond had consulted about his liver, they were expecting some kindly words from those who dined at Magny's; nothing of the sort happened, they had to content themselves with hearing that their book was 'fairly well put together'. Taine took them to task for words that were not in the dictionary, but gave them credit for a few descriptions. He did not find the end interesting; he had read Saint Theresa. 'The author of the *Voyage en Italie* told us this in an acid, irritable, and staccato tone of voice, and with a little more sickly sallowness than usual in his complexion. That is our only success. It must be admitted that our book has hardly had much spoiling up to the present.'

On February 19, they went to see Sainte-Beuve, whom they found in a melancholy mood, sad on account of his condition, sad about the state of politics and literature, sad because of the intrigues among Academicians. He confided to them with bitterness about his lonely life and his melancholy evenings. Night was falling, and the old man's words seemed gradually to fade into the shadows, 'speech drawing nearer and nearer to the great silence'. On March 2 they went back to see him again. He had just finished reading their novel and they had grounds for believing he was well disposed towards it. Had he not written to them when they were in Italy: 'This novel of Rome will come very opportunely, and it seems to me that opinion in literary circles is about to wake up and is showing a lively curiosity concerning you.' Now, kindly and carping by turns, he took them to task for developing their style and their characteristic qualities to an exaggerated degree. Given a skilful reader, and in a certain setting, their works might possibly meet with appreciation, but books were made to be read by everybody. Theirs were no longer literature, they were music, they were painting, and he instanced Rousseau, Bernardin de Saint-Pierre, Chateaubriand, Hugo, Gautier, and Saint-Victor, who had already gone far in this direction. They themselves wished to go farther still, to interpret movement in terms of colour: that was impossible. 'I don't myself know,' he said, 'how people will regard that later, but, for the moment, you must restrict and tone down your effects. Take, for instance, your description of the Pope dressed all in white, away in the background... No, emphatically no...' He would not listen to them. 'You must succeed... I want you to succeed,' he insisted. He exhorted them to write for the public, while

Their Two Last Novels

finding fault with them for their ambition, their constant labours, their sense of duty, and the passion they put into their efforts to satisfy themselves. They replied that for them there was only the public for whom they had worn themselves out in writing this novel: that is to say, posterity. This made him shrug his shoulders and 'blaspheme': posterity, that was a thing which did not exist! They went away from this interview thoroughly discouraged. 'It is rare for those who give opinions on art and literature not to submit themselves to the tyranny of fools; the guides of popular taste are generally its servants.'

On March 22, they went back once more to the rue du Montparnasse, for they were anxious to get an article out of him. For an hour he lectured them again, accusing them of not having understood anything in the *Imitation of Christ*, a copy of which, in the Latin text, full of arid flowers of speech and copiously annotated, he placed open before them. He began to read them some of its pages in a 'clerical' tone, remarking as he finished: 'Oh! there is a kind of love in this work, enough to make you drunk with its sweetness all your life!' They laughed up their sleeves at him. They were wrong. The author of *Port-Royal* had an experience of spiritual things which they lacked. A month later, through Charles Edmond, he offered them two articles in *Le Temps*, on condition that they should accept beforehand both the pleasure and displeasure this might give them. 'My uncle,' wrote Charles Edmond, 'would be very happy for you to reply to him in the *Temps*, as Flaubert did about *Salammbô* . . . you would do well to go and see him and say (if such is your opinion) that this arrangement suits you . . . He would take such an action on your part very kindly. Please be accommodating and tractable. Two important articles are well worth it.'

A courteous and truly friendly offer which they accepted. But some time later, the Princess, annoyed with 'M. de Sainte-Beuve', but having asked them how he was, Jules answered: 'M. de Sainte-Beuve? Oh . . . he's not so ill as people think, he's busy slating us.' Sainte-Beuve, however, had only a few months to live and his temper, which had never been very good, was affected by this. The remark about 'slating' them, which was repeated to him by someone—Taine, so the Goncourts thought—made him angry. 'I've never slated anyone!' he cried . . . 'These are bad literary habits I leave to others.' On April 9, 1869, on Jules asking for a clear statement on the matter,

Sainte-Beuve wrote to them: 'Dear Sirs, It really seemed to me after thorough reflection that I was embarking on a difficult and almost impossible operation: that of developing, amidst much praise of details, objections to methods employed and to the work as a whole, not only without offending the authors, but also avoiding a clash with the more or less kindly and certainly intelligent remnants of their circle of friends... Since my intentions and the spirit in which I reckoned to write these articles were very plain and frank... I should take it ill if anything in them were attributed to a variation in the temperature of the surrounding atmosphere, as our friend Taine has put it. No one, doubtless, is to blame in all this, but once doubt has been awakened, the safest thing for me to do is to refrain from comment. Besides, the very uncertain and very slight use these articles can have is already manifest in this sense that, having outlined them to you in advance, you can perfectly well judge if anything in them seems to you right and fair or if everything has been in vain.' Sainte-Beuve had nothing to fear; the prudence he affected was only a way of disguising his spleen.

This did not involve a breach of their friendship, for we have a letter from Sainte-Beuve, dated July 16, 1869, sent to Jules on his return from Royat: 'I am very sorry to hear that the waters of Royat have not done you any good. With me it is very simple: at a certain age, illness is a matter of course; at your age, it is an injustice, and you should rebel against it... Go on working, but don't work too much'.

They were away from Paris when he died. At Trouville, on October 15, 1869, they wrote in the *Journal*: 'We learn here of the death of Sainte-Beuve. The deceased has certainly not been repaid for all his courtesy and kindness to less important members of the press.' Nor, indeed, for that which he had shown to them.

On the subject of *Madame Gervaisis*, Philippe Serret wrote in *L'Univers*: 'One does not make a study of piety, one does not analyse it in cold blood as if it were the most ordinary of scientific phenomena, one practises it or else one is condemned to the sad state of knowing absolutely nothing about it.' From the point of view of sound logic the conversion of their heroine is apparently valid, but logic is scarcely in question with a woman who passes from philosophy to mysticism run mad! The explanation of her conversion by the influence of the mental climate of Rome is hardly convincing either. Rome provided

Their Two Last Novels

as many reasons for taking an aversion to Catholicism as for being attracted towards it. We agree with Barbey d'Aurevilly's judgement of the book. 'Conceived according to the objective methods of Renan, this mummified intelligence, with its coldly lifeless processes, *Madame Gervaisis* is no more a true study of the conversion of a soul that has turned to Christianity than Renan's life of Jesus Christ is actually his life. MM. de Goncourt had no knowledge of anything beyond the superficial characteristics of Catholic matters.'

George Sand wrote in a letter on March 6, 1869: 'It is possibly the life history of Liszt, it is also that of Mme Plessy. It is most certainly, on the grand scale—for you are great idealists—a full summing-up, carried through to its most positive expression, of conversions in this present age.' But she did not hide her opinion of their style. 'I hate neologisms, adjectives turned into adverbs, unnatural things that appear pretentious and which I have not met with in your previous works... You think that the subject should make the expression conform to and identify itself with it. For my part, I do not believe it should... A style which tries to adapt itself to the matter is no longer a real style.'

Renan did not write to them until December 4. 'My dear friends, will you forgive me for this long delay? It is only today that I have been able to continue the reading, so many times to my sorrow interrupted, of *Madame Gervaisis*... I will give a short notice to the *Débats*, a notice very unworthy of the book but in which will assuredly be seen the friendship I feel for the authors.'

Jules Levallois, in *L'Opinion Nationale*, to which he had returned, tried in vain to swim against the hostile current. In official and bourgeois circles the book had been judged dangerous, immoral and anti-religious. In the Tuileries Benedetti, the Ambassador in Berlin, was rebuked by the Duchesse de Sagan for having read it.

On the whole, it was a disappointment whose stinging blow to their pride an enthusiastic letter from Flaubert was only able to soften in some slight degree. Did they guess their friend's secret disapproval? At the same time, Flaubert had said in writing to George Sand: 'What an odd folly is this of trying to be witty where there is no occasion for it and of wanting to distinguish oneself, to be smart in fact, instead of admiring things with the dumb simplicity of a bourgeois! That's what a craze for originality, the common abuse of literature, leads to.' And to the Princess: 'What is your opinion of

Madame Gervaisis? Between ourselves, I dare not tell you that I find this book very remarkable, since you yourself have an exacting taste.'

Jules Claretie said that at the time of its publication *Madame Gervaisis* sold a hundred copies at the most. Edmond made Philippe Burty a present of the manuscript. He burnt the manuscripts of all the other novels he had written in collaboration with Jules.

XVII
The House at Auteuil

Towards the end of 1867, in order to increase their accommodation, the brothers had rented a small flat adjoining their own. 'An infernally hectic life, during all this month of November: publishing a book, putting a flat in order, coping with tradesmen of every sort, arranging a library, composing a brain-racking work on the vignettists of the eighteenth century, and each of us following a diet and trying to renew our strength a little. Our motto in this vile world should be: *In spite of everything*. While waiting to adopt it for ourselves, we are giving it to the hero of our play [*Mademoiselle de la Rochedragon*].'

It was not long before they regretted their new move. 'Our flat is the only one in the house in which there are any *objets d'art*, and it is also the only one which the rain comes into when it's raining. We have just extended it by a small set of rooms and we thought we had arranged our little home most admirably; and now there is an ostler who makes it impossible for us to sleep in the early morning or to work during the day by shouting, bellowing and whistling every day for six hours on end.'

In this early part of 1868 Jules developed a positive phobia about noise. Edmond, perhaps out of sympathy, was similarly afflicted, and so they decided to sell their farm at Breuvannes and buy a house where they would be sure of silence.

Poor Jules had lost his appetite and could not sleep. The least movement, the least exercise of will, required an enormous effort. 'The little things, the trifling matters that poison private life, the accumulation of pin-pricks that in the long run amount to torture, seem at this moment to be falling upon us from all sides. Mother Bazelaire has a husband who is dying. Old Marguérite [these were two peasants from Lorraine], whom we have called in, falls ill on her arrival. We have to slip away from our work to warm up some broth for her and take it up to her room. We cannot make final arrangements for selling our farm to that obstinate peasant. A swarm of troubles comes from our flat, it's like a pantomime where everything goes against some unlucky fellow, children scampering overhead, dogs barking furiously in the courtyard, cabmen whistling and singing, silence incessantly shattered around us, a kind of perpetual conspiracy of everything against our work. It makes us ill and affects our stomachs, which have become, so to speak, a trouble-centre of quivering sensibility, of nervous agitation; and in all this we have to find the peace, the composure, the inward silence necessary for the work we want to write.'

In May, Flaubert having announced in a very graphic letter that he was returning to Croisset, driven away by noise from the boulevard du Temple, from the Grand Hôtel, the Hôtel du Helder, the neighbouring baths, and du Camp's flat, Jules wrote to him in reply: 'I met someone who told me you had gone mad. I answered angrily that you had the right to do so. Oh! noise, noise, noise! I cannot... endure the sound of birds any longer! I have got to the point of crying out as Deburau did to the nightingale: "Won't you shut up, you horrid creature!" Put everything aside! We are setting off *to sleep three whole days* at Fontainebleau.'

There they felt so dejected, so deserted by everyone, that they rushed into each other's arms without being able to utter a word.

They had caught sight of Jeanne de Tourbey for the first time on December 11, 1859, at the first night of *La Tireuse de Cartes*, by Victor Séjour and Mocquard, at the Porte-Saint-Martin. Later on, in 1865, Flaubert had taken them along to see her at home. 'A stage courtesan's flat with various accessories. The woman herself talks in a cutting, staccato nervous way, with forced attempts at wit; a livid face, eyes horribly encircled, and an air of death about her, a lingering, self-intoxicated agony.' They learnt from Hector Crémieux of her intention to sell a house she owned in the Parc des Princes on the edge of the Bois de Boulogne. Trees and silence, this would be their salvation. With their farm at Breuvannes sold at last, they made Jeanne de Tourbey an offer. Whilst they were taking the waters at Vichy in July, 1868, she wired to them that she had agreed to the price of 48,000 francs.

'Do you know this particular house?' wrote Jules to Flaubert. 'It looks like a week-end cottage owned by the Sultan Misapouf, but its comical quaintness has completely infatuated us; there is a little bit of garden and, with the addition of a studio we shall build next year, we shall have somewhere we can sleep and work... Fortunately there is a spare room.'

The House at Auteuil

What Jeanne de Tourbey did not know was that the house had just been sold by her lover, Baroche, to someone else. This was a bitter disappointment to them, in spite of Sainte-Beuve's attempts to point out the disadvantages of the house; Jeanne de Tourbey's doctor, for instance, had said it was unhealthy.

The Princess undertook to search with Gautier for a little house in the neighbourhood of Enghien. Gautier told them in confidence that she would have made them a present of it. However, they did not have to refuse this gift, for on August 4, while they were staying at Saint-Gratien, on their return from Vichy, another house, 53 boulevard du Montmorency, was suggested to them. They immediately decided to acquire it. 'We are there, on the front steps of this longed-for house in Auteuil. The sun is still shining and the leaves on the bushes glitter under a shower from a garden hose. "Eighty-two thousand francs?" asks my brother, and both our hearts are beating.—"I will write to you tomorrow," says the other, "and will probably accept your offer." "Eighty-three thousand francs, and your immediate reply?" The owner thought it over for five endless minutes, then he let fall a melancholy, "It's agreed".'

The price, almost twice that of Jeanne de Tourbey's little cottage, was unreasonably high, but they liked the house so much. And what a retreat for their work! What a feeling of superiority their remoteness from Paris would give them! As if intoxicated by this impression they added a crowning touch to their folly by buying a Japanese bronze that cost 2,000 francs.

The house ran alongside the boulevard. Besides a garden, it had on the ground floor a dining-room, a drawing-room, a cloakroom and a kitchen. On the first floor it had three bedrooms, two dressing-rooms, and two rooms for servants; on the second, two bedrooms with sloping ceilings, an attic and a boxroom. Jules's bedroom was on this floor.

Their purchase of this very bourgeois dwelling in the style of Louis Philippe is rather surprising. As lovers of the eighteenth century, why should they not have preferred a house of that period, which might have reminded Edmond of the Courmonts' lovely house at Ménilmontant? There was no lack of such houses in Passy. And what a strange idea for neurasthenics, driven from the centre of Paris by its noise, to go and live alongside a railway 'rumbling, whistling, creating a disturbance on sleepless nights'. To be near the recently built station was an advantage; but on the other hand how disadvantageous!

The description Frantz Jourdain has left of this quarter of Paris helps to explain what may have decided the Goncourts to settle there. 'It is one of the most charming quarters of Paris, with a bit of open country twenty minutes away from the boulevard, and a hundred leagues removed from the hubbub of the capital, a modern oasis where the pretty little villas are tactfully built not more than two storeys high, so as not to hide from anyone the charming panorama bounded only by the horizon, with Mont Valérien, the slopes on the banks of the Seine, and the forest of Meudon as a background. No factories, no shops, no businesses, no heavy waggons, very few passers-by, and hardly any sign of life. With its trimly correct appearance, its lavish parade of good form, its sunny aspect, its elegant tranquillity, its atmosphere redolent of the sharp odour of the neighbouring woods, Auteuil gives me the impression of one of those winter gardens, far away from ceremonial drawing-rooms, where you go to rest and take your ease on nights when there is dancing, and where the noise of merrymaking and the sound of the orchestra penetrate only as a dim and indefinable echo. You feel that Paris is there, that you have only to turn round to get the impression of its fiery breath, but you do not see it and you scarcely hear it.'

XVIII

Self-Portraits

'The two brothers not only loved each other, they were also bound to each other by mysterious links, ties of the spirit, interlocking particles of their twin natures . . . although they were of very different ages and had characters diametrically opposed. Their first instinctive impulses were identical. They felt equally sudden sympathies and antipathies, and, if they went anywhere, would come away from the place with completely similar impressions of the people they had met. Not only individuals, but also things, in . . . their pleasing or displeasing qualities, appealed to each of them in the same way. Finally, as regards ideas, those creations of the brain whose birth is so entirely a matter of caprice and which often astonish you by their arrival "from heaven knows where", those ideas which as a rule are seldom simultaneous . . . in partnerships founded on love between men and women, such ideas came into being simultaneously with the two brothers, who very often would turn to each other after a period of silence to say the very same thing without being able to discover any explanation of the curious chance of meeting with two remarks from two mouths that only amounted to one.'

On this fraternal companionship between the Zemganno brothers Edmond lingers with visibly tender emotion. Both brothers suffered by separation from each other, they felt 'odd man out' when not together. Whenever he left the house the younger brother seemed to take the elder one's mind away with him. If the absent one was late coming home, the other was assailed with gloomy forebodings of some accident, which made him open the door of their flat so as to hear his brother's step from as far off as possible. The natural kinship of brothers had become still closer through successes and failures shared between them. 'Thus it was,' says Edmond in his novel, 'that these two beings had arrived at the point of possessing between the two of them—a fact almost unique in human friendships—one vanity only, and one pride which was at the same time either wounded or flattered in each.'

Edmond and Jules

This intimate sense of brotherhood, so deeply rooted in their common sensibility, is openly declared by Edmond in the preface to the *Journal*: 'This diary is our nightly confession: the confession of two lives inseparable in their pleasures, their work, and their sorrows, of . . . two minds receiving from their contact with people and things impressions so similar . . . so homogeneous, that it can be considered as the outpourings of a single *me* and a single *I*.' He should have added that almost the whole of the first part of the *Journal* is in the younger brother's hand; his own is rarely met with. It is Jules who here analyses himself and makes his own confession, analysing and confessing for his brother at the same time. Edmond nevertheless recognized that they were very unlike in character: Jules with a quick and lively mind, given to making pert and witty remarks, full of whimsicality and zest; Edmond, less sparkling and more dispassionate, rather taciturn and reserved, seldom eager for enjoyment, but fundamentally more warm-hearted, more mature as well, less of an artist but more of a human being. It is not certain that Edmond always agreed with Jules, but he admired and adored him and made it his duty to adopt and ratify his opinions and impressions, though not without sometimes making adjustments to them.

Jules fair, Edmond dark, both of them wearing their hair like an artist's, both with monocles, both inveterate smokers. Less stiff and less upright in his carriage than Edmond, more lively in his ways and in his mind, Jules was a fine young fellow. Edmond was a handsome man.

They delighted in their exemplary fellowship as brothers, prided themselves on it and were excited by it. 'Yesterday,' wrote Jules, 'I was at one end of the big table at the château. Edmond was chatting . . . at the other. I could hear nothing, but when he smiled I did so involuntarily with the same inclination of my head . . . Never have souls so similar been put into two bodies.' This is a touching confession, but here is a passage perhaps even more significant: 'We are not surprised at not being famous. I am not referring here to our books, our qualifications, our literary talent. I am considering our moral worth and strength. First of all, this great *impedimentum* of man; love and woman, reduced to its simplest terms. None of these low, promiscuous associations we see everywhere around us, those snug little partnerships, those counterfeits of married life which hinder a man in his career, occupy his thoughts, and turn him aside from a single-minded and free exercise of his will; love with us takes up five hours a week, from ten o'clock till eleven, and not a thought before or after. Another source of our strength, and one that is also rare, is a faculty of observation, of weighing and judging men, an expert knowledge and an intuitive sense as readers of character from outward appearance, which enables us to uncover personalities at first glance, to get right inside the people we rub up against, to manipulate all the strings that work these puppets, to divine and deduce each man's human characteristics; a great faculty for getting the luck all on our side, of faking the cards with which we play, of loading the dice and making game of our neighbours. Then there is also the advantage of a positive cast of mind, a fixed point in the will and the understanding, this quality that gives substantial form to acts and consistency to life. Above all, even above the perpetual tension of one's mind and heart... our utter devotion to one single end. We are two: *he and I*, egotism in a fraternity of minds. Imagine, if you can, two men, two brains, two souls, two active spirits, two wills linked, and riveted, and knit together... even in their self-conceit! Leaning on each other, drawing strength from each other, acting as each other's support, with no need to confide in or surrender themselves to any other person, and finding in themselves an outlet for emotion, a double cannon-ball that follows the same course, even when it describes a curve—how is it then it has not yet found its mark?'

In April, 1864, still sitting opposite each other at the table where they had just had dinner, they began a kind of examination of conscience: 'We who, in point of fact, are not two persons, we who suffer at the same time from the same fits of despondency, the same anxieties, the same illnesses, who together form a single lonely, splenetic, and sickly individual. Through all this in both of us there pass stray inclinations to diversion and longings for amusement. With the elder, these longings are those of a man who has little appetite for pleasure, with the younger... that of a young man whose youth has been spent without experiencing any enjoyment. But with both of us this has happened through lack of initiative, of worldly wisdom, and even for want of courage to enter into conversation with women. Thus we find a savour of insipidity in life and perpetual disgust in the troublesome business of living.'

Does that mean that they resembled each other absolutely, that they actually formed one single and identical personality? No, their characters afforded very marked contrasts. Jules wrote: 'I have not the same aspirations as the other one of us two. For him, if he were not what he is, his inclinations would be towards married life, towards that bourgeois dream of life in communion with a sentimental wife. He is a passionate, tender, melancholy individual, while I am a mournful materialist... I also feel something in myself of the eighteenth-century abbé, with little cruel sides to my nature belonging to the Italian Renaissance, not however with a taste for blood or physical suffering in other people, but somewhat inclined to a spirit of malice. In Edmond, on the contrary, there is almost an excess of simple good-nature. He was born in Lorraine, he has a Germanic temperament. I am a Latin, a native of Paris. Edmond can perfectly well imagine himself as a soldier in another century, with no dislike for fighting and with a fondness for idle dreaming. For my part, I rather see myself engaged in chapter house business, in the diplomatic schemes of religious communities, taking great pride in deceiving men and women for the sake of the ironical spectacle they afford... In short, a curious thing about us is the absolute difference in temperament, tastes and character, and identically the same ideas, the same sympathies and antipathies concerning other people, and the same intellectual point of view.'

Their mutual understanding did not exclude a few rare clashes of humour, or more precisely of ill-humour: 'Between us, there is no other cause of offence... of irritated nerves, than is produced by the desperate anguish of a literary career and of bringing out a book. This puts us into a state of fretful annoyance with ourselves which sometimes rebounds from one to the other in mutual bitterness. This happens when our work is not going well, when we are incapable of... attaining that ideal which in literature is always rising higher and higher and withdrawing itself farther from your pen. Then come gloomy fits of despair when... we are tempted by ideas of suicide... we review all the denials of justice we have both experienced... all the bad luck, the disappointments, the failures... the sickly state of health which does not leave a single day without one of us being ill or feeling anxious about the other's sufferings.'

There was nothing, even including criticisms and attacks, that they did not attribute to what they called their unparalleled fraternity. 'A fresh symptom of the envy and the hatred provoked by the success of our name and our books. Open indignation is now directed not only

Self-Portraits

against the form of our work and our ideas, but also against our duality, our unexampled brotherly association. In a twelve-page slating in the *Revue des Deux Mondes*, in the long attack on us in *Le Figaro*, there is flagrant and shameless animosity ... against the twin characteristics in our ideas and works ... it is this marriage, this union of ours in brotherhood which they attack. They hate us for loving each other!'

What is certain is that people did not like them. Their disappointed literary ambitions, their bitterness as unappreciated authors was all too evident. What real men of letters they were! No one has ever been so to such a degree as they.

A study of their system of collaboration would be a difficult task. Robert Ricatte has ventured on it, and not without some success. 'Every evening,' so Edmond confided to Alidor Delzant, 'one of the brothers, but more often Jules, would begin to write while the other, standing behind him, would suggest a picturesque touch, or give more liveliness or force to a phrase by the addition of a word or epithet'. The first part of the *Journal* is almost entirely in Jules's handwriting. He made current use of the term 'I'; so too, did the Tharaud brothers. One would not swear that this 'I' delighted Edmond, even though he allowed it to remain in his definitive edition of the *Journal*. In *En 18* . . . their respective contributions have not been satisfactorily blended; on Edmond's own admission, two distinct styles of writing can be recognized in this work. In the notes made while they were in Italy M. Max Fuchs has identified some differences in manner and inspiration, Jules, frequently a violent colourist, instinctively inclining towards broadly comical sketches of things and people, and homely and picturesque comparisons. Edmond on the other hand showing himself more sensitive to half-tones and chiaroscuro, also more methodical, a trifle pedantic at times in his treatment of pictures, and given to making insulting generalizations. In the historical works and the biographical studies of artists, Edmond's part is more important than Jules's, while the contrary holds good in *Charles Demailly* and *Manette Salomon*, especially with regard to style. In *Sœur Philomène*, *Renée Mauperin*, *Germinie Lacerteux* and *Madame Gervaisis*, the particular tendencies of the two brothers, if we can go by Edmond, are perfectly balanced, but Ricatte points out that his evidence on this matter is given at a late date and his other admissions contradict it.

According to Alidor Delzant, when it was a question of writing

Edmond and Jules

a book, the two brothers, plentifully supplied with cigarettes, would draw up a plan, put their heads together and agree about some descriptive fragment they remembered having 'pressed' in their *herbarium* of notes. The subject would next be broken up in their minds into a number of distinct pictures. The work, with all its various developments, would begin to come to life. First they attacked the beginning and the end, each of them shut in his own room and composing the same chapter. Then would begin long sessions in which the two texts were blended and the salient features of the style precisely fixed. This method explains the reason for the accumulated epithets and the repeated juxtaposition of similar expressions which did not meet with Sainte-Beuve's approval. 'But from this also comes the exuberant complexity of the period,' says Delzant, 'its solid structure, its muscular strength, and the undertones of meaning that develop and go through their evolutions freely beneath the gymnastics of the style'. In these gymnastics, Jules showed himself more exacting and more eager than his brother: 'I see him still,' writes Edmond, 'going over passages we had written together and which had satisfied us at first, working again at them for hours, or for half a day at a stretch, with an almost passionate obstinacy, changing an epithet here, there giving rhythm to a sentence, further on revising a turn of phrase ... wearing his brain out in pursuit of that perfect form of the French language so hard and sometimes so impossible to attain in expressing modern subjects and sensations.' No workmanship of this kind appears in the manuscript of the *Journal*, where only a very few things are altered or scratched out. Much of it, however, is probably only a fair copy of the original.

The *idée fixe* of a general hostility towards them of which the *Journal* gives proof certainly had a pathological origin. When it was not because of their fraternity that people hated them, it was because they were neither office-holders nor bureaucrats, neither married nor fathers of families, or else because they were thought to be rich, because their names had the prefix 'de', because the age was opposed to them, or, quite simply, because it was so. 'A kind of league against us prevents us from taking possession, in our lifetime, of our little portion of fame. This does not deprive us in the least of our confidence in or of our intuitive knowledge of the future, but it makes us feel bitter that during the whole of our lives nothing, or almost nothing, will be repaid to us for all that we have contributed that is new and human and artistic; while... the racket raised by the smallest little talents makes so much noise and these little talents earn such a prodigious income.' On March 28, 1869, they remarked: 'To be respected and hated, such is our lot...' At this date, the exacerbation of this state of mind is certainly to be explained by Jules's illness.

There is little doubt that this disease, contracted in 1859, found in him a soil that was favourable to its growth and prepared for it by his literary labours. As far back as April 26, 1859, he had confessed that he suffered from abnormal irritability. 'It seems to me that everything around me is like music out of tune. I suffer from contact with others... My servant, my mistress, both appear more stupid to me than they once were. My friends bore me and seem to talk about themselves more than usual... Everything I approach, everything I touch, everything I perceive rubs my nerves up the wrong way.'

On March 10, 1866, comes this confession: 'We are bored with everything, wounded by everything, suffer from everything, and yet find nothing in the lives or position or fortune of other people that we... desire, or envy.'

Did their strenuous habits of writing have anything to do with their discontent? They believed so, they were convinced that observation, instead of dulling their sensitivity, had increased, refined, developed it and left it exposed. 'The unceasing study... of one's sensations, of the inclinations of one's heart, the perpetual and daily anatomical dissection of one's whole being, ends in uncovering its most delicate fibres, in making them vibrate in the most surprising way... By dint of studying oneself, instead of getting harder one becomes a sensitive sort of being with a mind stripped of its skin, wounded by the least touch, defenceless, exposed, and dripping with blood.'

As almost always happens, this hyper-sensibility was accompanied by an insurmountable tendency to boredom, a tendency from which they sought relief by working and by expeditions to second-hand dealers, old curiosity shops, and dealers in autographs. They also reacted by telling themselves that this boredom, together with lack of success, was a proof of their superiority. 'One thing reassures me of our worth: the boredom that haunts us. That is the measure of men's worth in modern times. It was the death of Chateaubriand, Byron died of it before he was born. The essential quality of bourgeois talent is gaiety.'

Edmond and Jules

This nervously tense and bored frame of mind, aggravated by conceit and readiness to belittle others, was not calculated to win them friendships, sympathy, or visitors. They congratulated themselves on this and at the same time complained of it. On February 25, 1865, they wrote: 'It is impossible to imagine the isolated life we lead at present while our book makes a stir, a noise, and a scandal. Fewer letters, fewer visitors, less unexpected news by post or rings at our door-bell than the most insignificant little bourgeois in the Marais. Our life seems bent on being dull.'

Dull and sad. Sadness with them was inherent in their constitution. How could it have been otherwise? 'All observers are sad and needs must be so. They look on at life. They are not actors in it, but eye-witnesses ... Their normal state of mind is of mournful serenity.' At other times, however, they refused to accept this distressing fatality inherent in their natures. 'This evening we say to each other that we have been sad, bored and dejected all day. Why?... Is sadness possibly a thing for which there is no reason, an aimless impulse? Or rather is there not beneath one's ill-disposed temper always some hidden cause that escapes our notice? Could it be resentment of the increasing monotony of a life that for some time past has been even less eventful than usual? A life in which nothing unexpected happens, where there are no letters in the porter's lodge, where you are not disturbed ... and the people you see appear as hackneyed as twice-told tales? Would it be the pause in our work, the rest in the middle of our novel that gives us this feeling of emptiness and stagnation? Or could it simply be something one does not admit to oneself, the fact that among two lines of novelists' names that I read in a newspaper this morning—ours is not mentioned? I prefer to believe it is all of these things; for, apart from physical ills, money troubles, wounds to our pride, and sad misgivings on other people's account, if boredom alone possessed our minds it would be a very desperate business.'

When writing to his friend Chavannes and confessing to him that there is something indescribably lymphatic, some weakness of fibre, in himself, Charles Demailly adds that in order to react against the monotony of life, he needs a breath of keen air, a little sharp gust of wind: 'I appreciate, as giving health to my mind and a fillip to my work, the excitation and stimulus of society, a society of intelligent minds, you understand, of people interested in ideas.' 'A host of things in our age,' he remarks elsewhere, 'make for numbness in life and in ideas. The brain, like the earth, grows cold. There is an incubation of the mind that can only take place in the heat, in the tumult, in the contact with other minds.' The brothers therefore were fond of discussion, and all the more because they were generally alone in their opinion.

This weakness of fibre they sometimes attributed to their education, without however realizing that this timid attitude towards life had come from an education too exclusively feminine and too much under a mother's influence; a father's authority had been lacking, but they did not think of this when they wrote: 'It is a great misfortune to have been born, as we were, in this present century, at the wrong moment, astride two types of society, to have been brought up and educated according to those ideas of reason, prudence and good sense held by our parents... This out-of-date education makes us apply a scrupulous caution to everything in life, a shyness, a trepidation not to be found in young people of today. In short, we lack that dare-devil quality, that capacity to stake our all, that dashing recklessness of the present age.'

Although sad, discontented and sick at heart, these unfortunate propensities did not prevent them from having a decided liking for women, but they liked them only for the pleasure they afforded their eyes and for the sake of a few favours accorded at certain fixed times. 'What delightful moments,' notes Jules referring to Maria, 'such as seeing her in one's bedroom in her dressing-jacket with her skirts tucked up and billowing round her, a little bare flesh showing here and there; or sunk in an arm-chair, purring like a cat, or again, in a secluded path in the park, lying full length, her arms around her head and her dress flowing about her—white and lazy, arresting the envious glance of the sunburnt woman selling cocoa-nuts...' This same Maria inspired some other observations by Jules. 'A woman is not self-sufficient. She does not go of her own volition. The heat of her passion needs to be roused, to be instigated, to be given the right key-note. You have to whip up the tempo, her thoughts, her conversation, her nerves. If she is not sternly held in breathless suspense you will find her immersed in idle, foolish dreams.' Charles Demailly's diary contains a paragraph which should be placed beside this. 'A woman always seems to have to defend herself against her own instinctive weakness. In relation to everything and to nothing there arises in her a conflict of contrary desires, a riot of rebellious little whims . . . a war of eternal little decisions that seem to be made wantonly. Contrariness, in her eyes, is the real proof of her existence. Capriciousness is her way of exercising her will. In these furtive, polite, but irritating battles a woman wins a shameless ascendancy . . . over her wearied opponent . . .'

Charles Demailly cannot forgive himself for having got married. He gets indignant because the contemporary novel exalts and pities the wife who is misunderstood and tied to a coarse and selfish husband. 'In married life a wife is almost always the solvent of her husband's honour, I mean honour in its highest, purest and most foolishly ideal sense. She is the counsellor who, in the name of material interests, prompts men to lower their standards, forcing them to accept mediocrity, acts of meanness, in short, all those wretched, petty compromises with conscience.' But what sort of experience, indeed, had they themselves had? Had they not heard of devoted wives keeping artists and writers of the Bohemian world from drink, from debts, from sloth and poverty? Of wives who were flouted, deceived, deserted, left alone with their children to look after, or devoting themselves to preserving, at least in appearances, the dignity of a home?

Their own vow of celibacy seems to have proceeded as much from their attachment to their vocation as artists as from their misogyny. The opinions they ascribe to Coriolis in *Manette Salomon* are in fact their own. 'According to him, celibacy was the only state that left the artist his liberty, his powers, his brain, his conscience . . . He saw, indeed, all sorts of servitudes, abdications and weakening influences in the innocent but foolish happiness of marriage, that gentle, comfortable state, that soothing atmosphere, in which the nervous system is relaxed and the fiery passion that makes men create extinguished.'

Melancholy, disgust, boredom, disquietude, misanthropy—none of them impaired their satisfaction with themselves. Fundamentally sceptical and disillusioned, they had no doubts about either their talent or the nobility and independence of their own characters. 'There are spirits that are menials born and created for the service of those in authority . . . of that terrible dominator of man's conscience, success— and these are in the majority and are the happiest of men. But others are born, and we are of that number, with a feeling of revolt against those who triumph, with a warm sense of sympathy and kinship with those who are beaten and trampled underfoot in the vulgar victory

Self-Portraits

of mass ideas and opinions, in short, with that generous and unhappy pugnacity, which, from the age of eight or ten, leads them to fight the tyrant of their class and obliges them to remain for the rest of their lives in the opposition party in politics, literature and art.'

That essential superiority which they ascribed to themselves lay in the sensibility proper to their aristocratic character. 'As for talent, possibly we have some... but we draw less pride from having talent than from considering ourselves a species of sensitive beings of infinite delicacy, who vibrate in a superior fashion, and are veritable artists in our appreciation of the braised pullet's wing that we are eating at this moment, of a picture, a drawing, a lacquer box, a woman's linen headdress, and the supreme and exquisite qualities of every delicate object that lies beyond the coarse perceptions of the general public.' Their great merit was, as they themselves said, and we must admit they were right, that of having been the first 'who write with their nerves'.

How could these aristocrats fail to have been severe towards the more ordinary of their colleagues? We call to mind the preface to the *Journal*. 'We do not conceal from ourselves that we have been passionate, nervously excitable, morbidly impressionable creatures, and because of this sometimes unjust. But... if we sometimes express ourselves with the injustice that comes from prejudice or blind, unreasoning antipathy, we have never knowingly lied about any of the people we mention.' It is to be feared, however, that the full text of the *Journal* (still to be published) gives the impression of general and systematic denigration.

So gloomy a view did they take of the servile obligations imposed on ambition that it appears naïve: 'Yes, indeed, in order to succeed one must be a mediocrity and a menial, with a personality as amorphous as regards talent as regards character, in a carriage one must sit back to the horses, hand people their hats from the hat-stand, etc., and do such things never out of politeness, but always in a spirit of servility. Nothing takes one farther, under this régime of servitude, than dancing attendance on its ministers.'

When they write in praise of the man of letters as such, it is, make no mistake, of themselves that they are thinking: 'Great moral force in a writer... enables him to lift his thoughts above everyday life, and lets them work freely... He must hold himself aloof from the cares, the worries, the tribulations and discomforts of existence in order to rise to that serenity of mind in which he can conceive and create ... And this is not, believe me, a mere mechanical operation as simple in application as the adding up of numbers.'

A matter on which they have very rightly given themselves their due is that of their cult of art and their high standard of integrity as men of letters. If, when they started, their need of money had made them look to the theatre for a financial success, their vocation as pure, disinterested artists had made itself plain from the time they turned away from journalism; their difficulties and disappointments only had the effect of strengthening it. Already on October 16, 1856, Jules, then aged twenty-six, was writing in the *Journal*: 'These fits of despair, these doubts, not of ourselves but as to whether the time and the circumstances are favourable, create a more obstinate, more intractable, and more prickly literary conscience, instead of making us stoop to make concessions. And, for a brief moment, we consider whether we should not think and write absolutely for ourselves alone, leaving renown, the publisher and the public to others. But, as Gavarni says: "No man is perfect".'

To write for oneself alone, to forgo success and even the idea of publication was a temptation that would never have occurred to a writer of the romantic age. Aggravated, however, by the disillusioning experiences of the revolution of 1848, the misunderstanding between artists and bourgeois society had grown all the greater. We see here the beginnings of an evolution whose graph does not seem to be nearing its end. The Goncourts and their companions, men like Gautier, Flaubert, Saint-Victor and Baudelaire, kept a belief in art that we have lost.

Remarking on the general deceitfulness of politics, Jules writes: 'This leads in the long run to disillusionment, to a distaste for belief in anything, to a toleration of any sort of government, and a lack of interest which I find in all my fellow writers, and in Flaubert as well as myself. You realize that you must not die for a cause, no matter what, you must put up with whatever government exists, however antipathetic it may be to you, and believe in nothing but art and profess nothing except literature. All the rest is a snare and delusion.'

Art was for them the first and last word of all: 'I believe that since the beginning of the world there have hardly ever existed any living beings so entirely swallowed up by or so engulfed in matters of art and the intelligence as ourselves. Where this is absent, we should lack something like the power to breathe. Books, pictures and engravings limit the horizon of our vision. Reading, gazing, this is the way we spend our lives; *Hic sunt tabernacula nostra* . . .'

Consciousness of their moral superiority was naturally accompanied by an equal consciousness of their importance in the spheres of taste and historical studies. 'Now and then feelings of pride arise within us on noting what we have contributed of ourselves, our tastes and our particular crazes to this age which we have trained to follow these new fashions: art-collections, autographs, history in a graphic form, and the eighteenth century.' If their contemporaries did not do them justice, they at least discharged this duty.

Had their love for art stifled a love for nature to the extent that they claimed? They themselves made many declarations to this effect. 'In front of a good landscape I feel myself more in the country than in the midst of fields and woods. What a tame, uninteresting thing the country is, and how little it suits a combative frame of mind. This calm, this silence, this absence of movement, these tall trees with their leaves curling up in the heat like the feet of web-footed birds, this is something to delight the hearts of women, children and solicitors' clerks. But does not a thoughtful man feel ill at ease here, as if face to face with the enemy, as if confronted by that work of God which in the end will devour him, making fertile mould and green vegetation out of his philosopher's brain? Among the stones of great cities you escape from these ideas ... In ancient times, the country was neither a mother, nor a sister, neither a comforter, nor an intimate friend; it was not, as it is for us, an elegy on Nature, nor that region of romance, that land of dreams, coloured by the pantheism of a bourgeois Sunday. It was a place of rest, a respite from business, an excuse for idleness, a place where conversation escaped from the ordinary concerns of life and the town, and where thought took a holiday. One very characteristic thing in our dispositions is that of seeing nothing in nature but what is an echo or a reminder of art. Here's a horse in a stable, and immediately one of Géricault's studies is recalled to mind; and the cooper hammering away at a cask in the neighbouring yard brings one of Boissieu's sketches before our eyes ... Nature for me is an enemy. The country seems to me redolent of death. This green earth appears to me a great cemetery lying in wait. This grass feeds on man. These plants spring up and grow green on things that die. This sun which shines so bright and clear is the great corrupter ... nothing of all these things in nature appeals to me, nothing has any meaning for my heart. No, this sort of thing does not move me, as did that woman at dinner a short time ago who had a forehead like that of Andrea del Sarto's *Charity*, and the mouth of a ghoul in the *Arabian Nights*. No, that does not move me like the talk I heard yesterday, the brisk and cruel gossip B ...'s son retailed on the subject of Mirès.[1] A woman's face and a man's conversation; in these alone I take pleasure and interest.'

They were bored in the country, but possibly they did not find this boredom so unpleasing. Take, for instance, this note on a visit to Gretz. 'Here from day to day a foolish sort of gladness wells up in me more and more ... I feel as if the sun were under my skin, and lying in the orchard under the shade of the apple-trees, on straw from the washer-women's baskets, a gentle, happy dullness grows within me ... It is a delightful state, thought is suspended, your eyes gaze nowhere, dreams are unbounded by a horizon, days drift aimlessly by, and ideas follow the flight of white butterflies among the cabbages.' In short, they loved the country as they loved women, from a physical point of view, without giving their heart to it. They have, however, described certain landscapes, among them those of the Seine in *Charles Demailly*, modelled on their memories of Bar-sur-Seine, too well to have been always bored and melancholy in the country; also they themselves were too fine as painters of pictures not to have understood and experienced the love of nature that was in favour among the artists of their day.

Music, very much more than nature, was for them a world hermetically sealed. 'What I like above all in music,' says the *Journal*, 'is the women who listen to it ... On the great number of lunatics —shut up or at large—among musicians, Berthelot remarked very subtly: "They are people who feel but who do not think".' Charles Demailly, who is not ashamed to admit that he has absolutely no ear at all, makes the grossly stupid remark that 'a woman who does not like music and a man who does are both imperfect beings'. Edmond himself, however, was not so proud of not having an ear as might be believed, since he withdrew from the *Journal* this note by Jules dated June 1861: 'Edmond has never been able to remember any tune except one: *Rendez-moi ma patrie*. This comes back to him

---

[1] Jewish banker and newspaper proprietor of scandalous reputation.

whenever he is sad and he sings it almost in tune—a strange effect of the mind on the body.'

★ ★ ★

In religion they never varied. Scepticism, or, to put it frankly, atheism, began with them in adolescence, if not in childhood. There is no sign in their work of any faith that they, like so many others, might have abandoned on their initiation to life and to philosophy. Not only were they sceptics but often a trace of anti-Christian feeling breaks through in their writings: 'The greatest strength of the Christian religion,' they wrote on one occasion, 'is that it is the religion for the sad occasions of life, its misfortunes, disappointments, diseases, and everything that troubles the heart, the mind and the body. It addresses itself to people who suffer. It promises consolation to those who need it, hope to those who despair. The ancient religions were religions of man's joys and the festive occasions of life. Since then the world has grown old and sorrowful. The difference here is that between a garland of roses and a pocket handkerchief. Christianity is of service to those who weep.'

Like most unbelievers, they came up against the problem of evil: 'Sometimes God appears to me as an executioner and a torturer, and sometimes as a practical joker who amuses himself by cutting the stuffing out of this world's bed, in short, a poisoner with fevers, savage beasts, and insects, of all earthly Paradises, blue skies, fair climates and countries warmed by the sun ... We are roused to revolt against a God who has created death and pain for all living beings, against a God more wicked even than man himself and who does more evil things. As for man, what specific evil, what wickedness, what cruelty is he the author of? War and the judicial system, that is all. Death we can let pass, but what of sickness, suffering, sorrow and everything that tortures our lives? To be almighty and to have created all these things!'

Were they materialists then? Their case was a little more complicated. 'At heart,' wrote Jules on May 2, 1858, 'I am deeply interested in things of the spirit.' In the following October he wrote: 'I am not so fortunate as those people who wear their belief in God like a flannel under-waistcoat which they never leave off, even at night. A spell of sun or rain, fresh fish or game that is rather too high, these cause me now to believe and now to doubt. Survival after death appeals to me when I think of my mother or of ourselves; but an impersonal survival, a *hotch-potch* survival, as I described it to Saint-Victor, leaves me cold. And thereupon I become a materialist... But when I begin to think that my ideas spring from the impact of sensations, and reflect on all that is supernatural and spiritual in me, then my senses kindle a light within me, and immediately I become a spiritualist.'

One evening in 1859, they and Saint-Victor dined at Charles Edmond's house in Bellevue, and as they went down the road from the gare Montparnasse to the rue de Grenelle in brilliant moonlight, they scrutinized the heavens as millions of other human beings had done before them and have done since. But no revelation! And yet! 'It would have been so easy for God... great letters across the sky, a heavenly brightness clearly stamped in characters of fire. Ah! the burning bush should indeed light up again... Well then, we shall have to fall back on Kant. After seeing all the systems and all the creeds he was trying to construct collapsing under his hand and in his mind, he came to the conclusion that nothing was left but morality and a sense of duty... Yes, but that is very cold and very dry. Why are we on this earth? Why does death exist? And after death, what then? That is the most important consideration... and since no one, once dead, has ever returned in those dreams where we are loosed from life, to warn his son or his mother... Ah! my dear fellow, *diis ignotis;* that is the finest altar of the Athenians.'

On the evening of Good Friday, 1868, when they were dining with the wealthy courtesan, La Paiva, the conversation turned on metaphysics and ethics and this gave them an opportunity to define their position. 'Given infinity, what becomes of man's conscience? What becomes of morality? If infinity really exists, what is man? Nothing! Can you imagine a cheese-mite guilty of incest or other crimes?'

Certainly they were materialists. 'Nothing is less poetical than nature and natural concerns. Birth, life, and death, these three things that happen to every living creature are chemical operations. The motions of animal life in this world consist in a process of decomposition and then of recomposition from the heap of decaying matter. It is man himself who has covered all this wretchedness of nature with a veil, with images, symbols and a spirituality that ennobles it.' What then was life? A life-interest in an assemblage of molecules.

Self-Portraits

Their system of metaphysics was limited, but to anyone who might have reproached them for this they would have answered that for their own purposes it was still too extensive, that they even flattered themselves on having none at all.

On July 17, 1891, Edmond made the note: 'In the course of this morning's walk Daudet happened to ask me if my brother had worried about what lies beyond this life. I answered no, and that during his illness he had not once alluded to this after-life in any of his conversations with me. Then Daudet asked me what my convictions were on this matter and I replied that in spite of all my desire to meet my brother again I believed in a complete annihilation of individual personality after death... And Daudet told me that he thought exactly as I did.'

★   ★   ★

As for industrial progress and the industrial system, they had no faith in things of this kind any more than in the Republic; in fact they regarded them with horror. 'Progress, indeed, is simply this: in place of subjecting people to mental torture and wrecking their bodies, it has effectively ruined their brains... Progress has made paupers of all those who had a modest fortune!... What, in fact, does Paris owe to progress? A few boulevards, a few great arterial roads... Yes, it has not left any of those little corners in out-of-the-way streets where formerly you could live happy and hidden from the world... And in everything and everywhere, misrepresentations of the truth, and casuistry, and lies...' But the greatest scourge of all, in their opinion, was education. 'Every mother of the lower classes wants to give, and by dint of pinching and scraping, manages to give, her child the education she has not had herself. From this universal folly, this mania among the lowest ranks of society for thrusting one's children up above oneself, for lifting them up above one's own level, as one lifts children up at a display of fireworks, springs the inevitable lack of respect in this child for its parents. Faults in spelling discredit the father and mother in the eyes of the child who has been to school... and it necessarily follows that the son or the daughter comes to blush for its parents. Then, every career gets overcrowded and blocked by this vulgarization of talents and skills. A day will come when there will no longer be anything except heads and pens. In this tendency of everyone to rise above the family into which he was born, we are on the way towards having no more hands and arms, since workmen are no longer producing a race of workmen, or farm-labourers people of their own stock.'

But if they repudiated the idea of progress, they did not dispute the benefits of civilization, which is a trifle contradictory. 'I am more strongly convinced than ever that everything that is good in mankind comes from civilization, from education, from priding oneself on doing well, a form of vanity that exists only when a particular society is nearing its end. I stand firm also in the belief that a real sense of equality among men is not due to natural, spontaneous pride, but is the result of comparison and reflection, and that the lower classes, who demand it most eagerly, are the people most completely lacking in this idea of equality; among the lower classes, in fact, a man is not the creature of his ideas but of his senses. In everything he sees in society, rank, fortune, and even clothing, he sees everywhere and in everything nothing but a continual show of inequality.'

In an entry of November 18, 1860, the *Journal* contains a surprisingly clever forecast: 'There is perhaps no true liberty for the individual except when he is not yet incorporated in a completely civilized society in which he loses entire possession of himself, his family and his property. The State more especially, since 1789, has been infernally absorbent, and has nicely encroached on every man's individual rights, to the profit of the community; and I wonder whether the future does not hold in store for us, under the name of absolute government by the State, aided by the despotic control of a French bureaucracy, a tyranny far greater than that of a Louis XIV.'

An incident in 1867 inspired them to this prophecy: 'At the World Exhibition, a death blow to the past: the *Americanization* of France, industry awarded priority over art, the steam-driven threshing machine whittling down the space for pictures, articles of vulgar domestic use under cover and statues exposed to the air; in a word, the Federal Republic of Matter.' That same year, in a letter dating from their visit to Rome, this passage occurs: 'I was sitting at dinner yesterday at the Embassy next to a young American woman, the wife of an envoy from the United States in Brussels, and seeing this free-and-easy, jaunty grace, this tireless energy proper to a young nation, this hint of coquettishness that still retains the compelling charm of a flirtation in the young maid who has become a wife, and calling to mind the vivacity and the insinuating ways of certain Americans in

Self-Portraits

Paris, I said to myself that these men and these women seem destined to become the future conquerors of the world.' Referring to the future dominance of America, the *Journal* remarks elsewhere: 'It will be the barbarians of civilization who will swallow up the Latin world just as the horde of uncivilized barbarians devoured it in a former age'.

What they would have liked was an aristocratic society, 'but an aristocracy of talent, open to the common people and recruited on broad lines extending to intelligent minds among the working classes. It would be my dream to have a government that would attempt to wipe out poverty, abolish the pauper's common grave, decree that justice should be administered without fees, appoint poor men's lawyers, whose sole reward should be the honour of occupying that position; a government that would establish before God in the Church freedom from payment and equal conditions for baptisms, marriages and funerals; a government that would provide munificent hospitality for the sick in the hospitals—a government, in short, that would create a Ministry of Public Suffering.' Was there in them then an undercurrent of the humanitarianism of 1848? We would almost be tempted to believe it. 'The sight of a poor man's face,' says the *Journal*, 'saddens me for the rest of the day'.

In politics their views could be summarily defined as consisting in a hatred of Napoleon III, a hatred whose reasons, on Edmond's admission in a note to Jules's *Letters*, were entirely personal: 'The Caesarean socialism of the Empire, and the hostility of its government towards us when we were summoned before the courts during our law-suit to defend the honour of our name at the time of the performance of *Henriette Maréchal*, these have always prevented my brother and myself from ever becoming partisans of this imperial régime, but the sincere and tender and delicate friendship of the woman who happened by chance to be a princess has made *Mathildists* of us, *Mathildists* both affectionate and devoted to her cause.'

In the realm of history their point of view can be briefly summed up as consisting in a horror of the Revolution. 'The mind, supposing it has some little delicacy, is more revolted than the heart by these pages, which are more packed with follies than with crimes. What predominates in this welter of murders is an odour of stupidity. The Revolution presents itself as terrible to no purpose, it is fundamentally silly... And what a host of hypocritical fallacies and lies this

Revolution amounts to! ... What a book remains to be written on the *Humbugs of the Revolution*. For where is opinion about it founded on the real and absolute truth? Who has ever gone back to verifying the documents?' They admired their friend Michelet without sharing his beliefs, and undoubtedly they considered his documentation less reliable than their own. With regard to the Revolution, no one except themselves, so they affirmed, had clearly seen through its lies. 'One man only has handled the history of the Ancien Régime with some trace of impartiality, M. de Tocqueville, and he was too close to the passions of that time.'

Their hatred of democracy might have been roused by the spectacle of 1848. At that period, however, they had held themselves aloof from the struggle, inclining to accept the advent of socialism and communism fairly soon as a fatal necessity. Subsequently a study of the Revolution made them 'reactionaries', but Orléanists, legitimists, or Bonapartists, they certainly were not. They were like those innumerable artists and intellectuals who in our own time find themselves unable to side with democracy because of its vulgarity, its stupidity, its lack of a sense of order, but who are nevertheless disgusted by the self-centredness of bourgeois society. 'There are only two main currents in the history of mankind,' they affirmed; 'meanness which makes men conservatives, and envy which makes them revolutionaries.' In reality, they dreamt, as did Renan, of an intellectual oligarchy. Undoubtedly it was after listening to their table companion at Magny's that they wrote in May, 1868: 'Among the élite of men who think, a visible reaction against universal suffrage and the principle of democracy is taking place; and certain minds begin to see safety for the future in a subjection of the mob to the benevolent rule of an aristocracy of intellect.' Exiles in time, misanthropists, misogynists, melancholy, bored, disdainful, out of their element in their century, irascible, insolent, and highly-strung, pleased with themselves and dissatisfied with others, proud of their own aristocratic temperaments and their acute sensibility, embittered by lack of understanding on the part of critics and the public, sceptics in regard to all political and religious dogmas, if not deliberate atheists or materialists, artists and living only for art, ambitious of success and yet despising it, in short, entirely unadapted for happiness, they were above all neurasthenics. We would, indeed, be tempted to say that their neurasthenia explains them completely, if the physiological determination that was fashionable

Self-Portraits

in their day was still valid. In any analysis of mental phenomena rather more than this must be attributed to mysterious forces, but if Jules's liver complaint and Edmond's stomach troubles cannot completely account for their boredom, their pessimism, their misanthropy, their misogyny, their spleen, and their incapacity for happiness—they were not far from thinking that this explained their talent—these disorders had a good deal to do with it.

Their obsession with illness is one of the most significant manifestations of their neurasthenia. It appears in *Charles Demailly*, in which the hero presents an exact parallel of their own case, in *Sœur Philomène* and its descriptions of hospital life, in the study of pathological traits in *Germinie*, as in *Mme Gervaisis* and *Renée Mauperin*; it is also apparent in the pleasure they took in analysing their own infirmities in detail, and in transcribing, from conversations at Magny's and elsewhere, everything concerning other people's maladies.

The accounts of Edmond by his contemporaries increase considerably as he comes to acquire authority and fame; before Jules's death they are relatively few.

Gautier describes Jules as not looking his age, thanks to his fair complexion, his silky, flaxen hair, and the little pale golden moustache that softened the vivid colouring of his mouth; he was always carefully shaved and dressed as a gentleman should be. In manner he was gayer and more animated than his brother, to whom he was in some ways a source of amusement, always walking in front of him in the street with an impatience to which Edmond indulgently deferred.

Philippe Burty remembered his pupils as being deep blue (not black as Gautier described them) and either flashing or grave with thought, his mouth with an ironical but not at all an acrimonious twist, a hand eagerly stretched out to friends. Given to sudden outbursts of temper, he was quick to jeer at others and lavish with frank and sometimes blunt opinions which were tempered by perfect politeness.

Edmond, says Gautier, was dark and taller than his brother. In their youth, they each wore a square monocle on a black cord, and both of them were dressed alike. Jules, says Judith, Gautier's daughter, talked with much liveliness, and whenever he paused for breath his brother would continue the sentence, developing the idea, to which the other would subsequently return. 'It was a peculiar kind of duet

Edmond and Jules

in which the voices alternated without clashing, only in talking Edmond said *we*, and Jules always said *I*. When the conversation got well under way and my father was getting warmed up, they ... would almost cease talking and listen with the greatest pleasure and attention.'

Judith found them very polite and well-bred, but too studious. 'You would think you were in a classroom.' Gautier, who shared this impression, went even further. 'In spite of the charm of their conversation, their ease of manner and apparent nonchalance, you feel they are somehow preoccupied ... They do not talk as I do, for instance, simply for the pleasure of talking, they study, they observe ... Indeed, I have the impression that they are taking notes; that when no one is looking, they must be writing things down on the sly.'

The similarity of their characters was such, says Gautier, that people sometimes took Edmond for Jules or Jules for Edmond and by mistake would continue a conversation with one that they had begun with the other. All their letters, he said, though this was not strictly accurate, were signed with both their names. 'During more than ten years of close friendship we have only received one letter that departed from this pleasant social habit; this was the one in which from the depths of his despair the unhappy survivor announced the death of his beloved brother.'

In September, 1868, Zola commented in *Le Gaulois* on a medallion of the brothers: 'Their profiles placed side by side present the same delicate contours. The salient features are toned down by a subtle arrangement of foreground and background and their two faces have taken on a more striking resemblance in the cold bleak lines of the gold. With their hair flung back, and bare-necked they have the air of delicately voluptuous princelings ...' Continuing, he seems to indicate that he was somewhat envious of their material independence. 'I imagine them indifferent to gain ... working solely to satisfy their literary ambitions and not thinking about the profit they will make on a work until it is completed. Thus they have created a place for themselves aside from the commercial inclination of present-day literature. They are able to explore an idea at their ease and express it in a cleverly figured style; they have days, months, years of leisure in front of them, and if necessary will only write ten lines a week, working like skilful, meticulous lapidaries, intent on polishing their books. In their absolute freedom, they can indulge in proud impulses, fertile periods of idleness, with the artistic conscience of true and genuine writers.'

André Theuriet, having met them in 1867 at Philippe Burty's, describes them thus: 'Two men aged forty to forty-five were talking turn and turn about in a curt and almost peremptory way, and people were listening with obvious deference to them. The one, short in stature and delicate in appearance, had polished manners and a very Parisian, very refined, face; the other gave the impression of a bluff and intelligent country squire, tall and strongly built, with a dense crop of brown hair, a stubborn forehead, keen, penetrating eyes under thick eyebrows, a prominent jaw and a heavy moustache half hiding a mouth that showed little kindness.'

XIX
The Death of Jules

One night, in their house in Auteuil, which was still far from being completely furnished, Jules, profiting by his insomnia, imagined a story in the manner of Edgar Allan Poe: the tale of a man continually persecuted by noise, renting flats, buying houses, fleeing from his own country into forests and as far as the Pyramids, but finding silence nowhere, and finally committing suicide to escape from noise, but in his tomb still kept from sleeping by the worms...

It was a terrible blow to discover that even at Auteuil they were not safe from noise. Before buying the house Edmond had inspected its surroundings without noticing any sign of a stable. But alas! on the very first night they had been woken by the stamping of a horse which seemed to be lodged in the cellar, but was really in a sort of closet in their neighbours' house on the right. The cries of three little girls from their neighbours on the left drove them out of their drawing-room, their garden, and from all the coolest rooms in the house and eventually Edmond had shutters fixed inside the windows.

At the beginning of 1869, they were almost killed in an accident. They had taken a cab the driver of which was drunk. On the hill above the embankment in Passy, he drove them full-tilt into a cart and Edmond's face hit one of the carriage windows. Blood poured from a wound over his eye so as to make them wonder whether the eye itself were not split, but a chemist reassured them.

They had got to the pitch of thinking themselves under a curse. Flight seemed essential. They took refuge at the Grand Hôtel, and then in Passy, in the sort of room occupied by commercial travellers. '... here we are, we who have our own house, our Beauvais furniture, and those princely beds in which we shall doubtless never be able to sleep. Ah! the ironies of fate!' As was to be foreseen, they found it impossible to remain in Passy. After staying with their cousin Béhaine, they set off for Royat, to which they had made a trip on their way back from Vichy in July, 1867, and arrived there after breaking their journey at Clermont-Ferrand because of Jules having a liver attack.

The Death of Jules

At Royat they had the good luck to find a doctor who knew something about them, but the place itself was grim: no casino, no concerts, no distractions of any kind. Medical treatment, and nothing else: taking the waters, mineral and ferruginous baths, cold douches, hot douches, and wearisome walks along goat tracks.

The people at the spa, suffering from skin troubles, nerves, hysteria and partial paralysis, were not calculated to improve their morale. Arriving there on June 11, they left this 'region of gloom', these 'waters of affliction', these 'noise-infested hotels', these 'dinner-tables getting longer every day with extending ranks of fools' on July 2, but only to return to Auteuil and be met once more with the stamping of horses' hooves and the cries of a trio of children! They who had always found their greatest pleasure in work, who felt they had fully mastered their genius and perfected their philosophy, now believed themselves incapable henceforth of producing anything.

'Princes do not like sick people', they had written a short time before. However, they went back to Saint-Gratien. Here, as Jules Levallois relates, 'on one occasion Chesneau had to lead Jules to the dining-room because he could no longer find the way there himself.'

The Princess had sung the praises of Adolphe Franck, a historian and philosopher, and a person of importance, but a man who, in the eyes of the Goncourts, had the unpardonable defect of being a Jew. 'Princess, you should become a Jewess!' ejaculated Jules, who was evidently becoming unable to control his opinions. Once he had let the words slip, however, he became conscious of his misdemeanour; as they were getting up from the table he kissed the Princess's hand and offered his apologies, weeping. She took him in her arms, kissed him on both cheeks and said, 'Why now, it's nothing! You know very well that I love you.'

On September 6 they were at Bar-sur-Seine. 'What a deep feeling of melancholy you experience on seeing once more those banks of the Seine that you have seen in the full flush of health and creative energy, and treading once again those paths, but with a lagging step, and without hearing nature speak to the man of letters within you!' They were moved to pity Napoleon III when they heard he had been driven from his palace at Saint-Cloud by the tumult of the fair, for noise did not cease to harry the unlucky Jules. 'We have reached the point of crying out against the rain, the wind and the tempest, in which all human and animal noises are smothered and drowned.'

Edmond and Jules

The sound of barrels being hammered in preparation for the vintage drove them away again.

In a villa with a pleasant little garden, they spent three weeks at Trouville, 'the worst twenty days of our lives', but, nevertheless, treatment prescribed there by a certain Dr Helloco seemed to have produced a slight improvement in the sick man's condition. There they heard of the death of Sainte-Beuve, on which they made a harsh and acid comment, but allowance must be made for their own state of health and for the strain imposed on the invalid Jules by his desperate anxiety to finish their book on Gavarni. On June 20, 1872, Edmond wrote: 'These last days while looking through the *Journal* [as printed in *Le Bien Public*] my thoughts have been centred on the mad rage for work with which my brother accelerated the completion of this book. I remembered him, during our sad winter visits to Trouville and Saint-Gratien, tied to a chair from which I could not drag him away, one hand digging into his forehead as if he had to extract with painful labour the turns of phrase, the epithets, the apt expressions that once used to flow so freely from him...'

At Trouville, Jules was still pursued by noise. On October 7, he wrote to the Princess: 'Where indeed is silence to be found on this earth?... A more shrill and noisier lot of brats swarms here than you can find anywhere else. Imagine that Trouville is Rabelais' Ringing Island, that its great Catholic bells sound their peals more often than in Rome—and horrible little bells of sharp tinkling bronze which grate harshly on your ears.'

One morning, while Edmond was still in bed, he saw Jules coming into his room to read to him the last paragraph of their *Gavarni* which he had written during the night. 'I felt that in weeping over Gavarni he was weeping for himself, and the sentence: "He sleeps close beside us in the cemetery in Auteuil" became, without my being able to explain it, a constant memory... for ever ringing in my mind. For the first time I had an idea, which had not occurred to me till then, that he might die.'

On November 1, yielding to the Princess's entreaties, they took possession of the Catinat lodge, with their maid, Pélagie Denis, who had been in their service since the beginning of 1868. Hell and damnation! The priest, in order to try out his new bells, made them ring incessantly all day!

On December 14 they were back again in Auteuil; 'Empty days

The Death of Jules

and entirely dark, filled with douches and distressing walks along the endless avenue which runs from Auteuil to Boulogne.'

The year 1870 began very drearily for them: 'Today, the first day of the new year, not a single visit, not a glimpse of anyone who loves us. No one. Solitude and pain.'

Visits to the baths had begun again. 'We spend a part of each day at the hydropathic establishment, in that little house of suffering and torture where whimpering complaints and little stifled cries mingle with the rush of water and the cruel hiss of the douche. Along the corridor shoals of queer, misshapen creatures pass each other, and across it comes the doctor's question: "How did you sleep?" and the answers, "Very badly"—"Not at all well!"'

Here are the last words that fell from Jules's pen: 'How strange and singular these nervous disorders! Take for instance Vaucorbeil, the composer, who has a phobia about velvet, and is anxiously preoccupied when he is invited to dine at a house for the first time, by whether or not the dining-room chairs are upholstered in this material.'

It is distressing to read Edmond's notes in the *Journal* telling of his brother's gradual decline. Those in *Les Frères Zemganno*, in which Gianni plays his sad part of sick-nurse to Nello, are only a pale reflection of them.

At nightfall, they would walk in silence through the Bois de Boulogne. One evening, Jules suddenly stopped and made a little speech to Edmond, which the latter reproduced in his preface to *Chérie*: '"It makes no difference, you know, people can deny it... but one day they will have to recognize that we wrote *Germinie Lacerteux*, and that *Germinie Lacerteux* is the standard work that has served as a model for everything that has been cooked up since ours in the name of realism, naturalism, etc. That's one thing. Now who is it who, by writing and talking and buying things, has imposed a taste for the art and the furniture of the eighteenth century on a generation addicted to mahogany wardrobes? Where is the man who will dare to deny that it is we who did this? That's a second thing. Finally, take the description of a Parisian drawing-room furnished with things from Japan that was published in our first novel *En 18*... which appeared in 1851, yes, in 1851—and show me the amateurs of Japan at that date... And the bronzes and lacquers we acquired in those years when we used to go to Mallinet's shop and a little later Mme Desoye's... and the discovery in 1860 of the first album of

Edmond and Jules

Japanese drawings known in Paris; or at least in the world of men of letters and of artists... and the pages devoted to things Japanese in *Manette Salomon*, in *Idées et Sensations*... don't these make us the first to spread the knowledge of this art—this art on the way, without anyone suspecting it, to revolutionizing the point of view of the Western nations? That is a third thing. Now the search for truth in literature, the revival of interest in eighteenth-century art, the victory of the cult of Japan, these are, you know," he added after a moment's silence and with renewed signs of intelligent animation in his eyes, "these are the three great movements in literature and art in the second half of the nineteenth century, and it is we, poor, unknown individuals, who have guided all three. Well now! when you have done that, it is really difficult not to count as *someone* in the future."'

On another occasion when Jules was more depressed than usual, Edmond tried to cheer him up by insisting upon the years that would remain to him for writing books when he was well again. It was then that Jules, amazed at finding his thoughts so well divined, said to Edmond: 'I feel I shall never be able to work again! Never again!' For him literature was over and done with. Edmond now understood why his brother had worked so hard in the previous months 'goading himself on with stubborn pertinacity, hastening to make full use... of the last hours of a mind and a talent on the verge of extinction.' Philippe Burty came to Auteuil to listen to a chapter of their *Gavarni* read by Edmond. 'Jules,' he relates, 'was present at this reading. In his slow, drawling voice, and with gestures that were already stiff and awkward, he reminded his brother at moments of characteristic incidents concerning a night they had spent with Gavarni when the latter had lost the son he adored.'

It was not only Jules's intelligence that was failing, it was also his sense of tact, that aristocratic faculty he possessed to so eminent a degree, and even plain politeness. He mispronounced certain letters, *r* and *c* for instance, and this made his talk sound like that of the child he once had been. He would stand the whole afternoon in front of a tree with his hat over his eyes, not saying a word, sunk in his own thoughts, and so sad, so sad! He no longer took an interest in anything except the colour schemes of nature and the differing aspect of the skies. He did not recognize where he was, forgot how Watteau's name should be spelt, and could no longer distinguish the weights he used for his gymnastic exercises, although he did not fail

The Death of Jules

at times to surprise his brother by a remark such as a true novelist would make. Fixing his attention on anything called for a painful effort of concentration. He would either say nothing to questions or give an answer that was beside the point. But reading *Les Mémoires d'Outre-tombe* aloud had become an obsession with him; he pestered Edmond with it. He was gradually losing interest in everything and everyone. Even his capacity for loving and for feeling sympathy was affected. He was drawing apart from his brother, so much so in fact that the latter, in a letter to Flaubert, confessed to a temptation to which he had almost yielded: 'Pray believe that I had the idea of putting a sudden end to things. Everything had been arranged... even the letter to the police: I was going to blow his brains out, and after that my own. But at the last moment... having seized him by the collar in a momentary fit of impatience, anger or despair at some silly piece of wilfulness... my brother, I might say my child, looked up at me with eyes so amazed and so full of childish terror at the sight of my violence and the expression on my face that my hands let go of him and I felt myself altogether and for ever incapable of killing him. This is for yourself alone; not a word to anyone whatsoever. One must therefore go on living.' Living to see this fondly cherished brother, his other self, sinking by slow degrees into a state of drivelling lunacy!

They went back again to Bas-Meudon where they had been so happy with friends and women and wine; they wandered there like ghosts in a landscape of the dead. The sick man's expression had grown humble and shamefaced. Everything about him was deteriorating. It was as if a stranger had been put in his place. If anyone addressed him directly he seemed to rouse himself from a dream and had to have the question repeated three times. One evening Edmond announced that he was going out without being able to say exactly when he would return; the sick man let him go with such a show of indifference that poor Edmond began to wander haphazard through the Bois, withdrawing to a distance whenever he saw the roof of their house through the trees. He came home very late, to be welcomed by Jules in his night-shirt, and to feel an absurd delight on hearing the affectionate tone of his voice.

They went to dine at Saint-Cloud, not far from the house in which Charles Edmond lived so happily. Some hurdy-gurdies playing close by sent Edmond flying to the side of the road where he burst out sobbing under Jules's astonished gaze. On Monday, May 9, Jules, still busy reading *Les Mémoires d'Outre-tombe*, stumbled over a word and gave way to a quick burst of temper; as his brother was lifting him up to embrace him, he made a painful effort to say something. Had he lost his speech? He took up his book again and read aloud, 'Cardinal Pa-...'; he found it impossible to finish the word *Pacca*. Agitated, he took off his hat, passed his fingers over his forehead as if trying to ransack his brain. 'The despair in this desire, the anger in this effort,' says Edmond, 'cannot be expressed in writing. No, never have I watched so painful, so cruel a scene. It was the wild fury of a man of letters, of a maker of books, when it dawns on him that he cannot even read them any longer.'

Made happy by an appetizing dish or something new to wear, Jules would fidget with different objects, then at times suddenly draw back like a child afraid of being scolded. 'Where are you, my dear chap?' Edmond would ask him, disturbed by his silence. 'Away in space... in empty space,' would be his answer. Once in a restaurant as he was serving himself clumsily from a bowl his brother said, 'Please be careful or we shall not be able to go out anywhere.' Jules burst into tears. 'It's not my fault! It's not my fault!' he exclaimed. His trembling hand took hold of Edmond's across the table, and they wept together in front of the astonished diners.

On June 16, Jules was still reading *Les Mémoires d'Outre-tombe*. His brother advised him to take a rest and suggested a walk in the Bois. As they were going out of the room Jules stumbled and collapsed into an arm-chair. Edmond carried him to his bed, and asked what was troubling him; he replied with inarticulate sounds. But when his brother asked him if he recognized him he burst into loud laughter. Suddenly he uttered a hoarse cry, a terrifying gutteral noise. His face was convulsed, his arms writhed, he foamed at the mouth. Sitting on his bolster, Edmond took his hands and pressed his poor head, dripping with sweat, to his bosom.

Some less violent attacks were followed by fits of delirium. The sick man would raise his arms and send appeals and kisses to some invisible being, writhing and twitching like a wounded bird, and with an enigmatic expression on his face that made him look like one of da Vinci's figures. At other moments, seized with terror, he would cower beneath the sheets and cry out, 'Go away!' to heaven knows what ghostly visitor. Then would come a fresh spate of words,

The Death of Jules

sentences cut short, imitative gestures of fixing a monocle in his eye, picking up dumb-bells or writing a letter. At moments Edmond and Pélagie had the impression that he recognized them, but immediately he would become absorbed by his visions.

The next day Doctor Béni-Barde, his physician, said, 'This is the end,' and explained that his brain had disintegrated at the base of the skull, that the nerves in his chest were injured and a fatal attack of pulmonary consumption would follow.

The death-agony lasted for five days. During the night of Saturday, June 18, Edmond came at two o'clock in the morning to relieve Pélagie at the bedside. In spite of three doses of bromide, Jules could not sleep. He was tossing about and from the corners of his mouth letting slip fragmentary sentences, broken words and syllables, bursting forth to end in sighs.

On Sunday morning, at four o'clock, his breathing grew more rapid. At ten o'clock it was coming in gasps. By the afternoon it was stertorous, a gutteral rattle broken by groans, and cries of 'Mother, mother, come to me, mother!' Twice he called to Maria: 'Maïa! Maïa!' At eight o'clock in the evening his breathing became shrill. A new night began. By five o'clock on Monday morning his face had taken on the yellow hue of death. His eyes, deep and full of shadows, were wet with tears. At nine o'clock they cleared and his distant, wandering gaze seemed to light on Edmond. At 9.40 all was over. 'God be praised,' said Edmond. 'After two or three sighs he died, breathing like a little child going to sleep.'

The dead man's eyes were open once more. His face wore a faint look of sarcastic sadness, 'an earthly sadness,' says Edmond, 'such as I have not yet seen on the face of anyone dead. On this young face you seem to see, continuing after death, inconsolable regret for interrupted work.' Beside this description we can place these lines by Philippe Burty: 'I saw him in Auteuil, on his death-bed, quiet and grave, dressed as if he were ready to go out. His forehead had become wrinkled; his eyes had opened again; his glassy stare seemed full of terrible meaning, of inexpressible astonishment, of heart-broken indignation at a fate that shattered both his cherished hopes of fame and the ties of an unparalleled friendship between brothers.'

Edmond gazed for a long time at the corpse, and just as he had noted down from day to day, almost from hour to hour, the various phases of his brother's illness and his last agony, so he noted his

Edmond and Jules

impressions, which are of a tone and character unique in literature, up to the very moment of Jules's body being placed in the hearse, of arriving at the church and at the cemetery in Montmartre, where they had often walked together when they were writing *Germinie Lacerteux* and *Manette Salomon*, and where their father and mother were buried. Let us admire the twofold strain in Edmond's nature as an act of faith in an ideal to which he was convinced that his brother had sacrificed his life. For this zeal for literature that possessed him was the very thing he denounced as having killed Jules. 'At this moment I hold literature accursed. Perhaps, but for me, he would have become a painter, and gifted as he was, would have made a name for himself without tearing out his brains... and he would still be alive.'

Théophile Gautier, arriving in haste from Geneva, conveyed very well the impression made on him by Jules's death and his brother's terrible grief at the funeral. 'Edmond, in his tragic stupefaction, looked like a spectre turned to stone; Death, who habitually puts a mask of serene beauty on the faces he touches, had not obliterated an expression of bitter sorrow and inconsolable regret on Jules's features, none the less so delicate and regular. The dead man in his coffin wept for the living... Past all the stations on this dolorous way we followed poor Edmond, who blinded by his tears and with his arms supported by his friends, stumbled at every step as if his feet were enwrapped in the folds of his brother's shroud. Like men condemned to die, who undergo a terrible change on their way from the prison to the scaffold, so on the way from Auteuil to Montmartre he had aged twenty years and his hair had turned white!... this is not an illusion.. many of those present remarked it too... growing gradually paler on his head as we came nearer and nearer to the inevitable end of the journey at the little low doorway where the everlasting farewells were said. It was a grim and pitiful occasion, never has any funeral procession been accompanied by such heart-rending grief. Everyone wept or sobbed convulsively, and yet those who walked behind this hearse were philosophers, artists and writers inured to sorrow, accustomed to mastery over their souls, to keeping their nerves under control and to showing a fitting reticence in expressing their emotions.'

On his return to Auteuil Edmond went to bed, and covering the bed-clothes with portraits of his dead brother, gazed at them intently until nightfall.

The Death of Jules

The next day he had a few visitors: Maria, Edouard de Béhaine, his cousin Marin, and the Princess, who wept on his neck.

To spare him the frightful experience of being alone in the house, which he had decided to sell, Marin Labille took him off to Bar-sur-Seine. Charles Edmond and his wife had offered him a room at Bellevue and Flaubert one at Croisset.

The two brothers had become estranged from Paul de Saint-Victor, who, as the husband of a Jewess, had possibly taken offence over *Manette Salomon*. Jules's death reconciled him with the survivor.

Zola was deeply grieved by it. This writer, says Maurice Le Blond, 'always seems to have had a marked preference for Jules... It was one of those mysterious attractions that are as much physical as spiritual. It also came from a sort of certainty that, of the two Goncourts, Jules was more particularly the creative genius. As a witness to this unequalled collaboration in literature, this interpenetration in brotherhood of two hearts and two minds, coupled in a patient, laborious moulding of art, Zola had always been eager to study the part each of them played. Nothing but the fear of grieving the old master who was still alive prevented him from carrying out his plan.'

On June 27 Zola wrote to Edmond: 'His death, don't you think, was largely the result of the indifference of the public and the silence that greeted those books of his that were most true to life? It was art that killed him. When I read *Madame Gervaisis* I felt very strongly there was something of a dying man's last gasp in that impassioned, mystical story; and when I saw the astonished and frightened attitude of the public towards the book, I said to myself that this would bring about the artist's death. He was one of those whom stupidity stabs through the heart.'

From Bar-sur-Seine Edmond wrote in answer: 'In my opinion, my brother's death was due to his work, and more especially to his efforts to cultivate form, to produce finely polished phrases, and a carefully wrought style... I still think this method of composition is the only good one for a novel; but I fear it is not good for one's health. Consider, indeed, that all our work, and this is perhaps an original quality in it that has been dearly paid for, is based on neurasthenia, that these pictures of this disease have been drawn from ourselves, and that by dint of analysing ourselves in detail, probing into and dissecting ourselves, we came to possess a kind of super-intense sensibility that was wounded by the most infinitesimal accidents of life. I say we, for when we wrote *Charles Demailly* I was more ill than he was... I look again, and I find another cause. I myself was a collector; I was often distracted from my professional work by some bibelot, by some silly trifle or other; he, for his part, much less passionately eager to possess artistic objects, was more particularly a collector out of deference to what I liked, in a touching sacrifice to my tastes. He did not care for the country or for society; he showed a certain indolence over violent exercise, like fencing, hunting, or physical activities in general. His thoughts were therefore never for a moment distracted from literature by any kind of pleasure, hobby, passion, and what-not—love for a woman, for instance, or love of children. And when literature thus becomes the exclusive mistress of a certain type of brain, the doctor, sad to say, sees in this fixed preoccupation with one single object the first stages of monomania... The unlucky fate of *Henriette Maréchal* and of *Madame Gervaisis* undoubtedly aggravated an already morbid condition... As to those first causes that have neither an intellectual nor a moral origin, I know nothing about them! He only occasionally indulged in womanizing when quite young; he never drank a single glass of liqueur. I find nothing in his life but over-indulgence in tobacco; true, this was of the strongest and the most unhealthy kind, with which we stupefied ourselves in intervals between working... I have always in mind the terrible thesis formulated by Béni-Barde, the doctor who attended him and who has made a study of so many nervous disorders. "Ten years of excessive womanizing, ten years of excessive drinking, of over-indulgence in anything, will sometimes do less to destroy a man than one hour, one single hour, of mental excitement."'

Was Edmond sincere when he said he did not know what causes, apart from those connected with mind and character, could have caused Jules's illness and death? Had he not read that entry made on August 12, 1864, in which his brother admits to having contracted syphilis in 1850?

Apparently Gautier did not reject Edmond's explanation. 'Jules died of his profession just as all of us die; from having a mind in a perpetual state of tension, from working without relaxation, from a struggle with difficulties of his own devising, from the strain of rolling along this boulder of sentences that is heavier than the stone

The Death of Jules

of Sisyphus.' To this should be added a secret grievance: Jules missed not having the approbation of fools. 'One despises the common herd or keeps them at a distance; but such people take this for granted and do not gather round, which makes even the proudest natures very sad.'

Here then is Edmond, all alone, or, as someone expressed it 'a widower'. He is forty-eight. He has never been young. The grief that has lately aged him before his time will continue to consume him; but in spite of his frail nervous system, it will not kill his spirit. Edmond will slowly gain mastery over circumstances and find in his passion for literature, as in his voracious appetite for fame, the strength he needs to secure for his own name and his brother's that chance of survival which had been their supreme ambition from their first entry into the world of letters.

Part Two

EDMOND ALONE

I
The Siege and the Commune

Edmond spent July at Bar-sur-Seine, the little town on whose manners and customs he was to make such caustic comments in his *Journal* a few years later. The brothers had stayed there with their cousin Labille after the death of their mother and of their old servant Rose. Every year for twenty years they had wandered along the roads and footpaths, and they had taken notes there for the descriptive passages in *Charles Demailly*. They had sketched the stained glass window in the church showing the procession of the Fatted Calf. It was in this vat-room that they had learnt of Gavarni's death, it was on this bed that Jules had been lying when he received Thierry's letter summoning them urgently to rehearsals of *Henriette Maréchal*, and through this door that they had set out in white smocks and with knapsacks on their backs on their great journey across France.

As if paralysed with grief, incapable of fixing his mind on anything that did not directly remind him of Jules, and sometimes to his surprise finding himself thinking about him as if he were still alive, Edmond mused, and smoked, and went bathing in the river. He had conceived a horror of any sort of activity and found pleasure only in remaining as motionless as a fakir, with a strange feeling of emptiness at the pit of his stomach. Though he would have liked to dream of the dead, his nights remained empty of this dear image.

With the somewhat vague intention of going to live in a large studio in the place Vintimille or the avenue Frochot, he had put the house at Auteuil up for sale, convinced that he would never have the courage to go back there again; however, he did not sell it. Then an opportunity came for him to let the house, but he did not let it. All decisions and all action seemed to lie under a ban.

He was back in Auteuil by the beginning of August. Mechanically he wandered up and down amidst all the disorder, but it was when night came, when formerly they would have been smoking together and letting their ideas take haphazard shape, that he felt himself most deserted.

The Siege and the Commune

On August 6 he was looking through some portfolios of engravings when people in the street began running towards the Bourse, and coming out of the library he began to do the same. Under the colonnades and on the steps the crowd, bare-headed, were singing the Marseillaise. The next day, which was a Sunday, a deathly silence fell upon the town. The cutting down of the trees in the Bois de Boulogne, where cattle and sheep were grazing, provoked Edmond to an outburst of rage against the Prussians. At Neuilly Gautier lamented the fate of the house which he had made into a refuge for his old age. Did Edmond feel as strong a desire to see his own house saved, with his books, engravings and drawings?

On the 31st the demolition of houses in the outer zone of the city began. In September, lost among the mob, Edmond saw the names of the provisional government inscribed in red letters on a column. On another column someone had scrawled in charcoal: *The Republic is proclaimed*. The great door of the Tuileries bore the inscription in chalk: *Protection for the citizens*. In the neighbourhood of the Palais Bourbon and in the place de l'Hôtel de Ville there was a swarm of inquisitive spectators.

On the 6th, at Brébant's, whither the fortnightly dinners at Magny's had been transferred, there was an atmosphere of gloom: 'The Germans have little idea of enjoyment,' said Renan, 'except what they find in hatred, in the idea of vengeance and wreaking it on others.' Then, an instant later, he exclaimed: 'The Germans are a superior race...!' And later still: 'Let France perish! Let our country perish! Above all this the kingdom of Duty and of Reason still exists!'

During the siege and the Commune, Edmond continued to go for long walks, bringing back observations on things he had seen which are among the best pages in his work.

On September 18, his servant Pélagie was only able to buy a halfpennyworth of bread. The next day, the sound of gunfire could be heard, and on the 20th, as Edmond stood beside his brother's grave, his thoughts of him were interrupted by the militia drilling all round the cemetery.

On the 29th, Edmond set out to look for a shop where he could move his pictures. The next day, he was woken up by gunfire and on the boulevard Saint-Jacques the first of the wounded appeared.

On October 3, he writes: 'How is it that I, for whom life holds so little... do not seek to die? Is it cowardice that has made me avoid joining the National Guard? No... it is the feeling proper to a proud and singular nature, which would make me lay down my life if I by myself alone could do something great... in short, become a personality in this war, but which prevents me from resigning myself to being a mere cipher, an anonymous fragment of cannon-fodder. Such a death, however glorious it may be, I consider below my rank in literature... Yet... this feeling might have been suppressed if I were faced with an amicable, "Won't you come?" from a friend whose companionship would have protected me from the dirty and repulsive nobodies of the National Guard.'

On October 4, the bombardment of Paris began; there were only five people at Brébant's. On the evening of the 7th, a voice addressed him in the darkness; it was Pouthier. They went off to a café to talk about Jules. Pouthier was trying to get into the National Guard so as to earn twenty sous a day.

On the 15th, Edmond was present in the ballroom of the *Reine Blanche* at the founding of the Club de Montmartre. On the 18th, driven from home by the noise of gunfire, he prolonged his walk as far as the Mortemart battery in the Bois de Boulogne. On the 21st, from one of his windows, he observed every detail of the artillery in action.

During the following days, his impressions take on a gloomier tone: 'Will civil war, with famine and bombardment, be our fate tomorrow?'

On November 7, Edmond went to visit Victor Hugo. The poet had written to him at the time of Jules's death to express his sympathy, and he was anxious to thank him for it. 'There are some fine rebellious locks in his hair, like those on the head of Michelangelo's prophets, and on his face is an expression of singular and almost ecstatic placidity. Yes, indeed, ecstasy *in excelsis*, but from time to time there come flashes, almost immediately extinguished, from an eye as black as night.' Hugo talked to him about his books, which had been a distraction for him in his exile. 'You have created types, and that is a faculty people of great talent do not always possess.' He also preached to him about work, and spoke of a kind of collaboration with his beloved dead. He believed that the dead are present with us. On the whole, Hugo showed himself both friendly and natural, and not at all pompous or oracular.

On November 18, Edmond had a nightmare: he said his brother

was condemned to death. In order to ask Sainte-Beuve for a letter of recommendation he waited for a long time in a huge room full of Dresden china in which the critic strode up and down without saying a word to him. Then he went to see Princess Mathilde who told him with a kindly smile that the Emperor was no longer emperor and could do nothing for his brother, and the dream ended in incoherence and absurdity.

The violence of the bombardment now obliged him to take down his pictures and pack up his books. Inside the house everything had a look of desolation.

On January 4, he wrote: 'Still out of sorts. I am spending the whole day in a vague state of semi-slumber. Unformed ideas float through my brain, ready ... to turn into dreams, but halted on the verge of sleep by a burst of firing from Mont-Valérien, or the egg-laying squawks of three little hens I have in a coop close beside my little greenwood fire. These three fowls are my last resource against the flesh of cabmen's hacks to-day, and against to-morrow's hunger. (A few nights before, at Voisin's, he had been given elephant sausage for dinner.)

In *La Maison d'un Artiste* Edmond has told how, when Pélagie had refused to carry out the execution, he cut off the head of his little hen Blanche with a Japanese sword. This hen, which lived in the little ground-floor drawing-room in which he ate and slept, 'pure white, and delicately balanced, with a coquettish little top-knot', would jump up on his table while he was lunching and peck at his plate. Every morning he used to comb her with a fine comb, and was so much attached to her—she had such saucy manners and such amusing impudence—that he hesitated a long time before making up his mind to eat her. In the garden he cut off her head with one blow but, though headless, she began to run about. 'This murder,' he writes, 'is one of the things I most bitterly regret ... and all the more as I must confess she was frightfully tough, this poor Blanche!'

On January 10, there were many people dining at Brébant's. Charles Edmond gave terrifying descriptions of the rain of bombs on the Luxembourg. Because of a shell that had fallen in the place Saint-Sulpice, Saint-Victor left his flat in the rue de Furstenberg every night, and Renan had emigrated to the Right Bank. On the 12th, all along the road to Passy, the snow looked pink, reflecting the fires at Saint-Cloud.

Edmond Alone

On the 14th, no longer having the courage to go and dine in Paris, Edmond ate a blackbird he had shot in his garden. 'There crept into my mind ... a kind of superstitious conviction that something of my brother had passed into this little winged creature, this mournful denizen of the air, and I felt a vague sense of chill at having destroyed ... something from beyond this world, something friendly that watched over the safety of my house and myself.'

Every night, as he was coming home, he tried to make out from as far off as possible whether his house was still standing. It astounded him to find that in spite of the whistling of the shells, there was not a hole or a chip in its structure. The door was left half-open so that he should not have to wait too long on the pavement.

On the 16th, a shell-splinter damaged the roof of the house next door, but by the 18th the few stray shells had become a regular rain of cast-iron.

On the 21st, a great silence reigned over the whole of Paris. On the 22nd, under the bursting shells, he took all his most precious possessions to Burty's flat. On the 24th, at Brébant's, the company, scattered on the sofa and in armchairs, talked sadly under their breath, as though it were a sickroom. That evening they dined on dog's flesh.

New German batteries were now unmasked and shells were falling every minute on the railway lines. On his way to the naval battery at the Point du Jour, he went into Gavarni's garden, now cut up to make trenches and pitted with holes filled with unexploded shells. In the little green valley the last pine-trees were lying on their sides; its ivy-wreathed vaulted room had been converted into a casemate with a protruding stove-pipe.

The capitulation of the city on January 30 wrung cries of indignation from him. The proclamation of Wilhelm, Emperor of Germany, established, in his eyes, 'the end of all those things that had made France great'.

Seized with a rabid anger against his country and against the government, he shut himself up indoors, endeavouring to stifle thoughts and memories, not reading the papers any more, and avoiding people who had information to give.

On February 12 he went to see Gautier, who had taken refuge in the rue de Beaune in an attic which was filled with the smoke from his cigar. Théo, in a republican bonnet, was wearing the velvet jacket originally made for his visits to Saint-Gratien, but which was now

The Siege and the Commune

covered with spots like the coat of a Neapolitan cook; 'While he talked, and talked, just as Rabelais must have done, I was thinking of the injustice of the remuneration given to art. I thought of the sumptuous and execrable furniture of Ponson du Terrail [1] which I had seen moved from the rue Vivienne that morning, after the death of this man who had earned 70,000 francs a year, in some low quarter, during the siege.'

On the 23rd, he was hunting for books along the embankment for the first time for many months. On the 24th, he hastily jotted down on paper the first lines of *La Fille Elisa*, the 'book that we were to have written, he and I, after *Madame Gervaisis*.'

On March 1, he heard in the distance the dull sound of the Prussian drums, then, like a peal of thunder, came the rumble of the gun-carriages rolling past. Two helmeted soldiers stopped in front of his house. That night there was not a light, not a shadow of anyone in Auteuil. On the 3rd he was dragged out of bed by the Prussians' music: they were going away! Deliverance appeared to him in the shape of two gendarmes re-taking possession of the Boulevard de Montmorency at a gallop.

On March 18, he learnt that fighting was going on in Montmartre. At the gare d'Orléans, to which they had brought the body of Hugo's son, Hugo said to him: 'You have suffered a blow, so have I... But mine is more than an ordinary one: two sudden catastrophies in a single lifetime!' The funeral procession began to move forward, with Hugo's white hooded head looking like the head of a fighting monk. Burty annoyed Edmond, who was obsessed by dark presentiments, by making a jesting allusion to Thiers. Paul Verlaine, who had known Edmond since the time of *Henriette Maréchal*, asked him his opinion of present events. 'M. Thiers,' replied Edmond, 'is a shockingly bad writer, or rather not a writer at all, but at least with him in power one might be able to write in peace, but with these people we have now...' His bereavement in the previous year, says Verlaine, had left him completely indifferent to everything.

As they returned from the cemetery barricades were being put up everywhere, there were no carriages in the streets and the shopkeepers were putting up their shutters.

[1] A prolific and highly successful writer of crime stories.

Edmond Alone

On March 19, on the boulevard de Montmorency, a poster giving the names of the new government seemed to him to announce the final extinction of the Republic. 'The experiment of 1870, made with the pick of the basket, has been a lamentable failure. This latest one, made with the worst of the refuse, will be the end of this kind of government. The Republic ... is a fine, foolish dream of thoughtful, generous, and disinterested minds; it is not practicable with the evil, petty passions of the French populace. To them, Liberty, Equality and Fraternity mean nothing but the enslavement and destruction of the upper classes.'

On March 20 the gare Saint-Lazare was full of people trying to leave the city, but the next day the crowd seemed more orderly. Nevertheless, the mob were becoming dangerous, the National Guard at the Mairie Drouot were being hooted at, and all along the boulevard people were crying 'To arms!'

The morning of the 22nd was filled with the noise of gunfire. Pélagie announced that fighting was going on in Paris itself. On the 23rd, while Edmond was at Burty's, an officer of the National Guard came to inspect the flat to see about his men taking up a position on the balcony. 'I look at my marquetry furniture, my bibelots, my porcelain, my books half arranged on the shelves and half spread out on the floor, and I think that they are going to have a bad time when the house is stormed.'

During one of the following days he had a liver attack. 'Fourteen hours wriggling and writhing like a worm cut in two ... in all my life I have never suffered so much ... A curious thing; this disorder of the liver, which killed my brother and will doubtless kill me too, is not ... a hereditary complaint, but something acquired as a result of writing.' He seriously believed this was so.

On April 2 the fury of the bombardment was redoubled, but on the 4th it ceased, and for a moment Edmond feared that the Commune had become victorious; then the sound of machine-gun fire reassured him. On the 5th, the government of the Central Committee seemed to be nearing its end, though a great red flag was still floating above Fort d'Issy. The following day brought another outburst of gunfire such as had never been heard before, and volleys of musketry from Issy and Neuilly. Shells rained down on the rampart, driving back the crowd by the Etoile barrier who were watching three Versailles batteries bombard the barricade at the bridge and the rampart itself.

The Siege and the Commune

On the 7th, the men on the rampart replied with frenzied counter-volleys. Above Edmond's head a shell grazed the cornice of the Arc de Triomphe and a splinter fell close beside him.

On April 13, he notes: 'We begin to hear the plaintive whine of shells coming down on the Trocadéro, which is carrying on a fight with Mont-Valérien above our heads.' The next morning Pélagie announced that every man, whatever his age, would be compelled to march against the men of Versailles. 'And in Auteuil,' she added, 'people are speaking with terror about the house-to-house hunt that is going to be made for defaulters.'

On April 15, Mont-Valérien dropped a shell on Auteuil once a minute. Edmond decided to have a mattress put down on the floor of the cellar and to lie on it. During a lull in the bombardment he put his nose outside; the house next door was split from top to bottom. Near the station Pélagie was knocked down by the explosion of a shell that cut off the top of the station and tore up part of the line.

On the 17th the bombardment slackened: only three shells came down in the garden. Edmond, worn out by sleepless nights, decided to seek refuge in a flat in the rue de l'Arcade belonging to one of his cousins. Pélagie, however, remained at Auteuil. He notes with pleasure that the population of Paris are beginning to rebel. People are crying: 'Down with the Commune!' At Brébant's on the 21st there are four guests at dinner, among them Renan, who speaks in praise of Prince Napoleon. 'What a party spirit there is among party men,' writes Edmond. 'I heard Burty declare that he preferred the Prussian occupation to that of the *Versaillais!*' He continued to visit Burty regularly, though his political fanaticism was becoming more and more violent.

On May 4, bad news came from Auteuil. Shells were raining on the house; the railings had been smashed. From the balcony of Burty's flat, where Edmond was now sleeping, he watched the fight by the Madeleine and on the boulevards, following its different phases. The rough sketches that he afterwards drew from memory are strikingly true to life.

On May 24, thanks to a lull in the bombardment, Edmond managed to reach the rue de l'Arcade. The worthy Pélagie, who bore him no grudge for having left her alone in Auteuil, is waiting for him there with a huge bouquet of *Gloire de Dijon* roses from her tall tree. To bring it to him she has come right through the fighting. He goes back with her to the boulevard de Montmorency. There is a large hole on the first floor and the house is riddled with shell-splinters. The door has been raked with bullets and part of it has been hacked off. Inside, plaster, broken glass and shell splinters are everywhere. Repairs to the tune of four or five thousand francs will be needed.

When evening came they gazed through the trees at the sight of Paris on fire. Edmond spent the whole of May 25 wandering amid the ruins. On the 26th, near the station at Passy, a convoy of men and women prisoners was waiting, ready to set off for Versailles. The passage in which he describes this is a magnificent fragment, beneath which one is conscious of sincere and human emotion, completely free from anything trivial or precious. No less remarkable is the episode of the shooting of prisoners, in which Madame Verlaine is described coming to ask Burty how she could hide her husband.

Edmond spent the next few days visiting smoking Paris with his cousin Marin Labille. On June 10 he went to the funeral of Philippe de Courmont, killed during the attack on the Trocadéro, the only one of the cavalry officers on the side of the Versaillais who had fallen in the fighting. In the evening Edmond dined with Flaubert, who, still a man of letters more than anything else, had come to Paris to get some information for *La Tentation de Saint-Antoine*. 'This cataclysm seems to have passed over his head without drawing his attention away in the least from the calm, impassive occupation of writing a book.'

On June 20, the anniversary of Jules's death, he spent the whole day putting together the obituary notices written about him. On July 12, he was one of the first visitors to Saint-Gratien, which had been occupied by some of the German staff and where Mathilde had been in residence again since June 11. Life for him was about to resume its normal course.

II

Life Begins Again

The Princess received him with her accustomed animation, on which he congratulated her. She replied that all she wanted was to remain free and to look after Saint-Gratien. He noticed that she had lost her easy way of talking and that her conversation was interrupted by long silences. Popelin, her new lover, did not give the impression of being satisfied with his role and Edmond had a suspicion that in private he suffered from the autocratic temper of his mistress, whom he contradicted on every subject.

With her income reduced to 20,000 francs after the overthrow of the Emperor, the Princess dismissed part of her staff, kept only two or three carriages, and gave up her town house in the rue de Courcelles, installing herself instead at 18 rue de Berri, in 'a frightful little hole'. Here she gathered a new circle around her. But in spite of everything, how different it was from the old rue de Courcelles, the old Saint-Gratien!

Interested mainly in his house, which he had at last decided to put into proper order, and convinced that death would surprise him before this was finished, or that some accident would drive him out of it, Edmond had not been to the theatre for three years; now he began to go again. There were also fresh visits to Bar-sur-Seine, with nocturnal fishing or hunting parties, and more dinners at Brébant's. But he was still dominated by grief for Jules's death, from which the defeat of France and the Commune had been no more than temporary diversions. He had nightmares in which Jules appeared to him in his last illness and in which the suffering his death had brought was prolonged. Jules, in fact, continued to occupy half his life. He felt himself completely adrift.

On March 2, 1872, at a dinner at Flaubert's, Gautier, whom the Princess's doctor had already diagnosed as having heart trouble, made an alarming impression on Edmond. With eyes that seemed to be looking nowhere, a face as white as a Pierrot's, silent, eating and drinking automatically, he listened only when he heard talk of poetry. He had a feeling, he said, as he sank down on a divan, that he was already dead. On March 13, he did not appear at the Princess's dinner. He was expecting a visit the next day from Ricord, 'I do not like... Ricord at the bedside of an invalid,' Edmond wrote. 'At present he is our official gravedigger. His presence seems to hasten death. I am reminded of Murger, Sainte-Beuve, etc.'

Between Edmond's visits to his sick friend at the end of this winter of 1872, other visits, to Victor Hugo, took place. The latter overwhelmed him with compliments, but it was time, according to him, for artistic preoccupations to make room for higher concerns, metaphysical, sociological, etc. 'As I went downstairs,' writes Edmond, 'though I felt moved by the charm and courtesy of this great mind, deep inside me was ironical amusement over this mystical jargon... with which men like Michelet or like Hugo pontificate, trying to impose themselves on their immediate circle as prophets who are intimate with the gods.'

On May 8, Edmond noticed something in Gautier like 'a torpor of the brain'. At the beginning of July, the poet had a stroke. The first time he went out was to have lunch at Edmond's house. 'You would have thought,' said his host, 'that it was... someone walking in his sleep'. On August 1 the poet's daughter-in-law told Edmond that the night before his tongue had been paralysed for three-quarters of an hour. Two days later Edmond left for Schliersee, in the Bavarian Tyrol, invited by Edouard de Béhaine, who was now French Minister in Munich. He was struck by the stand-offish attitude of the German people. 'Seeing these Germans, one would say that it is we who have beaten them, they seem so much to harbour the bitter feelings aroused by a defeat.' All his sympathies lay with Ludwig II, 'this poor prince, with his love for those ages of French greatness under Louis XIV and Louis XV, compelled to work for the ruin of France on the orders of Bismarck whom he detests. Poor sovereign, reduced to saying to the French *chargé d'affaires*: "I earnestly pray for the restoration of France to its former greatness, and I am glad to tell you this without its coming to the ears of the Prussians."' The Bavarian mountains induced in Edmond one of his rare moments of exaltation. 'I have lived for an hour, translated above the things and ideas of earth, intoxicated by this grandeur, this altitude, this sublimity, this clear, untainted air.'

Life Begins Again

Did he go to see Gautier on his return? The *Journal* only mentions a conversation with the poet's son-in-law, Emile Bergerat, on October 13. On the 24th, opening a paper during dinner, he saw the news of Gautier's death. The next morning Bergerat showed him into the room where the body lay: 'His face with its faintly orange pallor, was almost hidden beneath his long black hair. On his breast he had a rosary whose white beads, lying round a fading rose, looked like the scatterings of a snowberry twig.' He had 'the wild serenity of a barbarian sunk to rest... Nothing about him spoke to me of a death in modern times. Memories of the stone figures on Chartres cathedral, mingled with reminiscences of the Merovingians, kept coming into my mind, I don't know why.'

The funeral was marked by pomp and ceremony. Trumpets sounded. Artists from the Opéra sang. An escort, chiefly of journalists, accompanied the hearse to Montmartre. 'Personally,' wrote Edmond, '... my corpse would feel horrified at having all this horde of the literary world behind my coffin... I ask only for the three men of genius and the half-dozen earnest shoemakers who attended the funeral of Heinrich Heine.' And that is all the funeral oration on the worthy, kindly Théo, that is in the *Journal*.

On November 19, 1872, Nadar appeared at Edmond's house and on behalf of Constantin Guys begged him to withdraw from his *Gavarni*, then appearing in *Le Bien Public*, certain expressions which showed Guys in an unfavourable light. Edmond suggested cutting the whole of his description of Guys, but this radical solution was not to Nadar's liking. 'What they really want,' said Edmond, 'is advertisement, and Nadar even insinuated that Guys would not be sorry if I said a word or two about his water-colours. Oh! the delicacy of these bohemians!' Next it was the widow of Maroy, the engraver, who came to make a protest: Edmond had said that her husband had engraved four of Gavarni's drawings abominably. In a fury, he agreed to everything he was asked to do.

Gavarni made its appearance in 1873, adorned with a portrait etched by Léopold Flameng, taken from a drawing by the artist himself, and with a facsimile of his handwriting. A fine article by Paul de Saint-Victor greeted the book in *Le Moniteur Universel*. 'Jules de Goncourt... has, so to speak, fallen dead at the foot of the mausoleum he was raising to the memory of the artist who was his friend.' There was also an unsigned article by Philippe Burty in *La République Française*, but the most important one was by Henri Delaborde in *La Revue des Deux Mondes*, an article in which the critic of this virtuous periodical wonders why the Goncourts, who had concealed none of Gavarni's misdemeanours, should not also have held them up to reprobation.

On the suggestion of Charles Blanc, the Ministry of Education bought 125 copies of the book at eight francs a copy. Far from pleasing Edmond, this made him furious. 'What a strange race of men these Blancs appear to be! Busy disarming hatreds on the sly, busy muzzling antipathies with a little money cribbed from the public purse. And yet what can one do about it?... As a well-bred man there is nothing I can do except express my thanks. How unlucky not to have been born a mountebank! To-morrow I might reject this offer in a way that would cause a stir in all the papers, and I should be looked on as a man of great integrity and should sell my whole edition.'

Gavarni was not the only work that Edmond published under their two names after Jules's death. In 1873, he had their drama, *La Patrie en Danger*, published, produced a new edition of *L'Art au XVIIIe Siècle*, drew up the catalogue of Watteau's work that Jules had so often thought of making, and had *Renée Mauperin*, *Germinie Lacerteux* and *Sœur Philomène* reprinted. In 1875 he brought out a limited edition with engravings of *L'Amour au Dix-huitième Siècle* (which is Chapter IV of *La Femme au Dix-huitième Siècle*). In 1878, he published the *Du Barry* and *Madame de Pompadour*, and in the following year, *La Duchesse de Châteauroux et ses Sœurs*, all of them developments of chapters in their *Maîtresses de Louis XV*.

III

Four Novels

The idea of *La Fille Elisa* had occurred to the two brothers in October, 1862, when they visited the women's prison at Clermont d'Oise with Edouard Lefebvre de Béhaine and his wife. Escorted by the governor and an inspector they began with the parlour, the kitchen and the refectory, and then came to the workroom, light but misty, decorated in a cold whitish blue. In spite of the harmony of the colours, a sensation of horror inseparable from the tortures of the penal system somehow made itself felt in this assembly of women prisoners. 'That philanthropic, mental torture that has surpassed the excesses of physical torture, but which makes no one cry out, excites no indignation, does not move one because one cannot handle it... because it is a dry, tearless torture... which, instead of crippling the body, mutilates the soul and kills the mind. This, so the deputy governor told me smiling... drives women mad, many of them every year. This torture is the rule of silence, which is a monstrous thing.'

Accompanied by the governor they afterwards went through the dormitories; thin little mattresses stretched over sacking, heavy grey blankets, brown sheets, brown chamber-pots and white nightcaps. Edmond's thoughts were of 'the unnatural passions which must expand and burst forth in this place; the jealousies, the fits of rage that make them get up at night and murder the occupant of the next bed... with their only weapon, a chamber-pot.' In the room allotted to mental cases, the only occupation was making shoes. 'Here there are witches, shrews, and women with fingers almost paralysed, lethargic brains, childish terrors, minds stirring restlessly... as do bodies in a nightmare...' Their visit ended in the infirmary where one young woman lay dying of a spinal disease and another of consumption.

What Robert Ricatte, in one of his studies of the Goncourts, calls the *Notebook of 'La Fille Elisa'*, is compiled of observations which either go back to the youth of their mistress, the midwife Maria, and to her daughter, a prostitute, who is presented as the heroine of the novel, or give a fragmentary picture of prostitution which includes extracts from letters found in a brothel in the Cité, anecdotes, background impressions, and jottings from various books on prostitution and conditions of prison life. This notebook was not all written during Jules's lifetime. After his death, Edmond made many entries in it, mainly from books he had read, but there are also pages that remind one of *Germinie Lacerteux*. It would seem, therefore, that they were considering both these novels at the same time. Why then did they abandon their plan of writing one on prostitution and the penal system in favour of *Manette Salomon* and *Madame Gervaisis*? Was it because of the poor reception given to *Germinie Lacerteux*?

It was not until February, 1871, that Edmond once more became engrossed in *La Fille Elisa*. In November of that year, the *Journal* records his desire to put into this novel 'something of the macabre character of the pastels of Guys and Rops.' But later he laid the book aside. On December 5 he wrote: 'Most decidedly I no longer take any interest in creating a book. Making a flower-bed, a room, or the binding for a book, is all that gives my brain any pleasure at the moment.' This fit of inertia, from which he was slightly roused by the example of Zola busy at work, ended a year later, as he was journeying back from Saint-Gratien. 'In the train, as I was returning home, the mist in which the embryonic idea of *La Fille Elisa* was floating was suddenly dispelled, and without having thought about it during these past few days, I had a clear ... revelation of the way in which I should construct and write my novel.'

During a walk through the Bois in the chill morning air, he decided to fuse the three projected sections of the novel into one, which Elisa would live over again in prison. He needed, however, to be encouraged by Alphonse Daudet in order to decide, on July 25, 1875, to write in large letters on the first page of a blank note-book, LA FILLE ELISA. '... once I had written this title, I was seized with painful anxiety, I began to have doubts about myself. It seemed to me, as I cudgelled my brain, that I no longer had either the power or the skill to write a work of imagination, and I feel afraid ... of a work no longer begun with the confidence I used to have when *he* was working with me.' However, on August 17, he was able to tell Daudet that he had written the first and last chapters.

There followed an interlude taken up with re-modelling *Sophie Arnould*, preparing *La Saint-Huberty*, and putting *Les Saint-Aubin* into shape for the third edition of *L'Art au XVIIIe Siècle*. When he had gone back to his novel he did not lay it down again.

His nightly walks to the pont de Saint-Cloud favoured his inspiration. He was pleased with himself. He read Zola the passage in which Elisa mounts guard and which he later accused his fellow-writer of having cribbed in *L'Assommoir*. Feelings of anxiety about his health did not prevent him from continuing his work, but he wrote the last chapters with the haste of one who fears that he will not have time to write all the clauses in his will. Apprehension of legal proceedings was an additional trial to his nerves. Huysmans, who had just published *Marthe, Histoire d'une Fille*, and who had learnt of his success in writing *La Fille Elisa*, sent him his book, expressing his regrets at this coincidence of subject and telling him that *Marthe*, which had been printed in Brussels, had been held up at the frontier. Edmond, racked with anxiety, dreamt that he was imprisoned and that from the depths of the prison, transformed into a theatre, two 'murderesses' from Clermont were ogling him.

La Fille Elisa was completed on December 30, 1876. 'Nothing now remains but to read it over. I had a plan for carrying things further ... but ... the thought that the work will be the subject of legal proceedings makes me disinclined to do anything more.' In January Edmond read the book to the Daudets, who approved of everything, except the final intervention of the author, and on the 21st the book was published by Charpentier.

On the advice of his 'young master', Daudet, he visited a few critics. 'I saw About at his flat in all the glory of gilded leather. I saw Barbey, who received me in his shirt-sleeves and pearl-grey trousers with a black stripe down the side. I saw Gille, Gille in his own person' (Gille being a critic and journalist well-known in his day).

At Charpentier's amidst the feverish bustle of the assistants, he packed up books to be sent off. Outside in the street, in a slight shower of rain, a man was reading *La Fille Elisa!* The book was on show everywhere. In a few days 10,000 copies had been sent out and five editions had been sold before printing was completed. By 1891 it had reached its thirtieth edition. The fear of its confiscation had given him terrible palpitations, but there was never a serious question of this. The Princess did not breathe a word to him about the novel, but only said: '... is there any fear of your being prosecuted?' He was touched by this anxiety on his behalf.

Edmond Alone

'I liked Goncourt's novel,' wrote Flaubert to the Princess. 'At the beginning of it, I was put off by certain affectations and careless slips in the style. Then I let it take hold of me. On the whole, I find this a work full of talent. That is my sincere opinion.'

Without having asked for authority to do so, *Le Nain Jaune* offered *La Fille Elisa* as a free gift to its subscribers, but coupled this offer with a 'prudish slating'. In *Le Gaulois* Edmond Tarbé, tacitly drawing the Attorney-General's attention to it, lamented the error into which Edmond had been led by his enthusiasm as a painter and novelist. 'Had it come from anyone but himself *La Fille Elisa* would not even have been mentioned in this paper. Written by this courageous and honest pen, it constitutes a danger that we have considered it our duty to point out. Nevertheless we do him honour by this expression of our indignation.' *La Nation* demanded that the author should be confined, as was the Marquis de Sade, in a lunatic asylum. The novel found an ardent champion, however, in Céard, writing in *L'Actualité*.

Besides being a philosophical study of the role of fate in the destiny of certain criminals, *La Fille Elisa* proclaimed that the system in women's prisons was so merciless that it caused numerous cases of insanity. The preface made no secret of the author's intention of appealing to the emotions of those who administered the law in order to mitigate the fearful torture imposed by the rule of silence, which parliament had recently re-confirmed for those serving longer sentences. Solitary confinement for those sentenced to a year or less was also re-confirmed.

To judge from certain authorities, however, it seems that cases of insanity attributable to this régime were less numerous than Edmond's preface would have us believe. One might therefore be tempted to accuse him merely of posing as a redresser of wrongs. Let us say that he sinned out of an excess of sentimentality and with an eye to the sensation to be produced, not that this artless deception could harm anyone. The documentation of the whole book is similarly exaggerated in everything concerning the behaviour of the women convicts.

'You have been thoroughly investigated,' Burty wrote to him after one of his friends had visited the Ministry, 'but there won't be any legal action against you.' And he added in a postscript: 'Between ourselves, don't do it again.'

Edmond has not concealed from us the pleasure he derived from the success of *La Fille Elisa*. 'Yes, indeed, whatever people may say, I think my talent has grown greater through misfortune and sorrow. Yes, indeed, my brother and I have brought about a literary movement that will carry everything before it, a movement at least as great as the romantic movement.'

As early as the end of 1876, and when it still remained for the final touches to be put to *La Fille Elisa*, Edmond introduced into his *Journal* the first sketch of a novel with which he counted on bidding farewell to this genre. 'I would like to create two clowns, two brothers loving each other as we loved each other, my brother and I. They will have pooled their spinal column and throughout their lives will try to perform an impossible feat of dexterity which for them will be what the solution of a scientific problem is for the scientist. There will be many details about the childhood of the younger brother and the fraternal affection of the elder, mingled with a hint of parental love. In the elder, strength, in the other graceful charm, with something in him of the poetry of the common people... At long last, the trick... would be discvoered. On the same day, the jealousy of an equestrienne whose love the younger brother had spurned would make him lose his footing... The two brothers would make, as it were, a religion of their muscles that would cause them to abstain from women and everything that weakens a man's strength.'

This is precisely the theme of *Les Frères Zemganno*. Edmond has not embellished it any more than he has departed from it. We see in this book the transposition of the rule of life which had been that of these two brothers; everything for the sake of their muscles, that is to say everything for style, everything for literature. Here too we see more intimate and personal analogies, such as the Zemgannos' dying mother placing the younger son's hand in the elder's. Like the elder Zemganno, the elder Goncourt understood his mother's preference for the younger; and just as Nello's training in acrobatics had been undertaken by Gianni, so had Jules's education in art and literature been undertaken by Edmond.

Edmond has given no explanation of why he made the two brothers into acrobats; but, on reflection, it can be seen that apart from literature no activity undertaken in common was better suited to his aim than that of acrobatics. Collaboration here is extremely close and is fraught with peril, which corresponds very well with the idea the

Goncourts had formed of the profession of letters and the torment it entails. 'To watch them [clowns] is to learn to write,' declared Barbey. We would add, with all due respect, that if acrobats performed as the Goncourts wrote they would sometimes break their necks.

Both Edmond and his brother had been amateurs of the circus. When, at the end of 1876, the idea of *Les Frères Bendigo*—this is what Edmond called them first before discovering in Bachaumont the name Zemganno which pleased him better—became fixed in his mind, fairs and circuses were in favour among young writers and artists, as they were to be after the First World War. There is nothing astonishing therefore in Edmond, attracted like Barbey by circus folk, having chosen to make the two brothers acrobats. Jules Claretie alleges that Médrano, known as Boum-Boum, was Edmond's own particular clown, as Boswell was Baudelaire's and Auriol Banville's, but there is no proof that he took Médrano or any other clown as his model.

On September 18, 1878, he sends his apologies to Burty for not having gone to see him; he has had to run round seeing jugglers and clowns in order to build up his first chapter. On October 2 he writes to tell Daudet that he has one chapter almost finished, 'in the second manner of the Goncourts, which I find infinitely amusing'. He will be happy to read the family what he has already written and receive the modest but well-deserved round of applause. On the 24th we read in the *Journal*: 'I ought to write my novel on the two clowns very well as I find my brain at this moment in a vague and fluid condition well adapted to this work, which is a little outside absolute reality.'

He asked Charles Franconi, the manager of the Cirque d'Hiver and the Cirque d'Eté for permission to go to rehearsals of a play in mime and asked him what kind of wood ·was used for a springboard. Frédéric Masson supplied him with a mine of information on acrobats and clowns.

He worked steadily, like a dumb beast, sometimes from morning till night and without going out for several days, enjoying seeing his manuscript grow larger. Again he went to have a look at the circus. 'The task of taking notes from life, of catching throughout a whole evening ... rapid and feverish impressions of little things that last only a second, throws me ... into a strange state of emotion ... of vague excitement ... restless twitchings in my body, and little nervous tremors in my hands.'

Four Novels

The novel was finished on March 10, 1879. The reading of it took place in Auteuil a few days later. Alphonse Daudet has given an account of it in his *Souvenirs d'un Homme de Lettres*. Besides himself, Zola, Turgenev and Charpentier were also there. Flaubert had broken his leg a few days before. 'We listened,' writes Daudet, 'moved, enraptured, but with a tightening of the heart, as we gazed ... at the tropical creepers, the rare shrubs with their glistening lacquered leaves in the little garden, still green in spite of the season. A thaw was beginning, twinkling like stars on the fountain, and damping the rockeries, as the sun of a departing winter cast its smile upon the snow ... "So you really like it?—You're pleased?" said Edmond de Goncourt, cheered by our enthusiasm, while ... the miniature of his dead brother in its little gilded oval frame seemed ... to be lit with a ray of belated glory.'

The book appeared on April 30. It was dedicated to Mme Alphonse Daudet, who, under the pseudonym of Karl Stenn, immediately reviewed it in the *Journal Officiel*. '... this work ... represents the Goncourts' second manner, which is no less interesting and artistic than the first ... There is the same process of compact analysis, the same truly poetic language. We find too that the constant habit of working together, of reviewing ... each chapter in turn, has resulted in blending the ideas and the style of MM. de Goncourt so well as to make a single literary character out of their artistic natures ...'

This article and a few lines from Victor Hugo compensated for the 'series of slatings' which, so Edmond wrote to Mme Daudet, had fallen on his head, particularly the one from Barbey d'Aurevilly in *Le Constitutionnel* reproaching him for his friendship with Zola and the naturalists. 'No one, I believe,' wrote Flaubert, 'realises better than I do what underlies your little book. It's bold, it has movement and colour. It's genuinely artistic and not, thank heaven! precious.' He disapproved, however, of the intention of the preface. 'Why do you have to make a direct appeal to the public? It's not worthy to receive your confidences.' This preface, towards the end of which Edmond seemed to repudiate naturalism, did not meet with Zola's approval either. 'You told me one evening,' he wrote, 'that great efforts were being made to create ... dissension in the little group to which we belong. Well, that's just what the papers are beginning to say of your preface; it's cast into the teeth of young men who love you, and whom you are accused of repudiating at the very moment when they badly need your powerful protection. This pains me very much. I am going to reply to your preface by expressing all my admiration for you, but also by trying to clear up certain points which you appear to me to have left obscure.' Zola's article appeared in *Voltaire*. In it he rejects the term 'low and vulgar' as applied to the subjects favoured by the naturalists and warns Edmond that if he should try to remain a naturalist when he sets out to depict polite society, he will find himself up against the same misunderstanding of his work as occurred over *Germinie Lacerteux*. This preface of Edmond's and Zola's reply caused the first rift in their friendship.

Les Frères Zemganno is the most moving of all Edmond's novels because it is the most full of feeling, the most personal, and one would be tempted to say the most impassioned, if brotherly affection, carried to its extreme limits, can be described as a passion. Since they had never been seriously involved in a love affair, no novel, either written by both the brothers or by Edmond alone, had been inspired by a great love. *Les Frères Zemganno* takes the place of such a novel among their works. Its construction and tone and the simplicity of its theme are impressive. In it we find the defects of the other novels, namely a limited flight of poetic fancy and a certain lack of imagination, but it is bathed in a sort of twilight glow, the projection, as it were, of Edmond's inconsolable grief. At no time has he any intention of presenting us with real circus artists, with their particular psychology, their habits of mind, or the language and manners of their profession. His two brothers have no existence of their own, no real life; they are symbols, phantoms, painted figures, but it is precisely this sort of nocturnal and lunar unreality that gives this work its strength. Jules had more wit, more whimsical fancy and more imagination than his brother, but it must also be granted that in collaboration with him Edmond would never have written so sensitive and original a work as *Les Frères Zemganno*.

'... my fellow-writers fail to grasp that it is a different sort of book from those I have already published ... a completely new injection of poetry and fantasy into a true-to-life study, and that I have tried to make realism take a step forward ... to endow it with certain literary qualities of half-tone and chiaroscuro which it did not previously possess ... are not natural objects as real by moonlight as when they are seen in the rays of the midday sun?' Curiously enough, these lines which fit so well with the impression of twilight

Four Novels

that one notices in reading *Les Frères Zemganno*, were written by Edmond in referring to *La Faustin*.

The idea of a theatrical novel, that would be the psychological study of an actress had occurred to the two brothers many years before. At Burty's house, on May 14, 1871, Edmond was once more seized with this idea and jotted down an outline of the story to which, as it happens, he was to attach little importance. It was not until nine years later, on August 27, 1880, that the idea of *La Faustin* again appeared in the *Journal*.

On April 6, at the house of the painter and sculptor Guiseppe de Nittis, Edmond read the first part of his novel. In the vast studio where oriental carpets, Japanese wall-pictures, easel-paintings, pastels and Chinese umbrellas shone in the light from two chandeliers, a little company of friends had assembled. A silk lampshade cast a soft light over the couch where the mistress of the house had invited Mme Alphonse Daudet, Mme de Hérédia, Mma Zola and Mme Georges Charpentier to sit beside her. The men were standing, among them Philippe Burty, Huysmans, Céard, Alexis. Seated at a little table Edmond read in a trembling, staccato voice that occasionally broke down, the completed scenes of *La Fausta*, the title that he gave first to *La Faustin*.

A few days later he wept as he wrote the letter in which Blancheron gives warning of his intention to commit suicide. 'Will it have the same effect on the reader's nerves as it has on mine?' Blancheron's letter is moderately touching and so too is the bequest he makes of his dog to the actress, but it is doubtful whether many of his readers, even women, have been moved to tears by it.

In his search for a model for *La Faustin*'s dressing-room he went to the Théatre Français to visit Mlle Lloyd, Madeleine Brohan, Delaunay and other actors and actresses in theirs. Mme Arnould-Plessy gave him information on the various ways of interpreting a part, and Dinah Félix got him admitted to rehearsals of a tragedy. On the conflict between love and the theatre in an actress's heart Mme Arnould-Plessy said: 'Well, if she is young, sincere, good-natured, tender and simple-hearted, in fact, if she is a true woman, she will be a woman before being an artist, and her love, that is to say her faith in the person she loves, will keep her free from regrets. But if she is not so young, if her faith in men has suffered, in fact, if she

Edmond Alone

has learnt that giving oneself up to another person is less than giving oneself up to art, then she will have done wrong to desert her art for a man and she will suffer for it. People who have retired because of age, in other words when the power to act is beyond them, do not suffer so much. On the contrary, that is the natural order of things.'

Broadly speaking, La Faustin is Rachel, but the letter about different phases in the study of a role comes from another actress, Mlle Fargueil, and the remarks during a dinner party are taken from conversations at Magny's.

After negotiations with Jules Guérin, of *Gil Blas*, the novel was accepted for publication in *Voltaire*. The editor intended to cover Paris with posters and to have 100,000 portraits of the heroine distributed in the streets—if only the police had authorized the use of sandwich-men! The editor then had another idea: little banners hanging on the lamp-posts along the main boulevards saying: '*La Faustin*, November 1, in *Voltaire*'. This sort of circus publicity embarrassed Edmond, but what could he do? Having stuck his little finger in, he was caught in the machinery.

Alphonse Daudet did not conceal his disapproval. 'I am even more deeply grieved than you are,' Edmond replied, 'and my distress is mingled with an extremely disagreeable feeling of nervous suspense.' *Gil Blas* having asked for permission to give *La Faustin* as a free gift to its subscribers, poor Edmond was in the depths of despair. 'Is it possible that the publication of a book can cause a man of letters the same deterioration of physical and mental energy criminals undergo after committing a crime?' If only the manager of *Voltaire* could even have reaped some reward for his efforts! But the sale of his paper was far from equalling these.

The book was published on January 17, 1882, and was prominently displayed in the bookshops, but Gambetta's resignation almost compromised its success. 'Am I condemned to remain all my life the man who published his first novel on the day of a *coup d'Etat?*' Edmond asked. Very soon, however, Charpentier had to see about reprinting it.

Paul Bourget, in *Le Parlement*, Daudet in *Le Reveil*, Mme Daudet in *Le Temps*, Maupassant in *Le Gaulois*, Zola in *Le Bien Public* and Céard in *L'Evénement* defended *La Faustin* against Léon Chapron, Ulbach, Delpit and Barbey d'Aurevilly. Vallès compared Edmond to the Marquis de Sade and his book to the buzzing of a fly in a hospital nightcap. Discussion on the book extended as far as Sweden and Portugal.

In *La Revue des Deux Mondes*, Brunetière denounced its realism, but ended with the suggestion that Edmond was not a true naturalist. 'He represents all that is contrary to naturalism . . . almost always odd, sometimes ingenious, but never natural. It is not even rococo, it is the spirit of Japanese art introduced into a novel.'

Three of Léon Daudet's schoolfellows, having to write an essay on death, included in it the *sardonic* death-agony described in *La Faustin*. '. . . this sardonic death-agony,' we read in the *Journal*, 'is a piece of invention, of imagination, but possible and probable, and I would not have risked it if I had not had certain information. Here is what happened to Rachel. She had an old servant whom she was much attached to and on whom I have modelled my Guénégaud. This old servant was taken ill, very ill . . . and one night the tragedienne was woken up and told that she was dying. Rachel went downstairs weeping bitterly and most genuinely distressed, but not a quarter of an hour had gone by before the actress was entirely absorbed in studying the death throes of the woman who had become, as it were, a stranger to her and a subject of observation. I gathered these details from Dinah Félix.'

★ ★ ★

The first idea of *Chérie* had come to Edmond in October, 1878, while listening to the confidences of Mlle Abbatucci, one of the Princess's ladies-in-waiting. 'To-day Mlle Abbatucci was talking to me about her life as a little girl and I let her go on talking, while my thoughts turned towards the project for a novel that would deal with the life of a young woman of the Second Empire.' In the novel the grand-daughter of the Marshal is the portrait of this grand-daughter of the Minister of Justice, suitably transposed. When the book appeared, Edmond feared the young woman's reproaches, but she contented herself by saying: 'This evening, you know, you'll have to be especially nice to me!'

According to the elder Rosny, some of the letters that were used in the writing of *Chérie* (at first called *Tony Freneuse*) were unusual because of their subtle psychology, others remarkable for a realism which at times was a little startling, and others because of certain odd touches, extraordinary or comic revelations, or physiological details that would have appeared only in medical books. Edmond told Rosny that these letters had taught him a good many things '... it's a gold mine for writers that I've discovered here,' he said, '... Try your hand at it, you are fond of truth! It's too late for me... My brain is no longer capable of a great effort of concentration, I am going to settle down with my notes and probably write a play.'

The collected correspondence reveals that Pauline Zeller, the daughter of the history professor whom Sainte-Beuve had got a position for in Princess Mathilde's household, helped Edmond to write *Chérie*. On March 10, 1883, she wrote to him: 'I am sending you my poor little red notebook by the same post. It is a sacrifice of my moral coquetry I am making for your sake, and I am now much more of a coquette morally than physically. You will find a lovely example in it of the vanity and frivolity from which I believe no little head of sixteen years who considers herself pretty can be free... I give it you, just as it is, knowing only too well you would be terribly distressed if I touched it up. The last page has been torn out, I haven't taken it out. I remember having torn it up almost as soon as I had written it... If at times it shocks you... don't be misled by it, and be quite sure that a young girl of sixteen, brought up in our particular environment, is completely ignorant of everything and acts almost entirely out of ignorance. Knowing nothing, one dares do anything. Reserve comes later.'

Pauline Zeller also gave Edmond letters from completely uninteresting little girls. She had a feeling of tenderness, possibly one of love, for the old writer. She used to scold him for being melancholy. 'What you tell me,' she once wrote to him, 'is horribly sad and I do not wish people to write me things like that!... if it is to make yourself seem interesting... you have no need to do that. You make your sorrows and your misfortunes bigger than they are, and one would really believe that the more unhappy you find yourself the better you are pleased.'

With *Chérie*, Edmond reached the final phase of a long evolution that had begun with *Charles Demailly* and tended towards the elimination of everything romantic in favour of a literal representation of everyday life. He realized it was not possible to go any further in this direction. On March 3, 1883, he wrote: 'In *La Petite-fille du Maréchal* [Chérie] I am looking for something that will no longer resemble a novel. Absence of plot is no longer enough for me; I would like the texture and the form to be different, and this book to have the character of a young woman's memoirs written by a friend. Certainly, this term *novel* no longer describes the kind of books we are writing. I would prefer a new title, which I am looking for but cannot find, in which it would perhaps be well to introduce the word *histories*, in the plural, with an appropriate adjective, but this adjective—there's the snag! No! No! to rechristen the novel of the nineteenth century, one would definitely have to find a new word.' One wonders why Edmond, who was a painter, did not happen to think of the word *study*, already used by Balzac, and later by Bourget.

In March, 1884, *Chérie* appeared as a serial in *Gil Blas* and Edmond read the preface to Daudet. In it he said that he had tried to describe 'refined reality' and that *Chérie* still included too many incidents, situations and intrigues to suit his taste.

Chérie has been considered a minor work. It is not a novel but is what is known to-day as a 'documentary', and a singularly lively documentary on life in society at the time of the Second Empire. The character of the heroine, at once so original and so simple, is portrayed very truthfully, and the analysis of her sensations shows remarkable subtlety and insight.

Eight thousand copies of the book were printed and when it was published in April, 1884, it was accompanied by a manifesto that defended that original and artistic style of writing which had been criticized by the Press. Edmond felt it was necessary to rally the little group of which he was the recognized head. 'Should we, the novelists, the artisans of that literary genre which has triumphed in the nineteenth century, should we renounce what has been the trade mark of all true writers in every age and in every country, lose all ambition to have a language capable of rendering our ideas, our sensations, our portrayal of men and things in a manner different from everyone else, in another tongue, in a language bearing our own signature, and descend to using the common vehicle of journalistic news items! . . . always, always, the novelist must write with an eye to those who have the most refined and subtle appreciation of French prose, and French prose of this present day, and always he will try to put into what he writes that indefinable something, exquisite and fascinating, which the most intelligent translation can never convey in another tongue.'

Was he so sure of the merits of an artfully polished style? Did he not sometimes have doubts about it? On May 24, 1888, he writes, for instance: 'Beauty in literature comes perhaps from being a writer without feeling conscious that one is writing.' Even more significant is this passage in the *Journal* of 1875 in which he condemns Mallarmé for his 'chinoiseries' and other 'baroque adornments of vocabulary and syntax'. 'This over-meticulous concentration on little points of style dulls the most gifted minds and while they are busy setting some insignificant gem of a phrase in position, turns them aside from those powerful, great and passionate things that give life to a book'. If this is not a condemnation of artistic style, what is it?

Chérie found no more favour in Pontmartin's eyes than *Germinie Lacerteux, La Fille Elisa,* and *La Faustin*: 'Since the death of Jules... the survivor's literary productions have so deteriorated that if he were not attached to the most gregarious of all coteries and adopted by the new school, not exactly as a progenitor, but as an uncle from whom one has expectations, he would no longer be considered. In all the copious repertory of the naturalist novel I know of nothing worse than *La Fille Elisa, La Faustin* and *Chérie.*' 'They are idle strollers,' wrote Barbey d'Aurevilly apropos of *Chérie*. 'They look around and are dazzled by what they see. They are not observers. Seeing is not observing.' Edmond Biré, the Royalist writer, was not any more indulgent, neither was the critic Anatole Claveau, nor Jules Levallois, nor the whole body of critics either at home or abroad. 'The slating becomes international,' wrote Edmond, '*La Fanfulla,* from Rome, declares that my sensibility makes me see phantasmagoric visions of the truth. In fact, there is a hue and cry throughout all Europe against my book.'

Having no more characters to create, or notes to take for a new work of imagination, Edmond was conscious of a strange feeling of emptiness after writing *Chérie*. 'I am suffering for the first time, perhaps, since my brother's death, from finding myself alone. When I was writing novels, when I was creating characters, my creations kept me company, supplied me with a circle of friends, and peopled my solitude; I lived with the good folk, men and women, of my little book. History, with its dead characters, does not give you this illusion...' A few days later he added: 'To-day, with the Sichels away at Eaux-Bonnes and the Daudets in Champrosay, to-day when those who remain of my little Sunday society have said goodbye to me with the words: "Till next October", I felt myself alone, all, all alone!—and for the first time I experienced a kind of dread of my isolation.'

IV
'La Maison d'un Artiste'

After Jules's death the furnishing of the house in Auteuil had remained incomplete. Mme Daudet relates that in 1874 the attention given to every detail of the garden contrasted with the rough and ready appearance of the house, and it is true that at this period Edmond believed himself to be quite detached from it and his collections. 'I wander aimlessly among my books without opening them, among my flowers and my drawings without casting a glance at them. The ties that existed between me and all these things seem to be broken. My house does not seem to me any longer what it was six months ago, I take no pleasure in being there. I know not what mortal lethargy has taken hold of me before its time.' It was not until three years later that, satisfied at last with the interior of the house, he took up his pen to describe it.

In 1860, the first exhibition of his drawings had been held in the Salle Martinet. In May, 1879, Charles Ephrussi, the collector, had appealed to his expert knowledge of old drawings at an exhibition at the Ecole des Beaux Arts, and Philippe Burty had given two lectures on drawings Edmond had lent. In 1884, a third exhibition of his drawings was held at Georges Petit's. This exhibition was a great success. The *Journal*, however, makes no allusion to it. This silence is all the more curious since in 1879 Edmond was busy writing *La Maison d'un Artiste*, forty pages of which had already been published a year before in the *Moniteur du Bibliophile*, and a chapter, *Les Marchands d'Estampes et de Dessins de 1848 à 1850*, had appeared in *Voltaire*. The book itself was published in two volumes in 1881. It divided into sections corresponding with the division of the house: on the ground floor was the hall, the dining-room, the little drawing-room and the big drawing-room, and the staircase; on the first floor, the study, the dressing-room, a bedroom, the Far-Eastern room, and a little sitting-room. Next came the second floor, and finally the garden.

The hall was paved with red and white marble, and its walls and ceiling covered in leather decorated with fantastic parrots. On the walls hung brass ornaments, pieces of gilded pottery, Japanese embroideries, weird and exotic objects of unknown origin, and standing out in the middle of all this a bas-relief by Clodion.

The dining-room, like the one in the rue Saint-Georges, was 'a real little den,' said Edmond, 'such as I love and in which neither wall nor ceiling can be seen beneath the decorations.' The walls were covered with panels of eighteenth-century tapestry and had two large gilt bronze brackets on them. The furniture was of the plainest: a table and eight chairs carved by Mazaros, a rosewood dinner-waggon, and a huge screen also marvellously carved. The mantelpiece was decorated with a little marble statue by Falconet and a pair of three-branched candlesticks engraved with a cardinal's coat-of-arms.

After the siege, when the little drawing-room had been turned into a combined bedroom, study, and hen-house, Edmond had had it hung with Turkey-red material and its woodwork painted with shining black enamel so as to show off the drawings that he and Jules had so patiently collected. In blue mounts and framed in old oak, carved and gilded, they filled the whole house. There were four hundred of them, many in portfolios that were stuffed to overflowing. They were his riches and his pride, witness to the fact that with plenty of time and little money, any poor fellow sensible enough to ignore paintings, even cheap ones, could accumulate little master-pieces that wealthier collectors had passed over. *La Maison d'un Artiste* contains the catalogue of them, commented upon with love.

The description of the big drawing-room is relatively short. Its ceiling was covered with a Boucher tapestry, bought with the royalties from *Germinie Lacerteux*. The sumptuous Beauvais furniture, representing the fables of La Fontaine, they had bought at Weil's in the days of their youth. There was also a Marie-Antoinette writing-table and a marquetry chest-of-drawers, two Sèvres vases on buhl stands, a Japanese bowl and on the mantelpiece a statuette and two terra-cotta vases by Clodion, and a clay model of Piron's bust by Caffieri. Standing on two small pieces of furniture inlaid with mosaic were gouaches and porcelains, and elsewhere various other ornaments and terra-cotta. In the middle of the room stood a tripod figured with sea-waves, and a large bronze Japanese vase bought for 2,000 francs before things Japanese came into fashion.

From the hall, through an opening hung with greenery, one could glimpse the staircase draped in coarse linen, maize-coloured and with a border in Persian style. The walls were covered with eighteenth-century drawings, Japanese wall-pictures and great dishes, and amongst all this the only framed engraving in the house, of Watteau's *L'Embarquement pour Cythère*, bought a long while before for eight francs. On the first floor landing, against a background of rusty yellow linen, Satsuma vases and other exotic curios stood on corner brackets close beside a little piece of red lacquer furniture containing albums enshrining the whole life of Japan. Thirty-five pages of *La Maison d'un Artiste* are devoted to a description of these. On the landing walls were Japanese panels encrusted with china flowers, ivory leaves, jade rocks, mother-of-pearl birds, stone cattle and coral suns.

On the study ceiling, against a background of black velvet, two Korean lions, stocky monsters with bloodshot eyes, gyrated among some peonies. The walls were filled with eighteenth-century books. In the centre of the mantelpiece, on a carved wooden base, stood Falconet's *Baigneuse* in Sèvres bisque, flanked by two Dresden pot-pourri jars and a pair of Japanese candlesticks. A gouache, *L'Epouse Indiscrète*, hung from the mirror, and on either side of it, beneath wall-brackets of green jade adorned with peacock's feathers, were miniatures of the family in gilded copper frames.

Did the books to which Edmond gave preference really reflect his tastes in literature? One dares not take what he said on this subject as literally true: '... the little piece of paper which was not itself a book and from which I made a book or at least a pamphlet, had a far superior attraction for me than some much vaunted work'; for instance, the little bulletin handed to the concierges of big town houses during Louis XV's illness. His list contains no philosophy, except one work by Helvétius, no science, except a treatise on geometry by Sebastien Leclerc, no jurisprudence, or theology; but works relating to art, private and official exhibitions, biographies of artists, reviews, catalogues, technical treatises, cookery books, autographs and manuscripts from which he quotes lengthy extracts with great satisfaction.

The buhl bookcase inherited from his mother, on which stood a statuette of Cupid in Mainz porcelain and a turquoise blue Chinese vase, was the Holy of Holies, which sheltered the most precious books, such as those illustrated by Boucher, Gravelot and Eisen, the Fermiers

Edmond Alone

Généraux edition of La Fontaine, the monumental Molière of 1734, and books stamped with coats-of-arms and magnificently bound in old morocco. Haphazard among these were the Goncourts' own works, on vellum, India paper and linen, some with watercolour illustrations by Gavarni, etchings by François Flameng, enamels by Popelin, and poems by Théophile Gautier, bound in.

On the poetry shelves were a copy of Dorat's verses, and also Sedaine's, both illustrated, and a few calendars containing songs; but on the whole there was very little. On the other hand, there were a great many novels, historical or pseudo-historical ones, novels on army life and on manners, nearly all the novels of Restif de la Bretonne, as well as Senac de Meilhan's *L'Emigré, Manon Lescaut, La Nouvelle Héloïse, Le Diable Amoureux*, the *Confessions du Comte de X*—by Duclos, *Les Liaisons Dangereuses, Les Amours de Faublas, La Religieuse*, and Marmontel's *Contes Moraux*, all in contemporary editions with engravings. Then there were books on manners, women, love, marriage, prostitution, a mixture of works in which Thomas's *Essai* on the characters, manners and minds of women stands out.

'There is in me,' wrote Edmond, 'a certain taste for the works of writers with deranged imaginations, extravagant concepts and peculiar ideas—for books which are slightly mad, those in fact in which, as Montaigne says, the mind, breaking loose from its reins, brings forth chimeras—and I have a little collection of such books on my library shelves.'

History begins with the twenty large volumes of Saint-Simon's *Mémoires*, continuing with the diaries and memoirs of the ducs de Luynes, Mathieu Marais, Barbier, Argenson, Grimm and Bachaumont, and ends with the collection of *Mémoires sur la Révolution*. Then follow other memoirs and biographical documents, first those written by women about women. Along another wall, one section is given to books on the theatre, the Opéra, the Comédie-Française, the Comédie-Italienne, etc., then on Parisian life, the cafés, the Palais-Royal, the Boulevards, the Champs-Elysées, the Bois de Boulogne, and so on.

In the rue Saint-Georges the finest books had been kept in the buhl bookcase in the drawing-room; those for which there was no room had been stacked on plain wooden shelves in a lumber-room next to Edmond's bedroom, which served as a study, and even after they acquired the house in the boulevard de Montmorency, the

'La Maison d'un Artiste'

paper-covered books and the pamphlets were piled in an attic on those same wooden shelves.

We pass now to the dressing-room. 'It is a peculiarity of mine,' said Edmond, 'when I am combing my hair or brushing my teeth, to like to have on the wall while I perform these boring operations, a gaily-coloured bit of paper or some little piece of shimmering pottery which brightens things up and reflects a light like that in the colour of flowers. And that is why my dressing-room is literally covered with porcelains or sketches in gouache.' The walls of this room were hidden by rush-matting stretched on bamboo frames and its woodwork was painted with red lacquer. The space above the doors was filled by a concourse of Boucher's women, and on each door a Japanese wall-picture quivered at every breeze. In the middle of one wall was an indecent little gouache by Mallet and Gavarni's *Débardeuses Londoniennes*, and on another, either side of a little rococo mirror, a landscape of a French park with a Japanese panel-picture underneath.

Edmond's bedroom was filled almost entirely by an enormous eighteenth-century bed with an oval head-piece. It was made of carved wood, heavily ornamented and except for some gilding on the legs, was painted white. There were two tapestry armchairs, a Louis XVI console table with a little clock on it of the same period and a pair of candlesticks with shades, also, besides a lot of sea-green porcelain from Madame de Pompadour's collection, a casket made of wood from the West Indies which had belonged to Captain Huot's mother. In this casket, which still contained an account book dating from the time of the Revolution, Edmond kept the contracts for his books, his share certificates, receipts from antique dealers, family papers, his father's cross of the Legion of Honour, his mother's wedding-ring, and a lock of his sister Lili's hair.

In this room, Edmond had the illusion of being transported to the preceding century; but it was chiefly at night, in the flickering light of the dying fire, that the wall-paper, printed with medallions of figures and flower vases suspended on blue ribbons against a white background, cast its spell. The pages in *La Maison d'un Artiste* in which the writer describes the nightly enchantment of his bedroom are one of the gems of this book.

The Far-Eastern room contained a show-case full of *netsukes*, and a great glass-fronted cabinet of Chinese porcelains. Near this stood a show-case filled with Satsuma bowls and on a table at the far end of the room stood a Japanese inkstand with a little arrangement of sabres and sword-guards above it. In the middle of the mantelpiece stood a large vase of pale green jade, and in this room too one of Edmond's great passions, a collection of swallow-tailed butterflies gleaming like porphyry, agate and jade. A great Japanese dish of red lacquer looked down from one wall, and in the middle of another, in a narrow glass-fronted cabinet, were little objects in gold, ivory, tortoise-shell, glass and rock crystal, snuff-boxes, scent-bottles, inkstands, and small cases of horn, ivory, wood and lacquered bamboo.

The inventory of the small sitting-room is a short one. It includes an immense *foukousa*, or piece of black velvet embroidered in gold, and a branch of magnolia fashioned in ivory on a lacquer panel, a green copper vase, and a sixteenth-century silk Persian carpet.

From the first to the second floor the staircase spiralled between drawings of the French School and Japanese *kakemonos*: tortoises disporting themselves on a beach at low tide, a cluster of poppies, river birds in the midst of aquatic plants, a female monkey holding her baby in her arms. Certain uninhabited rooms full of all kinds of junk and with cupboards stacked with works by modern authors, opened on to the landing.

One of the rooms on the second floor, the one Edmond later arranged to form the 'Grenier', was the room in which Jules had died and where there still remained a bed with its curtains drawn. On the walls were three or four drawings signed J.G. and the original drawing of *La Parisienne* with a dedication by Rops.

The last pages of *La Maison d'un Artiste* are devoted to the garden. From 1872 onwards, a taste for gardening had so taken hold of Edmond that he was sometimes tempted to sacrifice everything to it. 'At moments I am obsessed by the temptation to sell my collections,' he wrote on one occasion, 'to run away from Paris, and buy ... a great tract of land in some remote corner of France where I would live alone as a mad devotee of gardening.' This, however, was only a passing phase. In January, 1872, the frost killed his deodar, his laurels, his buckthorn shrubs, his spindle-trees.

In place of the ordinary trees and bushes that used to be in the garden Edmond planted rare evergreens. He made it into a painter's garden in which the colour scheme, ranging from darkest green to light, passed through tints of bluish-green and greenish-bronze. For

'La Maison d'un Artiste'

him his trees were *objets d'art*, placed as period furniture might be placed in a drawing-room. He added a trellis constructed on an eighteenth-century model, two earthenware statues, two bronze Cupids, a tall Japanese crane, and a bas-relief in terra-cotta. For his favourite corner—a little rock underneath his tall trees—he sacrificed a Dresden china dolphin, which provided a pleasant note of white amid the greenery moistened by the fountain. He was very proud of his yellow jasmine which blossomed as late as mid-December, his January-flowering heath, his February-flowering honeysuckle, his Japanese peonies, and his many-coloured roses.

Edmond undoubtedly loved his garden and prided himself upon it, but to Mme Daudet's question if he spent his evenings there he replied, 'No, I don't. Nature by night is deadly. You can bear it if there are two of you. It's too sad if you're alone.'

Nothing remains to-day of the things that he planted except a dwarf *arbor vitae*, four rhododendron bushes and a few trees from Japan or China which in the last century were considered rare. The Statue of Love that he put at the foot of the front steps has disappeared, so has the trellis which on fine nights resembled some construction in a dream and made him think of an imaginary palace built by Utamaro within the circle of the moon. Gone, too, is the little pond he hollowed out to put his goldfish in. A terrace with balustrades, which did not exist in his time, has now been put up, as well as a little building that faces the main gate.

V

The Cult of Japan

On July 27, 1877, Edmond and Gambetta had been witnesses at the wedding of Burty's daughter. Yet in 1882, Burty is represented as a treacherous creature 'with all the power of subversion he knows how to use against one without ... committing himself in words, and always doing so in the name of sacred friendship'.

What crime had this old friend committed? He had shown Mme Daudet a copy of her husband's *Les Amoureuses*, sent with his compliments to a mistress, and with the connivance of his wife had attempted to dislodge Pélagie in order to put a housekeeper of their own choice into the house at Auteuil. He had also written a novel, *Grave Imprudence*, in order 'to bring about the failure' of *Manette Salomon*, written thirteen years before—a ridiculous accusation. That of jealousy, however, is less so. The elder Rosny, who had met Burty in Auteuil, describes him as having a certain contempt for Edmond, who returned it. 'With Goncourt,' says Rosny, 'it was the scorn of a man of letters and a historian, and one who is sure of having been first in the field [in a love for Japanese things]. With Burty it was the scorn of a mind that is capable of forming concepts beyond his partner's comprehension'. For Burty took an interest in things beyond Edmond's understanding, anthropology, the study of prehistoric ages, and the fauna distributed throughout the world. But, just as their taste for eighteenth-century art had done earlier, a common interest in Japan drew them together. 'Japanese art,' said Edmond in his *Journal*, 'is as great as the art of Greece. What indeed is Greek art ...? A realistic interpretation of beauty. No fantasy, no dreams. It is line in its absolute sense. Not a grain of opium, so sweet and so soothing to the mind, in this representation of nature or of the soul.' These lines are in the *Journal* of January 10, 1862. But the Goncourts' taste for Japanese art goes back still further. In *En 18 ...* we read: 'On a white marble mantelpiece two incense-pans of Tonkinese bronze, stolen by some Buddhist priest from the temple of Say-Lo-Zam-Tay-Voug, distended their flopping gourd-shaped paunches above a curiously entangled wreath

The Cult of Japan

of hybrid vegetation. Serpents writhing in convulsive knots around the handles darted their crested heads towards a lotus flower expanding into a wondrously beautiful bud.'

The two brothers seem to have been the first customers at Mme Desoye's shop in the rue de Rivoli where they often went and whence originated 'the great movement in favour of Japan which to-day extends to fashionable paintings'. The period in which Mme Desoye flourished was also that in which second-hand dealers and junk-merchants did likewise. After the war of 1870, a marked change took place in the business of selling bibelots from the Far East. The junk-merchants of the Second Empire were transformed into well-dressed, cultured gentlemen, married to women of good position, and giving dinners at which the guests were waited on by servants in white ties. Auguste Sichel treated his customers, who were inclined to consider themselves under an obligation to him, as being on an equal footing with himself. He was on friendly terms with Edmond, who dined with him at his house every week, and later on no less regularly with his widow. Edmond considered Sichel's son, Philippe, to be the chief popularizer of Japanese art in France.

On March 20, 1884, the *Journal* speaks for the first time of Hayashi, the art dealer to whom Edmond was indebted for his introduction to Japanese engraving. In 1891, Hayashi brought Edmond the translation of certain important passages in Utamaro's *Maisons Vertes*, Utamaro being Hayashi's favourite artist, and Edmond told him of his intention to write biographical sketches of the Japanese artists. Later, Edmond expressed his amazement at Hayashi's lack of any sense of historical documentation; he had neither thought of showing him the portrait of Utamaro that he had among his portfolios, nor any idea whether poems composed by some women of the Yoshiwara, who figured on one of the plates in Utamaro's *Maisons Vertes*, were still in existence.

La Maison d'un Artiste gives us a glimpse of the Japanese articles collected by Edmond. But what was their real value? When they were put up for sale M. Gaston Migeon acknowledged that Edmond and Burty had been among the first to appreciate the charm of Japanese art, but that Burty's collection, like his friend's, showed excessive confidence in his own judgment and a lack of critical perception. Edmond's love for a precious and mannered style, says M. Migeon, always led him to overlook the finest things in Japanese art. It must be admitted, however, that when Edmond and Burty had begun collecting, nearly all the bibelots coming from Japan were relatively modern; importers of such things did not dare to risk bringing over examples of thirteenth, fourteenth or fifteenth-century workmanship, which were jealously guarded by noble families or preserved in temples, because it would have cost too much. French amateurs of Japan had therefore to content themselves with objects easily picked up in the shops in Yokohama and Tokio, whose antiquity went back no further than the eighteenth century and which were often not even very remarkable specimens.

Edmond had therefore no knowledge of really old pieces. 'Everything I like, and everything I see liked by people whose taste I respect, bronzes with the softness of wax, paintings from the life, delicately wrought ironwork, the enchanting ornamentation of Satzuma potters, lovely incrustations on wood, all this is... no more than eighty years old...' Towards the end of 1886 he became aware of a certain evolution in his taste; he was no longer enamoured of prettiness or exquisite finish, but was more attracted by a brutal strength in colouring.

Outamaro, le Peintre des Maisons Vertes, was published in 1891. In its preface, dated May 22 of that year, Edmond says: 'In this month, in which I am entering upon my seventieth year, I am publishing one volume of a series which is truly alarming in that it calls for investigations far afield and complicated work at home; a series which—I have no pretensions to carry to its end.' He clung firmly to his claim of being a pioneer in the discovery of Japan, and inscribed with pride on the cover of his *Outamaro* the names of some thirteen artists and craftsmen, painters, lacquerers, wood-carvers, potters, etc., whom he dreamed, though not very hopefully, of dealing with in subsequent volumes.

An admirer of *Outamaro* offered to provide information about Japan and Edmond asked him for a translation of a biography of Hokusai, which not one of the Japanese living in Paris had been able to give him. As soon as he received it—it was only a short account—Edmond had it published in *L'Echo de Paris*. Then an illustrated biography of Hokusai was published in Japan. But this was still not informative enough, and Edmond would not have been able to write his own study without help from Hayashi, who put his expert knowledge as well as his collection of prints and illustrations at Edmond's disposal.

The Cult of Japan

When in 1896 *Hokousai* finally appeared a certain scholar named Léon de Rosny came forward to challenge Edmond's views. Rosny, who had made a study of Japanese art, saw nothing in Hokusai but a common caricaturist who was 'crazy about drawings'.

Hokousai also formed the subject of a heated correspondence between Edmond and Arthur Meyer, who, having read the article only in proof, realized that it had nothing in it to interest the ordinary reader. The book also gave rise to another incident: Bing, a well-known dealer in Japanese art, had asked someone to let him have a biography of Hokusai, and his agent in Japan, having collected the necessary material which anyone interested in Japan could have procured and translated for themselves, put together two volumes on the subject. And now Bing, in *La Revue Blanche*, criticized Edmond's study as being nothing but a translation of this biography. Edmond replied that of the four hundred pages in his book, announced as long ago as 1891, only thirty had been borrowed from Bing's, the rest having been compiled from the *Vie de Hokousai* which he had published in *L'Echo* in 1892, from numerous prefaces to the artist's albums and books, and from a complete study of his prints and drawings, and from the account of his life for which he was indebted to Hayashi.

Bing's attack in *La Revue Blanche* was hardly calculated to make Edmond regard that periodical with a favourable eye. 'At one time, he remarked, 'the theatre was the department of literature in which most money could be earned. The Jews in the world of letters were then solely dramatists, for instance Dennery and Halévy. Now the young generation of Israelites has recognized the all-powerful influence of criticism, and the kind of blackmail that might be levied through it on the theatre and on publishers, and it has founded *La Revue Blanche* which is a veritable nest of young sheenies. It can be foreseen that with the co-operation of their elders, who supply the funds for almost all the papers, they will become the masters of French literature within the next twenty-five years.'

It was interest in Japan that had brought Edmond and Nittis the painter together. To the luxurious little house with its English standards of comfort where Nittis lived, surrounded by fine Japanese prints and pastels of Parisian life, Edmond was invited in February, 1878, to a dinner made more agreeable by seventeenth century songs. On another occasion, when the Princess was present, there were mandolin

Edmond Alone

players and Italian singers. Edmond also dined there with Oscar Wilde, 'an individual of doubtful sex, who held forth like a strolling player and told tales with his tongue in his cheek'.

'I have struck up a friendship with Nittis and his wife,' wrote Edmond in March 1889. 'They are charming friends.' Mme de Nittis, a little woman with a simple style of dressing, had something shrewdly cunning and quizzical and at the same time faintly peaky in her face.

Edmond and Nittis were soon on intimate terms. The writer went regularly to dine with the painter. But Nittis and his wife fell out with the Daudets: it had come to their ears that the latter were accusing them of preventing Edmond from marrying in order to become his heirs. They would have liked Edmond to stop visiting the Daudets, but this he refused to do.

In August, 1884, Edmond went to visit Nittis at Saint-Germain; a week later the painter was dead. Edmond kept watch throughout the night beside his body. The story of his death and funeral, related in detail in the *Journal*, is the work of a very fine reporter.

VI

'My Friends the Daudets'

One would say that if such a thing were possible Alphonse Daudet occupied the place in Edmond's heart that Jules had left empty. For twenty years, Edmond went twice and even three times a week to sit at the Daudets' table. On March 24, 1885, he wrote: 'I was telling Daudet to-day that my close friendship with him had given my mind its second youth, and that he was the only human being after my brother against whose mind my own liked striking sparks.'

The two had known each other by sight since the first performance of *Henriette Maréchal*, when Alphonse had been pointed out to Edmond. It was not, however, until 1873 that they first met each other, in Flaubert's flat. After a few meetings, Daudet and his wife came to lunch at Auteuil.

'A family partnership,' says Edmond, 'like the one I had with my brother. The wife writes and I have some reason to suspect that she has the style of an artist. Daudet is a handsome fellow, with a thick head of hair and a superb way of flinging back this mane ... he talks very amusingly about his shameless way of stuffing his books with anything that gives him a chance of literary reflections ... ' But Edmond made some reservations about his talent. ' ... in spite of his exuberance, and in spite of the intelligence and wit of his conversation, I believe he has a disposition to improvize, little given to ... thoughtful study and ... a temperament that condemns him permanently to a rather facile type of literature.' In Edmond's view, and this was a capital offence, Daudet was not a stylist. 'What he writes is very ingenious, very well set out, and yet this does not satisfy me, I should be much embarrassed to say why. But yes ... it is that his style ... has the quality of a well-written newspaper article.'

In July, 1874, Edmond paid his first visit to Champrosay. 'The house is made bright and cheerful by the presence of an intelligent and lovely child, on whose face one can see a charming mixture of both his mother and his father.' Mme Daudet read Edmond some of her poems. 'She is really extraordinary, this Mme Daudet. I have never met anyone, either man or woman, who read so well... a reader, too, with a thorough knowledge of... visual effects and of colouring, syntax, turns of phrase...' He appreciated this young woman's talent all the more because she had confessed to him that she had been initiated into literature by reading *Idées et Sensations*. 'This makes me proud, for she is the top pupil in my class.'

Unhappily he adds: 'And yet this place is... visited by hardly anything but artificial gaiety... stimulated by champagne... these delightful people, like their house, seemed sad to me because of the lack of any regard for what is elegant, artistic, quaint or comical. It is the most lamentable stronghold of *bourgeoisie* in which neither a picture, nor an engraving, or a bibelot is to be seen... nothing, absolutely nothing, that is not common, banal... I cannot acclimatize myself to this... environment which clashes so violently with an artistic calling that it drives me into a state of deep depression... it's idiotic, but that's how it is.'

Soon not a single week passed without Edmond and the Daudets meeting each other, either at his home or theirs. From 1885 onwards 'the charming family' lived in a flat in the rue de Bellechasse. The *Journal* gives a pleasing impression of their receptions and their hospitable table.

Edmond's and Daudet's affection for each other grew deeper from week to week, even though Daudet's successes, earned by 'too much pandering to the literary taste of the vulgar public, too much laying on of virtue in order to make the ugly side of reality acceptable', made Edmond feel slightly embittered. There were talks around the fireside, confidences about their work, memories of childhood, confessions of anxiety or sadness, interchanges of ideas on life, on illness and on death. There were also invitations to dinner with Mme Adam, a lady of letters, Charcot, the Daudet's doctor, Gambetta, or Coquelin, and readings of plays. New Year's Day was not allowed to pass without a visit to Auteuil by the Daudet family. Yet whether this intimacy authorized Edmond to set down in his *Journal* all that he could learn either directly or indirectly about the private life of his friends might be disputed.

It was Daudet who brought about a reconciliation between Scholl and Edmond, who, in spite of his dislike of the idea, agreed to dine with Scholl. He found him unchanged; he was still in a state of nerves, still cynical, still a boaster and a snob.

'My Friends the Daudets'

On May 1, 1883, Edmond wrote in his *Journal*: 'Lunch at Ledoyen's on the opening day of the Salon. Daudet sounds Zola and myself to know whether he should present himself for election to the Academy. We urge him to do so.' Daudet was probably conscious of his friends' tacit disapproval, for on May 17 Edmond writes: 'Daudet tells me to-day that he certainly will not present himself for election to the Academy and without letting me into secrets he mentions a host of unpleasant incidents that have already occurred in this connection. But it's like that with all elections, and Daudet is not so naïve as to be ignorant of this.'

The duel that took place in May, 1883, in which Daudet wounded Delpit, moved Edmond all the more because of its connection with a matter about which he was particularly sensitive: an article on the possibility of Daudet's standing for election to the Academy, in short, on his 'act of betrayal'. With what pleasure Edmond must have listened to his friend's complimentary remarks on the eve of the duel: 'It is strange how well you ... whose eyes are inquisitively intent on outward objects, can see right into people's minds. If you were not alive, I should consider myself the greatest man in the whole world of letters, the sole connoisseur of the human species.'

Before he went to fight Daudet wrote to his friend: 'My dear Goncourt, I write to you from the gare de L'Ouest, with my swords ready and the doctor expected. I hope all will turn out to your friend's honour; whatever happens I send you my warmest greetings and beg you, if there is a little accident, to give my dear wife the note I here enclose. After her husband, her children, and her papa and mamma you are the one she loves most dearly. Ever yours affectionately, Alphonse Daudet. Ebner [1] will write to you to-morrow, or I myself. Let's hope it will be me.' The following day he sent this express letter: 'My dear friend, I have just returned from Le Vésinet. I stuck my sword right into Delpit. Not a serious wound, it went through his arm without severing the artery. I am your devoted friend.'

That same year Daudet wrote *Sapho*, 'the most perfect work,' says Edmond, 'the most human, the finest of all those he has written ... a book that merits the title of masterpiece.'

He was delighted to see his friend's talent asserting itself. ' ... his faculty of observation is on the way to attaining heights of grand,

---

[1] Daudet's secretary.

austere and sternly cruel insight... my dear Daudet is like a polypus trying to suck the life out of every living thing... and he grows greater, and greater, and greater!'

It was in this same year that Edmond first read a few pages of his *Journal* to the Daudet family at his house in Auteuil. 'Throughout the close of this year,' he wrote, 'the country of my mind has been Daudet's dining-room and his little study. There I get from the husband a quick and sympathetic understanding of my thoughts, and from the wife tender esteem for the old writer, and from both of them an unchanging, constant friendliness...'

In the spring of 1884 Daudet's health, already in a bad state, grew worse. A course of treatment at Néris made no change. Coming away from a rehearsal of *Henriette Maréchal* Edmond and Daudet had gone to drink a glass of madeira at Foyot's and Daudet stumbled at the door, making his friend feel seriously anxious about his health for the first time. Was he possibly afflicted with the same disease as Jules? He was already speaking of 'a demi-wreck like myself'. Charcot, his doctor, diagnosed his case as hopeless.

In 1885, at the Daudets', Edmond met for the first time that great braggart', Barbey d'Aurevilly. 'He is dressed in a full-skirted frock-coat that makes his hips as large as if he wore a crinoline, and he wears white woollen trousers that look like a pair of flannel pants with understraps. Beneath this ridiculous costume, a person of excellent address with the soft, mincing speech of a man who is used to talking to women, and whose lack of teeth recalls at times the guttural intonation of Frédérick Lemaître, but in a minor key.'

In July, 1885, Edmond made his first long stay at Champrosay where he had been invited from time to time since the beginning of his friendship with the family. His first visit in 1877, with the publisher Charpentier, had been particularly pleasant. There had been games of bowls, a visit to Delacroix's old quarters, a walk in the forest of Sénart, a halt at a village inn round a bowl of mulled wine.

In April, 1885, Edmond met Drumont at dinner in Daudet's flat. The pamphleteer, referring to Jules's *Letters*, had represented Edmond as a corrupter of the young. He apologized for this, and from that time on they often met each other at their friends' houses and at Daudet's weekly dinners. *La France Juive*, which appeared in 1886, gave Edmond a shock, and as it mentioned *Manette Salomon*, which the Jewish press had condemned by its silence, and which had been fiercely slated by Albert Wolff, from then on he was only too ready to agree with Drumont's point of view. The two brothers had been anti-semites. Edmond became more and more so to the verge of obsession, but his anti-semitism was purely theoretical, and did not prevent him from being friendly with 'individuals of that race'. No less 'theoretical' was his opposition to the Republic, to democracy and the parliamentary system, for this was bound up with his aristocratic nostalgia for the old days of France, for the institutions, the manners and the people of the time of Louis XV. He prided himself on never having voted, in which he resembled many of his bourgeois contemporaries.

Edmond's visit to Champrosay in 1885 was a kind of consecration of the intimacy between the two friends. 'Daudet and I have arrived at that stage of intimate friendship in which we remain beside each other without saying a word or making a sound, happy to be together, and feeling no need to show this or to converse.'

At the beginning of 1886, Mme Daudet, who had long wanted to do so, came to dine in Auteuil after the meeting in the 'Grenier'. In June her daughter Edmée was born. Edmond was her godfather. 'This evening my god-daughter is presented to me in her best clothes by the nurse, who scolds me a little as I take the liberty of expressing astonishment at her being so small . . . the mother calls out to me gaily from her bed: "But she's very big, she weighs seven and a half pounds . . . as much as a leg of mutton for twelve." '

There was a marked difference in the mentalities of Edmond and Daudet, which was emphasized by the latter when he read in the *Journal* that scenes of natural life always reminded Edmond of a work of art. He himself was not an artist, far from it! Edmond certainly thought Daudet had great talent, but his gift of observation was always that of a man of the theatre. Also he did not approve of his commercial activities. 'I have children', was Daudet's answer. 'That's why a man of letters must remain a bachelor', was Edmond's private conclusion.

Daudet also had a Bohemian side which was quite unsuited to Edmond's taste. 'A strange nature, Daudet's: a liking for rusticity, a love of fields and woods . . . beershop appetites . . . and an inquisitive interest in unhealthy things and places.' On the other hand, they concurred in lamenting the subjection of French literature to Russian,

Edmond Alone

American and German influences. They also agreed about the final end of man and were equally pessimistic: we are ephemeral creatures, doomed to utter and definitive annihilation. '... speaking to Daudet of his wife's optimism, I said to him: "Yes, we two, alas! see things by day as others see them by night during a spell of sleeplessness or after a nightmare."' Another resemblance was in their methods of work, their habit of jotting down little notes from day to day, a habit that Daudet had contracted as far back as 1858, long before he became acquainted with Edmond.

As little Edmée grew older her godfather waxed sentimental about her, enlarging on the heavenly blue of her eyes, her pretty gestures, her little arms, her childish prattle. Here was another difference between the two men. Edmond believed only in immortality through books, Daudet saw it in children.

Months passed, bringing Edmond regularly and often to the Daudets' home, or the Daudets to Edmond's, without any trace of a misunderstanding. In February, 1888, Daudet read his play, *La Lutte pour la Vie*, to his friend. A few days later, in the rue de Bellechasse, they talked of Shakespeare, Macbeth and Hamlet, and reached the conclusion that only certain select coteries were able to appreciate literature 'of distinction'; but the next week Edmond was finding fault with Shakespeare for a lack of imagination almost equal to Molière's, and declaring that in all his work he admired only Lady Macbeth's sleep-walking scene and the graveyard scene in Hamlet.

On November 8, 1887, suffering from a bad attack of bronchitis and feeling seriously ill, Edmond had made some alterations in his will which he read aloud to Daudet, who until then did not know what was in it.

On June 3 in the following year, *L'Evénement* published under the signature 'Vertuchou', an article that created a scandal. In it Mme Daudet was accused of cultivating Edmond's friendship in order to inherit his money. Should Léon Daudet or his father send his seconds to Magnier, the editor-in-chief of the paper? Alphonse's age clearly indicated that he was the man to do it: he opted for a duel with pistols at fifteen paces until one of the adversaries fell. Edmond tried in vain to persuade him that such a solution was wanting in commonsense; he stood his ground. His seconds, Frantz Jourdain and a certain M. Glouvet, called on Magnier, who, after considering whether he should send them along to the author of the article,

'My Friends the Daudets'

decided to put them in touch with Scholl and Henry Houssaye.

The real point at stake, says Edmond, was professional rivalry. The publisher Ollendorff had remarked to Marpon, the publisher of *L'Immortel*, that Daudet, being as ill as he was, could not have written the book himself; it was obviously the work of his wife. However, a satisfactory settlement was reached, and *L'Evénement* published the apology Mme Daudet insisted on.

On February 24, 1889, Daudet coughed up blood. Edmond found him in bed with sad, sad eyes, his anxiety revealed in the way his hands gripped the sheet.

In October, rehearsals of Daudet's *La Lutte pour la Vie* began. Edmond spent half a day looking on. 'It's a kind of drama that sets your mind working on the moral conditions of society to-day, and that's not usual in a stage play. Daudet possesses ... to a superior degree that faculty of scenic invention that many accepted playwrights have in less measure ...'

Every year, on Edmond's return from Champrosay to Paris, there was a sort of ritual. Léon Daudet would travel in the train with his 'great master' Edmond to Auteuil, and then would stay on to dinner. What Léon wrote about Edmond as he showed himself to the Daudets, brings him admirably before us as one who was deeply attached to his friends, kindly and sensitive beneath a cold exterior, a man of infinite delicacy and tact, but rather shy, with a dread of familiarity and of over-hearty companions, and courteous as a nobleman in his behaviour to women; with a small appetite, but epicurean tastes in food, moderate in the use of wine and spirits because of his liver; often laughing, sometimes till he cried, easily saddened, highly strung, but fundamentally sane, with a soul as crystal clear as a child's and without a trace of anything low or commonplace; in politics and religion a traditionalist; devoid of any feeling for music and little interested in poetry.

As he grew older, Léon adds, Edmond thought more and more about Jules, associating him with himself in his work, his disappointments, and his successes. He would often read to his young friend the page he had just written. He read badly, with a sort of breathlessness and a nasal twang. When he had finished working he did not put anything in order, left his inkpot uncovered and everything on the table just as it was. He had little taste for antiquity and, like des Esseintes, preferred Petronius, Martial, Persius and other writers of the Silver Age to Virgil, Plato and Homer. He valued hardly anyone in the seventeenth century except Pascal, La Rochefoucauld, La Bruyère and Saint-Simon. Racine he found boring, Molière coarse, and Corneille pompous, but he greatly admired Diderot. His literary culture, less than that of Alphonse Daudet, was superior to Zola's, and his knowledge of art was extraordinarily wide.

Lucien Daudet, like his brother, has left memories of Edmond that portray him very well. At Champrosay, on the banks of the Seine, the real Edmond was revealed to little Lucien. His face took on the air of a countryman absorbed in his business, nothing mattered to him except the state of the water and the weather, and the contents of the hoop-nets which he counted with delight. Lucien stresses the provincial traits in Edmond's character, his habit of insisting, contrary to good usage, on his nobiliary prefix, of mispronouncing proper names and using slang expressions; how he was dazzled by a dinner at the Baronne Edmond de Rothschild's, and his annoyance at seldom being given a place beside Princess Mathilde at her Wednesday dinners. Yet this provincial was possessed of a miraculous devil: a passion for things rare and precious which he used his amazing dark eyes to seek out.

At the 'Grenier', on January 4, 1891, Alphonse announced that a grand idea had occurred to him: he would invest 100,000 francs in a review of which he would be chief editor, and which would serve as the organ of his friends. It would be called *La Revue de Champrosay* and would pay a high price for contributions and would publish a large number of interviews, always an excellent means of propaganda. Edmond made no reservations except with regard to the title.

In this same month Drumont launched a violent attack on Daudet because of *L'Obstacle*, a play about hereditary insanity that had just been given at the *Gymnase*. Daudet received a most insulting letter from the pamphleteer. He replied that he was at his disposal for a duel; the encounter could take place at Champrosay, but since he could not stand on his legs he would fight him sitting down. Mad with fury, Drumont replied that there were men in fighting condition in the rue de Bellechasse. He forgot, remarks Edmond, the great service Daudet had rendered him in giving a guarantee of 7,000 francs to Marpon for the publication of *La France Juive*. Edmond offered to intervene on Daudet's behalf, but Daudet refused to let him. Whereupon Drumont demanded an interview with Daudet's secretary,

'My Friends the Daudets'

Ebner; this was to ask, by way of compensation, that *L'Obstacle* should be dedicated to him. The matter ended with Daudet signing a statement that Drumont's father had the sanest mind of any man that ever existed. This seemed to Edmond a good moment for inserting a eulogy of Daudet in his *Journal*, praising him for his kindness, his generosity, and his forbearance.

Standing as landmarks in his *Journal* come a series of dinners at Champrosay and in the rue de Bellechasse, conversation, confidences, almost always gloomy, following each other, rehearsal after rehearsal, first night after first night. Edmond went everywhere with Daudet, they were inseparable. When, in March, 1893, he had a liver attack that kept him confined to his house for five or six weeks, Daudet came two or three times a week to see him, sometimes leaning on his brother Ernest's arm, sometimes on that of his fellow author Hennique, until the day when he himself became too ill and had to discontinue his visits.

On August 2, 1893, the feast of Saint-Alphonse was celebrated at Champrosay. The entire Allard family, Mme Daudet's relations, came from Bourg-la-Reine, and in the evening to crown this happy day Léon read the article on Victor Hugo he had just produced in *La Revue Nouvelle*, 'an altogether remarkable piece of work, full of ideas, images and flashes of insight, written in a superb style. This young Daudet is incontestably the finest critic of the present time.'

The year 1894 was the twentieth year of the Goncourt-Daudet friendship. Mme Daudet commented upon it affectionately to Edmond on New Year's Day. But, like the liver of the one and the legs of the other, this friendship was beginning to fail and now it had to suffer one of those misunderstandings that give rise to gossip. On April 5, 1894, Goncourt makes this comment on Daudet: 'I very much fear that his excessive use of morphia and chloral causes dark thoughts to flit through his brain.' And he sighed. The doubts that possessed him about the depth of this, his most intimate friendship, made the idea of dying seem insupportable.

On July 29 the two men went for a long drive by themselves through the forest of Sénart. 'He shows himself very tender towards me,' says Edmond, 'he speaks of his wife's affection for me, which is like her affection for a member of her own family, and assures me that despite all that has been said, or done, or invented by those who are jealous of our friendship, this affection has not wavered for a single moment.'

'Not for a single moment' . . . this, perhaps, was saying a good deal.

VII

The Five Friends

It was in 1863, at one of the Magny dinners, that the Goncourts first met Turgenev, a gentle, charming giant of a man, 'handsome, nobly handsome, hugely handsome', who had been a friend of Flaubert's for the past five years. Edmond did not meet him again until 1872, at dinner in Flaubert's flat when Théophile Gautier was also present, in a no less dismal frame of mind than the Russian novelist. Death was the favourite theme of these two brilliant conversationalists.

Edmond often dined with Flaubert at the Princess's, at Daudet's, at Brébant's restaurant, at the Café Riche, or at Flaubert's own flat, and Turgenev was almost always present on these convivial occasions. It was he who, well before Vogüé wrote *Le Roman Russe*, revealed the Russian novelists to his friends in Paris.

Edmond and Zola were amazed that there should be so few guests at Flaubert's Sunday gatherings. 'He is famous, has talent, and is a very good fellow, and welcomes you so warmly. Why then, with the possible exception of Turgenev, Daudet, Zola and myself, is there no one at his Sundays which are open to everyone?' Flaubert suffered from attacks of melancholia in which he was often reduced to tears. Edmond naïvely attributed this condition to the fears that haunt those who follow the profession of letters, fears from which, incidentally, all of them said they suffered; they all complained of having hallucinations.

Flaubert's Sunday receptions gave rise to a dinner in which all the five friends participated. 'Flaubert's dinners are unlucky,' we read in the *Journal* of January 25, 1875. 'It was while coming away from the first that I got my attack of pneumonia. Today Flaubert is away ill. There are therefore only Turgenev, Zola, Daudet and myself.' This bout of pneumonia, at the end of December, 1874, was a serious attack and had almost carried Edmond off. For eleven days he had not closed his eyes, stirring restlessly, talking, raving, and dreaming in his delirium that he was going the rounds of all the antique shops in Paris, buying everything there and taking it away.

The Five Friends

The five friends were not always in sympathy with each other. Their common obsession with death did not prevent them from violent wrangling over questions of aesthetics. Flaubert could not understand Edmond's exclusive cult of Balzac, and he charged Zola with adopting flashy devices in order to make himself known, Zola excused himself on the grounds that he had to earn his living. Turgenev had no liking for either Zola or his art; he suspected him of never having read Shakespeare, and accused him of a lack of philosophy and poetic feeling. He was also amazed that Edmond should proclaim it unworthy of an artist to move the bourgeoisie to tears: making a bourgeois weep was not so easy as all that!

Edmond had made the acquaintance of 'young' Maupassant at Flaubert's flat during the winter of 1874–5. One Sunday in February, the young writer related the extraordinary memories he had of Swinburne on holiday at Etretat. These are to be found in the *Journal*. The first letter we know of from the future author of *La Maison Tellier* to Edmond is dated two years later; in it he thanks him for *La Fille Elisa*. 'Here indeed is the modern novel as you have taught us to understand it, so true to life and at the same time so artistic.' On the day after the production of Zola's *L'Assommoir*, in the restaurant Trop, at the corner of the passage du Navre and the rue Saint-Lazare, the dinner generally considered as the one that inaugurated Naturalism took place. Flaubert, Goncourt and Zola were the guests of Paul Alexis, Céard, Hennique, Huysmans, Mirbeau and Guys de Valmont, *alias* Maupassant, the organizer of this little reunion.

Maupassant has several times proclaimed his admiration for *La Femme au Dix-Huitième Siècle* and the *Portraits Intimes*. 'There is really only one kind of history, that which is written by novelists', so he wrote to Edmond about the latter work, which he said he was reading over and over again to try to learn the secrets of a style in which each epithet casts light upon the things it touches on. In February, 1879, Maupassant had a little play in verse, *Histoire du Vieux Temps*, performed at the Théâtre Dejazet and he invited Edmond to it. Three months later he congratulated him on *Les Frères Zemganno*, and two months after on his *Théâtre*.

On March 28, 1880, Daudet, Zola, Charpentier and Edmond went by train together to dine and sleep at Croisset where Flaubert was to read them some chapters from *Bouvard et Pécuchet*. They were a very

Edmond Alone

merry party and soon they were being welcomed by Flaubert in a Calabrian peasant's hat and a short jacket, but as he was too tired there was no reading of *Bouvard*.

On May 8 Pélagie had just asked Edmond: 'Are you going to M. Flaubert's on Sunday?' when her daughter Blanche put a telegram on the table: 'Flaubert is dead'. 'For some time,' writes Edmond, 'I was so shaken . . . that I did not know what I was doing or what town I was passing through in my carriage. I felt that a tie, sometimes loosened, yet always inextricably knotted, bound us secretly to each other. And I recalled with painful emotion the tear that trembled on one of his lashes when Flaubert embraced me as he was saying goodbye on the threshold of his door a few weeks ago . . . we were the old champions of the new school, and I feel myself very much alone to-day.'

On May 11 Edmond took the train to Rouen with Claudius Popelin. Daudet, Zola and others did not travel until the following day. We read in the *Journal*: 'A detail depicted by Daudet: he had just taken his seat in the train when Hérédia noticed him putting on his black gloves, and Daudet said to him laughing: "Already! that surprises you, doesn't it? But . . . for me a train means . . . the joy of a holiday . . . and these black gloves are entrusted with the task of reminding me where I am going."'

In Flaubert's study were his handkerchief, his pipe and the volume of Corneille opened a few days before. The funeral procession made its way in a straggling line towards the cemetery. People were talking of brill *à la normande* and duckling with orange sauce, or commenting on the absence of Hugo, Taine, Renan, Dumas, Augier, and, most of all, du Camp. 'And once the holy water has been sprinkled on the coffin, the whole thirsty crowd hurries down towards the town with faces animated by thoughts of vulgar jollification. Daudet, Zola and I set off again, refusing to take part in the carousal prepared for this evening, and we come back home, talking, on our way, with pious respect of the dead.'

A committee was formed to raise a monument to Flaubert in Rouen. Edmond presided over it, with Lapierre and Turgenev as vice-chairmen and Maupassant as secretary. But of the 12,000 francs the sculptor asked for, only 9,000 had been collected at the end of five years. They had the idea of a performance at the Comédie-Française, at that time under Jules Claretie's management, then at the Odéon which Porel kindly placed at the disposal of the organizers. In the meantime, Edmond had suggested to Daudet, Maupassant and Zola that they should join with him to make up the required amount, but on January 1, 1887, an article in *Gil Blas* signed Santillane attacked the committee, and especially Edmond, in a most disagreeable way. Flaubert's friends, it alleged, were ungrateful wretches. Should not Edmond have devoted to the monument the money he proposed to use for his future Academy? Maupassant, the point of the situation having escaped him, wrote to *Gil Blas* expressing his approval and announcing that he would contribute 1,000 francs to the committee's funds. He had no intention whatever of offending Edmond, who was away in the South of France, but Edmond, incensed by his having done this, sent him his resignation as chairman and with it a subscription of 500 francs. Maupassant offered his apologies: he had not noticed anything in the article that might be unjust to Edmond. On February 2, in an interview with Edmond at Auteuil, he managed, though not without some difficulty, to persuade his master and friend to withdraw his resignation.

Maupassant's *Pierre et Jean* appeared in 1888, with a preface containing a few lines aimed at 'artistic style': 'There is no need for the odd, intricate, harmonious, and peculiar vocabulary imposed on us to-day under the name of artistic style to develop fully every shade of thought.' The allusion did not escape Edmond's notice. 'Already, over the Flaubert subscription, I had found his sincerity left much to be desired. Today, this attack of his reaches me at the same time as a letter in which he expresses his admiration and affection.' Another note, on June 3, 1889, shows Edmond not much inclined to admire Maupassant's novels. '... a novel like *Fort Comme la Mort* now has no interest for me. I no longer like anything except... genuine extracts from life, without any thought as to how they shall be rounded off, and without any of that dressing up for the benefit of the unintelligent reader on which big sales depend.'

The unveiling of Flaubert's monument was finally fixed for November 20, 1890. In miserable weather Edmond took the train to Rouen with Zola and Maupassant, whose staring eyes and air of debility arrested Edmond's attention. They had lunch with the Mayor of Rouen, and after a visit to the Museum, where the writer's manuscripts were on show, the ceremony took place to the strains of an agricultural society's band, and in a squall of wind and driving rain.

Edmond Alone

Some twenty writers and journalists from Paris were present, among them Mirbeau, Bauer and Céard. Edmond, who had been afraid that he would not be able to make his voice audible to the end, trembled as he read his address, but did so without too much difficulty, in spite of the wind that wrapt his fur coat to his body and tore the pages from under his nose. At Mennechet's, where they dined, the conversation turned from Maupassant's pornographic play, *La Feuille de Rose*, to duck *à la Rouennaise* and the punctuation of asthmatic stylists. Maupassant had vanished.

What Edmond did not like in Maupassant, and what prevented him from being in sympathy with him was, apart from the young writer's success, the fact that he had not a sufficiently aristocratic and disinterested conception of literature. One day, so Frantz Jourdain reports, Maupassant came to the 'Grenier' to talk, not about literature, as was the accepted custom, but on a matter of business. It was a question of founding a society of authors which should take the place of publishing firms and bookshops.

'Then,' said Edmond, 'Zola, Daudet, you and I would have to eat from the same platter as Ponson du Terrail, Fortuné de Boisgobey, Paul Féval, Georges Ohnet, and other prose-botchers.'

Maupassant replied that such discriminations did not form part of his plan.

'That may be,' said Edmond, 'but there are contacts I should hardly find agreeable. And then, what will become of the young writers if we desert them?'

Maupassant did not press the point.

In December, 1891, the *Journal* notes the development of megalomania in Maupassant and a tendency to live in an unreal world. 'Maupassant is a very remarkable *novelliere*, a very charming teller of short stories, but a stylist, a great writer, no, no!' Elsewhere it says: 'I have never seen in any man of the world a more full-blooded complexion, commoner features, a more low-class bodily form, and on top of all this clothes that look as if they came from a reach-me-down store and hats stuck back as far as the ears.' In other places the *Journal* follows closely all the phases of the disease which carried off the author of *Bel-Ami* at the beginning of July, 1893.

Flaubert's death had not put an end to the dinner of the 'Five'. 'We keep his place among us,' said Daudet. On April 10, 1883, at Foyot's, someone echoed Charcot's mournful diagnosis: Turgenev

The Five Friends

was a dying man. He was operated on, and was buried on September 7.

Some of Turgenev's comments, reported by Isaac Pavloski, a somewhat shady character, and the Paris correspondent of the Russian newspaper, *The New Age*, appeared in *La Liberté* in October, 1883. According to this individual, Turgenev considered *Les Frères Zemganno* a silly book and *La Faustin* a farrago of nonsense. The private character of Daudet was judged no less severely. Apropos of this, Jules Huret interviewed Daudet, Edmond and Zola. Edmond thought to read between the lines of Zola's statement to Huret that the former had always taken an interest in Turgenev's disparagement of Daudet and himself. From that moment Turgenev was no longer mentioned in the *Journal* as anything except a writer inferior to his reputation. 'In our circle,' Edmond told Huret in confidence, 'there was no one but Flaubert and Zola whom he found entirely to his liking, and more especially Zola . . . It's a peculiar thing, and one I have remarked on, but this man who was so refined and had such delicate taste (I allude to Turgenev) was especially happy in the company of coarse and vulgar people.' The caustic and sceptical attitude of mind so highly esteemed in artistic circles in Paris could hardly have been to the taste of this Scythian astray amid the Latins of decadent Rome. In 1890, Goncourt no longer considered Turgenev of any value except in respect of his earlier works. The real Russian novelist, in his opinion, was Dostoievsky.

VIII
Differences with Zola

Five young writers, the eldest of whom, Paul Bonnetain, was not yet thirty, had joined together in a voluntary association. The most remarkable of them, the elder Rosny, had just published *Nell Horn*. The other three were Gustave Guiches, Lucien Descaves and Paul Margueritte.

One Sunday, after returning from Champrosay, Bonnetain took Descaves and Rosny back with him to his flat. They smoked a few pipes of opium, drank some rather ordinary white wine, and exchanged confidences. Bonnetain, chief reporter on the literary supplement to *Le Figaro*, was proposing to write a protest in it against Zola's *La Terre*, then appearing in *Gil Blas*. Zola was going beyond all bounds and assuming an air of too much importance; young writers ought to break away from him. The idea occurred to Rosny, and received immediate approval, of a manifesto signed by them all.

At the offices of *Le Figaro* Guiches pointed out to Bonnetain that this would mean a rupture with Zola, but Bonnetain replied that the matter was more than a personal issue, that it concerned their future, which had been compromised by the scandal created by *La Terre*, since Zola passed for their master. The text of the manifesto read as follows: 'We strongly repudiate this counterfeit of genuine literature, this straining after Gallic freedom of speech... We repudiate those puppet creations of *Zolist* rhetoric, those huge, queer, superhuman shadow-figures... rudely flung in clumsy masses against a background glimpsed by chance through the windows of an express. From this last work of that great brain which launched *L'Assommoir* on the world, from this spurious *Terre*, we resolutely disassociate ourselves, though not without a feeling of sadness. It grieves us to the heart to spurn this man whom we have loved too deeply. Our protest is the outcry of our integrity, the dictates of our conscience as young men anxious to defend their works—whether good or bad—against the possibility of their being compared to the master's aberrations. It is necessary for us to adopt with all the strength of our hard-working

Differences with Zola

youth, with all the loyal integrity of our conscience as artists, a certain bearing and a certain dignity in face of a type of literature devoid of nobility, and to utter a protest in the name of wholesome and manly ambitions, in the name of our worship, our deep love, and our supreme respect for Art.'

Margueritte found the wording of this protest too severe, Guiches considered it too solemn, the expression 'dictates of conscience', among others, seemed to him unfortunate, and this was also the opinion of Rosny. Nevertheless they signed it, though convinced that Magnard, editor of *Le Figaro*, would refuse to publish so violent a proclamation.

On August 18, the manifesto, signed with the five names, appeared. There was a fine to-do about it. The signatories were overwhelmed with scorn and ridicule. Anatole France pointed out in *Le Temps* that at least two out of the five—and notably Bonnetain, the author of *Charlot S'Amuse*—were hardly qualified to defend the modesty that Zola had affronted, certain comments on whose physical condition exceeded the bounds of legitimate criticism.

What interests us here is to know in what degree the manifesto may have been inspired by Edmond and Daudet. According to Rosny, the article that Bonnetain had talked of on their return from Champrosay was meant to please both these writers. That may be so, and anyway it is quite certain that Zola was severely criticized both in Auteuil and at Daudet's house. A note from Daudet to Edmond allows us to imagine the tone in which Zola was referred to: 'Oh, how lucky Zola is always to be able to begin the same book without getting tired and bored, and I think of the "Marie Salope" which dredges up filth from the harbour every day, goes and dumps it out at sea, slap in the roadstead, and then comes back and resumes her job without ever feeling a wish to scamp it.' It is a far cry, however, from a desire to please, that is possibly only hinted at, to direct inspiration.

Huysmans, who did not like Edmond and frankly detested Daudet, wrote to Zola: 'This affair seems to me to smell very strongly of something from outside Paris.' Henry Bauer, the dramatic critic, at that time hostile to Edmond, believed in the latter's responsibility. 'You can sense as well as I can,' he wrote to Zola, 'the touch of that lachrymose brother, the "widow", as Becque calls him.' By the evening of August 18, Céard, a 'police-agent in Zola's pay' according to the writer Geffroy, reckoning that the squib was hanging fire, advised Zola not to answer it. On the 21st, he clearly pointed to Edmond in writing: 'When I see you, I will tell you my opinion about the origin of this incident, which was imagined by certain artful minds and carried out by fools.'

In his *Journal* of August 18, Edmond expresses his surprise and annoyance: four of the signatories were members of the 'Grenier'! It was not to be long, incidentally, before the fifth member, Guiches, would be introduced to it. At Champrosay, Daudet knew no more about the affair than he did. They agreed in finding the manifesto ill-devised, marred by the use of too many scientific terms, and that it tilted at Zola's physical characteristics in a most outrageous way. In Auteuil, on the 21st, Geffroy read an article written in reply to the attacks of which Edmond had been the object; he was recommended not to publish it, the accusation was too vile; Edmond had been completely ignorant of the manifesto's existence. If he had felt the need to express an opinion on Zola as a writer, he would have written it himself.

One sentence of Zola's in a letter to Bauer indicates that he thought Edmond and Daudet were responsible. 'You make an allusion to very ugly things underneath, which I stubbornly decline to notice.' In an interview with Fernand Xau, who was on the staff of *Gil Blas*, Zola said he refused to believe in the treachery of those whom certain people were trying to implicate. 'Possibly, as some have said, one should see in this manifesto the echo of certain comments emanating from people whom I hold in high esteem as men and as writers, and who profess the same feeling with regard to myself. This I refuse to believe, whatever semblance of reality may be given to this interpretation by several passages of this document, some of which relate to the great literary battle that is still going on, and others of which concern me quite personally. On the contrary, I feel certain that the persons to whom I refer are deeply distressed by a publication which was neither inspired by them nor received their assent.' Zola could not have said anything better calculated to make it understood that he believed in Edmond's and Daudet's complicity.

On October 13, he and Edmond met at a performance of *Sœur Philomène* at the Théâtre-Libre. Edmond having looked anything but pleased to see him, Zola wrote an angry letter, affirming that he had always exonerated him, which gave him the right to hope for a little show of kindly feeling. (Mutual friends had told him that, on

Differences with Zola

the contrary, Edmond was resentful of his having pointed him out as the man who had inspired the manifesto.) To this Edmond replied: 'Two years ago, referring to entirely personal opinions expressed by Gayda under the signature of Parisis, you wrote a letter to *Le Figaro*, without asking me for an explanation, in which you treated me as a miserable little fabricator of water-colours and etchings, incapable of producing a fully-developed *psychology*. I showed your friends a letter from Gayda [editor of *Le Figaro*] in reply to a complaint from me in which he told me that it was Blavet [Gayda's co-editor] who had substituted my name in place of the vague impersonal pronoun "one" in the article, believing that my name would make the article more interesting to the public. Recently, referring to the article by the "Five" that appeared in *Le Figaro*—an article of which, I give you my word of honour, I had no knowledge—an article published at a time when I was so ill that on the morning it appeared I happened to be at Dr Potain's, asking him whether I had not a fatal disease of the stomach, you introduced in reply to the interviewer from *Gil Blas* a remark of this character: "Although everything gives grounds for supposing that Goncourt and Daudet are the inspirers of this affair . . ." a remark . . . which prompted everyone who met Daudet and myself to ask: "Have you seen the accusation Zola has made against you?" a remark, in short, that occasioned many savage and personal attacks on me in the papers, accusing me of being meanly jealous of the money you earn. What nonsense! Am I jealous of the money earned by Daudet, who earns at least as much as you? As for what you say about *intimates*, the most intimate of them all is Geffroy, who has taken your side against the "Five" and as for the others, such as Rosny, for instance, you are in a position to judge for yourself that he is unamenable to any imposition of ideas on literature, whether they come from me or from yourself. Yes, my dear Zola, this is the sort of behaviour that has filled me with great sadness and a little indignation, and unfortunately what goes on in my heart comes out in my face and in my way of shaking hands.'

Zola replied: ' . . . I have affirmed in all sincerity that you had had no knowledge of the manifesto of the "Five". The newspapers had already implicated you in the affair. Unless I had declined to answer, which I regret I did not do, I could not have said anything other than what I said.' A letter that Edmond considered disingenuously friendly and in which Daudet saw 'a cowardly retreat'. On the 17th

Edmond Alone

Edmond curtly suggested that all this should be forgotten, to which Zola agreed. On the 29th, he expressed his thanks to Edmond; the gift of his *Journal* had touched him to the heart. 'I love you all the more', he told him.

To avoid a complete rupture, Daudet agreed to meet Zola again at Charpentier's and persuaded Edmond to go with him. A little later a mutual understanding was reached. Having received a copy of *La Terre* with a cordial inscription, Daudet formally disowned the five signatories to the article in *Le Figaro*. 'What astounds me,' replied Zola, 'is that from being the victim you made me into the guilty party; and that instead of sending me your friendly greetings you almost broke with me. Confess that this was rather going beyond the bounds.'

In connection with the preface to *Les Frères Zemganno*, in which the author appeared to announce that he was abandoning naturalist principles, Zola, it will be recalled, had written to Edmond that he deeply regretted this preface, and had set forth at length in *Voltaire* the grounds on which they differed. In 1883, the coincidence between the passage on Chérie's puberty and certain pages in *La Joie de Vivre* had excited Edmond's suspicions. Did Zola not know of this chapter in *Chérie*? The most serious thing was that Zola was being continually referred to as the leader of the naturalist school, whereas Edmond claimed, and not without reason, to have been its precursor, and that the author of *Germinal*, on his own admission to Daudet, acknowledged himself to be, as it were, a mere assimilator of ideas.

The manifesto of the 'Five', which might have set them at odds with each other for good and all, had the effect of bringing Edmond and Daudet into closer touch with Zola, at least in appearance. And yet Edmond and Zola were never real friends, they were separated by too many divergences in taste, in temperament, in their careers and talents. Edmond's most serious complaint against Zola was that he knew nothing of life; that of Zola against Edmond was that he was only at home in the eighteenth century. '... naturalism,' said Mme Zola, 'is not his province... He does not study the subject... Take, for instance, *La Fille Elisa*... I and these gentlemen know that things do not happen like that in these establishments.'

When Zola presented himself for election to the French Academy, Edmond struck his name off the list of members of his own. This left Zola quite unmoved. The spirit of the future institution could not

Differences with Zola

possibly be his; why then should he have cast in his lot with it?

A letter from Daudet to Edmond, dated January 10, 1893, echoes the fundamental discord between himself and Edmond on the one side and Zola on the other. Daudet tells how on the previous evening he had had a visit from Jean Lorrain, and then from Zola, full of secret thoughts and designs, and appearing outwardly as good-natured and devil-may-care as ever. 'Unfortunately we were not able to talk for long, for my boy Léon arrived, and since his admiration makes him [Zola] feel ill at ease, he took out his watch with a gesture like a doctor in a hurry, and made his escape before I could say anything to him about the Academy... On top of this, I learn *via* Loti that they have agreed about him at the Academy and that he will be elected next time. I have a very great desire if, on that occasion, I am still living, to write you a nice letter about the Academy Goncourt. And to think this man has been counted a personality!'

The dramatic situation in the Zola ménage gave fresh reasons for censure to the Daudets, who had naturally taken sides with the distracted wife. In 1895, seized with a sort of recrudescence of friendship for Daudet, Zola gave the latter, who hastened to repeat it to Edmond, the inner history of his private life. It was frightful. He was never free from the fear of seeing his mistress and his children murdered by his wife. He himself ran the risk every moment of having vitriol flung in his face by this fury, whose howling forced him to have their bedroom padded. While he was telling Daudet this he had a kind of *crise de nerfs* and burst into tears.

Zola's lack of taste, no less than this conjugal drama, created a rather inhospitable atmosphere in the rue de Bruxelles. On January 25, 1896, Edmond wrote: 'Ah, that house, where there is never the joy of having a little flame on the hearth, where the electric light hurts your eyes, and where you freeze because of doors being left open to show off sarcophagi of Roman grocers on the staircase and altar-pieces roughly carved with a knife that should adorn a chapel in a home for the blind.'

IX

At the Odéon

In 1865, La Rounat, the republican, had joined in booing *Henriette Maréchal*. In 1882, as manager of the Odéon, he had the idea of reviving this play that had so much displeased him seventeen years before. Edmond insisted on its being presented in full.

In spite of the formal agreement which, according to the author, he had entered into and which would have allowed Edmond to issue a writ against him, La Rounat, imposed upon by 'Hugo's gang', let the matter hang fire. Porel, assistant manager of the Odéon, considered, like La Rounat, that *Henriette*, the victim of a political intrigue, deserved a fresh trial. Edmond was delighted.

Porel and he met at Daudet's flat on December 4, 1884. 'He tells me,' wrote Edmond, 'that he wants to produce my play like a play performed on the other side of the Seine in a theatre on the boulevards, and that he has engaged Léonide Leblanc, who creates an impression in the world of money and dandies. That does not seem to me such a silly idea.'

For Edmond, both apprehensive and full of enthusiasm, and moreover in a sufficiently poor state of health to fear he might die before his play was put on, the rehearsals brought to light Porel's amazing gifts as a producer. Among the cast, besides Léonide Leblanc, the handsome mistress of the Duc d'Aumale, were the younger Albert Lambert, Duményy and Mlle Réal. The first performance took place on March 3, 1885.

That morning an article in *Le Gaulois* by Charles Dupuy, one of the signatories of the manifesto of December 7, 1865, caused Edmond some anxiety. After spending the whole day in bed, he went out, impelled by the need to feel himself loved and supported, to invite himself to dinner at the Daudets'. After walking ten times round the theatre, he could no longer contain himself, and stole into the wings where the sound of frenzied clapping and stamping reached him. The play was a success. People were pointing out the Duc d'Aumale to each other in the audience. There were embraces in

At the Odéon

which the Princess took part. Supper with the Daudets was a merry one. In the morning *Le Figaro* gave a good review, but the rest of the press was inclined to pick the play to pieces.

At subsequent performances the house was less full and after a short-lived rise in the receipts, and in spite of a plan for touring the provinces, it became clear that the play would not last very long. On March 14 Goncourt wrote: 'The revival of *Henriette Maréchal*, this poor, harmless play, without anything really daring except in the first act, has resuscitated all those feelings of hatred my brother and I aroused in the press in the finest days of our literary campaign.'

Before long the takings had fallen to 500 francs; the announcement of the last performances brought them up to 1,500 francs, but the play would have remained with a run of thirty-eight performances but for the failure of *Le Divorce de Sarah Moore*, by Jacques Rosier, when it had to be put on again. This revival brought Edmond 1,200 francs.

It was probably at Zola's house that Edmond was introduced to Henri Céard. Born in 1851, Céard entered the civil service and later became friendly with certain other young officials bitten like himself by the literary bug, notably Huysmans, with whom he remained intimate up to the end. The few lines of the preface to the famous *Soirées* are from his hand; one of his short stories, *La Saignée*, was placed in this work between Huysmans *Sac au Dos* and Léon Hennique's *L'Attaque du grand 7*. *Une belle Journée*, published in 1881, is considered by some people to be the finest masterpiece of the naturalist school.

The first mention of Céard in the *Journal* is in connection with a eulogistic review of *La Faustin*, but as early as November, 1876, he had already sung the praises of the Goncourts in *Les Droits de l'Homme*.

Authorized to make a play out of *Renée Mauperin*, he let some months go by. In September, 1880, Edmond wrote to him from Saint-Gratien to say that two young men, Henri Sena and Bush, had the same intention. Did he still stick to his project? A second letter followed on September 22 granting Céard a year's respite. He settled down to work, and at Auteuil on October 11, 1881, and again at the end of December at the Daudets', the young writer, in a voice that left the end of every sentence inaudible, read an involved and rather melodramatic play in the presence of Zola, Charpentier and their wives. It was then read to La Rounat and his assistant manager,

Porel. In a furious temper, La Rounat declared that so long as he was alive the new school of literature would never set foot inside the Odéon. Céard took his play to Chabrillat, manager of the Ambigu, who shortly afterwards blew his brains out, and the manuscript was not retrieved without some difficulty. Céard then handed it to Sarah Bernhardt who was thinking of acquiring the Ambigu. This great artist, who had a horror of tobacco, was unwilling to present *Renée Mauperin* because the heroine smoked; though only in the novel, not in the play.

Lavoix, the play-reader at the Comédie-Française, happening to meet Edmond at Princess Mathilde's, expressed a desire to see *Renée Mauperin*, but when confronted with it he jibbed. Céard was at the time working in the offices of the Préfet of the Seine and his duties brought him in contact with Mme Thénard, the 'duenna' of the Comédie-Française. She considered the play possible, provided the fifth act and the longer speeches were cut out, which was done forthwith. René Deslandes, the manager of the Vaudeville, read the play in his turn and demanded that instead of dying Renée should marry Denoisel. Edmond would have agreed to this—'It can't be helped,' he said, 'there will be the Renée Mauperin of the novel, and the Renée Mauperin of the play'—but Céard would not hear of it. In the end, Deslandes definitely refused the play.

After the death of La Rounat in 1884, Porel had become manager of the Odéon, and through Daudet's intervention, and on certain conditions, he accepted the play. After innumerable alterations and excisions, it was reduced to three acts, the text having been remodelled and transformed seven times by Edmond, Daudet, Porel and Céard in spontaneous collaboration. After fresh delays, a preliminary reading was followed by an official reading to the cast, at the end of which Porel in a state of nervous irritation told Céard to revise his second act. In the meantime they would rehearse the third. With shoulders bowed, in the falling rain, Céard went off to take refuge in an alehouse, and wrote a new second act which he spent the whole night copying out. The next morning, Porel was satisfied; it would pass.

On November 13, 1886, Edmond got up at five o'clock in the morning to remodel the scene between Mme Bourjot and young Mauperin. Things were already beginning to go badly between him and Céard, whose style did not please him at all. 'Céard's idea of the spoken word is certainly peculiar. He puts into the mouth of his

At the Odéon

characters such words as *confidences, securities*, etc., etc. ... terms culled from some book or other on philosophy ... at every moment, he tacks on a tail to some cutting remark whose only value lies in its brevity ... Then too he is guilty of bad form and errors of taste as flagrant as Bercy's.' Porel did not hesitate to describe Céard as a blackguard, an estimate that Edmond considered apt when, on November 15, there appeared in *Gil Blas* an article signed by Massiac, an underhand attack that was obviously inspired by Céard. In it the Goncourts were accused of cowardice because in the preface to the Quantin edition of *Germinie Lacerteux*, Edmond had admitted that he and his brother had not had the courage to identify Rose's body. Now Massiac could not have read this preface except in the copy Edmond had given to Céard. 'From the point of view of caddishness,' said Edmond, 'our friend is outstanding. The whole of the article, indeed, is a dazzling example of boldness in telling lies.'

The dress rehearsal took place at two o'clock on November 17. Mme Bourjot created a bad impression. Zola took the script of the play and cut out the greater part of the scene of the explanation between herself and Henri, already brutally curtailed by Porel. The first performance went fairly well. After the show, Daudet gave a supper party: four tables in the dining-room and one table in the anteroom for the younger guests. The general feeling of confidence was such that Porel said to Edmond: 'You know, you are now one of the family at the Odéon.' Daudet embraced Céard. Edmond, unable to forgive him for the article in *Gil Blas*, contented himself with shaking his hand.

The next day there was a shocking press. Louis Ganderax, Edmond's friend, wrote in the *Revue des Deux Mondes:* 'A script that embodies the plot of the novel and revives the memory of some of those charming pages, that, on the whole, sums up M. Céard's experiment. On its first night it greatly pleased spectators familiar with the works of MM. de Goncourt; I am doubtful whether the general public will be equally interested by it.'

At the end of November, after twenty performances, *Renée Mauperin* gave place to a revival of *Michel Pauper*, by Becque. Edmond took Céard to task for not having had the text of the play printed; a book would have made it possible for it to be performed in the provinces, but the scripts had been left lying around and the author had not had the heart to collect them.

Edmond Alone

It has frequently been said that the failure of *Renée Mauperin* was the origin of the breach between Edmond and Céard. It is probable that if the play had reached a hundred performances the article in *Gil Blas* would have been forgotten. A year after the last performance Edmond, who had already struck him out of his will as executor, took his collaborator's name off the list of members of the future Academy. From that time onwards Céard became openly opposed to Edmond. He later claimed that he had stopped going to the 'Grenier' on account of the gossipy, provincial atmosphere one inhaled there.

The memory of one thing might have made Edmond less severe. He had commissioned Céard to write the preface to Jules's *Lettres*, which Céard had read to him in February, 1885. 'Great distinction of style with a tenderness of heart that fills me with emotion,' was Edmond's comment. Only one criticism: Céard, too much of a bookish writer, would never make a novelist, 'but one cannot deny him qualities as a critic and an analyst of the first rank.'

Through Zola's kindly intervention Edmond and Céard were reconciled in 1890 at the unveiling of Flaubert's monument in Rouen: a reconciliation for the occasion only, and a purely formal one; they did not meet again until the banquet of 1895.

After the first performance of *Manette Salomon* in 1896, Céard received this note from the author: 'My dear Céard, I am very grateful to you for your article in the *Matin* and altogether happy to feel that a misunderstanding which has kept us apart from each other for years is now completely at an end.' Then followed a visiting card inscribed 'With all my thanks and the satisfaction of knowing I have been mistaken about your feelings towards old Goncourt.'

Edmond had authorized Arthur Byl and Jules Vidal to make a play of *Soeur Philomène* for the Théâtre-Libre. The first performance took place on October 12, 1887, and the audience gave the play a warm welcome. 'People are almost unanimous,' we read in *Souvenirs du Théâtre-Libre*, 'in extolling this success. Certain critics, however, say it is all very gloomy and ask for plays that are gay. In the first scene in the hospital there was a "nom de Dieu" that created a sensation, but I had slipped it into the sentence with so little emphasis that it roused no opposition, and M. de Goncourt was delighted with such easy acceptance of this daring.' Edmond had come to the theatre with Descaves and Geffroy. He noted the bold expletive in his *Journal* and the great effect Antoine produced in the role of the house-surgeon Barnier, also the impression made by the scene of the prayer interrupted by a song from the dying Romaine. 'It was a tremendous success.'

Sœur Philomène was revived in the following month at the Théâtre Molière in Brussels, then in two or three little local theatres in Paris and subsequently in January, 1898, at the Théâtre-Antoine.

In a volume of his dramatic works, published in 1879, Edmond had announced that he would not be producing any more new plays. But in the autumn of 1886, at Champrosay, Porel suggested to him the idea of making a play from *Germinie Lacerteux* that would faithfully follow the structure of the novel. In Edmond's view drama should no longer be anything but an adaptation of novels.

On January 15, 1888, the play, held up by the author's occasional bouts of ill-health, was ready. It was divided into ten scenes with a prologue and an epilogue. The next week Porel and Daudet came to lunch at Auteuil, and Edmond read them his *Germinie*. Porel, rather reticent, contented himself at first with asking for an alteration in the scene at the Boule-Noire, and the suppression of the seventh scene. The author willingly agreed to the alteration, but gave a grudging consent to the suppression. The very same day Porel went to see Réjane at the Variétés: it was she who was to play the part of Germinie at the Odéon. The play would be put on in December.

The reading of *Germinie Lacerteux* took place on November 14. Edmond, it goes without saying, had got up that morning in a terrible state of nerves. 'Porel reads the play very well. The reading produces a great impression. It makes them laugh and brings tears to their eyes. Duményi, who, before he knew what the play was like, had let me see how apprehensive he was about his role, accepts it with joy. As for Réjane she seems to be altogether tempted by her part, in a spirit of fearless curiosity.'

Rehearsals began. The scenery was insufficiently realistic, but what a marvellous producer Porel was! The author had decided that there would be only one interval; he had not foreseen the dissatisfaction of the café proprietors, who added their protest to those of the newspaper reporters.

The picture Léon Daudet has sketched of Edmond at rehearsals and performances of *Germinie* is something of a surprise; knowing his pessimistic and nervous disposition, it is not as we would have imagined him in such circumstances. 'He found everything perfect, the interpreters of his drama excellent, his audiences the very pick of audiences, his manager an angel in a lounge suit. Sitting far back in his ground-floor box, completely enveloped in a big winter overcoat of fur, and his eyes looking very dark and keen above a white moustache like a retired cavalry general's, he laughed at the amusing passages and was moved to tears by the more dramatic ones.' Réjane's acting enchanted him.

L'Evénement having published an extract from the play, Magnard, editor of *Le Figaro*, refused to publish the preface. At last, the dress rehearsal having been cancelled, a thing that put the whole body of critics in an ill temper and made the author fear that the affair had started off badly, the first performance took place in front of a distinguished audience such as had never before been seen at the Odéon. Among those present were Zola, Clémenceau, Rodin, Alphonse Daudet and his wife (whom Porel had placed in his stage-box with Edmond, who remained invisible), Léon Daudet, Geffroy, Scholl, Raffaëlli, Céard, Alexis, Rosny, Margueritte, Descaves, etc.

Céard's review in *Le Siècle*, although patently unsympathetic, seems to have described the reactions of the spectators accurately. 'A fairly representative audience, exasperated at length by certain infelicitous touches in the production of the play, interrupted with a frightful clamour a children's dinner and an old wives' tale of which at one moment we feared we should never see the end. This same audience, a few moments later, rendered striking justice to the noble and beautiful scenes in *Germinie Lacerteux* and its ill-temper quickly changed to expressions of approval wherever the author showed some power or some feeling. The scene in which Germinie brings Jupillon the money she has borrowed deeply affected the audience, which never expressed annoyance except at redundant episodes or side-issues that had no immediate interest. This double current of satisfaction and dissatisfaction manifested itself afresh at the fall of the curtain, and it was amidst a tumult of hooted dissent and loud cries of "Bravo!" that M. Duményi managed, though not without some difficulty, to utter M. Edmond de Goncourt's name.'

Although obsessed with the idea, which he and his brother had never relinquished, that they were not born under a happy star, and though he was to be informed by an anonymous letter that Sardou, Halévy, and Dumas had 'chuckled' over his ill-success, Edmond had not flinched. A hearty and encouraging handshake from Henry Bauer, who up till then had been hostile, did him good. At the Daudets' supper some twenty people were present. 'The supper was not a great success,' says Léon Daudet. 'People wished to congratulate the author on producing a fine work, but could not go against the evidence. They had to fall back on the vile standards of criticism and the lack of understanding among philistines.'

With the second performance the play rallied in spite of the critics and seats to the value of 2,500 francs were sold. 'So I wasn't mistaken,' reiterated Porel, 'and I'm not a blasted idiot!' But *Le Figaro*, *Le Temps* and *Le Petit Journal* refused to advertise it.

The famous critic Faguet's review of it was severe. 'I would not say that this play of *Germinie* is good; it is even bad, in the generally accepted sense of the term; I would not say it is entertaining, it is even boring; but it greatly tickles the fancy.' In other words, the author had relied too much on the intelligence and imagination of his audience. Sarcey's review, in *Le Temps*, was even less lenient: 'M. de Goncourt understands nothing at all about drama.' A regular indictment of the play by this same critic followed in *La France*, whereupon the senators on the 'Right', all of whom vied with each other in boasting that they had not seen *Germinie*, demanded the suppression of a play unworthy of the Odéon, which, in producing it, had rendered itself unworthy of its subsidy from the State. In authorizing this vulgar and immoral play the Board of Censors itself had also failed in its duty. Lockroy, the Minister of Fine Arts, replied that this was a question of literary criticism which should not come under discussion. President Carnot having intervened to prevent any more matinées of *Germinie Lacerteux*, Porel asked permission to put on the playbills: *Cancelled By Order;* this was refused. It was learnt a little later that during a performance of *Henri III* at the Comédie-Française Carnot had summoned the head of the Beaux-Arts to his box, and in the presence of several persons had declared that it was shameful to have allowed *Germinie Lacerteux* to be performed. The Minister had introduced police-agents into the auditorium to bring him a report.

Even Pélagie joined in the chorus of opposition: 'Really,' she said to her master, 'everyone in Auteuil thinks your play isn't at all nice.' The clergy of the parish also started a campaign against it.

Germinie Lacerteux achieved twenty-two performances, the last of which was on February 5, 1889. On the 11th, Edmond confided to his *Journal*: 'Those large half-rotted, yellow posters of *Germinie Lacerteux* which my eye still lights on in the streets, are sad as things that speak to you of a woman who has died.'

Germinie Lacerteux brought him 12,000 francs, thanks to which it was possible for him to suggest to Pierre Gavarni the idea of buying his father's lithographs and engravings. 'The collection, you need not doubt, will be kept until my death, and afterwards sold with a properly drawn-up catalogue.'

Edmond, who considered it unique at the age of sixty-seven to be 'abused, reviled and insulted like a novice', tells us that he was tempted to send his seconds to certain of his adversaries—possibly Jules Lemaître, or Sarcey, or Céard—but he had passed the age for fighting; a duel was all very well when a man was starting on his career. 'This haughty silence on which I am complimented is a sign of great superiority, but I should find even more of a triumph in a reply to criticism such as no writer of the present moment dares to make, a reply without mercy or pity.'

This reply was actually drawn up by him. With the exception of what concerns Sarcey and Vitu, it has remained unpublished. It is addressed first of all to Jules Lemaître who had written in the *Débats*: 'The play was applauded by M. Antoine [founder of Le Théâtre-Libre] because it is the most infamous of all the plays performed at the Théâtre-Libre.' Why this insulting judgment? 'It is,' said Edmond to Lemaître, 'because you were to follow me at the Odéon, and by killing my play you put yours forward by a few weeks ... you should have shown less hardness of heart towards my poor *Germinie Lacerteux*. As for me, I might have had her among my domestic staff, but you ... have had her in your family. For this Germinie was your wife and the pavements of Algiers are still at this very moment ringing with talk of your conjugal mishaps.' On reflection, Edmond judged it preferable not to publish such a reply.

In opposition to those who refused to see anything except vileness, filth and purulence in his play Edmond put forward Mlle de Varandeuil, the personification of honour and virtue. Obviously *Germinie* was not a 'jolly' play, and it even contained sentences that happy people and those who had grown rich would find hard to swallow, amongst others these words spoken by Mlle de Varandeuil at the hospital: 'Why, if the bourgeoisie of to-day did not build houses in which servants are lodged worse than dogs, you can be sure I should not be

At the Odéon

here.' Then, suddenly rising to a higher pitch and alluding to his *Journal*, Edmond cries out: 'Ah, my worthy calumniators, thanks to all the paper written on and carefully kept at this present time, and which in the hands of collectors take the shape of little private archives, the lives of all those men, both great and insignificant, who have attracted attention during this end of the century will one day be transparent, transparent, do you understand? ... I proclaim it aloud, I have nothing to fear from future biographers of our secret lives, from the comparison of my life with yours, whose foulness will then be public knowledge.' A fine apostrophe, but rather beside the point.

Edmond next attacked the paper which, in the 'war with knives' against him had, so he said, shown most animosity. This was *Le Figaro*, whose chief editor, Francis Magnard, at the moment when the 'Bravos' were drowning the 'Boos', had commissioned Auguste Vitu to write a cutting review, and had even taken a hand in it himself, besides doing his best to get the play ruined by revilers in his pay, such as Lemaître, and also enlisting one of the frequenters of the 'Grenier', M. Jules Case, to write an article on the use of dirty language in literature, refusing for twenty days to print Porel's announcements of *Germinie*, and boasting that with the aid of friends he would prevent the performance of *La Patrie en Danger* at the Théâtre-Libre. 'Besides,' added Edmond, 'whether it be Villemessant,[1] or whether it be Magnard, it is always the same paper, it is always the same gentlemen. At the time of *Henriette Maréchal* you half-murdered my brother, continue now with me, kill the man, kill the work, yes, continue my good gentlemen of *Le Figaro*, if it is your pleasure and your business to do so, for at bottom you are only keen and zealous manufacturers of fame for such men as Siraudin and Lambert Thiboust,[2] and when an original talent like Flaubert's comes under your criticism, you let fly at him with the expression "epileptic's style", when this great writer's disease was a secret everyone piously kept.'

Germinie Lacerteux was revived at the Odéon on March 21, 1891. Better acted than ever by the same cast as when it was first presented, within two days its receipts amounted to 7,872 francs. There were three curtain calls at the end of each act. Edmond was madly excited about it. There was a fresh revival on March 12, 1892, for fifteen

---

[1] Assistant editor of *Le Figaro*.
[2] Both dramatists.

performances. 'Never,' said Edmond, 'has Réjane shown herself a finer actress, more applauded, more mistress of an audience utterly under her spell.'

X

At the Théâtre-Libre

Edmond had met Antoine for the first time at Daudet's in 1888. 'He is a lean young fellow, frail and nervous, with a slightly perky nose, and eyes soft as velvet which are altogether charming.' Another description of him a year later runs: 'He has the look of an abbé who is tutor to a wealthy, right-thinking family, an abbé destined, however, to fling off his clerical habit, but with nothing in his expression or his bearing that denotes a man of the theatre.'

After a dinner at Auteuil to which the Daudets, Oscar Méténier and Paul Alexis were invited, Méténier, seated at the Japanese table, read the play he had made from *Les Frères Zemganno* in collaboration with Alexis and on Antoine's advice. Edmond and Daudet sat facing each other beside the fire with Alexis half hidden in the shadows. Edmond wept. The reading over, he talked at length of his brother. 'I think that I was made for works of imagination, for creating books on a grand scale, for accidents and surprises. Jules was more delicately refined, the stylist of us two: always scrutinizing, correcting and perfecting his work.' A remark on which Mme Daudet commented: 'Whenever Goncourt talks of himself and his brother, it is always to minimize himself.'

Les Frères Zemganno revealed itself as a very well organized, delicate and 'artistic' play. It appeared to prove that, contrary to Zola's opinion, it could do without a love interest.

With the centenary of 1789 approaching, Edmond, on February 19, 1887, expressed his bitter surprise that no theatrical manager had had the idea of putting on *La Patrie en Danger*, which had been in print since 1873. Antoine and Hennique therefore read this play to the audience of the Théâtre-Libre in the large auditorium whose red curtains, seen from outside, gave the effect of a house on fire. An audience of workmen, lower-class women and long-haired poets clapped vigorously at the end of each act. Rehearsals of the play began, on February 20, 1889, in the auditorium of the Menus Plaisirs. It was understood that if the play was successful at the Théâtre-Libre

Edmond Alone

Derenbourg would put it on again at the Menus Plaisirs with Antoine's company. The Board of Censors gave its approval to the play without asking for the suppression of a single sentence. The rehearsals, however, went badly, those who played the minor parts acted stiffly, and Edmond soon got sick of it; he was longing to return to his gardening and the book he was writing on La Guimard, the famous eighteenth century dancer. By a miracle the dress rehearsal went well. Antoine was excellent in the role of Boussanel. Certainly it was far from the interpretation the brothers had dreamed of, but the play as it was performed seemed to hold the audience. Alas, on the first night, the house remained cold as ice for the whole of the first two acts. The third act was applauded, however, and after the fifth the curtain rose several times, but the play as a whole was considered tedious.

Except for a savage onslaught by Céard, an attack by Félicien Champsaur, a review by Faguet that took a malicious pleasure in deducing from the construction of the play the safest rules for boring an audience, and finally an article in the *Petit Journal* demanding the suppression of a Board of Censors guilty of allowing a glorification of the surrender of Verdun, the press was not so bad as might have been feared. All the same, the receipts were pitiable and the play was taken off on March 24. If it had only depended on himself, Antoine would have continued to perform it; or at least so he told Edmond.

To comfort Edmond, the regular visitors to his 'Grenier' gave a dinner in his honour at Marguery's in a new dining-room decorated in medieval style. The guests numbered thirty-five. Rosny proposed a toast in affectionate tones that moved his old master's heart as much as Antoine's announcement of a performance of *La Patrie en Danger* in Rouen and of his intention to open the next season with *Les Frères Zemganno*. After a round of beer at the Café Riche the party broke up at about one o'clock in the morning. This manifestation of sympathy did not hide the truth from Edmond; he had a section of the younger generation against him: the decadents who in part derived from him, even though they would not acknowledge it and claimed to have discovered everything themselves. 'It is a younger generation in the image of the Republic; it wipes out the past.'

The first performance of *Les Frères Zemganno* took place at the Menus Plaisirs on February 25, 1890. The play was savagely attacked in all the papers. 'And to think,' sighed Edmond, 'that this fraternal

At the Théatre-Libre

feeling that fills it, presented in such a delicate and moving way, that this method of appealing to the heart, this thing that is absolutely new in drama and takes the place of that idiotic love-interest of all other plays, has not been noted as original by a single critic.'

On June 5, a lunch with Antoine's father brought the writer Ajalbert and Edmond together for a reading of *La Fille Elisa*, which the master had suggested one Sunday at the 'Grenier' to his young disciple because the latter was a lawyer. Ajalbert had read the first and third acts to him already. 'A fortnight later,' writes Ajalbert, 'I read the second act, containing Counsel's speech, to M. de Goncourt, who was thrilled by it; he was the same with each adaptation. But there was never enough of his text. Two-thirds of the novel are crowded into Counsel's speech, the rest of it had to be distributed among the first and third acts... From the scenic point of view one could only smile.' After inviting Edmond and Antoine (who was to play the lawyer) to lunch at the Palais de Justice, with a view to there being a scene in the Assize Court, Ajalbert read his three acts again at Daudet's on November 23, 1890.

The dress rehearsal was a great success, but on the first night, December 24, the house showed itself less well-disposed. 'Our only chance,' said Edmond during the interval, 'is for Antoine to put the play on its feet'. He did this so well that *La Fille Elisa* seemed to outshine Daudet's *L'Obstacle* which was being performed at the same time at the Vaudeville. A savage attack on the play by the president of the Cercle des Critiques, Hector Pessard, who admitted he had left the house after the first act, roused a protest from Ajalbert: 'Has a critic the right to criticize a work he has not seen?' On January 10, Edmond gave a dinner at his house for the adapter, Porel, Daudet, Réjane, and the actors in the play. At last he experienced, if only through the medium of a collaborator, a great theatrical success.

This success reached such a pitch that Félix Duquesnel offered to revive the play at the Porte Saint-Martin for the 'public at large'. Agreement was reached, and with what delight! The first night was billed for January 23. It was all too good, too contrary to Edmond's fate as a dramatist. Then, just when the advance bookings were promising marvellously, the Board of Censors banned the play and Léon Bourgeois, Minister of Education, refused to lift the ban.

On July 24, 1891, in the Chamber of Deputies, Alexandre Millerand demanded an explanation from the Minister. Even if the Board of

Censors was not mischievous, it was useless, but the immediate question was simply whether in this case it had used its powers tactfully and properly. The Ministry of Fine-Arts gave the Théâtre-Libre an annual subsidy of 500 francs in the form of a subscription for four seats. In reality this answered no purpose but that of enabling four officials to supervise performances. What had made them think that *La Fille Elisa* should be banned? Its form or its subject? Because of the ideas expressed in it or because of its language? Objections to its form must be set aside since the Board had not asked for any modifications, as they had with *Germinie Lacerteux*; besides, on this point agreement would have been easy since before the play was shown M. de Goncourt had told a journalist that the interior of a certain establishment would not be seen on the stage, nor would any coarse words, obscene expressions or smutty speeches be heard. *La Fille Elisa* was written in a language that was absolutely correct. Millerand had been present at the dress-rehearsal, he had read the play several times and had found in it four disputable passages in which the Board might have required some modification, but they had not done so. In reply to an interruption from M. Noël Parfait: 'But the subject itself is immoral!' the orator exclaimed: 'Do you think it is less demoralizing for a decent working-woman to see on the stage a rich and happy courtesan than a wretched girl chained to her brother like a convict to the hulks?' What shocked Millerand was not the shortcomings of the Board of Censors, but the contrast between what it sanctioned and what it forbade ... All the critics had remarked on the very real qualities in this play; not one of them had considered it so immoral that it could not be performed in public. Millerand cited a book by M. Yves Guyot, Minister of Labour, on the subject of prostitution, in which the police who inspected houses of ill fame were themselves accused of procuring. Was there any danger in letting social problems be discussed in the theatre? (A sign of dissent from the Minister). Would the play therefore have been banned in the interests of public morals? Did not the Board of Censors sanction, on six or seven stages every evening, the exhibition of half-naked women? And the songs at the cabaret shows? Millerand concluded that it was impossible to enforce the ban.

The Minister replied that the Board of Censors existed above all in the interest of the authors themselves, and he cited the case of the younger Dumas. M. de Goncourt himself had admitted that he expected to be banned, but he was mistaken in attributing it to personal spite. It was not because they did not want to see social and political questions treated on the stage that *La Fille Elisa* had been banned; it was not inspired either by class or caste prejudice; it was a question of moral scruples. To illustrate the gulf between the author's intentions and the form of his play the Minister gave a summary of it, subject to frequent interruptions, and concluded: 'Unless one threw open one of these establishments on the stage itself, I do not know how the author could have managed to give us a more intimate knowledge of them.'

Resuming his speech, Millerand referred to *Germinie Lacerteux*, in which the author's consent to certain modifications had been given, and once again roundly condemned the double-faced attitude of the Board of Censors, weak and indulgent with regard to ribald works, implacable towards those that were strictly austere. Thereupon the incident was closed.

During this time *La Fille Elisa*, cried in the streets by hawkers, was selling at the rate of 300,000 copies.

The Press started enquiries about the Board of Censors. Zola was the partisan of total liberty, Sardou, having scalded his fingers in his misadventure over *Thermidor*, took up a position against the government. Edmond, in an interview with a reporter, answered him in a way that had at least the merit of bringing the debate into the field of literature and taste... 'Now, is it really more often true that a play is amputated or refused by the Board of Censors on account of a few lively or vulgar expressions? No, it is usually rejected... because of antiquated "chauvinism" with regard to tragedy, and a religious respect for the nobility. In actual fact, the interest of the public has transferred itself in successive stages from the Agamemnons and monarchs of antiquity to the marquesses of the seventeenth and eighteenth centuries, and from the marquesses to the solid, substantial bourgeois of the nineteenth century, and they intend, do these Censors, that we should stop at this "nobility" of the present day. They have no idea, these gentlemen, that a hundred and fifty years ago, at the moment when Marivaux was publishing his novel *Marianne*, people were dinning into his ears the fact that the doings of the nobility were alone of interest to the public and Marivaux was forced to write a preface in which he proclaimed the interest he took in what public opinion called the *ignobility* of bourgeois affairs, and affirmed that people who had a slight turn for philosophy and were not the dupes of class distinctions would not be displeased to learn what sort of woman there was inside a well-to-do linen-draper's wife. Well, a hundred and fifty years from then—and here I will speak for myself—it is perhaps permissible for a philosophical mind of Marivaux's type to stoop to a general servant or a vulgar prostitute. And I say, in spite of the ban on *La Fille Elisa*, and the ill-will of the government towards *Germinie Lacerteux*, that before twenty years have passed these plays will be performed quite as often as plays about emperors, or marquesses, or substantial citizens.' As for the problem of censorship, this was his solution: no censorship and no banning on suspicion. A play that provoked hostility should at first only have its performance suspended; at the end of a week, if hostilities broke out again, then, and then only, should it be banned.

In March a parliamentary commission of enquiry began to function with M. Dyonis-Ordinaire presiding and M. Dujardin-Beaumetz as secretary. It heard evidence from Camille Doucet, president of the Society of Authors, the younger Dumas, Zola, Richepin and other dramatists, Carré and Antoine, theatrical managers, Got, the senior actor at the Comédie-Française, Léon Bourgeois, Minister of Education and Fine Arts, and Deloncle, a deputy. Two camps of equal numbers had formed themselves. Deloncle's amendment (a system of 'provisional legislation' for a trial period of three years) was adopted. This attempt at conciliation, however, did not lead to the drafting of a bill, and the Board of Censors' endorsement of the ban remained. Edmond, who thought it useless to go to any trouble about the matter, contented himself with writing a letter to the chairman of the commission.

In March, 1891, *La Fille Elisa* had been performed three times in Brussels. Antoine, so Ajalbert wrote to Edmond, had been extraordinarily good, his voice had not had its usual harsh, dry tones. It was a triumph! In Turkey, the play was banned as in France.

In October, 1891, Edmond read *A bas le progrès!* to Porel and Réjane. Interested at first, she had been quickly influenced by her husband's indifference. 'It has no dramatic quality!' was Porel's verdict. A few months passed, and on January 26, 1892, Koning, manager of the Théâtre du Gymnase, announced that he was putting *A bas le progrès!* on there with Noblet in the role of the thief. But the project was postponed indefinitely. On May 25 Edmond read the play to Antoine and Ajalbert. On August 14 a telegram from Royat informed him that *Charles Demailly*, adapted from the novel by Oscar Méténier and Paul Alexis, and considered unplayable by Porel, had been accepted by Koning. The affair had been hanging fire for more than two years, and Edmond had had to urge Alexis to make an effort to finish the play.

The reading of *Charles Demailly* took place on October 16 to the accompaniment of laughter and murmurs of applause, but the expression on the face of Sizos, the leading actress, and the attitude of Koning, who obviously wanted to tone down the play, made Edmond anxious. Then Sizos sprained her ankle; when would she be able to play? 'This sprain,' said Koning, 'is actually costing me 20,000 francs'. Then came the dress rehearsal. Duflos was excellent as Demailly, but in the middle of the fourth act there were signs of disapproval which did not augur well. Koning sent to warn the police. The next morning, in the absence of Méténier and Alexis, Edmond and Koning made some alterations in the third act. 'Dined at Marguery's,' wrote Edmond. 'The first and second acts were coldly received. The fourth was a triumph, the last scene ended with thunderous applause. But the journalists, so the man at the box office says, are furious.'

Three days later, Edmond learnt from his adapters that the play was not a success. The press combined in slating it, Sarcey's article being particularly violent. *Charles Demailly* was taken off on January 18, 1893. However, in the spring the play had some slight success at the Théâtre-Michel in Saint Petersburg.

On January 5, Antoine went to lunch at Auteuil to fix a date for *A bas le progrès!* The 16th was agreed upon, but that evening the weather was frightful, with snow and ice. From the Riche Edmond took a cab to the Menus Plaisirs, where he hid himself from view in Daudet's box. 'Here am I once again ensconced in my cupboard at the theatre. I had some fears about the political scene, but everything gets by, this scene and the others, and it seems to me that the audience is laughing and clapping ... in my wooden coffer I haven't a very precise idea of what is going on in the house. At the end my name is pronounced amid faint applause and I have the feeling that the play has not been such a hit as I thought it would be. But at that moment, like everyone in the audience, I am more preoccupied with the idea of getting home than anything else.' What a journey back! No cab available, his umbrella left behind at the Café Riche, and a fall at the gare Saint-Lazare. The next day but one, a volley of insults from all the papers: 'Out-of-date paradoxes, spiteful, senile twaddle, pretentious nonsense, meaningless incoherence, total lack of imagination', etc. Why such hatred? 'Because,' said Edmond to Rosny the following Sunday, 'I am an honest man and honesty is becoming a nuisance to the great mass of the public.' He firmly believed this was so.

On April 23, 1894, *A bas le progrès!*, acted at Frantz Jourdain's by Janvier and Saras from the Odéon, and Mlle Valdey, who had played in it at the Théâtre-libre, had a cold reception. The same play was also given in a little flat belonging to Mme Dardoize, a friend of the Daudets. This was not a success either.

The idea had occurred to Edmond of making a play from *La Faustin*. After a liver attack that had laid him low in the spring of 1893, he wanted to take advantage of a cure at Vichy to work on this play while he was there. Henry Bauer invited him to lunch with Sarah Bernhardt, and on October 17 there was a dinner at the actress's house for a reading of *La Faustin*, in the presence of her son, her daughter-in-law, Bauer, Jean Lorrain, and the actress Guérard. 'At last,' writes Edmond, 'we go into the studio. No lamps, only candles for lighting and a typescript of the play with the letters faintly printed, much less legible than the large round hand of the copyists, which hinders Bauer very much in his reading, and it is cold, very cold. In the end, after the seventh scene, I ask if I can read the eighth and last. I read rather badly, but with some vigour, and Sarah seems to me to be struck by this last scene.'

Sarah however did not come to a decision. 'Sarah is a romantic; she certainly has, with regard to this novel, and because of the fuss that is being made about Réjane, a faint inclination to experiment with modern drama, but her tastes in literature make her shrink from it, and then, in my play, she has a very horrid sister, and it happens that in real life she has a sister, which I knew nothing about.' A few days later, Jean Lorrain asked Maurice Bernhardt: 'Now, about Goncourt's play, what do you think of it?' 'It's very good, but do you really think my mother could possibly put it on?' Edmond asked the tragedienne to let him have the play back. She sent him an express letter, assuring him of her wish to play something of his, and asked for an extension of time. This left him sceptical, and not without reason: on February 22, 1894, he received the manuscript without a word from Sarah, but with a letter from Bauer attempting to find excuses for her want of manners.

At the Théatre-Libre

On October 30, he read his play to Porel; the latter thought that the part would not suit Réjane, whose voice, however, was more to Edmond's liking than Sarah's. Mme Segond-Weber, who wished to act in the play, got Montesquiou to introduce her to Edmond at Auteuil, and then went to see Porel. The latter found fault with the play because of a scene in which the actress had not enough time for a change of costume, but he had firmly made up his mind to produce the *Manette Salomon* which Edmond said he was about to adapt from the novel.

XI

The Rue de Berri and Saint-Gratien

In 1871 Giraud and Popelin, on behalf of Princess Mathilde, had rented the Duchesse de Lesparre's house in the rue de Berri, and at the end of 1872 Mathilde moved in. Standing between a courtyard and a garden, it was a fairly solid building in which a bronze statue of Napoleon, busts of Napoleon III, the Empress Eugénie and others of the Bonaparte family, among them the Princess herself, together with gilded chairs and red hangings, precluded any idea of friendly intimacy.

The conservatory and the big drawing-room were only thrown open for official receptions. These, resumed at the beginning of 1873 and suspended on the death of the ex-Emperor, began again a year later, on the same plan and with the same sort of ceremony as in the rue de Courcelles: Wednesday was reserved for writers, Thursday for artists, and Sunday for concerts and dances. With members of the Princess's family, almost all the former frequenters of her salon, Claudius Popelin, her unofficial prince consort, shining in the forefront, gathered together again in the rue de Berri: Edmond, Augier, the younger Dumas, Flaubert, Doré, Gounod, Renan, Taine and others, including the naturalist Blanchard, and Anastasi, the blind painter. Saint-Victor, however, was not among them. According to Flaubert, he had behaved like a cad to the Princess, though possibly he had simply contented himself with no longer coming to dance attendance on her. In 1875, when Edmond was ill, he went to visit him. The Princess happened to arrive, and fearing he might be met with insults, Saint-Victor withdrew. Edmond thought he ought to write and explain to him that the meeting had been accidental, though in the *Journal* he speaks harshly of this 'incorrigible fellow'.

The Princess's circle was becoming full of nondescript and incongruous characters as more and more people of fashion joined it and painters and doctors invaded the dinners reserved for writers. The famous salon, upon which men like Sainte-Beuve, Mérimée and Gautier had shed their lustre, was little by little losing its character and the food was mediocre.

The Rue de Berri and Saint-Gratien

On Edmond's fifty-second birthday the Princess invited herself to dinner at his house as she had already done the year before, and from that tmie on, every year before leaving for Saint-Gratien, she and Popelin came to lunch at Auteuil on Edmond's birthday. At other times she came to tea there with the whole of her suite.

Although the Princess cherished a friendly feeling for Edmond, she had some mental reservations. She could not form a very clear or very satisfactory idea of this shy, cold and reserved individual. His lack of trust, his inability to open his heart, barely redeemed by one or two spirited outbursts of feeling, were not at all in accordance with the spontaneity, frankness, and at times even downright rudeness that marked her own reactions. And his type of literature, in particular his novels, was not at all to her taste. When *La Fille Elisa* appeared, Edmond wrote in his *Journal*: 'After dinner the Princess, gazing at me with a rather puzzled sort of tenderness, says to me: "What a way you have of creating things that are so unlike yourself! It's abominable! Quite abominable!" And she refuses to listen to my reply.'

On March 13, 1878, in the rue de Berri, he had a fainting fit at table. They laid him on a sofa with his legs in the air and sprinkled his face with eau de Cologne, while the Princess fanned him with her fan. He thought his heart was affected. 'I must hurry to publish my work', he told himself. But it was a false alarm, though this fit had no doubt something to do with the nickname 'Delicate' given to him by the young women of Mathilde's circle. It was, in fact, Flaubert whose days were numbered. In September, 1879, after one of those visits to Saint-Gratien when the guests had nothing to do except stroll round the farm and read the *Revue des Deux Mondes*, Flaubert disclosed to Edmond plans for his future work: the last chapters of *Bouvard et Pécuchet*, a volume of short stories, a historical sketch of one or two families belonging to Rouen, a long novel on the Empire, and another dealing with the battle of Thermopylae.

In September, 1880, Mathilde read Edmond an article she had just written on Gautier. 'The Princess is utterly devoid of any talent as a writer; if one made a shorthand note of her conversation, of things she lets slip when she gets excited, one would sometimes come upon a ring of Saint-Simon's currency, but her ideas no longer show any boldness or colour ... Everything ... is commonplace, dull and worthy only of a silly, little woman!' He pointed out to her that she spoke of Gautier as if he were nobody in particular. 'Don't worry,' said Popelin to Edmond the next morning, 'I shall be making a fair copy of the manuscript and the Princess doesn't read things over. I'm going to change all that, and pay great honour to our friend...' A mediocre writer herself, the Princess was nevertheless jealous of her friends' successes. On September 1, 1881, Edmond remarked: 'The Princess has some very curious feminine traits. In a year when you are not causing a sensation her friendship for you does not lessen, but there is a little lowering of her regard for you in the years when you cause too much, she envies you your success and cannot keep herself from attacking the work that earns you this notoriety.'

His visit to Saint-Gratien in September, 1882, gave Edmond a chance of discovering even more about her private life. On September 24 there was a painful incident: Mathilde upbraided Edmond and Popelin for not having troubled to bow to her when out walking in the park. 'Oh, if it had been a beautiful young girl you would certainly have noticed her, while I, of course, am now just an old woman!' It was probably as a result of this that Edmond became the recipient of Popelin's confidences: he had been unbelievably assiduous in his attentions to the Princess, reading to her, massaging her, taking care of her, loving her as a lover and a husband, and preventing her from wandering like a mad woman all round Europe. Maxime du Camp had described her as a woman reputed to be of an amorous disposition. 'Well,' said Popelin, 'there is no woman more reserved in love, and no woman who shows less imagination in sexual pleasures...'

Three days later, the Princess in her turn unbosomed herself to Edmond. Popelin no longer loved her except out of a sense of duty; she suspected him of deceiving her. In spite of Edmond's reassuring words the matter ended in tears. In truth, relations between Popelin and herself had been getting worse ever since the beginning of 1879, when the *Almanach de Gotha* had announced their marriage.

As early as 1874, there had been a rumour of Edmond's marriage to Marie Abbatucci, one of the Princess's ladies-in-waiting. Had he shown her too much attention or was it rather that the idea of this marriage was a suggestion thrown out by Mme de Galbois, who ten years earlier had taken it into her head to arrange a marriage for Flaubert? Anyhow, in 1874, Edmond felt hardly any interest in this young woman. 'Mlle Abbatucci... a very charming and good-natured young person, is the perfect type of young woman of the

Imperial régime. Nothing counts with her but the Civil Service and, after that, the nobility. In her dreams of marriage she longs for a young highly placed official, or, failing this, a marquess or a count . . . ' By September, 1878, however, the young woman's charms were beginning to work on him. 'What a mine of pretty details, what a storehouse of rare and undiscovered human documents is this Mlle Abbatucci. If I were younger, I should be tempted to marry her in order to write about the woman, the young unmarried girl of this present age, novels such as are not and never will be written.' (Out of this, incidentally, sprang *Chérie*.) Another note, in 1883, depicts Marie Abbatucci as a charmingly artless girl full of surprise and merriment. Was it she, or was it Edmond's friend Pauline Zeller, or another woman, from whom he received a letter so tender that he was seized with a temptation to reply to it in the same tone? This would have been to enter on the road that leads to marriage; the thought of his Academy and of his promise to his brother held him back.

He asked Mme Daudet for a copy of her *Enfance d'une Parisienne* for Mlle Abbatucci. This was hardly tactful, because Mme Daudet had an idea of marrying him to one of her cousins. However, she sent him a copy of her book, at the same time referring to the young woman for whom it was intended as an intruder and not at all pretty. Having received from the latter a moss-rose that had adorned her evening-dress the night before, Edmond burnt the flower in a shovel and put its ashes into a white jade snuff-box. 'The future buyer of this snuff-box will not suspect that this little thimbleful of ashes are the ashes of the love between the novelist of *Chérie* and Mlle X.' He was haunted by thoughts of her beauty-spot and the golden down on the back of her neck, but he found her a woman of little intelligence and with a rather limp and peevish character; for himself, a man of melancholy disposition, this was not at all what he needed.

Having come to see him once before in Auteuil, she announced that she was paying him a second visit. Aghast at the idea of what this would entail, he ordered Pélagie to tell her that he was at Champrosay. She arrived, and waited on by Pélagie, lunched alone, while Edmond, lying in bed on the floor above, kept himself with some difficulty from coughing. At two o'clock she left and at last he could sit down to a meal. 'What adventures for a man of sixty-five! Though, on my word of honour, I yearn for a life without adventures.'

Marie made one last attempt; would he come down to the country to visit her on her birthday? Once again he made Champrosay his excuse, where he had to meet Porel. This time she gave up, but addressed these few words to him: '*Amen, dit un tambour en éclatant de rire. Coppée.* Read it again. Your friend.' The whole of that day this little note tormented him. After all, she was perhaps the only woman of good reputation who had really loved him, and he had behaved harshly, too harshly, towards her... But, good heavens! With the engagements he had undertaken on behalf of his Academy, what else could he do? And then, he was old. It was his duty to break with her.

The next year came a rupture between Mathilde and Marie Abbatucci. Had the latter not taken it into her head to tell Edmond that the Princess had accused her of going to bed with everyone, notably the Popelins, father and son, and even with himself? She had left the house, but the Princess had forced her to return, and, since her Highness was incapable of doing so, it was she who had nursed Popelin. Mathilde had said to her; 'I loathe you, my dear, but I cannot do without you.' To Edmond she said: 'I assure you, Goncourt, that, at this moment, I am drawing near to Heaven.'

Haunted by jealousy, the Princess was growing older and thinner. Mlle Abbatucci came to Auteuil to charge Edmond with having repeated what the Princess had confided to Popelin of her suspicions concerning Marie's relations with him. It was a repetition of the Princess's accusations against Mlle Zeller whom she had earlier on suspected of wishing to take Nieuwerkerke from her. The atmosphere in the rue de Berri, where Frédéric Masson had introduced some of Edmond's enemies, such as Anatole France and Ludovic Halévy, was becoming unfit to breathe. There were scenes at table between her Highness and Popelin, and fits of rage against Mlle Zeller, and then apologies because of her close friendship with Mlle Abbatucci. On December 31, 1888, Mathilde told Edmond that she had twice caught Popelin and Mlle Abbatucci together. The next day there was a fresh storm: Mlle Zeller had received a telegram from Mlle Abbatucci asking her if it was true that the Princess had found fault with her on her account. This had to end; otherwise it would be the death of the poor Princess. Popelin was no longer anything but a limp rag in her arms, but she was still attached to him and would do everything to keep him.

The Rue de Berri and Saint-Gratien

Completely at her wit's end, Mlle Abbatucci paid a fresh visit to Auteuil. The Princess had tried to bribe her concièrge, and Mlle Zeller, whom Edmond excused on account of her father's 'craven academic spirit', had deserted her. Whom should he judge to be in the right? He was rather inclined to believe in Mlle Abbatucci's innocence. She was not to be seen any longer in the rue de Berri and removed her things from Saint-Gratien. Edmond went to see Popelin, who was lying low. He was extremely depressed and complained of giddiness. The Princess had behaved abominably. She had a completely primitive nature. She had insulted him. He swore there was nothing between himself and Mlle Abbatucci. Go back to the Princess's house? Ah, no! Not that! Impossible! It was therefore she who put herself out to visit him and everything between them passed off in the best possible way. In a little while he would appear again in the rue de Berri. 'You are very fond of her!' remarked Edmond. Yes, indeed, he was fond of her, she had not stopped sending him little presents every day.

The following month the Princess is at Auteuil, still bewailing Popelin's infidelities. Edmond advises her to break with him, and that indeed was what she would have liked to do. Ah, this fellow Popelin, whom she had so dearly cherished! Two days later, conscientiously playing his ungrateful role as intermediary, Edmond visits the painter, whose attitude fills him with disgust. On April 24, 1889, Popelin returns to the rue de Berri, and a dinner is given to celebrate the reconciliation. Misunderstanding, however, persists between him and the Princess; new quarrels occur in which Mme de Galbois runs the risk of having her ears boxed by Popelin. Edmond, out of friendship for the Princess, has left off seeing Mlle Abbatucci.

Because of his *Journal*, certain people asked the Princess not to invite Edmond any longer on the same day as themselves. She herself harboured a grudge against him for having repeated a remark of Flaubert's on the stupidity of Napoleon III, while Popelin, who used to say that the Princess did not deserve her reputation, now ranged himself on her side. From now on Edmond was to visit the rue de Berri less and less often, until finally he ceased to go there at all. The Princess invited him to one of her Monday receptions. He begged her to excuse him; he had decided to withdraw from polite society and not to go out to dine any longer except with his intimate friends. Was this the final breach between them? In a letter 'tinged with melancholy', she uttered a lament: was she no longer counted among his friends? Through the mediation of Mlle Zeller they settled their grievances. One of these fine mornings she would visit him again at Auteuil. 'You are such a rascal!' she let fly at him in La Gandara's house as she gave him an invitation to Saint-Gratien. But what a sly rogue that fellow Popelin was!

Was it Mlle Abbatucci who, a few months earlier, had sent him a letter asking him to marry her? Is it Mlle Abbatucci who is referred to in these lines of the *Journal* on July 8, 1891? 'Recently, while out walking with her, I had it on my lips to say: "If you did not do me the honour of loving me, we could enjoy such pleasant companionship together!"' He was unhappy for a whole day about having refused to marry her. She did not give up so easily, and in July, 1893, he was obliged to make matters clear: he could no longer be in love with anyone, not even with her.

In May, 1892, Popelin, whose escapades had for several years made the atmosphere of the rue de Berri and Saint-Gratien barely fit to breathe, fell ill. On May 17 he died. 'Oh, Goncourt,' lamented Mathilde on receiving his condolences the next morning, 'how far away from us now are our happy years!' At the funeral, which was princely, Edmond found himself in the same carriage as Hérédia and Coppée. 'He died of the scenes she created with him,' said Hérédia, who was seldom kind. At the dead man's bedside, Mlle Abbatucci, who had flung herself into the Princess's arms, drew down upon herself this injunction: 'Go away, Mademoiselle, it is too late!' The following week Mathilde came to fetch Edmond to dine with her; she felt the need of giving vent to her sorrow. He saw her again at Saint-Gratien, dressed all in black, dejected, sunk in grief. Popelin's son had refused to give her back her letters.

Edmond had no desire to write an article on Popelin, who had become his enemy from the time he had broken with Mlle Abbatucci, but the Princess had asked him to do so. He reiterated his grievances, though he would write the article all the same, but let her weigh the consequences. In any case it would not be in *Le Temps;* he had fallen out with its editor, Hébrard. She roundly reproached him for having taken her request amiss. 'I see from your letter,' she added, 'that certain remarks reported to you, and of which I was unaware, have prejudiced you against him. I give up asking you for anything on behalf of our dear departed friend. I am sure that among his friends

The Rue de Berri and Saint-Gratien

there will be found some sufficiently disinterested to render him what is his due. Don't let us talk about it any more. Forget me yet once more, and allow me to express all my affection for you.' This 'forget me' might make one believe she was giving him his *congé*, but she had already written as much to him at the time of the publication of the *Journal* without their ceasing to meet each other. This time too their relations with one another continued. In November, 1892, she badgered him affectionately: 'I hope you are not ill, I did not see you at dinner with me on Wednesday. I hope to see you Wednesday next.'

He continued to go, as in the past, to dine in the rue de Berri or at Saint-Gratien when the state of his liver, which was getting increasingly worse, allowed it, but he was severely disillusioned. On April 24, 1894, he wrote: 'The Princess's lack of admiration for anyone with talent or for anything at all original, surpasses everything one can imagine ... truly, in the matter of art, one does not really know what the Princess likes, or rather, one knows only too well: it is everything that is vulgar and commonplace, everything that in a menial and conventional way is a spurious imitation of the beautiful.' If he had once hoped to influence Mathilde's mind or her tastes, he now measured the full extent of his failure.

XII
The Academy and the 'Grenier'

The foundation of the Academy that bears the name of the Goncourts can be explained by various motivations, first, by their temperamental disposition which caused the two brothers to hold themselves aloof, to seem cold and contemptuous. To be a candidate for the Academy on the Quai Conti meant, besides acting unworthily in order to get elected, agreeing to play a spectacular role; nothing was more opposed to their characters, and to Edmond's in particular. Another of their aversions to official recognition of their talent lay in their make-up as artists, their mixing with the Bohemian world, which they nevertheless held in abhorrence, and their frequenting of studios where ever since their youth they had breathed an air of freedom and independence. They had been opposed to the school of Ingres and were partisans of the colourists; colour was anti-academic. So too was realism; the academic spirit, on the other hand, was essentially conventional. The Academy had not accepted either Diderot or Balzac, whom they admired above everyone else, nor their friend Gautier; between it and them there was a fundamental incompatibility. Also the example of Flaubert was certainly not without some influence on their attitude.

As bachelors with no kith and kin except cousins, it was natural that the problem of what would become of their cherished collections should occur to them. As early as July, 1867, a vague idea of providing a destination for them seems to appear in the *Journal*: 'It is rather strange that no legacy has yet been left to an author, or bequeathed by a dying man to an intelligent mind. If ever a writer has inherited anything from a reader it must needs have been that the writer was personally acquainted with him, visited him frequently, and had some physical contact with his mind.' This is not as yet the idea of an Academy founded for the purpose of assuring the material welfare of ten or so good writers, but it is not very far off it. The first idea of their Academy must have occurred to them about this time.

It was certainly suggested to them also by the Magny dinners, this

The Academy and the 'Grenier'

gathering of free spirits around a restaurant table. But the idea of an Academy which should bear the name of Goncourt had its chief source in their desperate dream of survival after death and of passing in the eyes of posterity as creative artists. For these pessimists, sceptics, atheists and materialists believed in posterity; it was from future generations that they expected the recognition of their genius. For all the sad experiences of their lives, the instances of injustice, the senseless attacks they had had to bear, the indifference from which they had suffered, their Academy would requite them; it would be like a bastion erected in the mysterious, unknown domain of the future and over it would float, come what may, the flag of the literary revolution they themselves had incited.

The draft of a will, dated July 14, 1874, and which remained undiscovered until after Edmond's death, contained a provisional list of members of the future Academy and included the names of Flaubert, Saint-Victor, Veuillot, Banville, Barbey, Fromentin, Chennevières, Zola, Daudet and Cladel. Neither Veuillot, nor Barbey, Fromentin or Cladel were strictly speaking Edmond's friends. He had put them on his list because of their talent and because they had little chance of ever belonging to the Académie Française.

In *Le Bien Public* of June 23, 1882, the project for the Academy burst like a bomb. 'We have from a reliable source, with details that complete it,' wrote the poet Ernest d'Hervilly, 'the stupendous news we are publishing to-day . . . Each of the ten members will be allotted a yearly pension of 6,000 francs. Every year a prize of 5,000 francs will be awarded by the members of the Academy for the best work of imagination.'

The whole Press seized on the information. The list of the Academy's future members seems for a time to have been kept secret by Edmond, though Vallès learnt that he figured in it. This was not to his liking, and in an article headed *Les Dix*, he gave vent to his indignation in *Le Reveil*. According to Vallès, the best nurse of talent and genius was poverty.

Edmond was greatly distressed. On July 14 he wrote: 'Conceive an idea like that of the foundation I wish to make of a pension of 6,000 francs to ten talented men of letters whom the Academy does not want; sacrifice to this idea a number of things, such as a wish to marry, a longing to have Marie Abbatucci at your bedside when you die, to surround you with her loving attentions and her sweet company. And your reward will be an article in some insignificant newspaper accusing you of being a cunning rogue . . .' But just as he had forgiven Barbey d'Aurevilly for his 'bodysnatchers' of history, so he forgave Vallès and kept him on his list.

The list of members drawn up in 1874 had been modified. Fromentin, Flaubert, Saint-Victor and Veuillot, who had since died, were replaced respectively by Paul Bourget, Maupassant, Céard and Loti. Chennevières was replaced by Huysmans, Cladel by Vallès, and this last, on his death in 1885, by Geffroy. In subsequent lists, Céard, out of favour in 1889, was replaced by the elder Rosny; Barbey, who died that year, by Léon Hennique; Zola, who stood for election to the Académie Française in 1890, by Mirbeau. Banville, who died in 1891, Loti (elected a member of the Académie Française a few days later), and Bourget and Maupassant, were crossed off; only two names were substituted for these four—the younger Rosny and Paul Margueritte.

'Apart from three or four famous names,' Edmond told a reporter on *Le Gaulois*, 'the Académie des Goncourt will be open to young writers whom accidents of fortune and the exigencies of life place in an inferior position and oblige them to accept some indifferent sort of occupation in order to earn a livelihood . . . Our idea has been to assist the development of budding talents, to relieve them of the material problem of how to live, to put them in a position to work effectively and in short to make the task of producing a literary work more easy for them.' Edmond's solicitor, however, strongly advised him not to pursue his plan for a foundation, which was, in his opinion, unrealizable, 'a fantasy of a crazy brain.'

The effect of the will when its contents were disclosed was apparently to provoke a strong movement in the direction of Auteuil and to stir up rivalry between young writers who might eventually benefit by the legacy. The less important newspapers echoed and exaggerated these rivalries; if they were to be believed, the 'Grenier' was a nest of vipers.

We must now say something about the nature of this famous 'Grenier', a sort of *vivarium* in which Edmond kept his future academicians in reserve.

After Flaubert's death in 1880, the little group of friends that gathered at his house on Sundays, amongst whom, besides the 'Five' (Flaubert, Zola, Turgenev, Edmond and Daudet), Taine and Burty sometimes took their places, had been dispersed. Zola and Daudet suggested to Edmond that he should restore the tradition by throwing his house open to his friends on Sundays. This idea agreed well with his plan for an Academy and he hastened to put it into effect.

The ground and first floors were full of treasures; it would have been too risky to entertain young visitors there, who were mostly, when opportunity offered, irreverent and rowdy. The second floor, where Jules had died, would, in spite of its low sloping ceilings, answer the purpose, but it would be necessary to upset the interior arrangements and sacrifice the room once occupied by his beloved dead. Out of a spirit of literary good-fellowship and in order to make a setting worthy of his prestige as the leader of a school, Edmond made up his mind to it and commissioned his friend, the architect Frantz Jourdain, to turn the three rooms into two.

In the ninth volume of the published *Journal* (December 14, 1894), Edmond has given a minute description of the 'Grenier'. Turkey-red on the ceilings, turkey-red on the walls, and round the doors and windows black bookcases. Over the parquet was stretched a poppy-coloured carpet with designs in blue recalling the characters of Turkish script. Edmond wished to break away from the eighteenth-century type of furnishing and adopt the style of an artist's studio or a smoking-room. On the other hand, he had not broken with Japan; in the little room which looked out over the garden, a Japanese sash embroidered with white wistaria tempered the rather harsh red of the walls, and the red ceiling was toned down by a piece of Japanese drapery in grey, mauve, white and gold. *Kakemonos* were suspended from the bookcase and bibelots hung on the walls or were arranged on a whatnot.

In the larger room, which led out of the smaller, two *kakemonos* depicted effects of moonlight and against the walls stood little bookcases containing all the works of Balzac, Hugo, Musset and Stendhal in their original editions.

The uniform red of the room was broken up by Chinese and Japanese embroideries and brightened by a large rose-pink and green drapery with a flight of cranes across it. But, says Edmond, the most interesting thing in the 'Grenier' was a show-case displaying the portraits of friends either painted or drawn from illustrations to *editions de luxe* of their favourite works: Daudet, Zola, Banville, Coppée, Huysmans, Hennique, Henri de Régnier, Mme Alphonse Daudet, Princess Mathilde, etc.

Edmond Alone

The inauguration of the 'Grenier', which Edmond had begun to furnish in the middle of November, 1884, not without a heavy heart as he watched them knocking down the dividing wall in the room where his brother had died, was preceded in January of the following year by a sort of private rehearsal with the Daudet family. This lingered along until twilight, in affectionate outpourings of the heart that were encouraged by the encroaching gloom. The official inauguration took place on February 1. Twenty guests, according to Edmond, had received a card stating: 'The "Grenier" of the Goncourts opens its literary Sunday sessions on Sunday, February 1, 1885. It will be much honoured by your presence.' About fifteen came to it, Edmond adds, but the list of those present at this first Sunday gathering includes some thirty names, among them Popelin, Banville, Daudet, Zola, Hérédia, Bourget, Scholl, Mendès, Theuriet, France, Paul Alexis, Maupassant, Céard and Hennique. The *Journal* gives only meagre details of this first meeting. They talked about Vallès and Séverine, about Montesquiou and his Baudelairean love-affair with a woman ventriloquist. Daudet compared Renan's brain to a cathedral put to secular uses. The next day Edmond was amazed to read under the signature of 'Young Gayda', of *Le Figaro*, who had written his article before going to the session, that there had been some people at his house who were on bad terms with each other and would not at any price have consented to meet each other anywhere else. 'Poor twentieth century, how it will be deceived if it goes looking for information in the newspapers!' Did he himself place any greater faith in the newspapers of the eighteenth century?

Personal recollections of these Sunday receptions, the 'Auteuil Vespers' as Céard maliciously calls them, make it possible to reconstitute its ritual, its atmosphere, its chief priests and its supernumary adherents. All agree about the welcome Edmond gave his guests, his slightly frigid courtesy, his air of aloofness, his rather limp handshake, the incoherence of his rather colourless conversation, and his fits of yawning. 'It is terrible how bored one gets when Daudet isn't here!' he would say, without a thought of the offence that might be given to those present.

With a white silk handkerchief round his neck, setting off the blackness of his eyes, huddled up in a sort of thick, close-fitting jacket, Edmond would hold out two fingers to each new arrival, without getting up from the divan, on which Daudet had sunk down beside him. The latter had been brought there by his son Léon and Hennique, pale and staggering, his legs trembling, exhausted by the long drive and the two flights of stairs. He would have much preferred to remain in the rue de Bellechasse if Edmond had not counted on him so much. On his arrival the atmosphere would begin to thaw. His sufferings had not affected his genius for conversation, which was as sparkling as that of Scholl or Hébrard, but with more humanity and depth.

The feminine element was not altogether absent from the 'Grenier', but it did not make its appearance until the end of the afternoon, when wives came to fetch their husbands; Mme Daudet, for instance, Mme Charpentier and Mme Robert de Bonnières. On November 15, 1885, Edmond remarked: 'Women go very well against the background and are completely in tune with the harmonies of the furniture. But the majority of my public demands however that women should arrive late, late, late.'

Zola, sometimes good-tempered, sometimes sullen, his head on his hands, his neck sunk between his shoulders, was, quite as much as Daudet, the great man of the place, but he did not come often, especially after the manifesto of 1887. According to Léon Daudet, he irritated Edmond, whose nerves were set on edge whenever he heard him talk, so that his eyes would take on a metallic gleam and his fingers beat a tattoo. The elder Rosny noted this too: 'Goncourt, in his heart, detested him and Daudet did not like him very much. He knew this, resigned himself to it and showed no sign of hostility, but you felt he was ill at ease and reserved. And yet those who listened to him experienced an impression of power.' Léon Daudet says that he was intellectually inferior to both his father and Edmond, though this was not the elder Rosny's opinion. 'Zola revealed a manifest superiority over Goncourt and Daudet; he made use of general principles and kept to the point in his ideas ... in other words, he was able to reason and they were hardly able to reason at all.'

In the early days, many people came to the 'Grenier', but later on there were fewer visitors. Edmond's temperament was not sufficiently sunny. '... when a reception is as cold as in Flaubert's house or mine, once it ceases to be a novelty, no one comes except intimate friends and two or three persons not worth counting.'

On February 28, 1886, Princess Mathilde made her appearance at the 'Grenier'. She had heard much talk of those whom she called 'dirty rascals'. They did not make too bad an impression on her.

Edmond Alone

All they needed, she said, was to frequent the right sort of people and mix a little with good society. 'But you only have to invite them,' Edmond replied, 'they ask for nothing better!'

XIII
The *Journal*

The manuscript of the famous *Journal* is described in the catalogue of French manuscripts in the Bibliothèque Nationale drawn up in 1918 by M. Henry Omont. It consists of eleven volumes (the last in duplicate) running from 1851–1896. The first five volumes are in Jules's small, close and nervous handwriting, the others in Edmond's, more regular, more legible, more elegantly formed.

Although fragments of the *Journal* had appeared in 1863 in *Idées et Sensations*, it was not until July, 1883, that Edmond for the first time broke the silence in which his memoirs had been wrapped. 'The Daudets come to lunch with me to-day, with their children. I read them a few notes from my Memoirs; they seem to be truly amazed by the life of these pages that speak of the dead past.'

After he had read them other passages, one of which was an account of a visit to Michelet, the Daudets asked to hear more, and from that time onwards Edmond read them extracts at Champrosay every summer.

What had been the aim of the two brothers in writing this *Journal*, for which Bachaumont's *Mémoires Secrets* had supplied the model? 'In my *Journal*,' writes Jules, 'I have tried to collect all the interesting things that are lost in conversation'. They wanted however to do something else as well. 'In Saint-Simon, with his admirable portrayal of people, the portrayal of things is missing.' They wished to surpass Saint-Simon. While moralists, and no contemptible ones either, they always kept in mind the fact that they had a vocation for painting. Hence the many portraits and descriptions of interiors in the *Journal*. But anecdotes and the trend of manners interested them no less; they liked these to be hideously foul and gloomy, sharing the taste of writers of their day for the horrible, repulsive and atrocious side of human nature and of society.

Edmond divided his *Journal* into two parts: in the one he put everything that seemed to him fit for publication in his lifetime, in the other those things that called for postponement and which, some twenty years after his death, could no longer cause offence to anyone. Did he imagine that when this time had elapsed all his contemporaries would have disappeared and that their heirs, feeling the same reverence as himself for incidents taken from life or reports of conversations, would bow to the evidence provided by his brother and himself?

In 1886 the existence of these memoirs was no longer a secret; their publication was announced in February of that year in *Le Gaulois*. Daudet had mentioned the *Journal* to Francis Magnard, editor of *Le Figaro*, who printed some extracts from it, though these were too short for Edmond's liking. Half of the six thousand lines agreed on appeared without creating the success that had been hoped for. On August 19, 1886, Edmond expressed his disappointment. 'Six fragments of my *Journal* have now appeared in *Le Figaro*, and not a letter, not a card, to say "Well done!"' On the contrary; an aged Courmont cousin declared she was dissatisfied with the way in which Edmond talked of her father-in-law. Albéric Second, furious at seeing some remarks he had once made at the Café Riche reproduced, almost challenged him to a duel. Finally, the time arrived when Magnard could no longer guarantee regular publication of the work.

In the rue de Berri the *Journal* created an ice-cold barrier round Edmond. The Princess reproached him fiercely for decrying Gautier, and for using '*such language*'! The idea of daring to call Gounod 'an utter ass'! At this he exploded and was on the verge of picking up his hat and leaving the house, but Mathilde suddenly softened towards him; she was merely afraid that he would make too many enemies.

Magnard had given him a choice: either the memoirs would in future only appear at irregular intervals, or the author could be released from his contract. Edmond chose the second solution.

The first volume of the *Journal* appeared on March 3, 1887. At the 'Grenier' compliments rained down. Rosny was amazed that a simple *gentleman* should have produced a work of this kind. 'And why, in the eyes of certain people,' asked the author, 'is Edmond de Goncourt a gentleman, an amateur, an aristocrat who toys with literature, and why is Guy de Maupassant a real man of letters? I should very much like to know.'

An article in *Le Français* denounced the *Journal* as a masterpiece of self-conceit and complacency. A letter from Taine was still more displeasing to the author. The philosopher did not know what Renan and Berthelot would say of this first volume, but, said he, 'I know that I am still alive and that I have a horror of all personal publicity. May I beg you to leave out of your next volume everything that may concern me. When I was talking with you or when you were present, it was *sub rosa*, as our poor friend Sainte-Beuve used to say.' Edmond paid no attention to this discreet but firm injunction, which was perhaps what earned him the anonymous letter included amongst the correspondence, in which two young men alleged that they were in possession of certain notes by Taine on him and his brother and that they intended to make them public.

Three weeks after the book had been published only two thousand copies had been sold. 'Really,' said Edmond, 'for such a result it isn't worth the pain of narrowly escaping duels, of rousing so much anger, getting on bad terms with all your remaining kith and kin, and making all your acquaintances cool towards you ... But let me have patience, I put my trust in the future.' He was convinced, and rightly so, that posterity would see in his *Journal* 'the truest and most living pictures' of men and things in his day.

In the autumn of 1887, his second volume, given a good send-off by Daudet in *Le Figaro*, had an excellent press. Protests against it, however, were no less numerous. 'No matter, I love the truth, and I like to tell it in the way one is allowed to in one's lifetime, in homeopathic doses of one granule ... for this truth as it stands, I could die if need be, as other men die for their country ... do our celebrities, our academicians, our members of the Institut really imagine that they will be handed on to posterity like little household gods, without any alloy of humanity whatever?'

On November 15 the Princess paid him a visit, but, embarrassed by not knowing what to say, did not utter a word about his *Journal*. 'It can't be helped,' wrote Edmond, 'all princes, and even the most intelligent, are crassly stupid, and we are really utter dolts to make them a present of the posthumous fame they would not have without us'. She had, however, written to him a fortnight before. 'Everything, everything, in it is correct and gives a good account of events! Thank you for the words you devote to me.'

The third volume was on sale in the spring of 1888. 'This is my last volume, it represents the ultimate production of my life as a man of letters and I look at the poster advertising it with a certain sadness and an indescribable feeling of satisfaction at my release.' Did the moving account he gives of the death of Jules enforce silence? In spite of his apprehensions, which had been so great as to make him buy a life-preserver, no hostile reaction was immediately forthcoming. At the beginning of May, however, he received a letter from Sainte-Beuve's former secretary, Jules Troubat, in which he declared that he had been mistaken in thinking him a man of honour. The following year 'the husband of Sainte-Beuve's former cook and mistress' reproached the authors of the *Journal* for fawning on the great.

Edmond learnt from Mlle Abbatucci that at first Mathilde had been extremely annoyed with him, but the members of her circle had turned her in his favour. 'You extremely impertinent fellow!' she contented herself with exclaiming when she met him a few days later.

This first series, appearing at half-yearly intervals, had at least had the advantage of bringing Edmond new readers and of leading to the reprinting of *Charles Demailly*, *Soeur Philomène* and *Manette Salomon*. The year 1889 passed without the publication of a new volume. Edmond had only made arrangements with Charpentier for the period up to the death of Jules. The first volume of the second series appeared in *L'Echo de Paris* from March to July 1890. 'I beg of you,' Edmond wrote to the Princess, 'not to talk any more about me! I thank you for all you say about me, but there are people who do not like me and are spiteful about me because of my opinions. Pray forget me.'

He had moments of weariness and discouragement. People did not attack him any more, but they did not mention him either. On August 1, 1890, he wrote: 'From time to time I get tired of going on with this diary, but on sluggish days, when this weariness makes itself felt, I say to myself: "You should have the energy of those who continue to write though dying in frozen wastes or under the heat of the tropics, for this history of literary life at the end of the nineteenth century will really have a strange interest for later centuries."'

The volume on the siege and the Commune, which appeared on October 6, 1890, caused him to be accused of lacking in patriotism. 'They even deny my affection for my brother. Why? Simply because my sufferings for my country and the sorrows of my heart have been set down in writing. If this were not so, I should have—and in more than sufficient measure—all that I am said to lack.' The journalists—and they were wrong—were not the only ones to hold this opinion. 'What a terrible character your *Journal* is taking on!' wrote Raffaëlli, the impressionist painter, bluntly. 'One's heart is strangely offended by those first pages in which one sees a truly savage egotism developing in you under the sudden impact of your great sorrow. What a man you then become: insensitive to everything around you, nothing remains but maniacal fears and desires.'

In November Edmond asked how many copies of the fourth volume had been sold; the reply was three thousand, five hundred. 'It's all very well, but it's hard, when Daudet's *Souvenirs de la Jeunesse* is being printed at the rate of thirty thousand copies.'

Alarmed by the hostility aroused by the *Journal*, the Daudets, at whose house he had read his notes on the year 1877, advised him to suspend publication. 'Women will never be revolutionaries,' remarked Edmond, 'either in literature or in art!' Had his praise of Mme Daudet's talent been thought insufficient? The publication of a new section of the *Journal* in *L'Echo de Paris* did not bring him a single word of encouragement or friendship.

The conversations at Brébant's, reported in the fourth volume of the *Journal*, in the course of which Renan had flaunted the superiority of the Germans while the siege was going on, revealed the author of *La Vie de Jésus* in a light that did not please him. He addressed an open letter to *Le Petit Lannionais*, a newspaper of his native province: 'All those accounts that M. de Goncourt gives of dinners whose chronicler he has no sort of right to be are complete transformations of the truth. He has understood nothing and attributes to us what his own mind, closed to every sort of general principle, made him believe and hear. As to what concerns myself, I protest most emphatically against this sorry reporting... the senile drivel of dolts is not of any consequence.' On subsequent days, in interviews granted to *Paris*, *Le XIXe Siècle* and *La Presse*, Renan took up the same theme: M. de Goncourt was completely lacking in intelligence and in moral sense. 'He seems to me to be damnably angry, this unfrocked priest!' said Edmond, smiling.

Renan had in fact made, though with reservations and a more or less different shade of meaning, the remarks repeated by Edmond. The latter replied to Renan through the intermediation of Jules Huret, affirming that the conversations reported by him were, so to speak, shorthand transcripts, recorded the same evening or at the latest the morning after. The charge of indiscretion—a reproach that Taine had already made—he accepted without shame; his indiscretions were a disclosure, not of the private lives, but of the thoughts and ideas of his contemporaries; they were documents for a history of nineteenth-century thought. Ever since the beginning of the world, no interesting memoirs had been written except by indiscreet persons. His only crime was to be still living twenty years after the events and the words he recorded. He ended by insinuating that the real cause of M. Renan's annoyance was his intention of soliciting a seat in the Senate, and in this connection, his paradoxical remarks in the past ran the risk of causing him a little embarrassment.

Another reply to Renan was made in Edmond's preface to his fifth volume. 'I never said that M. Renan was delighted by the German victories, but I did say that he considered the Germans a superior race to the French, perhaps ... because he is a Protestant. Why, good heavens, the infatuation of our great French thinkers for Germany during the two or three years before the war is not a secret to anyone; for years on end the diners at Magny's have had their ears wearied with talk of the superiority of German science, the superiority of German sauerkraut, etc., etc.... and ... the superiority of the Princess of Prussia over all the princesses in the world.'

The fifth volume appeared in February, 1891. On the 22nd of that month, a frequenter of the 'Grenier', Robert de Bonnières, wrote a savage review in *Le Figaro*. '... for nearly twenty years, M. de Goncourt has only flown on one wing ... By the very fact of their spitefulness these *Mémoires de la Vie Littéraire* will be found diverting by men of letters. They divert us, but it must be admitted that if they do, it is only by flattering the least noble and the least pleasing side of our natures. In them M. de Goncourt "plays the spy on truth"—he himself has said so. It could not be better expressed. It is true that he "plays the spy" and that it is disquieting to have him at one's table; that a drawing-room which he enters is no longer safe; that meeting him in the street is calculated to alarm those people who love peace and quiet ... Let him beware, however! For the most part he listens and thinks he understands, he looks and thinks he sees, and then believes what he thinks and takes the species of literary tremor that has kept him in a state of convulsions these past fifty years for the free flight of ideas ... He has eyes like a fly, eyes with facets, and, like a fly, he alights on everything but penetrates nothing ...

Of the literary élite of his time, men such as Gautier, Sainte-Beuve, Taine, Flaubert, in short the very best of their kind, he has most of the time only managed to give us a grotesque and often repulsive picture...'

In the following month Octave Mirbeau answered Bonnières in *L'Echo de Paris*. 'We have, through his *Journal*, a very moving and very complete mental reconstruction of Edmond de Goncourt's noble figure. Sincere with regard to people, sincere with regard to things, in his treatment of himself he shows a sincerity carried to the extent of scrupulous and meticulous exactitude. And it is by this above all that his *Journal* captivates me. M. de Goncourt does not seek to dress himself up or make himself out a hero; his first thought is to reveal himself to us just as he is in the innermost recesses of his soul. In truth, my dear Bonnières, you have a daring that surpasses mine and I do not envy you for it. After reproaching M. de Goncourt with the death of his brother, after sneering at him for the distress of mind which he was thrown into by this death of one half of his soul, one half of his brain, one half of his life, you bring against him the curious and honourable reproach of having achieved success more slowly than his friends. For this there is a reason, the heroic nature of which you doubtless fail to understand: it is that M. de Goncourt has been faithful to his ideals, and has always refused to adapt his literary integrity to the making of easy concessions, to denials of his conscience, or to committing those little secret stratagems that oblige a man who wishes to rank high in the esteem of society and the admiration of the public to sink to... the nastiness of the one and the stupidity of the other.'

The sixth volume appeared on February 23, 1892, with a short preface. 'For forty years now I have been seeking to tell the truth in the novel, in history and the rest. This unlucky passion has stirred up so much hatred, and so much anger against me, and given rise to such slanderous misinterpretations of my writings that now, when I am old and ailing and anxious for peace of mind—I hand on the telling of this truth... to the younger writers, who have rich blood in their veins and whose limbs are still supple. This volume of the *Journal des Goncourts* is the last that will appear in my lifetime.'

It was not to be the last, however.

Two days after the publication of this sixth volume Mme Daudet said to him: 'Would you believe it, in the collections of articles from the *Courrier Français* that Forain has brought Alphonse to use in writing the article about his album, I read an interview ... in which he said that your posthumous *Journal* dealt very harshly with the Daudets.' Edmond immediately thought this must be one of Jean Lorrain's bits of idle gossip. '... it's really abominable ... what sort of underhand character is this fellow Lorrain? The Daudets, the only people I love, the only ones about whom, if there was anything in them that did not seem quite perfect, I did not choose to mention ...' In answer to Mme Daudet he wrote: 'But even if this were so, anything bad I might say about you would clash with all the good I have written ...'

The seventh volume began to appear in *L'Echo de Paris* in April 1894. The Princess was still full of apprehensions. Daudet tried to persuade her that Edmond was one of her best friends, and the *Journal* was the book in which she would cut the best figure in the eyes of posterity. 'There is promise of trouble,' Edmond wrote after the first fragment of the *Journal* had appeared. He was not mistaken. There was first of all a series of anonymous letters and then, on May 3, a sudden explosion by Ernest Daudet, Léon's elder brother, whom Edmond considered a 'tactless, churlish fellow'. In one passage of the *Journal* there was a reference to his mother, and in what terms! Goncourt treated her as 'a bohemian in religion'. Ernest was on the point of addressing a protest to the *Echo*, but Alphonse managed to dissuade him from doing so. Instead he wrote to Edmond. It was quite evident he had never known their mother! Never had any saintly soul been inspired by a more broad-minded or more intelligent idea of religion. There had been many other things in her life besides Mass and Vespers. 'If you had read what I have written about her in *Mon Frère et Moi*, you would not have drawn this portrait which is the exact opposite of the truth. I hope you will not let it remain in the book.' Edmond did not keep it in and Ernest Daudet was grateful to him for this. When they met each other again in Alphonse's house, Ernest held out his hand and Edmond, out of friendship for the younger brother, shook it.

No less disturbed than her husband by this exposure of their private affairs, Madame Daudet would have liked to dissuade Edmond from publishing the *Journal*, but he pointed out to them that it was the finest monument to a literary friendship there had ever been. This was probably not the Daudets' opinion, as they gave him to understand in the most kindly way. 'My dears,' he said, 'how sorry I am to have caused you pain'. He had not foreseen all this uproar. It was certainly not the opinion either of those who reproached Edmond in the newspapers for having dwelt on Alphonse's disease. Alas! the Daudet ménage lent an ear to the most scurrilous tittle-tattle, and this worked havoc in the brain of the poor invalid crammed full of morphia, who obstinately persisted in putting Edmond on his guard against Lorrain. Mlle Zeller did not make matters any better by repeating to Edmond what Maurice Barrès had told her—that the Daudets were furious with him for comparing his god-daughter Edmée to a leg of mutton. Edmond, henceforth more circumspect, submitted the eighth volume to his friends in manuscript.

In literary circles and on the boulevards there was talk of nothing but the *Journal*. Anonymous letters continued to pour in. Poor Edmond could not sleep because of them. He was most affected, however, by two articles that attacked him in December, 1894: one by Maurice Talmeyr in *Le Figaro*, the other, in *Le Jour*, by Fromentin who, among other points to censure, found fault with him for excessive use of the first person singular. Huret offered to interview Edmond; he refused, he had made it a rule not to answer criticisms. And he found consolation in telling himself that all this hostility could only be attributed to his blameless life. One tangible consolation was afforded him: Eugène Cros, Jaurès' secretary, brought him an article in *La Petite République* in which Jaurès had replied to Talmeyr's attack, and assured him at the same time of Jaurès' unreserved admiration.

The eighth volume appeared on May 8, 1895. On August 23, at Champrosay, he read his friends passages from the ninth and last volume, to which he was thinking of adding a revengeful preface. Noticing that Mme Daudet was looking irritated, he said to her: 'Between ourselves, don't you find here a quite unusual friendship in the field of letters, a friendship that has lasted without diminution for more than twenty-five years, a friendship that by its singularity, in this century of people engaged in destroying one another, will interest those who will read us fifty years from now? ... is there not some advantage in noting the moments of unease in such a friendship, whose tenderness has something of the inquietude of love?'

A few weeks before Madame Daudet had said to him: 'You don't know to what extent I am your friend. When I am dead, you'll weep for me—you see.' To which he had naturally replied, 'If heaven wills it. I very much hope that it's you who'll weep for me.'

Edmond Alone

Edmond was astonished and distressed that no editor had come forward to enquire about his ninth volume. Then, on January 6, 1896, Henry Simond appeared to discuss arrangements with him. *L'Echo de Paris* was going through a crisis. The rate would be only fifty centimes a line, instead of the one franc per line he had previously been paid. At this same moment, Charpentier told him he intended giving up his business. The death of his son and the fact that he himself was worn out, had robbed him of all inclination to carry on with publishing.

The ninth and last volume appeared on May 26, Edmond's birthday. It got going rather slowly. A letter from Forain threatened Edmond with legal proceedings if he continued to occupy himself with his affairs. Edmond replied that he would do as Forain wished. He attributed this letter, whose writer was now well-known in polite society, to the fact that he had revived the memory of difficulties at the beginning of Forain's career and the time when, having no settled home of his own, he had lodged with the sculptor Alexandre Charpentier.

XIV
Engagements and Recreations

The time that was not taken up with work on his *Journal*, Edmond spent at the Archives, in visiting dealers in antiques and Japonaiserie, in going to private views, art exhibitions or the Louvre.

The World Exhibition of 1889 afforded him considerable distraction. He thought the Eiffel tower hideous, and his judgement on the Exhibition as a whole was most unfavourable. A cardboard reconstruction of the East, everything giving an appearance of ostentatious trumpery. In a Paris conquered by Southerners and Jews, the Parisian man and woman were becoming a rare species. Paris was no longer Paris. Its very smell was different; a smell of musk rising from the crowd that would have been unbearable in a café on the boulevards.

And then it was too big, this Exhibition, it contained too many things, it was impossible to fix one's attention on anything, visitors circulated in a sort of terrified stupor, like cattle he had seen running about in the Bois in 1870.

He visited the Pavilion of the Forests, the sculpture gallery, the ancient relics of Cambodia and Egypt, the gallery of Foreign Art, the Annamite theatre. It would seem, however, that this Exhibition should have inspired a more inquisitive interest, if not enthusiasm, in this amateur of modernism and it is surprising not to find him more attracted by the examples of Far Eastern art, although his *Journal* was not necessarily a complete catalogue of his discoveries and impressions. The Exhibition coincided, moreover, with his beginning to feel a certain indifference towards Chinese porcelain and Japanese earthenware. He was turning back once more to the grace of the eighteenth century in France and Germany.

The time-table of his life was very irregular. When he was working on a book or a play he became absorbed by it; the rest of the time he rose late and went late to bed, idled, dreamed, went out for walks, lounged about, and dined in town. If he was at home, where he was mostly by himself, he ate his meals in the kitchen, waited on by Pélagie and her daughter Blanche, already over-tired, already ailing, assisted in these last years by Pélagie's niece, Marie Blaise, who, like both of them, was rapt in adoration of the great gentleman. He ate very discreetly, though he was particular about the quality of the cooking. No wine, no seasoning or sauces, at least towards the end of his life.

Born at Ruaux, near Plombières, where her father had a tobacconist's shop, Pélagie (*née* Noël) had first married an accountant of the name of Denis. Left a widow, she had obtained a situation in a butcher's shop, and then with a certain Mme de la Salle. In May, 1868, at the age of thirty-seven, she had entered the Goncourts' service. Tall, slender, pale and elegant, she was good-humoured or grumpy by turns. She wore her hair in plaits under a muslin bonnet in the Lorraine style, under a black lace coif with two streamers hanging down her back. Edmond, it seems, would entrust no one else with the task of curling his moustache, and he never invited anyone to lunch without first asking her permission. The usual cost of the housekeeping was from 500 to 600 francs a month. 'M. de Goncourt,' so Marie Blaise informed us, 'was neither mean nor extravagant. He was kind and generous and always thought that working-class people were badly paid.'

Charmed by his handsome and singularly interesting face, painters often asked him to let them paint his portrait. He had given sittings to Varin, Prince Gabrielli and Nittis, and also sat for Bracquemond, Rafaëlli, the sculptor Alfred Lenoir, and Carrière. Looking at all the various portraits Carrière made of him, Chéret said, frowning: 'You would need a Watteau.' Edmond himself, however, was not quite so severe. 'This portrait is possibly not a perfect likeness, but all the portraits made of me up till now seem to give an unintelligent, commonplace, bourgeois likeness of myself, and this portrait of Carrière's seems to me the first portrait that shows something of the head of the man who has written the books I have written, the first portrait giving a likeness of my mind.'

This somewhat morose yet well-mannered old bachelor was invited out nearly every day, regularly on Thursdays and Sundays for dinner with the Daudets, on Wednesdays with the Princess, and on Saturdays 'to the accompaniment of mildly scandalous talk', with Mme Sichel, the widow of the dealer in Japanese works of art. Besides these weekly engagements, there were the dinners at Brébant's, which had taken the place of those at Magny's and seem to have alternated with the dinner of the Spartiates that was held every other Tuesday, and also the dinners of the Friends of Japanese Art, to which, according to M. Maurice Feuillet, the last surviving member, 'each guest brought a print or a Japanese curio, the fruit of some recent happy discovery, which the company discussed over dessert.'

In spite of the lack of mutual trust that marked their relations and a host of mental reservations on either side, in spite of the lavish display of bric-à-brac that drew a smile of pity from him, Edmond went sometimes to dine at Zola's house. He dined too with his old friend Banville, with the publisher Georges Charpentier, and also with some of his 'Grenier' friends. He dined out, in fact, almost every evening, and this assiduous attendance at gatherings from which he invariably returned with a harvest of scandalous stories (but at which the sauces were rather too rich) makes it permissable to assume that the condition of his liver would have been less aggravating had he not imposed on himself the task of recording everything in the conversation that was amusing, piquant or scandalous.

In spite of his robust appearance, his health, and in particular his nervous system, had never been good. In hot weather his digestion suffered. He complained of abdominal pains. His bronchial tubes were brittle and he coughed a great deal. At one time he had inflammation of the lungs and at another influenza. He had an almost constant dread of fainting and was haunted by the fear of becoming blind. No portrait shows him with spectacles, however, though he admits he was short-sighted and sometimes had to wear glasses.

In October, 1891, he was attacked by rheumatism, but it was liver attacks that troubled him most. From 1892 onwards they became more and more violent, and more prolonged, bringing compassionate visitors to see him, the Princess and Zola among others. In February and March 1893 a severe attack confined him to his room for six weeks.

These attacks took him unawares. One evening in March, 1884, while he was going up the stairs to Daudet's flat, he had to turn back, and after scribbling a note in the concierge's lodge, flung himself into a cab that took him to the boat from Auteuil, an interminable journey. At the Point du Jour he still had half an hour's walk in front of him with this vulture gnawing at him. It was a night such as he could not remember ever having endured. He began to understand how it is that invalids sometimes fling themselves out of windows.

'I believe I am done for,' he wrote a few days later. There followed for three successive years an almost uninterrupted succession of attacks.

Just as Barrès had thrilled him in 1891 by telling him that in Nancy people were making pilgrimages to look at the plaque in the courtyard of the house where he was born, so in 1894 Roger Marx delighted Edmond with the news that a street in Nancy had been christened rue des Goncourts, and announced, to the old master's intense pleasure, that his friends intended giving a banquet in his honour. Each subscriber would receive a medal with the profile that Alexandre Charpentier had just modelled of him. The idea soon took shape and two months later Geffroy, Hennique, Lecomte, Carrière and Rafaëlli secured Daudet's co-operation. This happened at a most opportune moment: Zola and Daudet were at this time working to have the rosette of the Legion of Honour awarded to their friend.

'I was present,' wrote Frantz Jourdain later, 'at a series of the most painful discussions in order to get him to accept the rosette... that Alphonse Daudet and Emile Zola, with the most exquisite tact and the most touching affection, had obtained for him from M. Poincaré.'

Céard, who had been unfriendly since the failure of *Renée Mauperin*, claimed that Edmond actually owed this rosette to him. At a revival of *Antigone*, Poincaré, the Minister of Education, had jokingly declared that he felt inclined to decorate Sophocles. Céard pointed out, however, that Sophocles, being of Greek nationality, could only receive a decoration from the Minister for Foreign Affairs, and discreetly suggested that Poincaré should give the rosette to Edmond. Shortly afterwards Poincaré left the rue de Grenelle, but two years later was back in office again and it was then that he promoted Edmond to the rank of officer of the Legion of Honour. 'I would have preferred,' said Edmond, 'to have one of my plays performed by actors of talent'.

On February 10, 1895, Daudet informed Goncourt that he was going to receive the rosette and that Poincaré would preside at the banquet.

Daudet, who had accepted the office of chairman of the banquet committee, was anxious for the affair to be on a grand scale. February 22 was the date fixed, and the place was to be the Grand Hôtel. For the menus Willette drew a picture of Edmond leaning up against a bust of his brother, with figures representing Elisa, a Geisha girl and a pretty eighteenth-century woman seated at his feet. 'I have the eyes of a man impaled on a white-hot lightning conductor,' said Edmond, 'my brother looks exactly like a hairdresser's dummy, and as for those allegorical women, they are figures from a carnival in Montmartre.' Contrary to custom it was decided that women should not be admitted. 'In a crowd of two or three hundred guests,' Daudet explained, 'Heaven knows what motley and meretricious species of wenches we might see sitting down...' Nevertheless, Edmond afterwards received bitter reproaches from Mme Daudet, who in view of the occasion had had a dress made out of a lovely Japanese kimono. The Princess, too, did not say a word to him about either his rosette or the banquet.

An unfortunate event now occurred: Auguste Vacquerie, a member of the committee, died. The banquet was postponed until March 1, but at that time Poincaré had influenza, and Coppée a serious attack of bronchitis. Edmond would have preferred to hear no more talk of the affair. He was annoyed with Daudet because of all the high-sounding names with which he had swelled the list of the committee.

There are three accounts of the banquet: one by Goncourt in his *Journal*, another by Jules Renard in his, and a third by Robert de Montesquiou in his *Mémoires*.

The day began well for Goncourt. 'In the *Libre Parole* an article like those of the days when Drumont and I were bosom friends and in which he associates himself with those who will be entertaining me.' The hours seemed endless. Impatient, and with nerves on edge, he found it impossible to stay quiet. At the Grand Hôtel the queue was interminable, the organization so bad that after waiting for forty minutes Scholl went away, and Edmond himself only succeeded in squeezing his way through with difficulty. The great dining-room presented a magnificent appearance; three hundred places were laid beneath a blaze of unscreened lights. Edmond had Poincaré on his right, and Daudet on his left. During dessert Frantz Jourdain rose and read out telegrams received from Belgium, Holland, Italy, Germany and Scandinavia. Poincaré made a speech 'such as has never yet been made by a minister decorating a man of letters, excusing himself for being there as a minister and asking me almost humbly on the government's behalf to allow myself to be decorated'. Then followed speeches by Hérédia and Clémenceau, whose eloquence, says Edmond, created little impression, by Céard as the mouthpiece of the 'oldest young friends' and who now 'regoncourtized', had announced the banquet in *Le Matin*. Henri de Régnier, Zola and Gautier then spoke in turn. 'Incapable of saying ten words in front of ten people', the hero of the evening contented himself with a brief expression of his thanks.

Coffee was served on the floor above, and there were embraces, the exchange of recollections with people whose names and faces he had forgotten, introductions to Italians, Russians and Japanese. By eleven o'clock, not having swallowed a mouthful, Edmond was dying of hunger, and a scrap or two of chocolate that should have awaited him at Auteuil had been eaten by Pélagie, Blanche and Marie.

'I don't see you very often,' Edmond had remarked to Renard, who reports the occasion in his *Journal*. 'My dear Master, that's purely out of discretion.' 'Well then, it's very silly,' answered Edmond. 'He's a grand person, our Master,' adds Renard. 'He is moved, and when you shake his hand it feels ... charged with the current of his emotion. In front of him, on the table, is a superbly towering cake, which you would say is the Goncourt Academy modelled by a pastrycook on a smaller scale ... Daudet, remaining seated, reads his little tribute of friendship to Goncourt. He has very much the air of a schoolboy bent over his table, over his trembling sheet of paper, under the stern eye of the master. And yet ... our sympathy went out to them both when, during our cheers and clapping, Daudet and Goncourt grasped each other's hands under the table.'

According to Montesquiou, the celebration was a humdrum affair, cold and tedious, Clémenceau's speech lacked life and Daudet's was almost inaudible. 'When it was over Goncourt muttered something that seemed to mean: "You have made me wait a long time for this."'

After the pleasure of the moment had passed, Edmond drew up a balance-sheet of the affair: 'What my banquet has cost me, what it has brought me in the way of alms to distribute, what low tricks it has subjected me to by beggars, all sorts of beggars, as ingenious as the one I met last night ...'

In July, 1892, the idea of making a play out of *Manette Salomon* had been suggested to Edmond by Serge Chapoton, a young usher at the Lycée Michelet, but Chapoton would have preferred Manette not to be a Jewess; he feared—not for himself, he said, but for Goncourt— hostility from certain quarters. Edmond entrusted *Manette* to him on the condition that she remained a Jewess. 'I do not want to give the appearance of exploiting anti-semitism ... my hatred of the Jewish race is entirely platonic—but I should ... consider it too foolishly sensitive to give up the idea of dramatising a work that came into the world almost twenty years before La France Juive.' However, Chapoton's fall from a horse put an end to the project.

Edmond therefore settled down to work by himself and towards the middle of December 1894, having completed the play with a prologue and ten scenes, he told Porel. In January he wrote to him again, but Porel put off the reading until the 15th. To keep the author of *Germinie Lacerteux* waiting, this was a bit too thick! Another cause for impatience: he was without any news of *La Faustin*, which Mme Duse was to play in Vienna. At length a meeting with Porel was arranged to take place in Daudet's flat. At nine o'clock Edmond began the reading, but was too exhausted to finish it and he had to get Alphonse to take his place. At first Porel had been cold, but at the seventh scene he warmed up, though he declared that there were no actors to perform in such a play. And then scenery was so expensive, and his fellow-manager, Albert Carré, was utterly lacking in any artistic sense. *Manette Salomon* was a play of superior merit and required an interpretation to match it. A few days later he received Carré's refusal.

It was in the midst of all this that his banquet took place. Carré, who on that particular evening had suggested coming to see him, arrived at Auteuil on March 8. It appeared from his explanation that it was not he who had refused to produce *Manette*, but Porel. In that case, what did the latter mean by his admiration of the final scenes? What was the meaning of the letter in which he asked Edmond to let him have the play, and his promise to produce it in a good theatre on his return from the United States? This letter was a surprise to Carré. 'Then it's agreed,' he said, 'your play is accepted. As for a good theatre, that can only mean the Vaudeville or the Gymnase ... I am forestalling Porel. But business is business.'

In December Porel announced that he would produce *Manette* after *Les Viveurs*. But in January, both Porel and Carré demanded the suppression of a scene and other alterations. This seemed hard to Edmond, who had already cut out one scene. He could not allow that Manette should not appear in the last two acts.

A few days later, on a fine, cold afternoon, some fifteen people, among whom were the two managers, made their way to the 'Grenier'

Edmond Alone

to hear a reading of the play. There they were joined by the future members of the cast. The two managers, turn and turn about, carried on with the reading which, washed down with sherry and malaga, followed by a tea, was greeted with applause.

In February, Porel announced that the play would be performed on the 27th. The rehearsal on the 17th made a bad impression on Edmond and a dress rehearsal on the 26th was made impossible because of Candé losing his voice. After trying to force the door of the theatre, the critics, furious at having put themselves out to no purpose, agreed on a protest, which was published in *Le Temps*. Statements by Edmond quoted in *L'Echo de Paris* were not of a kind to appease their anger. Simond, editor of *L'Echo*, subsequently reported to Edmond that Céard had shown himself the most violent of the lot: he looked completely mad. 'I should not be astonished,' said Edmond, 'if he were slightly crazed. This man . . . who was my friend, suddenly becomes my enemy, then asks to be friends with me again, then once more makes himself my enemy without my having done anything to supply a motive for all these variations.'

On the 28th, the dress rehearsal came to an end with an impression of success. The prologue had been liked and although the studio scenes had been coldly received, the burning of the pictures and the scene in the Luxembourg, admirably acted by Galipaux, had been warmly applauded. In the scene of the 'anti-semitic' dinner a vague sense of opposition had made itself felt behind the cries of 'bravo!' and a row was to be expected. The Princess, who had asked for a box, sent her tickets back. So much the better; the attacks against the Jews and the Institut would certainly have infuriated her.

The next day Edmond had a severe cold and only got up in time to reach the theatre a few minutes before the performance. It was a splendid audience, but full of Jews. As on the previous evening, the prologue was greeted with applause; the audience gave a cool reception, however, to the scenes that followed it, though after one of them there were three curtain calls. People were already congratulating Edmond on his triumph and at the end he left the theatre feeling certain of a hundred performances.

Great was his disillusionment the next day: a 'venomous' review by Henry Fouquier in *Le Figaro* said the play was boring. Henry Bauer's review was full of praise, and so was the one by Catulle Mendès, but there were violent attacks from other quarters. At the

'Grenier' congratulations were all the warmer. That evening, the house appeared to be enjoying itself, though there were gaps in the dress-circle and the stalls. The Jews had taken seats in order not to occupy them.

On March 13, *Le Figaro* announced that *Manette Salomon* would not be performed after the 24th and would give place to a revival of *Amoureuse*, 'a play by a Jew succeeding a play against the Jews'. According to Daudet, Zola had behaved disgracefully; he had supplied two or three journalists with arguments against *Manette*. 'What I find odd,' said Edmond, 'is that Daudet tells me this as if the announcement of this rascally act should really astonish me, or come as a surprise, but he does not suspect that for years I have had a conviction, and also proof that Zola, in spite of his cordial handshakes, and his calling me "my dear friend", is working, with all the perfidy of the Italian that he is, to ruin my work which he sees as a threat to his own in the future.' His bitterness was aggravated by the listless attitude of the young friends who came to his Sundays; not one of them had felt compelled to answer the attacks by Fouquier and the others.

Such was Edmond's last unlucky venture into drama. He attempted to console himself by devoting his whole attention to his garden.

XV
The Last Months

In April, 1895, Edmond remarked: 'My friend Daudet's brain is haunted from time to time by dark thoughts inspired by morphia. Hasn't he written to me this very day to tell me, without rhyme or reason, that he has the notion that I believe he has broken with me, when, on the contrary, he has never had such need of my encouraging support?'

Already, in February of the previous year, Daudet had written him a similar letter, reproaching him for his surliness and for giving the impression that his visits to the rue de Bellechasse were an irksome duty. The two friends had come to an understanding. Daudet was the only one of all his contemporaries for whom Edmond felt any friendship, his house the only one in which he liked to be. But there it was—he himself suffered from his liver and repeated attacks had their effect on his temper. Daudet had a more expansive nature, but bottled up his imaginary grievances in silence.

The year 1895, however, had passed without a cloud between them. In the spring Daudet had made a journey to England and had come back fatter and full of vitality. Edmond's stay at Champrosay in August had been no less pleasant than the previous ones. But alas! a misunderstanding between the two friends had been brewing for a long time. It dated from 1883, when, while lunching at Ledoyen's, Daudet had asked Edmond and Zola what they thought of his eventually standing for election to the French Academy. (The project of a Goncourt Academy was, of course, already known to them all at that time.)

On March 21, 1896, conversation at the 'Grenier' having turned on the recrudescence of 'academic fever', symptoms of which had been apparent in literary circles since Flaubert's death, it happened that Daudet's name was mentioned. Had his refusal to stand for election been clear and categorical? That evening in the rue de Bellechasse Edmond, quite frankly, put his foot in it: having named Daudet as his executor in connection with the founding of his future

The Last Months

Academy, he needed to get things settled. 'What would you do,' he asked, 'if you were nominated to the Academy without the customary formalities?' It was Mme Daudet who replied, not without some vehemence: 'He would accept!' Daudet himself gave no direct answer. 'Really,' said Edmond to himself bitterly, 'I believe I am the only one who is not hungering or thirsting for an academic chair, and I'm damnably afraid that Daudet secretly desires one as much as Zola!'

After farewells that had some trace of melancholy—would they see each other again?—the Daudets set off for Venice. At the 'Grenier' their journey was described as diplomatic. '... there is no question,' says the *Journal* at this time, 'that he has a secret longing for this uniform and this ridiculous sword. I remember now his bad temper over the interview in which I said that neither he nor I had decided to stand in the way of Zola's election. Then, I recall him urging me one day to belong to the Academy ... that I had only to say the word, and that he had made his nomination conditional on my own.'

There now came a newspaper report that Daudet had been taken ill in Venice. For his own Academy, Daudet's absence and his own state of health were bad omens. 'I am really seriously affected with bronchitis and I think that if I happened to die while Daudet was still in Italy, the arrangements in my will might meet with opposition.'

However, a note now arrived from Daudet announcing his return from Italy 'slightly more damaged but with no serious break', though he had been very ill. Seized with remorse, Edmond rushed off to the rue de Bellechasse, to find poor Daudet shattered by serious stomach trouble.

A few days before all this, *L'Echo de Paris* had published a drawing by Steinlen representing Léon Daudet licking the feet of the Duc d'Orléans, and Léon had sent his seconds to Henry Simond, the editor, who had refused to fight. Whereupon Léon had gone to Simond's office and boxed his ears. Daudet reproached his son for striking Simond in front of his own staff; he should have done it in the street or at the theatre. Simond alleged that the drawing had appeared without his knowledge, but no one believed him, and Edmond wondered what the reason was for publishing it; *L'Echo* had no motive for quarrelling with the Daudets, though according to Mme Daudet, all her son's friends were envious of his successes.

Poor Edmond thus found himself in an awkward position. Just when his *Journal* was on the point of appearing in it, *L'Echo* found itself at variance with his dearest friends. On top of it all, Mme Daudet reproached him vehemently for having accepted invitations to dine with Zola and with Rodenbach, the symbolist poet, on the following Thursday and Sunday. He had no difficulty, however, in vindicating himself: he had accepted their invitations because he had not foreseen the Daudets' sudden return from Venice. But it was clear that Mme Daudet was annoyed about the publication of the *Journal* in *L'Echo*. Every friendly reference in it to Léon, she said, would be suppressed.

On April 20, under the first instalment, there appeared a note from Simond in reply to Léon's in *Le Figaro*. The next morning Edmond received a letter from Mme Daudet in which she accused him of trampling underfoot a friendship of five and twenty years' and of letting himself be influenced by her enemy, Mme Sichel. Edmond, overwhelmed, wrote to Daudet complaining of his wife's harshness to him. He had made arrangements with Simond a long time ago; how could he have foreseen what was to happen? He could not break with *L'Echo* unless they asked him to cut his manuscript. To this letter Daudet gave no reply.

Just at this time, Léon was stricken with typhoid which it was believed he had picked up in Venice, and Edmond went nearly every day to make enquiries about him.

On May 29, an article by Fromentin in *Le Jour*, to which Mirbeau replied in *Le Journal* with one of his most caustic sallies, referred openly to the rumour that Edmond had quarrelled with the Daudets, which provoked a curt denial from Daudet in *L'Echo* the next day: he had neither quarrelled with Goncourt nor was he a candidate for the Academy. Nevertheless, Daudet said to Barrès at about this time, 'It's all over; that friendship has ended. I have no more pleasure in it.'

(After Edmond's death, Pauline Zeller wrote to Primoli: 'For more than a month M. de Goncourt, who went every day to the rue de Bellechasse to enquire about his friends, was not once invited to a meal with them, and some reason was always found for cutting his visits short. One day, he came back saying: "They almost turned me out." They were suspicious that... he might have accidently overheard something, and the publication of the *Journal*... which they had urged him to undertake so earnestly that they bored everyone

The Last Months

and created a vacuum round its author, might at this moment become dangerous. Moreover, Daudet did not hesitate to say to his circle of friends that he was heartily sick of Goncourt. Poor Goncourt! If he had only known! But he alone knew nothing about it.')

On June 4, 1896, there was a great dinner at the Daudets' to celebrate Léon's convalescence. Both he and his father treated Edmond very affectionately. Mme Daudet's remarks, on the other hand, were full of hidden meanings and allusions to Fromentin's article, for which she seemed to hold him responsible. Again, Daudet assured Edmond that he would never be a candidate for the Academy, though this Edmond found it difficult to believe.

On June 7 all the Daudet family came with Barrès to the 'Grenier', and Edmond was given a pressing invitation to Champrosay for the end of July.

A week later, an article by Ernest Daudet in *Le Figaro* nearly ruined everything. 'I do not believe that the history of literature presents an example of such a mistake being made by so great and noble a mind. This mad persistence of a writer of M. de Goncourt's rank and merit in a course where scandal rubs shoulders so closely with indiscretion and calumny with truth . . . this morbid compulsion to say everything, write everything, publish everything, to divulge not only one's . . . mental anxieties, one's physical ailments, but also those of others . . . are matters without precedent, well calculated to astonish and sadden, and which it would be impossible to explain if one did not know to what an abuse of the *Ego* literature can lead those who let themselves . . . be mastered by it instead of becoming its master.'

Would Edmond go to Champrosay after this? Léon wondered anxiously. But Edmond bore him so slight a grudge that he invited Daudet and his family to lunch on the 16th, before they left Paris, and it was a very cordial meal. On the 18th he dined once more in the rue de Bellechasse. It was the last time . . .

July 11, he took the train for Champrosay at the gare de Lyon. As he had so often done before, Daudet (on whose account of these last days we have largely relied) came to meet him at the station. Preceded by Léon, who had travelled with him, and carrying the red leather bag which Daudet regarded as an inseparable part of his friend's personality, Edmond got out of the carriage slightly dazed —he had a horror of railway stations and of crowds—though, dressed in a grey suit and with a little brown sailor hat on his head, he had never looked so trim, so strong, so erect, so young.

Mme Daudet, her mother and Edmée gave him the affectionate welcome to which he was accustomed and after casting a glance over the surrounding country from the study window, he went up to his room. Soon he came down again to take a stroll round the garden with Daudet leaning on his arm, while Mme Daudet showed him her roses. He talked about his own, his espalier fruit-trees, his trellis-work and his house, now at the mercy of workmen repairing the roof.

'How lucky we are to be by ourselves!' he remarked as they sat down to a meal. 'These last few days I wasn't even thirsty, though my tongue was dry and I had a bitter taste in my mouth.'

He told them all about life in Auteuil, a banquet in honour of Fasquelle, the editor, an afternoon in the country with Montesquiou at Mirbeau's house, his meeting with Pierre Louÿs at Jean Lorrain's. Then they discussed the question of whether one was still the same self from childhood and youth upwards or whether one changed all the time. They recalled memories, among others a dinner with Flaubert and Zola.

Presently the atmosphere was heavy, there was a little lightning, and they could hear the frogs croaking. The clock of the little parish church struck ten. Edmée, the grandmother and Lucien went off to bed. When they had gone there came another string of memories, of Brandès, Turgenev and others.

The following morning, strolling round the garden with Daudet, Edmond complained of feeling thirsty and of suffering from the heat. July always brought on his attacks. He spoke of the anonymous letters, of notes besmeared with filth, that the *Journal* had brought him. He had enough of this *Journal*! He was not going to publish any more of it. Mme Daudet declared she was delighted to hear it and Daudet confessed that because of the *Journal* he had been feeling less at ease with him. Edmond then left them to go and have a game of billiards.

At lunch he still felt thirsty and no longer had the excellent appetite he had had the day before. When his afternoon nap was over, the landau was got ready and they set off for Corbeil by the road that runs alongside the Seine. (He was amazed that anyone could live outside Paris. He admired the countryside, but not with much enthusiasm.) He firmly believed, he said presently, in the chance of future fame, but Daudet said he set no value on anything but the

The Last Months

mere joy of writing. 'I am a man of feeling and a great talker,' said he.

'Jules was a little like that,' Edmond answered.

At dinner, he still had no appetite and the next morning, having slept badly, he announced that he would not be coming down before lunch. However, the desire to read the newspapers caused him to put in an earlier appearance. The talk turned to academic elections—a dangerous subject.

'If I presented myself for election, my dear Goncourt, you would be the first to hear of it,' said Daudet.

'What pleasure you give me!' Edmond answered. 'Some ten or twelve years ago, you were already one of my Academy. But I urged you to use your own discretion. When I was assured that you were applying for the chair that Dumas had occupied, I was deeply grieved, but I remained your friend, and I even realized all the more how much your friend I was.'

Daudet did not approve of the title of Academy. Edmond replied that it was with his brother that he had had the idea of this classification and this title. The decision had been taken by both of them jointly and he did not feel himself permitted to change anything. The French Academy had been rejuvenated by the admission of Loti and Bourget, but it still remained incapable of discovering new talents.

'It is a strange thing,' he added. 'Jules died in 1870: well, for fifteen years, I, who dream a great deal, never had a dream without him coming into it. Then suddenly he vanished out of my dreams. During the day, I used to think of him, the memory of him haunted me just as much as before, but in my dreams, in my nocturnal life, he did not exist any more. And this for the space of ten years... One night last year my brother came back. I was dreaming of I know not what, some nonsense or other; only Jules was there, and since then he has never ceased to be there. Last night again, he was in my dreams, and with me.'

At lunch, he did not feel hungry. He asked for some milk with the chill taken off, and then left it. After a nap, he seemed rested, but refused to go for a drive. They would just walk as far as the Seine. He told Daudet about his plans for work: to finish *La Camargo*, make a detailed catalogue of the collections which were not in *La Maison d'un Artiste*, revise a few scenes of *La Faustin* if Antoine was to produce it, and that would be all. He was more interested in his *Journal* than in a novel...

Edmond Alone

A melancholy dinner followed with three empty chairs, Mme Daudet's and Lucien's—they had gone to Douai—and Léon's. Daudet was feeling sad. 'Well, my dear chap,' Edmond said, 'what you are feeling to-night I have often felt walking round my garden in Auteuil. And you... are not alone here, or only for one evening, whereas from one year's end to another, I have only my collections to keep me company. It's dull, if you only knew it, and it doesn't appeal to you every day.'

The evening was spent in reminiscences of Jules, Saint-Gratien, Gautier, the Girauds, the rollicking parties at the Parrocels' house in Provence, and afterwards Daudet stayed up by himself waiting for the train that would bring the travellers home again.

Edmond slept badly and in the morning decided to spend the day in bed on a milk diet.

The next day, Wednesday, July 14, everything had been got ready for his bath, which he counted on prolonging for an hour. But this Daudet thought was too long, and he went to call to him through the door that he really ought to go back to bed. 'Well, perhaps you're right,' said Edmond. 'Send the servant to me. I'm going up to my room.'

The bathroom at Champrosay was a sort of wash-house in the yard with a zinc bath. To get to his room on the second floor Edmond had to cross the yard. Was it at this moment perhaps that he caught a chill? Half an hour later Daudet found him stretched, or rather flung across his bed, half-dressed, as if he had not had the strength to get between the sheets. He complained of a pain in his right side, shivers and cold feet; even though his teeth were chattering he tried to force a smile. Two or three times his speech failed him, but presently he had an impression that he was feeling better, the pain was bearable. 'If it should increase, I would get you to ask for a morphia injection' (two years before, in similar circumstances, he had been given one) and towards half past one he did so; then suddenly no longer felt the need of it.

He and Daudet talked about the next day's dinner. On Thursdays at Champrosay there were sometimes twenty-five people sitting down to a leg of mutton or a fish stew and these dinners were of interest to Edmond for his *Journal*.

'To-morrow,' he said, 'I shall be there and I promise to do you honour. I feel stronger, I shall not even need an injection.'

The Last Months

Such were the last words Daudet heard him utter.

An hour later Mme Daudet found him half-asleep, with his hands quivering restlessly.

'How do you feel, M. de Goncourt?'

'Better, better . . . ' he gasped, gazing vacantly into space.

Mme Daudet, alarmed, summoned her mother. Edmond's eyes were now closed, his face was flushed, his breathing laboured. At Mme Daudet's request, Ebner, Daudet's secretary, went off to send a telegram to Dr Barié, one of the doctors who had attended him before. Arriving at about five o'clock, the doctor diagnosed congestion of the lungs. The patient's pulse was 120. Possibly he had caught cold coming out of his bath; or perhaps the illness had been with him for some time. A month earlier he had had a cough, and had complained of having a weight like a cupboard on his chest and of feeling as though there was a litter of kittens in his bronchial tubes.

Mustard plasters and injections of ether and caffeine enlivened him a little, but his voice was no more than an indistinct babble.

'Do you recognize your friends the Daudets?' asked Barié.

'Certainly I recognize them.'

He fell back exhausted, murmuring, 'So tired . . . so tired.'

They thought of summoning Pélagie, but he had ordered her not to leave Auteuil because of the men repairing the roof. Should they inform his family? But where were they? He talked so little about them. However, they sent telegrams to his cousins Rattier and Lefebvre de Béhaine, and to a Dr Fort at Draveil to come and relieve Dr Barié.

At eleven o'clock that night Barié went off, leaving Fort installed. Edmond was now drowsy and though still feverish was calm. Twice while having a drink he had tried to smile.

Outside the night was stormy and the wind whistled. It had just struck midnight and everyone was asleep, except for the doctor and Daudet, when there was a knock on his door: the doctor begged Daudet and his wife to come up immediately, M. de Goncourt was *in extremis.*

Upstairs, as he hurried along the corridor, Daudet could hear the death rattle: 'He was breathing heavily and fast, his features absolutely still, his face red and swollen . . . his beautiful white hair spreading round him like damp silk on the pillow.' What had happened? The night had promised to be not a bad one, then suddenly Edmond's

Edmond Alone

pulse had quickened, his temperature had risen, his face had become more inflamed. The doctor tried yet another injection of ether, but it was useless: the death agony had begun.

On her knees at the foot of the bed, Mme Daudet prayed and wept, while Daudet clasped the dying man's hand. 'Goncourt, my friend... I'm here, close beside you.'

'I do not know,' writes Daudet, 'if he can hear me. At moments I have the illusion that he can, and especially when he pauses in his breathing and his handsome face with its heavy eyelids seems to be listening to what I am saying to him about his brother Jules, whom he loved more than anything else. Suddenly, his hand is withdrawn from mine, quickly, and almost roughly. The death agony, it seems, has spasmodic movements such as this. For me, it was like a departure hurried on, the leave-taking of a friend who is pressed for time and who tears himself abruptly from your farewell embraces. Ah! Goncourt, true and faithful companion...'

Edmond was dead.

At daybreak Daudet went off to get some sleep, leaving the body 'with a rosary entwined by his friend, my wife, about his beautiful, lifeless hands'.

Tall green palm branches and armfuls of roses, all the roses in the garden, were cut by Mme Daudet's orders to adorn the dead man's room and his bed.

In a letter to Primoli, cousin of Princess Mathilde, Pauline Zeller confirms that Mme Daudet's feeling for Edmond bordered on love. 'Yes, the death of my friend M. de Goncourt leaves a great emptiness in my heart, and great emptiness too in my head. He took possession of my mind, breathing into it ever-recurring impulses to activity, making it live, in short, with the kind of life he loved.' But what is of special interest in this letter is what concerns the relations between Edmond and Daudet in this last stage of their friendship. 'He had a liver attack and wished to take a bath which, carelessly prepared, was too hot for him. Having probably not dried himself properly, he took cold. From this moment everything is obscure, we do not know what happened... Dr Rollin, the most celebrated doctor of the day, is astounded at the treatment applied: "We have to-day," he says, "such powerful reagents that even old men can be cured of congestion of the lungs. Mustard plasters and injections were only calculated to give him pain." Pélagie, the only one who would have

The Last Months

known how to look after him, who would not have left him for a single moment, and whom he would have been happy to have there to give him the meticulous attention to which he was accustomed, was not summoned. She was only informed of what had happened by a cruel telegram. She would not have gone off to bed like all the Daudets, leaving the invalid in the sole care of a servant instructed to come and tell them if he was taking a turn for the worse, and of a country doctor ... Just as I am about to end my letter, I recall one more sinister little detail: the arrival in the dead man's room ... of the two young servant girls, Pélagie's daughter and her niece. They had hastened there, these two children, on Thursday morning, utterly overcome. They were made to wait a long time in the courtyard where his god-daughter, Mlle Edmée, was dancing about and singing to herself. Then, when at last they were shown into the room, Mme Daudet lifted the veil that covered his face for just a second, and then they had to go quickly and pack his trunk in the room next door; and as ... they were not quick enough collecting his things and his linen, the chambermaid treated them as idiots ... Then there was M. de Goncourt's writing-case, seized and ransacked by Mme Daudet and Geffroy, with all the papers in it spread out so as not to leave any compromising note inside, and there was Mme Daudet, saying to the young women: "Look, here is a hundred franc note and some small change, I don't want to incur any responsibility, you understand?" Responsibility for money, in such a place and at such a terrible moment! Then, Mme Daudet also asks: "Do you know if he brought a stick or an umbrella?" Could they remember anything, these poor girls? A stick, an umbrella, was that of any importance? And when the trunk was packed, as they were asking if they could see him again, the chambermaid answered that she would go and ask Madam, and they heard the reply: "Oh! let them come in and get the thing over." They went in but the nun who was keeping watch did not lift the veil that covered his face, and they went away without seeing their master again, shocked by the attitude of the household and the welcome they had received.'

★ ★ ★

'Goncourt died suddenly. Come quickly,' Daudet had wired to Frantz Jourdain. When the latter entered the study, Daudet, Geffroy and the writer Edouard Conte were already there, sitting in silence.

Edmond Alone

In a low voice Daudet repeated the account of the tragedy to Jourdain.

The shutters of the dead man's room were closed; near a vase with a palm branch in holy water, two candles cast a dim light upon the corpse, dressed in a black frock-coat, an embroidered waistcoat and a white silk neckerchief, lying at rest amongst the flowers, the hands clasping a little silver crucifix. His cheeks were terribly pale, his eyelids blue. He seemed to be wrapped in solemn, peaceful slumber. Kneeling down, Jourdain wept over the only being with whom, so he wrote, he had felt himself in complete communion of thought. As he left, he took with him a frond from a fern thrown upon the bed.

The next morning he returned to Champrosay with Roger Marx, the art critic, to bring the body back to Auteuil. At Daudet's side stood Gustave Toudouze, the novelist, the painters Raffaëlli and Carrière, Nadar and Mme Dardoize, a friend of the Daudets who kept a diary in imitation of Edmond. 'Now then, brave hearts!' said Daudet. Jourdain, Marx and Toudouze went upstairs. Two nuns were praying beside the bed. The leaden coffin was sealed up, the lid of polished oak screwed on, and down the narrow staircase workmen in their Sunday suits carried their load with many grunts and groans. The coffin was placed on the tiled floor of the hall and blessed by the curé of Draveil, who had been waiting in the drawing-room with Mme Daudet and a few others. 'Farewell, old friend!' said Daudet in tears as Lucien supported him, then he fell back into a chair, his face buried in his handkerchief.

At the station, the coffin was hoisted into the van and, accompanied by the curé, Jourdain and Roger Marx got into one of the carriages. Night had fallen when they reached Auteuil. Pélagie and Blanche guided the mournful procession through the garden with lamps. The drawing-room had been transformed into a mortuary chapel. There the coffin was placed and the next morning the dead man's friends began to file past it.

Throughout the Press unanimous homage was paid to Edmond de Goncourt's disinterestedness, his independence, his love for literature and the perfect dignity of his life. The final passage from Jean Lorrain's article in *Le Journal* deserves to be recorded: 'For the past three months M. de Goncourt has not had the tranquil existence nor the inner peace of mind to which he was entitled ... I do not here allude to the controversies aroused concerning his *Journal* or the insinuations

The Last Months

and palpable maliciousness of certain literary flunkeys... The petty nagging of certain sections of the press over childish traits in the last volume of the *Journal* had necessarily annoyed a man so highly-strung as M. de Goncourt, but the great grief that saddened his three last months had at once a nearer and a more distant source. M. de Goncourt has never even whispered a word to me of this grief, but I have noticed him much absorbed and much disquieted during these last days. This grief was known to everyone in his immediate circle; a letter from a woman [Mme Daudet], one of the women on terms of close friendship with him, was the cause of it, and this is no longer a mystery now that the newspapers have spoken of this letter... recently, in *Le Figaro*, under an ambiguous signature, there appeared an atrocious article manifestly written to wound the Master of Auteuil in all that he held most dear. This latest manœuvre has been given the lie by the friends the article aimed at, since it was in their house that it was given to him to pass away in that gentle, painless death he had always asked for and which we envy him, seeing that he, the sorrowing, clear-sighted witness of his brother's death agony, was at least spared the sadness of watching his own departure and of knowing that he was dying.'

On the eve of the funeral visitors came all day to the closely shuttered house. 'This house of his in Auteuil that Goncourt had so harmoniously arranged,' wrote Mme Daudet, 'now that he is no longer there, and living—is it the fault of my eyes suffused with tears?—seems to me narrow and shrunk to a smaller size. The catafalque takes up the whole of the big drawing-room; the great Japanese bowl, pushed into the background, is adorned with a huge bouquet of hydrangeas; wreaths and sheaves of flowers leant against the black drapery, and all around, as witnesses to his noble life as a writer, are sketches by Watteau, Baudouin and Moreau le Jeune, Carmontelle's gouaches and Gobelin tapestries, show-cases filled with eighteenth-century ornaments, bright and fragile, Japanese objects in warm golden tones, evoking memories of the writer's tall figure bending over a piece of lacquer-work or Dresden china, with that absorption, that hunching of the shoulders, that delicate play of hovering fingers characteristic of the amateur of art observing beauty!'

In accordance with the law, Maître Duplan, the solicitor, deposited the will with the President of the Civil Court, Pélagie handed over to Daudet an envelope found amongst the papers of the deceased that probably contained a codicil, and to the solicitor she handed various other papers, manuscripts, the play of *La Faustin* that Antoine had commissioned for the Odéon, a fantasy written in slang, and the notebooks of the *Journal*. On July 18, at Champrosay, Maître Duplan read the will and its codicils to the legatees.

The newspapers considered themselves in a position to divulge its contents. The whole of Edmond's fortune went to his future Academy, the residuary legatee being only entrusted with seeing to the carrying out of this wish. After various personal bequests of *objets d'art*, Pélagie received an annual pension of 1,200 francs as well as the furniture of her bedroom and the things in the kitchen, while various friends received legacies of less importance.

The weather was fine on the day of the funeral, July 20, 1896. A military picket formed a guard of honour. At Notre-Dame-d'Auteuil, among a large but not very quiet congregation, a sort of hum could be heard. *L'Echo de Paris*, the Society of Dramatic Authors, the Friends of the 'Grenier', Porel and Réjane ('From Germinie Lacerteux to Edmond de Goncourt') had sent wreaths. Princess Mathilde and Mme Daudet had taken their places in the front row which was reserved for ladies. Edouard Lefebvre de Béhaine, Zola, Léon Daudet and Bracquemond held the cords of the canopy. The head of the State, who, a few days before, had sent an aide-de-camp to the funeral of the Marquis de Morès, had not chosen to be represented. Outside the church, a bare fifty inquisitive spectators were watching to see the celebrities coming out.

It is a long journey from Auteuil to Montmartre and the heat and weariness weeded out some from the funeral procession which a privileged few were following in carriages.

At the graveside, Zola, beside whom Hennique was standing, ready to take his pages from him if emotion should cause him to break off, made a speech that everyone considered very fine: 'My loyalty to him, and my unalterable affection for him, springs from the fact that he was always a man of courage, and of a fiercely independent character. . . . this noble gallantry of the mind, the saying of what one believes to be the truth, even at the cost of sacrificing a life of peace and quiet . . . nothing is rarer, nothing is finer, nothing nobler. He loved literature to the extent of giving up his whole life to it, he experienced no joy, he endured no suffering but on its account. He leaves behind him the example of the noblest and proudest of

The Last Months

writers whose errors, if he were guilty of any, were errors arising only from his burning passion for literature. One day, in his *Journal*, this document so ill-understood and so full of poignant interest, he uttered the sublime cry of one whose whole life was devoted to Letters, a cry of distress at the thought that some day the earth will crumble to nothing, and his works be read no longer... on that day I loved him all the more because of his pride, that divine and lordly pride which expresses the faith of us other writers in the painful labour of bringing our works to birth. Dear and noble friend "our own" old Goncourt, this is the young man, the novice of 1865, who now bids you farewell; it is also the novelist whom you saw developing, who has remained your pupil even while becoming your rival, and it is also the man at this moment growing old, who, following your example, has found, like yourself, all his comfort in work. Today, at last, you are at rest, you come to sleep by your brother's side. And, just as our friend Daudet, distraught and sobbing, cried out to you in your death agony, so too I cry: "Depart, depart, poor, noble, sorrowing labourer, depart to be reunited with him in the grave and on the roll of fame."'

On behalf of the family Villedeuil thanked Zola, and the company having slowly dispersed, Edmond remained alone with his brother in that vault before which he had so often come to weep and to call down upon both their heads the blessing of future generations.

★ ★ ★

The nineteenth century, the century of Chateaubriand, Flaubert, Théophile Gautier and the Goncourts, was the century of outstanding excellence in the field of literature. Viewed both as an art and an independent profession, literature had then a prestige, and inspired a devotion, of which no other period affords a similar example. The importance of the Goncourts, and the significance of their lives, derives from this. They were, of all writers, the most representative of an ideal unknown before their day and which has since become debased. From this point of view, they rightly deserve first place. No other writers attempted with such conviction to subordinate moral values to purely literary ones. Mallarmé alone could be compared with the Goncourts in this respect.

As with every faith that is sincerely and scrupulously practised, their faith in literature deserves our admiration. We, for whom other

Edmond Alone

problems besides disinterested inspiration and those of style unhappily present themselves, may smile at it, but we must not lose sight of the fact that Edmond and Jules de Goncourt cannot be relegated simply to the role of seekers after the right epithet and phrase-polishers, to which they are too often restricted. They made literature 'take a step forward', and they did this in a sense that was strictly their own; by investigating, observing and expressing the truth. The merit, which they jealously claimed for themselves, of having cleared the way for naturalism must be granted to them, and whatever is said to the contrary nothing can alter the fact that naturalism has had its day and that since then the French novel has never been what it was.

We have described in this book the extent, according to others and to themselves, of the Goncourts' influence in various other domains: in the cult of Japan, in appreciation of the eighteenth century, in a graphic and anecdotal presentation of history. The painful aspect of their case is their conception of 'fine writing' of which they rightfully flattered themselves to have been the initiators, and which today causes one merely to shrug one's shoulders. Yet Paul Souday, who could not be suspected of harbouring a prejudice in their favour, claimed to distinguish in many writers of his own day, Proust, Colette, Barbusse and even Duhamel among them, a sort of impressionism similar to that of the Goncourts. We will not go so far as this, but admit that, before 1900, this impressionism, this studied care for vocabulary and grammar, had had a profound influence on the style of prose writers of the Symbolist school, including Mallarmé. If we wish to be fair to 'Goncourtism', moreover, we must carry it back to the moment when it was in favour with all young men of letters and call to mind what Anatole France, who certainly did not practice it, and in fact abominated it, wrote in 1889 of Goncourt's disciple, Léon Hennique, and which could have been exactly applied to his master: 'I do not understand the art and management of style in the same way as M. Léon Hennique. But at least, I hope this difference of opinion will not make me either bitter or unfair. In his own way he likes art, I like it in mine. Is not that a reason for us to come to an agreement and to turn our common scorn against those wretches who spend their lives perpetually among ugly things? When I think that at this very moment he is writing such books as *Le Docteur Rameau*, *La Comtesse Sarah* and *Le Dernier Amour* I am tempted to cry out to M. Léon Hennique: "What! You know the value of words, the worth of style, the nobility of art, and here am I picking a quarrel with you because you are too elegant, too finical, too precious, because you wander off into sparkling nebulosities. I ought, on the other hand, to say that all this is beautiful, all this is good. For your worst faults are preferable to the vulgarity of those authors beloved by the crowd."'

What has become most out of date in the Goncourts is their method of composition, which is all too apparent in the structure of their works: a system of little notes taken straight from life and used just as they come. They were not the first to make notes, everyone did so, but their anxiety to present the naked truth made them slaves to a literal transcription at variance with a certain vital rhythm the novel requires. On the other hand, they excelled in reproducing the eye-witness's point of view, and possibly the most successful pages in their works are examples of direct reporting. Their vision of things was undistorted, keen and trenchant. Their portraits and their interiors have an astonishing relief such as no writer of their period succeeded in producing and one that makes them comparable with their two favourite masters: Saint-Simon and La Bruyère. Their psychology, like their philosophy, was limited in range, but it was accurate, and free from conventionality and commonplaces. There is no parrot-like imitation of others in the Goncourts, indeed one of their most salient features is a natural, and instinctive, originality. As delineators of character they are often excellent, particularly with regard to women, though these had little place in their private lives. But is it not precisely their indifference to women that made them so clear-sighted in their attitude to the coquetry and the blandishments of the opposite sex?

They were, as has been pointed out already, men of letters in a sense that no one else has ever been or ever will be. This it was that welded them together in unalterable affection for each other. If their art had not been their exclusive preoccupation, if love and politics had created a division in their hearts, their extraordinary sense of identity would have been destroyed; this fraternal couple, to whom no period in literature presents a parallel, would have ceased to exist.

Their passion for literature explains Edmond's reactionary tendencies. Democracy, for him, implied by its very nature the reign of politics, and the reign of politics was the negation of that priority which he believed should be given as a right to literature; it meant phrase-making and ideology, and he held in abhorrence humanitarian phraseology and ideology, which sprang from a lack of realism that he repudiated from the depths of his soul. Politics, in short, was rhetoric, and he despised rhetoric, as necessarily empty of meaning and deceitful.

We do not believe we shall be accused of having concealed the defects of the Goncourts, or their errors, but egotistical as they may have been, caustic, indiscreet, imbued with a sense of their own superiority and naively complacent about themselves, would they have appeared so to the same extent if they had not multiplied the evidence of these failings in their *Journal?* Have such defects less real existence in those who confess them less ingenuously? Apart from all this, what fineness there is in their own attitude of mind, what dignity in their lives! Edmond's pride and integrity, his aristocratic bearing, his scorn of intrigue, his disinterestedness, his independence, all these have been too unanimously attested by those who met him for us not to feel obliged to take them largely into account. Nor must we either fail to interpret to his credit his disillusionment and his melancholy, signs of an idealism of which perhaps he was not fully conscious, but which radiated from all his personality and made it truly noble.

He had no capacity for contentment. Would he be content with his biographer? The latter does not venture to think so.

Index

Abbatucci, Marie, 231, 290–4, 297, 306
About, Edmond, 95–6; *Gaétana*, 146
Académie Française, 296–8, 322–3
Académie des Goncourts, 296–8; inauguration of the Grenier, 298–302
L'Actualité, 224
Adam, Mme., lady of letters, 248
Ajalbert, writer, 281, 284
Alexis, Paul, 229, 257, 274, 279, 285, 300
Algiers, the Goncourts in, 33–4
Allan, Mme, 40
Ambigu theatre, 270
Amyot, publishers, 76
Anastasi, painter, 288
L'Année Littéraire, 134
Antoine, actor-manager, 276, 279, 280, 284, 285, 327, 334
D'Arcosse, Fossé, 90
L'Art, 143
L'Artiste, 64, 65, 114
D'Artois, Comte, 13
Asseline, editor of *La Mousquetaire*, 53
Asselineau, friend of Baudelaire, 147
L'Assemblée Nationale, 65
Atheists' dinners, at Magny's, 103
Athénéum, 44
Aubryet, Xavier, 60, 65, 87, 88, 96–7
Augier, Emile, 258, 288
D'Aumale, Duc, 268
Auteuil, the Goncourts' house at, 169–70; description of, in *La Maison d'un Artiste*, 235–41
L'Avenir National, 136

Bachaumont, *Mémoires Secrets*, 303
Balmont, M. de, 38
Balzac, Honoré de, 81, 88, 139, 233, 296; *Les Illusions Perdues*, 77
Banville, Théodore de, 44, 98–9, 140, 226, 297–300, 315; depicted in *Charles Demailly*, 98

Barbey d'Aurevilly, J. A., 67, 68, 77, 165, 223, 227, 230, 234, 297, 298; meets Edmond, 250
Barbusse, Henri, 336
Barié, Dr, 329
Baroche, lover of Jeanne de Tourbey, 169
Barrès, Maurice, 311, 316
Barrière, 54, 55, 67
Baschet, Armand, 57, 58
Bassigny, Goncourt family origins in, 11–12
Baudelaire, Charles, 50, 73, 87, 182, 226
Baudillart, Henri, 55
Bauer, Henry, 260, 263, 264, 274, 286, 320
Beaufort, manager of the Vaudeville, 75, 140
Beaulieu, Anatole de, 154
Beauvoir (pseudonym of Eugène Roger de Bully), 92
Beauvoir, Roger de, 45
Becque, *Michel Pauper*, 271
Béguin, Albert, *Le Romantisme et le Rêve*, 65
Béhaine, Alphonse Lefebvre de (cousin), 50
Béhaine, Armand Lefebvre de (cousin), 46
Béhaine, Edmond Lefebvre de, 133
Béhaine, Edouard Lefebvre de (cousin), 15, 17, 30, 79, 150, 152, 158, 159, 194, 203, 218, 221, 329, 334
Béni-Barde, Dr, 201, 204
Béranger, 15
Bergerat, Emile, 219
Bernhardt, Maurice, 286
Bernhardt, Sarah, 270, 286
Berthelot, M. P. E., 122, 305
Bertin, Edouard, 161
Bien Public, Le, 219, 230, 297
Bing, art dealer, 245
Biré, Edmond, 234

339

Index

Blaise, Marie, 314, 318
Blanc, Charles, 159, 220
Blanchard, naturalist, 288
Bocage, actor, 126
Bohemians, the Goncourts' hatred of, 77
Bonheur, Rosa, 132
Bonnetain, Paul, 262, 263
Bonnières, Mme Robert de, 301
Bonnières, Robert de, 308
Boschot, Adolphe, 90
Bouilhet, Louis, 79, 114, 145; *La Conjuration d'Amboise*, 150
Bourbon, Collège, 20
Bourgeois, Léon, 281, 284
Bourget, Paul, 230, 233, 298, 300, 327
Bracquemond, artist, 157, 314, 334
Brassine, actress, 53
Brébant's restaurant, 120, 209–12, 215, 217, 256, 307, 314–15
Breuvannes: Goncourt family house at, 23; the house sold, 167
Brindeau, actor, 40
Brohan, Madeleine, 229
Brunetière, critic, 231
Burnouf, Orientalist, 132
Burty, Philippe, 72–3, 89–90, 104, 124, 191, 198, 201, 212–14, 216, 220, 224, 226, 229, 235, 243, 298; rift with Edmond, 242
Bush, writer, 269
Byl, Arthur, 272
Byron, Lord, 83

Caboche, schoolmaster, 20
Candé, actor, 320
Café Riche. *See* Riche
Carnot, President, 275
Carré, Albert, 284, 319
Carrier, miniaturist, 90
Carrière, painter, 314, 316, 332
Case, Jules, 277
Céard, Henri, 100, 152, 224, 229, 230, 257, 260, 263, 276, 298, 300, 316, 320; meets Edmond, 269; *Une belle Journée*, 269; dramatises *Renée Mauperin*, 269–71; inspires underhand attack on the Goncourts, 271; rift with Edmond, 272; reviews play of *Germinie Lacerteux*, 274; attacks play of *Les Frères Zemganno*, 280; and the Legion of Honour for Edmond, 316, 317

Censors, Board of, 281–4
Cercle des Critiques, 281
Chabrillat, manager of the Ambigu theatre, 270
Chambe, dealer in old iron, 89, 90
Chambord, Comte de, 68–9
Champrosay, the Daudets' house at, 247, 250
Champsaur, Félicien, 280
Chapron, Léon, 230
Chapoton, Serge, 318–19
Charavay, dealer in autographs, 66
Charcot, Daudet's doctor, 248, 250
Charpentier, Alexandre, 312, 316
Charpentier, Georges, 134, 135, 223, 227, 230, 250, 257, 269, 315
Charpentier, Mme Georges, 229, 301
Chateaubriand, 162
Châtelet Theatre, 153
Chauchard, General, 128
Chenavard, painter, 159
Chennevières, art critic, 105, 125, 126, 297, 298
Chéret, 314
Chesneau, critic, 108
Chiromancie, La, 44
Chronique de Paris, 145
Cladel, 297, 298
Claretie, Jules, 90, 137, 226, 258
Claudin, novelist, 68, 96, 97
Claveau, Anatole, 234
Clémenceau, Georges, 274, 317, 318
Clermont d'Oise, women's prison at, 221
Cloquet, Dr, 80
Colette, 336
Collardez, Paul, 13, 17, 25, 26, 29, 34, 46, 48, 70
Colmant, Alexandre, 85, 89
Comédie-Française, 40, 140–1, 148, 150, 152, 258, 270, 275
Compardon, historian, 69
Constitutionnel, Le, 107, 108, 227
Conte, Edouard, 331
Coppée, François, 294, 299, 317
Coquelin, 141, 152, 248
Corbin, Colonel, 24
Corsaire, Le, 44, 155
Courbet, Gustave, 157
Courmont, Alphonse de, 158
Courmont, Cornélie Le Bas de (cousin), 16, 304

340

Index

Courmont, Jules de (uncle), 15, 21, 46, 47, 53
Courmont, Nephthalie de (aunt), 22; depicted in *Madame Gervaisis*, 158
Courmont, Philippe de, 216
Courmont Pomponne, le Bas de (grandmother), 16
Courtois, Mlle de (first wife of Marc-Pierre Huot), 13
Croissy-Beaubourg, Jules de Courmont's house at, 53
Cros, Eugène, 311
Curmer, publisher, 36
Curt, Fanny (cousin), 30
Cuvillier-Fleury, critic, 134

Dailly, Mme, Blanche Passy's half-sister, 133
Dardoize, Mme, friend of the Daudets, 286, 332
Daudet, Alphonse, 81, 94, 97, 144, 187, 222, 223, 226, 230, 258, 259, 261, 270–1, 273–4, 279, 281, 297–9, 321; friendship with Edmond, 247–55; duel with Delpit, 249; his *Sapho*, 249; ill health, 250, 253; *La Lutte pour la Vie*, 252, 253; Drumont attacks his *L'Obstacle*, 254; at Flaubert's Sunday gatherings, 256–7; and the manifesto against Zola, 264–7; performance of his *L'Obstacle*, 281; at the Grenier, 300–1; his *Souvenirs de la Jeunesse*, 307; and the Legion of Honour for Edmond, 316–18; misunderstanding with Edmond, 322–5; entertains Edmond at Champrosay, 325–8; and Edmond's death, 329–32
Daudet, Mme Alphonse, 227, 229–30, 235, 241–2, 247–8, 251, 255, 274, 279, 299, 301, 306, 317, 324, 326, 328, 333–4; accused of wishing to inherit de Goncourt's money, 252–3; ideas for Edmond's marriage, 291; and the Goncourt *Journal*, 309–11; upbraids Edmond, 324; and Edmond's death, 329–32
Daudet, Ernest, 310, 325
Daudet, Léon, 231, 252–3, 273–5, 301, 323–5, 328, 334
Daudet, Lucien, 254, 332
Decamps, painter, 73, 157

De Fly (or Defly, or Dieudé-Defly), Mme, 125–6, 127, 129
Delaage, Henri, 44
Delaborde, Henri, 220
Delaunay, actor, 141, 142, 229
Deloncle, politician, 284
Delpit, critic, 230, 249
Delzant, Alidor, 79, 140, 144, 155, 175, 176
Denis, Pélagie. *See* Pélagie
Dennery, Adolphe, 97–9, 245
Dentu, bookseller, 49, 52, 59, 64, 66, 71, 76
Derenbourg, theatre manager, 280
Descaves, Lucien, 262, 272, 274
Desgranges, Clémence. *See* Gisette
Deshayes, 43
Deslandes, René, 270
Desoye, Mme, printseller, 243
Diderot, 296
Doche, Mme, actress, 93–4, 114
Domergue, Rosalie, 80
Doré, Gustave, 88, 288
Dostoievsky, 261
Doucet, Camille, 142, 284
Droits de l'Homme, Les, 269
Drumont, pamphleteer, 250–1, 254–5, 317
Du Camp, 258
Duchesne, Albert, 155
Ducrot, General, 151–2
Duflos, actor, 285
Duhamel, Georges, 336
Dujardin-Beaumetz, M., 284
Dumas, Alexandre (the elder), 20
Dumas, Alexandre (the younger), 50, 113, 258, 274, 284, 288; *L'Affaire Clémenceau*, 20
Dumeny, actor, 268
Dumineray, publisher, 37, 39
Duplan, Jules, 155
Duplan, Maître, 333–4
Dupois, art teacher, 29
Dupuy, Charles, 268
Duquesnel, Félix, 281
Duse, Mme, 319
Du Terrail, Ponson, 213
Dyonis-Ordinaire, M., 284

Ebner, Daudet's secretary, 249, 329
L'Echo de Paris, 244–5, 306–7, 309–10, 312, 320, 323–4, 334

341

Index

L'Eclair, 42–4, 49–50, 87, 93
Edmond, Charles, 88, 96, 114, 122, 155, 163, 169, 203, 211, 298; friendship with the Goncourts, 95
Eggis, journalist, 44
Enault, Louis, 44–5
Ephrussi, Charles, 235
Esquirol, *Mental Diseases*, 77
L'Événement, 147, 230, 252–3, 274

Faguet, Emile, critic, 275, 280
Fanier (or Fagniez), Maître, 24
Fantin–Latour, 157
Fargueil, Mlle, actress, 230
Fasquelle, editor, 326
Fechter, actor, 42
Félix, Dinah, 141, 229, 231
Félix, Père, 146
Feuillet, Maurice, 315
Feydeau, dramatist, 65, 99; *Monsieur de Saint-Bernard*, 140
Figaro, Le, 134, 155–6, 175, 262–3, 265–6, 268, 274–5, 277, 300, 304–5, 308, 311, 320–1, 324–5, 333
Figaro-Programme, 147
Firmin–Didot, Ambroise, 67
Flameng, Léopold, 219
Flaubert, Gustave, 64–5, 79–82, 88, 96, 99, 106–8, 112, 131, 145, 150, 159–60, 168, 182, 199, 203, 261, 288–90, 293, 296–8, 309; friendship with the Goncourts, 114–16; *Madame Bovary*, 116, 139; the Goncourts' reservations about him, 116–18; on *Renée Mauperin*, 134; on *Germinie Lacerteux*, 137; on *Henriette Maréchal*, 149; on *Manette Salomon*, 155; on *Madame Gervaisis*, 165–6; his *Tentation de Saint-Antoine* 216; on *La Fille Elisa*, 224; on *Les Frères Zemganno*, 227; his Sunday gatherings, 256–7; his *Bouvard et Pécuchet*, 257–8, 289; death of, 258; monument to, 258–60
Follin, Dr, 80
Forain, 312
Forgues, translator, 44
Fort, Dr, 329
Fosca, François, 33, 157
Fouquier, Henri, 320
Foyot's restaurant, 260

Frack, Professor, 146
Français, Le, 304
France, Anatole, 263, 292, 300, 336
France, La, 103, 147, 275
Franconi, Charles, 226
Fromentin, Eugène, 72–3, 297–8, 311, 324–5
Fuchs, Max, 175

Gabrielli, Prince, 314
Gaïffe, Félix, 45, 76
Galbois, Mme de, 129, 290, 293
Galipaux, actor, 320
Gambetta, Léon, 230, 242, 248
Ganderax, Louis, 271
Gaulois, Le, 161, 192, 224, 230, 268, 298, 304
Gautier, Théophile, 37, 64–5, 72–3, 88, 90, 92, 96, 99, 106, 108, 120, 130, 134, 156, 160, 162, 169, 182, 209, 212, 256, 288–9, 304, 309, 318; friendship with the Goncourts, 112, 113; alleged poverty, 112; obsequiousness, 113; and *Henriette Maréchal*, 144, 147, 151; on the Goncourts' appearance and character, 191–2; and the death of Jules, 202, 204–5; illness, 217–18; death, 219
Gavarni, Paul, 21, 43, 45, 49, 51, 59, 72, 90, 92, 99, 105, 109, 114, 125–6, 182, 208; friendship with the Goncourts, 100–3; appearance and character, 100–1, 103; decline in health, 102–3; poverty, 103; death, 103–4; Princess Mathilde's outburst against, 128
Gavarni, Pierre, 102, 104, 276
Gayda, editor of *Figaro*, 265, 300
Gazette des Beaux-Arts, 124
Gazette de France, La, 149
Gazette de Paris, La, 65
Geffroy, writer, 69, 263–5, 272, 274, 298, 316, 331
Geroult, editor, 133
Gil Blas (periodical), 230, 233, 259, 264–5, 271–2
Gille, critic, 223
Girardin, publisher, 125
Giraud, Eugène, 125, 288
Giraud, historian, 125
Gisette (Clémence Desgranges), 97, 98
Gisors, Jules' childhood days at, 24

Index

Glouvet, M., 252
Goncourt, Annette-Cécile de (mother), 15, 16, 19, 20, 26-8
GONCOURT BROTHERS
(1) Edmond and Jules
paternal antecedents, 11-15; their father, 14; maternal antecedents, 15-17; take style of 'de Goncourt', 17-18; their mother, 19-20; money difficulties, 29; decide to become painters, 30; early love episodes, 30-2; journey to South of France, 32-3; at Algiers, 33-4; at rue Saint-Georges, Paris, 35; in Switzerland and Belgium, 35-6; first literary efforts, 36-7; at Louèche, Valais mountains, 37; first publication, 37-9; ill-success with plays, 40-1; and L'Eclair, 42-3; admiration for Gavarni, 43; contribute to Paris, 44-50; work on L'Histoire de la Société Française, 51-3; in Bordeaux, Croissy-Beaubourg and Sainte-Addresse, 53-4; and Montalembert, 54-5; and Barrière, 55; with Célestin Nanteuil at Bougival, 56; journey to Italy, 57-9; discovery of Edgar Allan Poe, 59; interest in Marie Lepelletier, 61-2; and the bookseller Dentu, 64; engage a groom, 64; and Gautier, 64-5; leanings towards lyricism and symbolism, 65; meet Flaubert and Feydeau, 65; with Passy at Gisors, 65; introduce private life into criticism, 66-7; life of Marie-Antoinette 67-9; with the Courmonts at Croissy-Beaubourg, 69-70; sell holdings in Breuvannes, 70; L'Art du Dix-Huitième Siècle, 71-3; etchings by, 71, 72; as art critics, 72; rejection of their play La Guerre des Lettres, 75-6; first novel, 76-7; Jules' illness, 78; reception of Les Maîtresses de Louis XV, 79; origin of Sœur Philomène, 79-81; and the death of Rosalie Malingre, 83-6; life in the boulevards, 87-91; hunt for bibelots, drawings etc., 89-90; undeserved reputation for 18th century matters, 90; and the Marcille family, 90-2; their at homes, 92; and Scholl, 93-4; and Mario Uchard, 94-5; and Charles Edmond, 95; and Edmond About, 95-6; and Murger, 96; and Aubryet, 96-7; and Adolphe Dennery, 97-8; and de Banville, 98-9; and Feydeau, 99; and Gavarni, 100-4; and the Magny restaurant dinners, 104-6; and Sainte-Beuve, 106-11; and Gautier, 112-13; and George Sand, 113; and Flaubert, 114-18; and Saint-Victor, 118-21; and Taine, 121; and Renan, 121-2; and Berthelot, 122; and Michelet, 122-4; and Philippe Burty, 124; and the Princess Mathilde, 125-30; meet Napoleon III, 130; origin and publication of Renée Mauperin, 131-5; and the attacks on Germinie Lacerteux, 135-9; and the outcry against Henriette Maréchal, 140-51; their La Patrie en Danger rejected, 152-3; at Marlotte and Gretz, 154; Manette Salomon published, 154-8; in Rome, and the reception of Madame Gervaisis, 158-66; and Zola, 161; sell the house at Breuvannes, 167; search for a house, 168-9; system of collaboration, 175-6; buy a house in Auteuil, 169-70; involved in cab accident, 194; Jules' liver attack, 194-5; at Bar-sur-Seine and Trouville, 195-6; return to Auteuil, 196-7; Jules' last days and death, 197-203

(2) Edmond
birth, 19; at the Pension Goubaux, 20; at Lycée Henri IV and Collège Bourbon, 20-1; on his aunt Nephthalie de Courmont, 22; on his cousin Augusta, 22-3; memories of childhood at Breuvannes, 23; enters solicitor's office, 24-5; buys works of art, 25-6; enters Ministry of Finance, 26; witnesses Revolution of 1848, 26-7; bitterness about his youthful days, 28; no desire for fame, 29; at art school, 29-30; etchings by, 71, 72; his original drawings not extant, 73; and Jules' illness, 78; nominated to the Legion of Honour, 160; and the cause of

343

Index

Jules's death, 203–5; at Bar-sur-Seine, 208; returns to Auteuil, and life during the siege and Commune, 209–16; resumes normal life, 217; in the Bavarian Tyrol, 218; and Gautier's death, 219; his *Gavarni* published, 219–20; origin and success of *La Fille Elisa*, 221–5; visits to circuses, and writing of *Les Frères Zemganno*, 225–9; mixed reception for *La Faustin*, 229–31; *Chérie*, and Pauline Zeller, 231–4; first exhibition of his drawings, 235; description of his house at Auteuil, 235–40; his garden, 240–1; rift with Burty, 242; cult of Japanese art, 242–6; and Nittis, 245–6; friendship with Daudet, 247–55; meets Barbey d'Aurevilly, 250; godfather to Daudet's daughter, 251; at Flaubert's Sunday gatherings, 256–7; meets Maupassant, 257; and Flaubert's death, 258; and the monument to Flaubert, 258–60; opinion of Maupassant, 260; opinion of Turgenev, 261; and the manifesto against Zola, 263–4; quarrels with Zola, 264–7; and the first performance of *Henriette Maréchal*, 268–9; and Céard's dramatisation of *Renée Mauperin*, 269–71; breach with Céard, 272; and the dramatisation of *Sœur Philomène*, 272–3; and the dramatisation of *Germinie Lacerteux*, 273–8; and the dramatisation of *Les Frères Zemganno*, 279–81; and the banning of the play of *La Fille Elisa*, 281–4; and the reception of his play *A bas le progrès*, 284–6; and the dramatisation of *Charles Demailly*, 285; and the dramatisation of *La Faustin*, 286–7; in the Princess Mathilde's circle at the rue de Berri, 288; fainting fit, 289; opinion of the Princess Mathilde, 289–90, 295; relations with Marie Abbatucci, 290–2, 294; and the Abbatucci-Popelin affair, 292–3; less friendly with the Princess, 293–5; and Popelin's death, 294; promulgates an Académie des Goncourts, 296–8; inaugurates the Grenier, 298–302; publication of the *Journal* (see below under Works); at the World Exhibition of 1889, 313; Pélagie's care of him, 313–14; sits to portrait painters, 314; dines out regularly, 314–15; ill-health, and attacks of rheumatism, 315–16; his profile on a medal, 316; officer of the Legion of Honour, 316–18; and the dramatisation of *Manette Salomon*, 318–21; misunderstanding with Daudet, 322–5; at Champrosay with the Daudets, 325–8, death, 329–31; obsequies, and homage to, 331–5; influence and place in literature, 335–8

CHARACTER, HABITS, etc.
taciturnity and moroseness, 31–2; pessimism, 77; gourmet, 92–3; fraternal companionship, 171–4; appearance, 172; Jules on their character-contrasts, 174; system of collaboration, 175–6; *idée fixe* of public hostility, 176–7; boredom, 177; dullness and sadness, 178; weakness of fibre, 178–9; liking for women, 179–80; self-satisfaction, 180–1; severity towards colleagues, 181–2; a neurasthenic, 190–1; contemporaries' impressions of, 191–3

BELIEFS, INTERESTS
realism, 31–2, 136, 138; love, 60–1, 63; hatred of Bohemians, 77; misogyny, 156; anti-semitism, 156, 195, 250–1; painting, 156–7; cult of art, and integrity as man of letters, 182–3; attitude to nature, 183–4, 241; deafness to music, 184–5; atheism and materialism, 185–7; repudiates idea of progress, 187–8; on benefits of civilization, 188; on the State, 188; on the Americanization of France, 188–9; liking for an aristocratic society, 189; hatred of Napoleon III, 189; attitude to history, 189–90; hatred of democracy, 190; interest in the circus, 226; on style, 233–4; taste in books, 237–9; aversion to official recognition, 296

Index

(3) Jules
at the Collège Bourbon, 23; bad health, and schooldays, 23–4; at Gisors with the Passy family, 24; and the death of his mother, 27–8; contracts syphilis, 36; and Céleste Laveneur, 51–2; affair with the woman Dubuisson, 53–6; love affair in Venice, 57–8; illnesses, 78, 167–8, 194–5; pardoned by Princess Mathilde after his outburst, 195; last days, and death, 197–202; influence, and place in literature, 335–8

CHARACTER, HABITS, etc.
gaiety and liveliness, 32; pessimism, 77; fraternal companionship, 171–4; appearance, 172; self-contrasted with Edmond, 174; humour and ill-humour, 174–5; system of collaboration, 175–6; idée fixe of public hostility, 176; irritability, 177; boredom, 177; dullness and sadness, 178; weakness of fibre, 178–9; liking for women, 179–80; self-satisfaction, 180–1; severity towards colleagues, 181–2; a neurasthenic, 190–1; contemporaries' impressions of, 191–3

BELIEFS, INTERESTS
realism, 31–2, 136, 138; on love, 60–1, 63; hatred of Bohemians, 77; misogyny, 156; anti-semitism, 156, 195; on painting, 156–7; cult of art and integrity as man of letters, 182–3; attitude to nature, 183–4; deafness to music, 184–5; atheism and materialism, 185–7; repudiates idea of progress, 187–8; on benefits of civilization, 188; on the State, 188; on the Americanization of France, 188–9; liking for an aristocratic society, 189; hatred of Napoleon III, 189; attitude to history, 189–90; hatred of democracy, 190; interest in the circus, 226; aversion to official recognition, 296

(4) Works (E, J denotes joint authorship; E works by Edmond, and J those by Jules).
A bas le progrès (E), 284–6

Abou-Hassan (E, J), 37
Les Actrices (E, J), 64
L'Amour au Dix-huitième Siècle (E, J), 220
L'Art au Dix-Huitième Siècle (E, J) 71–2, 83, 220, 223
Biographie de Sophie Arnould... See *Sophie Arnould*
Boucher (E, J), 71
La Camargo (E), 327
Le Camp des Tartares (E, J), 49, 51
Chardin (E, J), 71
Charles Demailly (E, J), 25, 38, 43–5, 77–8, 88, 98, 155–6, 158, 175, 191, 204, 208, 232, 306; quoted 27, 51, 105, 178–80, 184; dramatisation of, 285
Chérie (E), 197, 231–4, 266
Cochin-Eisen (E, J), 71
La Cuisinière (E, J), 36
Debucourt (E, J), 71
La Du Barry (E, J), 79, 220
La Duchesse de Châteauroux et ses Sœurs (E, J), 79, 220
En 18.. (E, J), 37–9, 42, 49, 106, 156, 175, 197; quoted 36
Etienne Marcel (J), 24
La Faustin (E), 54, 229–31, 234, 261, 269, 327, 334; dramatisation of, 286–7, 319
La Femme au Dix-huitième Siècle (E, J), 82–3, 107, 220, 257
La Fille Elisa (E), 59, 62, 97n., 135–6, 213, 221–5, 234, 257, 266, 289; dramatisation of, 282–4
Fragonard (E, J), 71
Les Frères Bendigo (original title of *Les Frères Zemganno*), 226
Les Frères Zemganno (E), 63, 171, 197, 225–9, 257, 261, 266; dramatisation of, 279–81
Gavarni (E, J), 196, 219–20
Germinie Lacerteux (E, J), 16, 62, 84, 109, 135–9, 144, 158, 175, 191, 197, 202, 220, 222, 228, 234, 236, 271; dramatisation of, 273–8, 282, 284
Greuze (E, J), 71
La Guerre des Lettres (E, J), 75–6
Hégésippe Moreau (E, J), 36
Henriette Maréchal (E, J), 140–51, 189, 204, 208, 247, 250, 268–9, 277

345

Index

Histoire de la Société Française Pendant la Directoire (E, J), 53, 54
Histoire de la Société Française Pendant la Révolution (E, J), 44, 48, 51, 52–6, 106
Hokousai (E), 245
Les Hommes de Lettres (E, J), 76, 80, 96, 113–14, 140
Idées et Sensations (E, J), 118, 198, 303
L'Italie d'hier (E, J), 57
La Jeune Bourgeoise (original title of Renée Mauperin), 134
Journal (E, J): its fragmentary appearance in Idées et Sensations, 303; aim in composition, 303; division into two parts, 303–4; its existence become public, and extracts appear in Le Figaro, 304; first three volumes, and its reception, 304–6; stimulates demand for Goncourt writings, 306; fourth volume attacked for lack of patriotism, 306–7; Renan's objections, 307–8; Edmond's reply to Renan, 308: de Bonnières' attack, and Mirbeau's defence, 308–9; sixth and seventh volumes, and reactions of the Daudets, 309–11; eighth volume, 311; ninth volume, 311–12
Letters (J), 51, 250, 272
La Lorette (E, J), 49
Madame Gervaisis (E, J), 158–66, 175, 191, 203, 204, 213, 221
Madame de Pompadour (E, J), 69, 79, 220
Mademoiselle de la Rochedragon (original title of La Patrie en Danger), 152
Mademoiselle Tony-Freneuse (original title of Madame Gervaisis), 158
La Maison d'un Artiste (E), 235–40, 243; quoted 21, 211, 327
Les Maîtresses de Louis XV (E, J), 79, 220
Mam'zelle Zirzabelle (E, J), 41
Manette Salomon (E, J), 65, 119, 124, 142, 154–8, 175, 180, 198, 202–3, 222, 242, 251, 306; dramatisation of, 272, 287, 318–21
Marie-Antoinette (E, J), 67–9, 75, 106, 125

Moreau (E, J), 71
Les Mystères des Théâtres (E, J), 49
La Nuit de la Saint-Sylvestre (E, J), 40, 49, 75
Outamaro, la Peintre des Maisons Vertes (E), 244
La Patrie en Danger (E, J), 152–3, 220, 277, 279–80
Pages Retrouvées (E, J), 50
La Peinture à l'Exposition de 1855 (E, J), 56
Les Portraits Intimes du XVIIIe Siècle (E, J), 64, 66–7, 106, 257
Prud'hon (E, J), 71
Quelques Créatures de ce Temps (E, J; formerly titled Une Voiture de Masques), 59
Renée Mauperin (E, J), 65, 131–4, 158, 175, 191, 220, 316; dramatisation of, 269–72
La Révolution dans les Mœurs (E, J), 52
Les Saint-Aubin (E, J), 71, 222–3
La Saint-Huberty (E), 222
Le Salon de 1852 (E, J), 49
Sans Titre, (E, J), 36–7
La Société Française Pendant la Directoire. See Histoire
Sœur Philomène (E, J), 61–2, 80–2, 88, 107, 114, 175, 191, 220, 264, 306; dramatisation of, 272–3
Sophie Arnould (E, J), 66–7, 222
Tony Freneuse (original title of Chérie), 231
La Tour (E, J), 71
Venise, la Nuit (E, J), 65
Les Vignettistes Gravelot (E, J), 71
Une Voiture de Masques (E, J; later titled Quelques Creatures de ce Temps), 50, 57, 59
Watteau (E, J), 71
Goncourt Academy. See Académie des Goncourts
Goncourt, Lorraine, Huot family of, 11
Got, actor, 141–2, 144, 284
Goubaux, Prosper-Parfait, 20
Goubaux, Pension (later the Collège Chaptal), 20
Goudchaux, manager of the Vaudeville, 75
Gounod, 288
Grenier, the, 298–302, 320–3, 334

Index

Gretz-sur-Loing, the Goncourts take lodgings at, 154
Guérard, actress, 286
Guérin, Alphonse (uncle), 15, 31
Guérin, Annette-Cecile (mother), 13 (*for later references see under Goncourt*)
Guérin, Armand (uncle), 15
Guérin, Jules (uncle), 15
Guérin, Jules, of *Gil Blas*, 230
Guéroult, Adolphe, 146
Guiches, Gustave, 262–3
Guyot, Yves, 282
Guys, Constantin, 219
Gymnase-Dramatique, 40

Hachette, publisher, 137
Hafner, 43
Halévy, Ludovic, 96, 245, 274, 292
Harmand, manager of the Vaudeville theatre, 140
Haussmann, Baron, 126
Hayashi, art dealer, 243–4
Hébert, writer, 106
Hébert, painter, 159
Hébrard, Adrien, 155, 294, 301
Heine, Heinrich, 37
Helder, Café du, 75, 87
Helloco, Dr, 196
Hennique, Léon, 257, 269, 298–301, 316, 334, 336; *L'Attaque du grand 7*, 269
Henry IV, Lycée, 20
Henrys, Fédora (cousin; married Léon Rattier), 37
Henrys, Virginie (wife of Pierre-Antoine-Victor Huot), 14
Hérédia, José-Maria de, 159, 258, 294, 300, 317
Hérédia, Mme de, 229
D'Hervilly, Ernest, 297
Hostein, manager of the Châtelet Theatre, 153
Houssaye, Arsène, 40, 65, 88, 90, 97
Houssaye, Henri, 253
Hugo, Victor, 52, 73, 117, 122–3, 162, 210, 213, 218, 258; *Les Misérables*, 135–6; on *Germinie Lacerteux*, 137
Huot, Antoine (great-grandfather), 12
Huot, Bathilde-Antoinette-Augusta (cousin; married Léonidas Labille), 14, 22

Huot, Jean-Antoine (grandfather), 12, 53
Huot, Marc-Pierre (father), 12–14, 19
Huot, Pierre-Antoine-Victor (uncle), 14
Huret, Jules, 261, 307, 311
Huysmans, J. K., 229, 257, 263, 298–9; *Marthe, Histoire d'une Fille*, 223; *Sac au Dos*, 269

L'Illustration, 83

Jacobé, Ambroise, 17
Jacottet and Bourdillat, publishers, 88
Janin, Jules, 39–40, 43, 46, 76, 92
Janvier, actor, 286
Japanese Art, Friends of, 315
Jaurès, Jean, 311
Jour, Le, 324
Jourdain, Frantz, 170, 252, 260, 286, 299, 316, 317, 331–2
Journal, Le, 332
Journal des Débats, 39, 54, 55, 76, 134, 161, 276
Journal Officiel, 227

Karr, Alphonse, 35, 44, 47–8
Koning, theatre manager, 285
Kuhn, Joachim, 129

Labille, Léonidas-Eugène, 14–15, 17 22–3, 28, 208
Labille, Marin, 203, 216
Lacaussade, judge, 47
Lacaze, senator, 110
La Charité Hospital, 80
Laclos, novelist, 104
Lacroix, Paul, *Le Moyen Age et la Renaissance*, 33
Lacroix, publisher, 161
Lafontaine, actor, 141
Lafontaine, Mme Victoria, 141, 145
La Forge, Anatole de, 146
Lagenevais, critic, 134, 136
Lagier, actress, 97
La Gondole, Café de, 101
La Guéronnière, M. de, 146
Lamartine, Alphonse de, 118
Lambert, Albert, 268
Landelle, novelist, 49

347

Index

La Paiva, courtesan, 186
La Roncière, Admiral de, 126
La Rounat, Charles de, 76, 268–70
Latour–Dumoulin, controller-general of printed publications, 45, 47
Laveneur, Céleste, 51–2
Lavoix, play-reader at the Comédie-Française, 270
Lapierre, 258
Lebarbier, managing director of *Paris*, 44, 48
Leblanc, Léonide, 94, 268
Le Blond, Maurice, 203
Le Chanteur, Mme, 18
Lecomte, 316
Ledoyen's restaurant, 322
Legonidec, judge, 46
Legouvé, 20
Lemaître, actor, 126
Lemaître, Jules, 139, 276
Lemoine, Edouard, 55
Lenoir, Alfred, 314
Lepelletier, Maria, 32, 61–2
Lermina, Julia, 155
Lescure, François Adolphe de, *La Vraie Marie-Antoinette*, 69
Lesparre, Duchesse de, 288
Levallois, Sainte-Beuve's secretary, 108
Levallois, Jules, 123, 136, 165, 195, 234
Lévy, Michel, 76, 81, 116–17
Lia Félix, Mlle, actress, 119–20
Liberté de Penser, La, 42
Liberté, La, 261
Librairie Nouvelle, 81–2, 88
Lireux, journalist, 40
Lloyd, Mlle, actress, 229
Lockroy, Minister of Fine Arts, 275
Lorrain, Jean, 267, 286, 311, 326, 332
Loti, Pierre, 298, 327
Louys, Pierre, 326
Ludwig II, of Bavaria, 218

Magnard, François, 274, 277, 304
Magnier, editor of *L'Evénement*, 252
Magny's restaurant, 87, 92, 103; the dinners of free spirits at, 104–5, 107, 109–10, 113, 117, 130, 161, 209, 256, 296–7, 308, 315
Mail, Café du, 102
Malingre, Rosalie (known as Rose), 21, 64, 79, 83–6, 135

348

Mallarmé, Stéphane, 335, 336
Manceau, engraver, 113
Manet, Edouard, 157
Mangin, Françoise, 19
Marcille, collector, 90
Marcille, Mme Camille, 91
Margueritte, Paul, 262–3, 274, 298
Marguery's restaurant, 280
Maria, midwife, 201, 203, 221
Marivaux, *Marianne*, 283–4
Maroy, engraver, 219
Marpon, publisher, 253, 254
Marx, Roger, 73, 316, 332
Massiac, journalist, 271
Masson, Frédéric, 226, 292
Mathilde, Princess, 83, 87, 89, 92, 97, 108, 110, 113, 118, 121, 159, 160, 163, 169, 196, 203, 216, 223, 254, 270, 305, 315, 320, 334; first meeting with the Goncourts, 125–6; her house, 126; second meeting, 126–7; the Goncourts' character sketch of, 127; outburst against Gavarni, 128; her character, 128; and *Germinie Lacerteux*, 137–8; and *Henriette Maréchal*, 143, 147, 149; pardons Jules' outburst, 195; changes her town house, 217; her circle in the rue de Berri, 288; reservations about Edmond, 289; article on Gautier, and Edmond's opinion of her, 289–90; relations with Popelin, 290; and Edmond's relations with Marie Abbatucci, 290–2; and the Abbatucci-Popelin relationship, 292–3; and Edmond's friendship, 293–5; and Popelin's death, 294; at the Grenier, 301–2; and the *Journal*, 304, 306, 310
Matin, Le, 318
Maupassant, Guy de, 37, 230, 258, 298–300, 304; meets Edmond, 257; his *Histoire du Vieux Temps*, **257**; and the monument to Flaubert, 259; Edmond's opinion of, 260
Mendès, Catulle, 143, 300, 320
Menus Plaisirs theatre, 279–80, 285
Mérimée, Prosper, 73, 288
Méténier, Oscar, 279, 285
Meyer, Arthur, 245
Michelet, Jules, 69, 82, 122–3, 190
Michelet, Mme, 122, 123
Migeon, Gaston, 243

Index

Millerand, Alexandre, 281-2
Mirbeau, Octave, 257, 260, 309, 324
Mirès, owner of *Le Pays*, 77, 184
Moniteur, 97
Moniteur Universel, Le, 219
Moniteur du Bibliophile, 235
Monnier, Henri, 72, 102
Monselet, Charles, 53, 82, 99, 134, 136
Montalembert, 54-5
Monteil, Alexis, *L'Histoire des Français des Divers Etats*, 66
Montépin, 50
Montesquiou, Robert de, 287, 300, 317-18, 326
Montigny, Lemoine-, manager of the Gymnase-Dramatique, 40-1, 75
Montigny, Edouard Lemoine-, 75
Morère, friend of Gavarni, 88
Moulin Rouge, 88, 105
Mousquetaire, La, 53
Murat, Joachim, 128
Murger, 44, 88, 92, 96, 99, 154; *Scènes de la Vie de Bohème*, 158
Musset, Alfred de, 126

Nadar, artist, 43, 147, 219, 332; depicted in *Charles Demailly*, 43
Nain Jaune, Le, 224
Nancy, rue des Goncourts in, 316
Nanteuil, Célestin, 56
Napoléon III, 130, 146, 195, 288, 293
Napoléon, Prince, 130, 146
Nathalie, Mlle, actress, 45-6
Nation, La, 224
Neufchâteau, Jean-Antoine Goncourt's house at, 12, 23
Neveux, Pol, 72, 90
Nieuwerkerke, lover of Princess Mathilde, 46, 48, 125-7, 130
Nisard, critic, 132
Nittis, Giuseppe de, 157, 229, 245, 314
Nittis, Mme de, 246
Noblet, actor, 284
Nouvelle Revue de Paris, La, 137

Odéon theatre, 258, 268, 270, 273-5, 277, 286, 334
Odinot, Paul, *Les Goncourts et le Bassigny Lorrain*, 11, 70
Ollendorf, publisher, 253
Omont, Henri, 303

L'Opinion Nationale, 133-4, 146, 165
Orliac, Edouard, 50
D'Osmoy, Comte, 145, 148

Parfait, Noël, 282
Paris, during the siege, 209-16
Paris, 44-8, 49-50, 93, 98, 307
Parlement, Le, 230
Passy, Blanche, 131-3
Passy, Louis, 24, 29, 36, 57, 65, 131, 133
Paul, Prince, of Wurtemberg, 125
Pays, Le, 77, 118
Pélagie Denis, 196, 201, 209, 211, 214-15, 242, 258, 275, 291, 313-14, 318, 330-4
Perrot, M., 51
Pessard, Hector, 281
Petit Journal, Le, 275, 280
Petit Lannionais, Le, 307
Peyrelongue, picture dealer, 30, 43
Pissarro, Camille, 157
Plessy, Mme Arnould-, 141-2, 144-6, 229
Poe, Edgar Allan, 37, 59, 194
Poincaré, Raymond, Minister of Education, 316, 317
Ponsard, François, *Horace and Lydia*, 144; *Le Lion Amoureux*, 152
Pontmartin, critic, 39, 52, 234
Popelin, Claudius, 129, 258, 288-90, 292-4, 300
Porel, theatre manager, 85, 259, 268, 270-1, 273, 275, 281, 284-5, 287, 319-20, 334
Porte Saint-Marin theatre, 281
Poulet-Malassis and de Broise, publishers, 66
Pouthier, art teacher, 29, 42-4
Préault, sculptor, 147
Presse, La, 76, 118, 134, 147, 307
Prévost-Paradol, 24
Primoli, cousin of Princess Mathilde, 324, 330
Proust, Marcel, 336-7

Rachel, Mlle, actress, 45, 119, 230-1
Radziwill, Prince, 112
Raffaëlli, painter, 274, 307, 314, 332
Rambaud, Iveling, 147
Rattier, Léon, 37, 121, 329

349

Index

Réal, Mlle, actress, 268
Régnier, Henri de, 299, 318
Réjane, actress, 273-4, 278, 284, 286, 287, 334
Rémusat, 52
Renan, Ernest, 106, 113, 121-3, 159, 165, 209, 211, 258, 288, 305; objects to the Goncourt *Journal*, 307-8
Renard, Jules, 317, 318
République Française, La, 220
Reveil, Le, 68, 230, 297
Revue Blanche, La, 245
Revue des Deux Mondes, La, 39, 134, 136, 144, 147, 175, 220, 231, 271, 289
Revue des Lettres et des Arts, 156
Revue Nouvelle, La, 255
Revue de Paris, La, 37
Ricard, Louis-Xavier de, 143
Ricatte, Robert, 175, 221
Riche, Café, 87-8, 95-6, 118, 256, 280, 285, 304
Richepin, dramatist, 284
Ricord, 218
Robin, Dr, 161
Rodenbach, poet, 324
Rodin, 274
Rollin, Dr, 330
Rome, the Goncourt brothers in, 158-60
Roqueplan, writer, 143, 147
Rose. *See* Malingre
Rosier, Jacques, *Le Divorce de Sarah Moore*, 269
Rosny (the elder), writer, 67, 231, 232, 242, 262-3, 274, 280, 286, 298, 301, 304; *Nell Horn*, 262
Rosny (the younger), writer, 298
Rothschild, Baronne Edmond de, 254
Rouland, M., advocate, 48
Rousseau, J.-J., 162
Rousseau, Théodore, 157
Rousset, Camille, 152
Royat, 284-5
Royer, M. de, Attorney-General, 46, 48, 50
Rue, La, 145

Sagan, Duchesse de, 165
Saint-Antoine's Hospital, 80
Saint-Aubin, Augustin de, 71, 73, 124
Saint-Gratien, Princess Mathilde's house at, 126

Saint-Pierre, Bernardin de, 162
Saint-Victor, Paul de, 75, 82, 88, 90, 96, 99, 106, 109, 114, 117, 124, 127, 134, 147, 154, 156, 162, 182, 186, 211, 297-8; friendship with the Goncourts, 118-19; the Goncourts' criticism of, 119, 120; and Lia Félix, 119-20; quarrels with the Goncourts, 120; reconciled to Edmond, 120-1, 203; on *Gavarni*, 219-20; offends Princess Mathilde, 288
Sainte-Beuve, C. A., 45-6, 50, 52, 66, 68, 82, 103, 113, 117-18, 121, 126, 159, 169, 176, 211, 232, 298, 309; at the Magny dinners, 105, 107; the Goncourts' dislike of, 106-7; friendship with the Goncourts, 107-8, 162-4; his secretary's opinion of, 108-9; on *Germinie Lacerteux*, 109; the Goncourts at variance with, 109-11; on *Henriette Maréchal*, 150; on *Madame Gervaisis*, 162-3; death, 164, 196
Sainville, actor, 36-7
Salon des Refusés, 157
Sand, George, 77, 81-2, 88, 113; on *Madame Gervaisis*, 165
Saras, actor, 286
Sarcey, critic, 142, 161, 275-6
Sardou, Victorien, 274, 283; *Thermidor*, 283
Scholl, Aurélien, 44, 51-3, 58, 88, 93-4, 114, 253, 274, 300-1
Second, Albéric, 304
Segond-Weber, Mme, actress, 287
Séjour, Victor, and Mocquard, *La Tireuse de Cartes*, 168
Sena, Henri, 269
Serret, Philippe, 164
Servin, painter, 30, 43
Séverine, 300
Sichel, Auguste, 243
Sichel, Mme Auguste, 314, 324
Sichel, Philippe, 243
Siècle, Le, 274
Simon, Dr, 83
Simond, Henri, 312, 320, 323
Siraudin, dramatist, 277
Sizos, actress, 285
Souday, Paul, 336
Soulié, courtier, 129
Spartiates, the, 315

350

Index

Steinlen, artist, 323
Stenn, Karl (pseudonym of Mme Alphonse Daudet), 227
Sue, Eugène, 20
Swinburne, A. C., 257
Symbolist school, 336

Taine, H. A., 106, 121–2, 156, 159, 161, 163, 258, 288, 298, 304–5, 308–9
Talmeyr, Maurice, 311
Tarbé, Edmond, 224
Temps, Le, 142, 155, 163, 230, 275, 294
Théâtre–Antoine, 273
Théâtre Dejazet, 257
Théâtre Français, 143, 229
Théâtre du Gymnase, 284
Théâtre-Libre, 264, 272, 276–7, 279, 282
Théâtre–Michel, Saint Petersburg, 285
Théâtre Molière, Brussels, 273
Thénard, Mme, actress, 270
Theuriet, writer, 300
Thiboust, Lambert, 277
Thierry, Edouard, 140–3, 148–9, 153, 208
Thiers, Adolphe, 160, 213
Thimot, historian, 69
Tocqueville, Alexis de, 190
Toudouze, Gustave, 332
Tourbey, Jeanne de, 168–9
Tournemine, Orientalist and painter, 154
Trop restaurant, 257
Troubat, Jules, 306
Trouville, the Goncourts at, 160
Turcas, M., Cherubini's grandson, 53
Turgenev, Ivan, 227, 258, 298; at Flaubert's Sunday gatherings, 256; antipathy to Zola, 257; death, 260–1; opinion of Edmond, 261

Uchard, Mario, 75, 88, 90, 94–5, 114
Ulbach, Louis, 17, 230
L'Univers, 164

Vacquerie, Auguste, 317
Vaillant, Marshal, 143, 147, 149
Vailly, M. de, 60

Valdey, Mlle, actress, 286
Valentin, artist, 43
Vallès, Jules, 145, 155, 230, 297–8, 300
Valmont, Guy de, 257
Vapereau, critic, 17, 134
Varandeuil, Mlle de, 276
Variétés theatre, 273
Varin, painter, 314
Vaudeville theatre, 75, 140, 270, 281
Venet, a 'tartuffe', 44
Verlaine, Mme, 217
Verlaine, Paul, 213
Veuillot, 297, 298
Veyne, Dr, 103, 105
Vichy, 160
Vidal, Jules, 272
Vidalenc, junk dealer, 89
Vieil–Castel, official writer of memoirs to salon of Princess Mathilde, 125
Villedeuil, Laurent de, 16
Villedeuil, Pierre–Charles, Comte de, 49, 93, 335; launches *L'Eclair*, 42–3; launches *Paris*, 44–5; and the court action against *Paris*, 45, 47; and cessation of his papers, 50
Villedeuil, Marquis de, 27, 41
Villemessant, publisher, 146
Villemessant, assistant editor of *Figaro*, 277
Villetard, critic, 136
Villiers de l'Isle-Adam, 156
Viollet-le-Duc, 126, 155–6
Vitu, Auguste, 276, 277
Vogué, *Le Roman Russe*, 256
Voillemot, colourist, 43
Voltaire, 228, 230, 235

Whistler, J. M., 157
Wilde, Oscar, 246
Wilhelm I, Emperor, 212
Willette, 316
Wolff, Albert, 155, 251
World Exhibition (1889), 313

Xau, Fernand, 264

Zeller, historian, 69
Zeller, Pauline, 232, 291–4, 311, 324
Ziem, painter, 97

Index

Zola, Emile, 81, 161, 222, 227, 230, 249, 258-9, 261, 269, 271-2, 274, 279, 283-4, 297, 299-300, 315-16, 322-4; defends *Germinie Lacerteux*, 136-7; impressions of the Goncourts, 192-3; and the death of Jules, 203; his *L'Assommoir*, 223, 257, 262; onnaturalism, 227-8; at Flaubert's Sunday gatherings, 256-7; young writers' manifesto against, 262-4; quarrels with Edmond, 264-7; at the Grenier, 301; and the Legion of Honour for Edmond, 316, 318; and the dramatisation of *Manette Salomon*, 321; speech at Edmond's funeral, 334-5

Zola, Mme, 229